Education, Change and Society

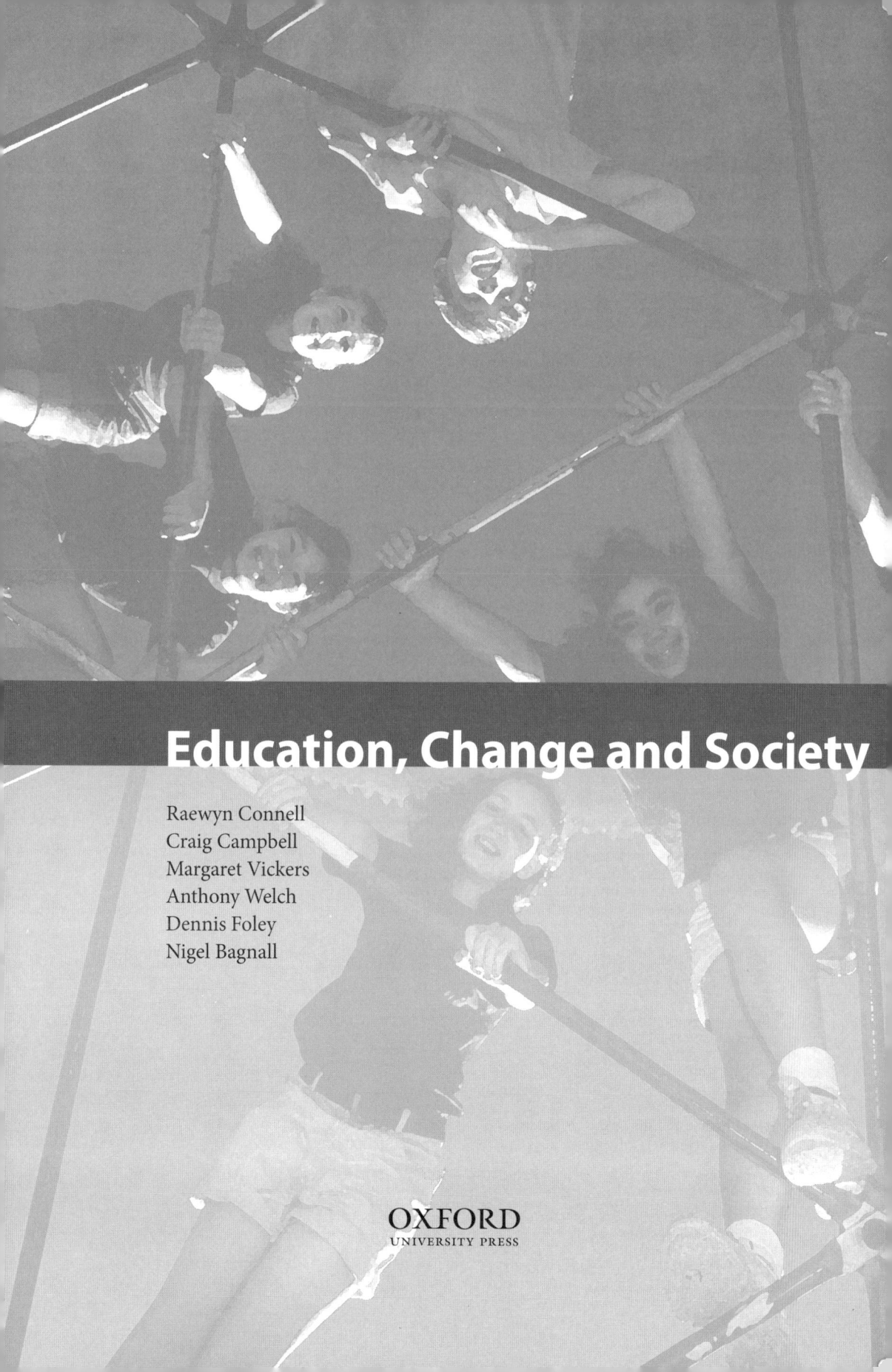

Education, Change and Society

Raewyn Connell
Craig Campbell
Margaret Vickers
Anthony Welch
Dennis Foley
Nigel Bagnall

OXFORD
UNIVERSITY PRESS

OXFORD
UNIVERSITY PRESS

253 Normanby Road, South Melbourne, Victoria 3205, Australia

Oxford University Press is a department of the University of Oxford.
It furthers the University's objective of excellence in research,
scholarship, and education by publishing worldwide in

Oxford New York

Auckland Cape Town Dar es Salaam Hong Kong Karachi
Kuala Lumpur Madrid Melbourne Mexico City Nairobi
New Delhi Shanghai Taipei Toronto

With offices in

Argentina Austria Brazil Chile Czech Republic France Greece
Guatemala Hungary Italy Japan Poland Portugal Singapore
South Korea Switzerland Thailand Turkey Ukraine Vietnam

OXFORD is a trade mark of Oxford University Press
in the UK and in certain other countries

National Library of Australia Cataloguing-in-Publication data:

Education, change and society.

Bibliography.
For undergraduate education students.
ISBN 978 0 19555 528 8.

ISBN 0 19 555528 7.

1. Educational change - Textbooks. 2. Educational change -
Study and teaching (Higher). 3. Education - Social aspects
- Textbooks. 4. Education - Social aspects - Study and
teaching (Higher). I. Connell, Raewyn.

371.2

Edited by Liz Filleul
Typeset by Linda Hamley
Proofread by Peter Cruttenden
Printed in Hong Kong by Sheck Wah Tong Printing Press Ltd

Contents

Contributors

Raewyn Connell is University Professor at the University of Sydney. She is author or co-author of nineteen books, including *Teachers' Work*, *Making the Difference*, *Gender and Power*, *Schools and Social Justice*, *Masculinities*, and, most recently, *Gender*. A contributor to research journals in sociology, education, political science, and gender studies, her current research concerns social theory, changing gender relations, neoliberal globalisation and intellectuals. Email: r.connell@ edfac.usyd.edu.au.

Craig Campbell teaches and researches the history of education at the University of Sydney. Before 1990, he was a teacher and teacher union leader in South Australia. His research concentrates on adolescence and secondary schooling during the twentieth century. Books include *The Comprehensive Public High School*, *Towards the State High School in Australia 1850–1925* and the co-edited *Ethnicity and Education*. He is currently working on a project linking the history of middle-class formation to changing patterns of school choice over the last fifty years and on a book reviewing the educational histories of nations in the South-West Pacific.

Margaret Vickers is Professor of Education at the University of Western Sydney. She is active in both community service and research on social justice issues, gender, early school leaving, and youth in transition. Margaret began her working life as a high school teacher, and her career includes senior appointments in the Australian Public Service and the Paris-based OECD (Organisation for Economic Co-operation and Development).

Anthony Welch has published widely on Australian and international education. He has also undertaken consultancies with governments in Australia, Korea, Japan and Viet Nam; the United Nations; and other agencies. He has been visiting professor in Germany, the USA, France, and Japan and has project experience in several Asian countries. His books include *Australian Education: Reform or Crisis?*, *Globalisation and Educational Re-Structuring in Asia and the Pacific*, and

The Professoriate: Profile of a Profession. Recently a Head of the School within the Faculty of Education and Social Work (University of Sydney), he has also directed its International Institute for Educational Development.

Dennis Foley has published across a wide range of disciplines within the humanities and management. His work has reviewed the education of Indigenous Australians within Australian settler society, advocating the inclusion of an Indigenous epistemology and pedagogy. He is a Fulbright Scholar, having studied the links between education, successful microeconomic reform and improved life chances. He recently completed postdoctoral fellowships at the Australian National University's Centre for Aboriginal Economic Policy Research and the National Centre for Indigenous Studies. Books include *Repossession of Our Spirit* and *Successful Indigenous Australian Entrepreneurs.* Currently he is teaching and researching at Swinburne University in Victoria.

Nigel Bagnall has extensive professional and consulting experience in a wide range of educational settings. He works in the Faculty of Education and Social Work at the University of Sydney. His work in international schools and his research on the International Baccalaureate has established his reputation in the field of international curriculum in cross-cultural settings. His current research interests include youth transition and the role of international schools as agents for change. In 2005 his book *Youth Transition in a Globalised Marketplace* was published.

Publisher's Note

Oxford University Press Australia's Higher Education textbook publishing delivers the quality teaching and learning resources that lecturers demand and students need.

Education, Change and Society is published to reflect Oxford University Press's commitment to knowledge, knowledge transfer and learning. The book is grounded in the decades of teaching experience of all of its authors, and reflects their skills at applying sound research methods to practice. In particular, the book owes its existence to 'Social Perspectives in Education'—the subject that Nigel Bagnall and Craig Campbell have been teaching successfully to their second year education students at the University of Sydney.

In publishing this textbook, we expect that students and lecturers from across Australia and New Zealand will benefit from the information contained within, helping them to achieve their goals of becoming better teachers and educators.

Acknowledgments

Raewyn Connell wishes to thank Molly Nicholson and John Fisher for unflagging and inventive research assistance.

Craig Campbell wishes to thank Kay Whitehead for permission to use extracts from journals written by teaching students at Flinders University. He also thanks Nigel Bagnall for permission to use extracts from research conducted by him, Sandra Nicholls and Peter Cuttance on parental school choice. Philippa Crosbie, social sciences librarian at the University of Sydney, provided timely assistance with the production of SEIFA tables from the Australian Bureau of Statistics.

Margaret Vickers would like to thank Cherry Collins, Raewyn Connell and Craig Campbell for their generosity in responding to drafts and supplying work that has been absorbed into her thinking and writing. She also thanks Florence McCarthy, whose patient support and expert readings of her work are always invaluable.

Anthony Welch thanks his co-authors for helpful feedback on drafts, especially Craig Campbell, Raewyn Connell and Margaret Vickers. He also thanks John Fisher and Jacqui Hicks for research assistance and Jill Gientzotis and Peter Welch for discussions on patterns of Vocational Education and Training enrolment and outcomes.

Dennis Foley thanks Jill Barnes for her enthusiastic and untiring support in reading and commenting on his work, and the Aboriginal Elder, Uncle John Budby, for his approval of content.

Nigel Bagnall would like to thank the two teachers at the international school in Hanoi, who agreed to their interviews being published in the chapter on globalisation.

All the authors thank the anonymous readers of the original book proposal and chapters. Their suggestions and positive responses were much appreciated. We also thank Debra James of Oxford University Press for her enthusiastic support for the project.

All the authors acknowledge and thank their undergraduate and graduate students over many years who have engaged with their teaching, and especially those who have boldly told them when a particular approach has or has not worked. This book would not exist without you.

Introduction

Education, Change and Society has at least two major purposes.

One is to help its readers situate educational activity in its broad social and policy contexts. The study of education can do more than help us understand how individuals may learn and how teachers may teach. The way any society educates its people provides important opportunities for understanding how those societies work; how they are made and ordered. It helps us understand what is valued in that society, and how 'winners and losers' are created. We only have to look at the life-consequences of the results gained by young people at the end of secondary school to see that the way our society organises the education of young people has very broad social as well as individual consequences.

As readers of this book will already know, Australia is experiencing a period of major change in education. The way that schools, school funding, school markets, universities and the responsibilities of government for education are organised have all been subject to quite radical reform in recent times. This turmoil in education is also occurring in Europe and North America. There is a great need to develop our understanding of the nature and consequences of such change. We also need to prepare ourselves for informed intervention if necessary, whether as students, teachers, parents or simply as active citizens.

As a consequence, this book ranges in focus from the local to the global contexts of educational change. It focuses on young people and families at one level, and high policy, national and international, at another. It has never been more important for students of education to be able to understand the connections between the local and the global in explaining contemporary educational change. Perhaps unusually for a book of this nature, there is also a strong contribution from history in explaining the current operation of education in Australia.

This book has been organised in a way that encourages the discussion, indeed contesting, of its text. Some chapters include boxed text that often provides evocative comment, illustration, and grounded examples of matters that the main text discusses more generally. They are meant to provoke reflection on the themes of the chapter. At the end of each chapter a number of focus questions are offered. They not only help readers identify some of the writers' key points, but hopefully will provoke thought and discussion beyond the text. Where this book is used as part of a course of study, some of these questions could easily be used as starting points for students' own essays, tutorial discussions, and even research if the suggestions for a research project as outlined in chapter 13 are taken up. Then there are the further reading references, also suggested at the conclusion of each chapter.

If *Education, Change and Society* is used as a textbook it should not be seen as self-contained. This is where the suggestions for further reading are significant. The book provides a platform for discovering the wealth of research and writing that has been done on the social contexts of education and policy studies in Australia and beyond. There are also some suggested web sites to explore. These and other sites must be read critically. As with all texts, web sites vary dramatically in terms of credibility and authority. Some belong to interest groups, not so much focused on looking at all sides of a question, but to support very specific agendas in education.

Readers will notice that the authors of the different chapters are named. Although this book is a cooperative effort, and although we have discussed each other's work, you will notice there are noticeably different styles from chapter to chapter. Probably the chapter most unlike the others is the chapter on Aboriginal experience and education in Australia. This chapter is charged with an urgency deriving from the great social justice questions that remain unresolved in that area. Unlike the other chapters it specifically targets one group of readers, those who are or would be teachers. As you will read, there are very strong reasons for this. This chapter more than any other demonstrates the general argument of this book; that is, that the study of education cannot be pursued successfully without the parallel study of society, politics, policy and economics.

The general contents of this book point to the issues that all the authors consider highly significant in understanding Australian education today.

What impact has globalisation had on Australian schools? How do Aboriginal students get on in Australian schools? What impacts do neoliberal and neo–conservative policy agendas have on school choice, selective schooling and the public or private funding of education—and the curriculum? Who writes policy documents in education? What impacts do they have on students, teachers, parents, administrators and the broader community? How do national policy agendas work in a world that is apparently witnessing a diminished role for the nation state? Why did state, private and corporate schools emerge as they did in Australia? How has this history of schooling affected the development of education? Why do more students in Australian schools attend non-government schools than in most other developed nations in the world? What are we to make of the gender wars in education? What truth is there in the argument that boys are the 'new disadvantaged', and that the historic struggle for girls to participate on an equal basis has been won? How do cultural differences among different groups in the population affect their schooling? How responsive are Australian education systems to the different languages, cultural origins, and ethnic and religious identities of families and students? How do schools participate in the making and unmaking of a class society? How does the transition of youth from school to work operate? And how does what is taught in schools, the curriculum, relate to such questions?

A special feature of this book is the suggestion that for those who use it as a textbook, a research project could usefully be developed. In chapter 13 we offer a model that requires working closely with a fellow student on a topic of interest to both partners. We argue that the role of research has become increasingly significant in education, and to teachers in particular: for example, the days of gaining some teaching qualification and then heading off into the classroom for the next thirty years without staying abreast of developments in education are over. Teachers, schools and school systems increasingly need to be well informed about what works, what does not, and why—and more to the point with this book, what social and policy developments in and around education affect the way they operate. It is crucial that education professionals understand the potential contribution of well-conducted research for useful reform. The research assignment outlined in this book is conceived as a 'first' project, one that begins to raise the levels of awareness about what constitutes useful research questions, methods, data, and conclusions.

We wish you well in the use of this book. We hope that it will provide a stimulus to good thinking and provide some useful perspectives that will help you understand the way that education in Australia operates, especially in terms of its contribution to the making of Australian society.

Nigel Bagnall

1
Making Education Policy

Anthony Welch

'There is no use trying,' said Alice; 'one can't believe impossible things.'
'I dare say you haven't had much practice,' said the Queen.
'When I was your age, I always did it for half an hour a day. Why, sometimes I've
believed as many as six impossible things before breakfast.'
LEWIS CARROLL

1   Making policy, making democracy

The world of education has changed profoundly over recent decades, so as to re-shape all who interact with it, whether educators, students or parents. Educational institutions, too, have been reshaped in particular ways, sometimes by forces well outside education, and all too often, it seems, according to principles that have little to do with education.

As prospective educators, and current students of education, it is critical that you understand the context of the system in which you will work. In addition to the key themes such as race, gender, and class, this includes far more than just public and private schools. It also includes Technical and Further Education (TAFE), universities, and other institutions of education (zoos, transport systems, and commercial organisations that include training as part of their business). It is also important to understand something of the policy process itself, not merely so that you can make informed decisions about the rationale for specific policies in education (for example, the kinds and quality of evidence upon which they are based), but also so that you can play a role in the policy process, if desired. Indeed, it is quite possible that you will be invited to play a role in developing or assessing policy within a few years of beginning your career in education. This may be at institutional level (school, TAFE, or in other educational settings) or as part of wider actions (such as taking part in trade union campaigns).

Much of the argument developed in this chapter, and the concepts on which it draws, are not unique to the world of education, but reflect key ways in which contemporary families, society, and the state are being reshaped. It is only to be expected that changes in education, at times, originate from political or economic arenas—indeed it is argued in chapter 6 that education more often responds to change than initiates it. Nonetheless, many educators now feel that these changes are often outside their control, and that their views are rarely sought and little appreciated. Civil servants involved in the policy process sometimes also feel that their expertise and experience is little acknowledged or appreciated. Changes, it is felt, come from 'on high', or from remote authorities, which seem to have little appreciation of the purposes of education as educators see it, and often seem to create more work, but bring little benefit. This leads us to the question of what are the purposes of education within a democratic society and, perhaps, how is democracy itself changing?

2 Understanding the policy process

Many of the individual chapters in this volume are examples of educational policy in action: gender, multiculturalism, rural–urban differences. So it is important that we understand something of the policy process. How are policies made in education?

Policy is the name we give to deliberative, 'official' statements about social goals (which are in effect both images or ideas about social goals) and the strategies to put these in place. Policy, then, is about means and ends—perhaps a better way of expressing this is that it is about means towards ends. Put simply, policy is about what is to be done. Policies are not made unless something can be improved, something we value is threatened, or we feel that there is a problem of some kind that prevents certain specified goals from being attained. Policies are, then, a response to change, an attempt to guide or manage change. They may be either an attempt to preserve or restore threatened (or lost) values or an attempt to realise as yet unattained values, or both. They attempt to regulate, or (re)shape, social reality in specific ways. Nonetheless the policy problematic consists of different facets: policy, as *an embodiment of a set of values*, is distinct from policy in the sense of an analysis of the *obstacles to value realisation*, and distinct again from the *strategy for realising values* in the teeth of the obstacles, which is in turn distinct from the *process of implementation*, in which strategies sometimes come adrift.

This more recent characterisation of the policy process emphasises this link between means and ends. It was not always so. Earlier explanations were more linear, often outlining separate stages in the policy process—along the lines of formulation, adoption, and implementation (perhaps also with some subsequent evaluation). The problem with such traditional, technicist accounts is that they make the process remote from our intervention—policy becomes external and reified, something that is done to us. Such views also tend to reinforce a traditionally managerial conception of policy (for more on managerialism, see below), in which the generation of policy is strictly separated from the implementation phase

(Bowe, Ball & Gold, 1992, p. 7). Such characterisations also ignore the fact that policies are not static, but often evolve even after their 'official' promulgation.

These older accounts of policy also often saw the process as 'value-free'. That is, it was assumed that policy was just about the technical process of implementing social goals, without consideration of the underpinning social values, their effects, or where they came from. A key problem with the assumption that policies are unrelated to values, or are 'value free', is that it ignores the question of power in society, in particular the notions that policies are not neutral, but rather help to empower and disempower specific groups differentially in society, and, moreover, that at specific moments in the history of policies, intervention by key interest groups may become possible. Cracks, fissures, and crevices may open up in policy discourses, into which wedges may be driven, which can splinter the apparently smooth and united face with which a policy is often presented. Beyond this, the managerial approach fails to allow much role for differentiation—that is, that different readings of a policy are possible, indeed predictable.

Contemporary accounts of policy often stress its contingent and changeable qualities. The British policy analyst Stephen Ball (1990, 1994; Bowe, Ball & Gold, 1992) sees it as follows:

> A policy is both contested and changing, always in a state of 'becoming', of 'was' and 'never was' and 'not quite'; for any text a plurality of readers must always produce a plurality of readings (Ball, 1994, p. 16).

Clearly, however, despite this multiplicity of possible readings (policies are inherently neither closed nor complete), authors of policies do make strenuous efforts to control the proliferation of meanings and in particular to legitimise their reading and undermine others'. Once again, this reminds us of the fact that policies involve politics, and emerge in specific circumstances, at a particular time. Powerful figures can at times act as virtual 'gatekeepers', interpreting policy to those around them (or not). In school settings these could be Principals or Departmental Heads, for example. But policy, which often attempts to redistribute power relations, can also be effectively undermined, perhaps by those charged with its implementation at school level. The example on national assessment policy in Britain given by Ball (1994, p. 18) amusingly reveals this process. Despite this, and the recognition that one policy may well contradict other policies, nonetheless policy 'matters: it is important, not the least because it consists of texts which are (sometimes) *acted on*' (Ball, 1994, p. 18). Ultimately:

> Given constraints, circumstances and practicalities, the translation of the crude, abstract simplicities of policy texts into interactive and sustainable practices of some sort involves productive thought, invention and adaptation. Policies do not normally tell you what to do, they create circumstances in which the range of options available

in deciding what to do are narrowed or changed, or particular goals or outcomes set. A response must still be put together, constructed in context, offset against other expectations. All of this involves creative social action, not robotic activity' (Ball, 1994, p. 19).

State, and increasingly global, policy, then (for more on ways in which globalisation sets policy agendas at the national level, see chapter 12), sets the rules of the game, but does not determine the outcome, which is often settled by competing interest groups. Moreover, as with other arenas such as health and welfare, educational policy often confronts the realities of social inequalities, lack of resources, and other resistant elements of the local context that it is powerless to change.

On occasion, Ball refers to policy as discourse. In so doing, he intends to highlight the way in which policy is deliberately presented as 'truth', its meaning as fixed or given. Discourses, according to the French theorist Michel Foucault, shape what may be said and by whom, and with what legitimacy; they are practices that produce 'knowledge' and 'truth', and express particular ways of thought, language and practice (Ball, 1994). They contain particular value systems. Policy ensembles such as 'marketisation', 'ability', 'management', and 'efficiency and effectiveness' each contain their own truths, values and practices, according to this view. They create their own new sciences (and associated technologies) of education, with the assistance of specific 'experts' or 'intellectuals' who help to create the machinery of this new science, and elaborate its rationale. Thus the discourse creates a reality, and it may be (at times) difficult or impossible to 'see' (talk, write) beyond the boundaries of this reality. The discourse may render it difficult to think 'otherwise' (oppositionally):

> The essence of this is that there are real struggles over the interpretation and enactment of policies. But these are set within a moving discursive frame which articulates and constrains the possibilities and probabilities of interpretation and enactment. We read and respond to policies in discursive circumstances that we cannot, or perhaps do not, think about' (Ball, 1994, p. 23).

Might this lead to simple pessimism, a perception of powerlessness or loss of agency based on the assumed determinism of the discourse? Do the limits of the discourse form the limits to what we can think and do? Not necessarily, on this account, since in practice we are enmeshed in a variety of contradictory discourses, some of which may well be starting points for opposition. Nonetheless, some discourses contain more power (in certain settings) than others, and it is arguably currently the case that 'market liberalism', 'economic rationalism' and the like are powerfully influential on social policy.

Another useful way of thinking about the purposes and effects of policy draws on a fundamental distinction often used in the social sciences: between critical and functionalist styles of theory. Traditionally, policy analysis was often tied more or less closely to the machinery of policy-making, and thus often echoed its values. Thus the generally functionalist values of maintaining the social system and fostering values that promoted social harmony, consensus, and integration were often (implicitly) incorporated into policy analysis. This was not different from the situation of the social sciences in general, where, in the pre- and post-World War II era, such values underpinned mainstream social analysis. From around the 1970s, however, these values were less likely to be taken for granted, and were often replaced by principles based more around the struggle of competing interests for power and control. From this view, personal and social emancipation are prime values, and confront modes of domination in society that are oppressive for the many (who are disempowered in society) and advantageous for the few (whose powerful positions in society give them disproportionate influence). This gives policy a very different role.

Who makes policy?

Tennis clubs as well as Departments of Education and the World Bank are engaged in the policy process: that is, they attempt to achieve certain goals by setting and attempting to implement policies. (Clearly, however, not all policy decisions are as world shattering as others—more people are affected by policy decisions made by the World Bank or the Department of Education than by one devised by the local tennis club). But in another sense, there is no one answer to the question of who makes policy, since different policy contexts involve different dynamics, in which specific processes and individuals become important. This again reminds us that policies always need to be seen in their social and institutional context. For while abstract discussions of policy may be interesting, a close examination of the actual, historically concrete political and social context, and in turn who are the major players in that episode, is more likely to yield knowledge of what the policy was actually designed to achieve (and not merely its stated objectives), and why certain historical figures were important in the determination of that specific policy, at that time, and in that setting. This applies in education as well as in other areas of social policy (health, environment, transport, welfare etc.). To take an obvious example, we may all hold views on media policy, but James Packer's views, or those of Rupert Murdoch, will be much more influential than yours or mine. For this and other reasons, it is important to carefully scrutinise policies for their underlying aims and effects, which are by no means always congruent with the stated ones!

In the end (after reading and thinking about the problem) it is up to you to decide whether you see policy as ultimately being about ethics and politics, or whether you think that values should be left out of the policy equation. But as students of policy, we are required to critically scrutinise evidence adduced and omitted, research methodologies employed, underlying assumptions, and the emphases, silences, and omissions of policy documents. This is all the more important for the significant proportion of students who undertake policy-related research projects (see chapter 13).

3 Politics of reform or the reform of politics? The changing nature of the state

It was argued above that policies have a concrete history (or, as Foucault might have it, an 'archaeology' or 'genealogy'). They are produced at a particular time, for a particular purpose, and by a complex social and political process. In short, they are embedded in their time and place, while seeking to make specific changes. In addition, they are promulgated with some sort of legal/administrative force, and they are elaborated, evaluated, implemented (or not implemented), and revised or jettisoned. They are, above all, social artefacts, usually forged in a struggle between competing interest groups, and often ultimately satisfying no single interest group entirely. But what role does the state play in this process, and how has this role changed in recent times?

It is this question that makes analysis of the role of government, the 'state' as an apparatus in a nation, including the bureaucracy, and other organisations, important. By state here, I do not intend to refer to a particular state (Tasmania, for example), but rather the complex web of public authority and public institutions that regulate (and for much of the twentieth century generally provided) basic services such as health, education, and welfare, and that also provide a degree of legitimacy for the system as a whole.

It is argued here that the neoliberal project of reform that has been the focus of policy realignments in most of the Anglo-American democracies over the past two decades, and to a lesser extent elsewhere, has reshaped the state in two particular ways. The first is that the so-called crisis of the state has led to a significant reduction in what is often called the 'public good' function of education. (The 'public good' of something refers to the notion that it has worth and is of benefit to the whole of society, and not just for the 'private good' of the individual.) In Australia, more than in many other countries, the onslaught on the public good functions of key social policy arenas has licensed considerable privatisation of services in education, health, transport and welfare, while at the same time presiding over a process that has seen responsibility for (problems in) delivery exported to the local level.

The second form of change is the degree of control that the state exercises over the operation of education, and institutions and individuals that deliver education. Paradoxically perhaps, while the state has reduced substantially its responsibility for delivering and funding the education system—in part a reflection of a wider, monetarist set of economic reforms (Codd, 1997)—it has increased the detailed regulation of institutions and individuals, under the name of accountability. The latter phenomenon is generally called managerialism. Each of these trends is treated below.

The crisis of the state

Michael Pusey's groundbreaking *Economic Rationalism in Australia* (1991), as well as Anna Yeatman's *Bureaucrats, Technocrats and Femocrats* (1990), focused on ways in which the policy climate in Australia had changed significantly over the past decade or so. Each of these works uses changes in the nature of the Australian state as a key part of their explanation, and each, particularly the first, provides a useful starting point for your reading into the policy context in Australia, and some similar trends overseas. While each uses different terms, both are characterising similar trends that have occurred in Australia, and some other parts of the world over the last decade or more (Ball, 1998; Henry et al., 2001). Pusey speaks of the change in Australia from an earlier state-building set of values that saw the economy as in the service of social policy, to something more like the reverse. Under the current ideology, he argues, an economistic techno-logic dominates all forms of social policy. In some of her work, Yeatman characterises the changes as from a welfare state to a competition state, in which, under the latter, the only real rationale for intervention by the state is to maximise economic competitiveness, in the new, interconnected, globalised world:

> The state is no longer in a position anywhere to pursue the general welfare as if it were mainly a domestic problem. As the world economy is characterised by increasing interpenetration and the crystallisation of transnational markets and structures, the state itself is having to act more and more like a market player, that shapes its policies to promote, control and maximize returns from market forces in an international setting (Yeatman, 1993, p. 3).

Both works analyse and evaluate the changing role of the state in social policy arenas such as education. Both books should be high on your priority list for early reading, as they characterise the changes in the Australian policy context. You may disagree of course; but not without reading them first. In Australia's case, we have also often been influenced by reforms in other (English-speaking) countries, but there are also international economic patterns of globalisation and restructuring (Welch & Mok, 2003; Welch, 2005), which continue to be influential, as well as modern theoretical currents, such as postmodernism (Welch, 1996b; Apple, 1997), which may be influential at times in helping to cast policy in particular moulds.

Just as there are international trends that are reconfiguring the modern state, there are many aspects of policy in Australian education that reflect local influences. Sometimes too much perhaps—the narrow parochialism and needless duplication of separate state education departments has long been lamented, both by practitioners and analysts of the Australian system. The structure of Australian government is distinctive. The traditionally strongly centralised, and sometimes sclerotic central bureaucracies that inhabit each of the Australian capitals, and at times act as a dead hand upon worthwhile reforms; the role of national and state governments in a federal system and the often adversarial relationship between them; trade unions and voluntary associations such as parents' groups, are all important local influences. So, too, is the economic and political situation of Australia, located close to Asia, at a time of rapid changes in the global economy. Cultural factors and multiculturalism, and broad generic changes in communication and information management, are also important elements of the contemporary policy context.

Of all these changes, those that have reshaped the nature of the modern Australian state are central. A key element in Pusey's account is the specific ways in which the Australian state—'the complex of legal, political and bureaucratic institutions' (Pusey, 1991, p. 14)—has been transformed over the past two decades or so. In earlier times, he argues, Australia was engaged in a state-building exercise, which was crucial to the development of the infrastructure and services that we currently take for granted—roads and railways, hospitals, schools and universities. Indeed, in a country with a land mass of 7.7 million square kilometres, and a population in 1880 of only 2.25 million, it is hard to imagine any other way that this infrastructure could have been developed, beyond major, sustained intervention by the state. The ratio of costs to profits meant that no private entrepreneur, however wealthy, would have dreamed of establishing schools, hospitals and railways in the many small hamlets that were beginning to occupy the vast Australian continent. Even today, Australia's population is only around 21 million (a little less than that of Taiwan), which yields an average of only about 2.6 individuals per square kilometre. This is the lowest population density of any advanced country in the world. Such low population density makes a substantial difference to the range and quality of services such as education and communications that are available to rural and remote communities (especially Indigenous), as chapter 4 details. It also means that there is little incentive for private providers to establish and maintain services such as education in areas with small and scattered populations. There is cost, but no profit, in providing services to the bush, however important it is to those communities, and however beneficial to the nation.

The end of World War II in 1945 saw a commitment to open up opportunities to the wider populace, in ways that had not occurred before. In education, this embraced the new migrant communities that were such an important feature of postwar Australia (see chapter 7). It also embraced the development of state high schools for the rapidly growing population (Australia's population grew at an average 2 per cent per annum over the period 1945–75, half of which was due to immigration and the other half to fertility).

Education was becoming more available than ever before, and was widely seen as a key means to achieve equality in society. Arguably the apex of this commitment came with the publication of *Schools in Australia* (1973), colloquially known as the Karmel Report (Karmel, 1973). Commissioned by the incoming, reformist Whitlam government, it was one of the first systematic national reports to attempt to measure the state of education. It became a landmark document, and was used to redirect educational resources and priorities. In particular, the report pointed out that the postwar policy of expansion had not equalised opportunities in higher education, for example. Equally, attendance at different school types was strongly correlated with greater retentivity: those attending a private Anglican high school were over three times more likely to complete year 12 than those attending a state high school (Welch, 1996b, p. 146; Karmel, 1973, p. 19). Rural and female disadvantage in education was also charted. Overall, the committee found that just opening up opportunity by making an unchanged education more available had not worked, and argued that equality of outcomes should now be the measure of educational reforms and progress. To achieve this bold vision, they argued that 'certain additional measures have to be taken with those who lag behind' (Welch, 1996b; Karmel, 1973, p. 23). In the aftermath of the report, impressive resources were devoted to equalising education, including specific schemes such as the significant Disadvantaged Schools Program (Connell, White & Johnston, 1991).

However important, such initiatives proved to be brief. The publication of the *Quality of Education: Report of the Review Committee* in 1985, often called the QERC Report, signalled a move to more outcomes-based education, and a lesser emphasis on equality of opportunity, compared to its predecessor in 1973. By the mid 1980s, Pusey's argument, based on a close study of the federal civil service, revealed that a very different policy landscape was becoming evident, the contours of which have only deepened since, according to many. For Pusey, Australian 'reality has been turned upside down' (Pusey, 1991, p. 10), via a radical hollowing out of traditional state functions. The notion of the 'social good', according to this new ideology, has become marginalised: a 'buried discourse' (Pusey, 1991,

p. 166) replaced by a new economistic rhetoric of individual rights, and ideologies of 'efficiency', and 'choice'. As some have pointed out, notably the American author Raymond Callahan (1962), we have seen such efficiency ideologies before in education, and with predictable results (see Welch, 1998).

This is the heart of what Pusey dubbed 'economic rationalism': the domination of social policy by the language and logic of economics. But it is important to understand that this is a very particular form of economics: modern 'positivist' economics, which perceives itself as a value-free science (rather like the mainstream physical sciences), simply applying specific theories and techniques to economic problems, and eschewing value judgements about social goals. This is very distinct from political economy, for example, where social and political elements are an integral part of any economic analysis.

The domination of social policy by positivist forms of economics, including in education, distorted the policy process, simply adopting certain goals as given, or self-evident, and then 'rationally' implementing these goals in the leanest, most economically efficient manner, ignoring moral concerns about the quality of people's lives, and the impact on society. In the process, whole programs, or specialist units and agencies, often designed to focus on marginal groups, disappeared.

A recent example was the axing of the Department of Women in the 2004 New South Wales state budget, one in a series of decisions taken over the last two decades by all state and federal governments, of whatever political persuasion, which have steadily dismantled specific equity programs, or special purpose offices and agencies, in areas such as women's affairs, Indigenous affairs, or multicultural affairs. The decision may well save money—which is often why it is done. And it is regularly accompanied by an assurance from the relevant Minister, or Director General, that 'mainstreaming' the policy—for example, making all departments add women's equity issues to their agenda, rather than having a special agency or Ministry responsible for monitoring the policy and ensuring progress is made— will be just as efficient. In practice, key specialist personnel and resources are often lost, and the focus of the policy diffused. In the case just cited, a single person was retained from thirty-two specialist staff, many with years of irreplaceable expertise. The former Deputy Director of the department now works in New Zealand.

Changing the civil service

This process has been aggravated by the politicisation of the public service over the last two decades or so, leading to what Anna Yeatman (1987) termed 'teleological promiscuity' (that is, an amoral openness to any social goal). The 'Westminster' system of parliamentary government has, as one of its core principles, the independence of its civil servants. Traditionally, such individuals would commence their career at low levels within a particular state or federal department, and work their way up, acquiring valuable experience and 'corporate memory' along the way. Hence, senior civil servants, charged with giving the Minister advice in key areas, could be assumed to know their policy area intimately. Now, however, management skills are increasingly seen as generic, and career paths much less confined to a single department or Ministry. So it is perfectly possible to move from a senior management role in, say, transport, or water resources, to one in education. (In a sense, this is beginning to parallel the transition that state or federal Ministers make, from one portfolio to another—perhaps starting in Transport, or Regional Affairs, then to Education, and perhaps ultimately to Finance.) This has undoubtedly diminished the authority of senior civil servants in the policy process.

A second trend has been for Ministers to develop special (policy) units within their own office, staffed with their own appointees, who in practice sometimes take the place of the specialist civil servants, at least to some extent. Such staffers are commonly quite young, often with a background in the Minister's own political party, and exhibit primary loyalty to the Minister and their office, rather than the portfolio. Indeed, it is relatively rare for such individuals to have great experience in the policy portfolio at all—they often have much less work experience of any kind than the specialist civil servant, whose career has been within the area. Nonetheless, if the staffer rings with an urgent demand from the Minister's office, it would be a foolhardy public servant, even a very senior one, to ignore it or even to delay responding, however many other work demands there are. If the Minister moves portfolio, such 'staffers' are likely to accompany them, while the civil servants remain within the department.

With one important exception. A third trend is the creation of a higher echelon of civil servants, collectively often known as the Senior Executive Service (SES), somewhat similar to the 'Next Steps' agencies introduced into the UK civil service during the late 1980s. This small and select group of senior bureaucrats within a Ministry comprises the uppermost ranks of the civil service, with titles such as *Director, Assistant Director-General, Deputy Director-General,* and *Director-General.* Such positions may be filled from outside the specific Ministry, or, less commonly, from outside the civil service (for example, from industry, or the non-government or 'third' sector). Unlike the lower and middle levels of the civil service, SES employment contracts do not include permanence, but are for a specified term (perhaps 5 years). Renewal, and perhaps a financial bonus, is conditional upon achieving specified performance targets.

This causes at least two problems that clearly relate to our understanding of how the policy process is changing. The fact that each individual within the SES has their performance monitored, annually, by their superior, can entail a certain loss of independence, since the individual who is being reviewed may expend a significant amount of their energy and time ensuring that their superior is 'happy' with their performance. This is important, since the renewal of their appointment may well depend on favourable reviews, but the process can compromise their capacity (or willingness) to deliver independent advice 'without fear or favour', as was the expectation under the older system. Most civil servants are still strongly committed to the public good aspects of policy alluded to above, but have become constrained by the much more instrumentalist values and practices of the newer system (Yeatman, 1994, 1997). The second problem is that colleagues at lower echelons, upon whose work the attainment of SES performance targets ultimately depends, may feel no such commitment to meeting such performance targets, which bring them no rewards, just additional work.

In effect, civil servants, at least at the senior levels, have become incorporated into government in ways they had been protected against previously. Senior civil servants have had to take on the role of politicians, who expect them to answer external queries about operational aspects of specific policies (Clarke, Gewirtz & McLaughlin, 2000, p. 73). The 'minister soars above the ruck, pristine, uninformed and therefore untouchable, a distant observer of the follies being played out below' (*SMH*, 2006, 7 February). This does not prevent those same politicians interfering routinely in the day-to-day operation of the public agencies or state departments. But it certainly leaves senior public servants much more exposed when an inquiry finds that there are problems with services in education (or health, or welfare, or immigration affairs). How often is it now the case that when problems are found with schools or hospitals, that a senior civil servant loses their job, rather than the relevant Minister, who righteously remarks that he or she 'was not told' of the problem?

> ... civil servants have been positioned as political scapegoats by ministers who have been unwilling to take responsibility when matters have gone amiss, and who have been able to define the problem as an 'operational' issue (Clarke, Gewirtz & McLaughlin, 2000, p. 73).

Under the traditional Westminster system, it was the job of the Minister to know, and if problems were found to be serious, it was the Minister, rather than the civil servant, who fell. Now it is 'not *Yes, Minister*, it is *Don't ask, Minister*' (*SMH*, 2006, 7 February).

4　The rise of economics: markets, managerialism, and the knowledge economy

If Pusey's argument has force, it should be possible to trace the influence of rising economic effects on ways of thinking about educational policy and on measuring their effects. There are at least three areas in which clear effects can be seen: markets, managerialism and performance indicators, and the knowledge economy.

The rise of markets in education has had a profound effect on Australian society in recent years (McKnight, 2005) as educational institutions (both private *and* public) increasingly compete for students, or at least for a greater share of certain kinds of students. It is now often said that, rather than students choosing schools, schools are often choosing students, in carefully orchestrated marketing campaigns. Universities are also enmeshed in this market, competing for both local and international enrolments.

But individuals and families also compete for advantage in education. Within market discourses education is seen as a positional good, in which those who have the knowledge and opportunity use education for purposes of achieving greater status and a better position in the socio-economic hierarchy (Gewirtz, Ball & Bowe, 1995). Choices are often made more according to the status of an educational institution, whether school, college or university, rather than the quality of education it offers. Individuals gain advantage through gaining access to prestige education, but this is at a cost to others: 'Positional competition ... is a zero-sum game. What winners win, losers lose' (Hirsch, 1976, p. 52). For a more detailed illustration of the operation of educational markets, see chapter 9 on school choice.

Managerialism

Much of this is reflective of a broader change that has significant implications for how policy is done—the incorporation of a culture of managerialism among the public service. Educators, social workers and health workers all feel the impact of this 'new work order' (Gee, Hull & Lankshear, 1996). Managerialism is a core feature of what is called New Public Management (NPM), under which governance in the modern state becomes a form of entrepreneurship. The implications for civil servants involved in the policy process, as well as teachers, pupils and academics, are substantial.

Under this new regime, the public sector is no longer 'about the delivery of public values but about the management of scarce resources' (Yeatman, 1993, p. 3). In practice, this means doing more with less, in a context where public resources are being redirected away from social welfare towards the prime requirement of enhancing economic competitiveness. Accountability is transformed under such an ideological regime—from political accountability to financial (Clarke, Gewirtz & McLaughlin; 2000, p. 73). Agencies and departments become responsible for the prudent management of declining resources (in relative, if not in absolute terms), in a setting where their effectiveness is measured by quantitative performance indicators. Current examples of such indicators include how many patients had to wait more than a year for elective surgery, or how many pupils achieved in the top 10 per cent in nationally mandated performance literacy or numeracy tests (*SMH*,

2005, 4, 12 May; *Australian*, 2005, 3 June, 30 August). Nothing is usually said about the quality of the measures themselves, although it is generally assumed that success in meeting performance targets, as measured by the indicators, equates to good quality, whether of health, welfare, or education. Qualitative assessments of policy outcomes—slower to do, but often richer, and more meaningful and effective in getting at the experience of pupils, their parents and teachers (or doctors, nurses and patients)—are almost never part of the proliferating panoply of performance indicators. Not only are they too slow and costly, it is argued, relative to quick, quantitative measures, they are often wrongly thought to be too 'unscientific' (See chapter 13 (part 1) for a sketch of how such an ideology of scientism and empiricism arose, and its meaning for educational research.)

The effects on both the policy process, and those who must work with it and within it, occur on a daily basis. According to one specialist, '... the first consequence is to turn public servants into economic managers working inside a permanent depression mentality' (Yeatman, 1993, p. 4). Under this new ideology, heads of civil service departments, and to an extent, school principals, deans of university faculties and the like, can become more like 'bean counters'. This is not to say that such individuals lack traditional commitment to their policy portfolio, or relevant groups with whom they interact: rather, that the technologies of surveillance and performance assessment, key elements of modern managerialist models, distort and detract from the traditional educational missions of teaching and learning. This is because of the increasing levels of resources that must be devoted, at an individual and institutional level, to meet their never-ending demands. The performance of educational managers such as department heads is measured against their peers, in the efficient and unquestioning achievement of pre-set agendas in the most economically lean manner (Retallick, 1991). In turn, they must exhort their staff to compete in conforming to an ever-larger and more intrusive panoply of performance indicators. In the increasingly market-oriented world of education, whoever has the neatest, most efficient results, as measured by performance indicators, wins. In the process, accountability has become transformed into a species of accountancy (Peters, 1992; Welch, 1998).

Payment by results

A key technology of managerialism is the idea of rewarding workers according to quantitative performance targets. How do performance indicators work, why were they introduced, and what influence do they have on educational policy? In the Anglo-American democracies described above (such countries as New Zealand, Canada, the UK, and Australia), performance indicators have flourished in recent decades, to the point where they have become an integral element of managerialism within education, just as in health, welfare and other public policy arenas. But not for the first time. As indicated above, the fever for business efficiency has swept through education before. Such past episodes serve not merely as good examples of the effects of this ideology, but as excellent reminders of how history can usefully inform contemporary policy.

The first example is drawn from the mid nineteenth century, and was, like much educational baggage of the time, imported from England. (Among other things, it also serves as a timely warning to current hyper-globalists, who insist that the impact of globalisation effects on current policy agendas is an entirely novel phenomenon. Importing policies from the UK, or elsewhere, is by no means new!)

The Revised Code, or *payment by results* as it came to be known, was introduced into British education around the 1860s, and in various forms into some of the Australian colonies at much the same time (Turney, 1969, pp. 229–32). The defence of the English scheme was encapsulated in the proud boast of its proponent to the British parliament: 'If it is not cheap it shall be efficient; if it is not efficient it shall be cheap' (Maclure, 1973, pp. 79–80). Its legitimacy stemmed from the strong prevailing current of business accountability and efficiency that informed education inquiries of the time: 'The Commissioners held the common view of the period, that the notion of accountability, so vital to a well-run business, should be applied vigorously to all forms of government expenditure' (Musgrave, 1968, p. 35).

The scheme, largely inspired by middle-class fears of rising calls upon state funds for elementary schools (which were provided for the working class) and the needs of a 'business age', specified a 'standard' that each child had to attain to pass at that level (Musgrave, 1968, p. 36). This standard was based upon the assumed needs of industry for a literate workforce, and bourgeois assumptions of the knowledge needed by the working class: '... a Christian version of the three Rs for boys and girls up to the age of ten or twelve' (Musgrave, 1968, p. 36). Once implemented, the scheme justified steep cuts to the state budget for primary education—the grant promptly fell by more than a quarter, from £813,441 in 1861 to £636,806 in 1865—and also led to a sharp decline in numbers of pupil teachers and teachers' college trainees (the latter from 2792 to 2403 within 6 years of the scheme being introduced). That this decline occurred at a time of demonstrably increasing need meant a profound worsening in the ratio of pupil teachers to students in schools: from 1:36 in 1861 to 1:54 5 years later, a fall of precisely 50 per cent (Maclure, 1973, p. 81).

It also had other perverse effects. It encouraged cheating by teachers, whose annual salaries were now tied both to the numbers of pupils in their classes and to their performance in particular exams. Her Majesty's Inspectors (HMIs) reported that teachers 'stuffed and almost roasted' (Hyndman, 1978, p. 34) their pupils on test items once they knew that the inspector's visit was imminent. Other teachers secretly trained their pupils so that when they were asked questions, they raised their right hands if they knew the correct answer, but their left hand if they did not, thus creating a more favourable impression upon the visiting inspector. Another teacher proudly proclaimed that his entire class would pass the test, because 'any one of them can copy three desks off' (Hyndman, 1978, p. 34), while yet another teacher (wrongly) caned his entire class for leaving the 'd' out of 'pigeon' on the test. Other teachers falsified their enrolment registers, inflating the numbers of pupils so that the numbers were kept artificially high. Evidently sick children were dragged along to school to satisfy attendance requirements, upon which teachers' salaries were dependent (Hyndman, 1978, p. 37). (Pupils had to have 200 attendances per year to their credit before they could take the test.) Moreover, teachers, who had previously been paid directly, now had to negotiate with school managers 'as to their rate of remuneration' (Musgrave, 1968, p. 37).

Cramming (of the facts needed to pass the test) rather than teaching became the means to ensure one's livelihood as a teacher, and there is no doubt that pupils, teachers, and the process of education were impoverished as a result: 'Now there is always a tendency both in teachers and pupils to confine themselves to the minimum of requirement. Attention is paid to the subject which pays, to the exclusion of all others' (Hyndman, 1978, p. 30). Hence, a further product of the Revised Code was a narrowing of the curriculum and a narrow instrumentalism with respect to educational aims. Overall, while the scheme was justified by appeals to the principle of 'efficiency', it was in fact introduced largely as a means of curbing justifiable growth in state expenditure on education.

The Australian schemes largely aped the British. The introduction of the so-called 'Standards of Proficiency' into New South Wales by William Wilkins entailed scrupulously close following of the set requirements by teachers, and a similarly close examination of those requirements by the inspectors. Teachers' promotional prospects were directly tied to the results obtained by their pupils in the test, hence one of the major effects of the scheme was that of 'encouraging rote learning and the use of mechanical modes of instruction' (Turney, 1969, p. 230), while the role of inspectors changed from that of mentor to more of an assessor: 'The work of the inspector largely became one of mechanical examining and his reports became mainly based on statistical analysis of results' (Turney, 1969, p. 231).

Teachers' work came to be dominated by the 'Standards', leading to mechanical forms of pedagogy that slavishly followed key texts. A critic of the time argued that the fault lay not with the teachers, many of whom did not wish to teach in such a narrow and instrumental manner, but were nonetheless:

defeated by the machinery which they were obliged to employ. They were bound by the books prescribed to them; the inspectors, upon whose reports their bread depended, were perhaps bound by the same books in testing the proficiency of the scholars. The schoolmasters who would fain teach in a more rational manner, are afraid to displease their inspectors, whom they suppose to be strongly in favour of this kind of (mechanical) teaching (Turney, 1969, p. 232).

In the colony of Victoria, *payment by results* was acknowledged to have achieved 'the encouragement (of) … memorization rather than reasoning, (of) formal, mechanical teaching methods, and … keeping the curriculum narrow' (Barcan, 1980, p. 107; see also Rodwell, 1992).

Taylorism or scientific management

The 'payment by results' scheme in England, and similar schemes in various Australian colonies at much the same time, were not the only ones to use appeals to efficiency as a means to promote business-style reforms in education. A second episode occurred with the introduction of Taylorism or *scientific management* into American schools and universities in the period around World War I. Originally introduced into manufacturing industry in an attempt to increase productivity (the amount of work achieved per worker), the success of scientific management in extracting more output per input made it attractive to those concerned to hold back or reduce spending on education. The impetus stemmed largely from business interests, which were concerned, under the banner of efficiency, to reduce costs (termed 'wastage') to the state in education, and at the same time to shift the financial burden of training workers, through apprenticeships, away from industry, which had been their traditional training ground.

Once again, the *cult of efficiency* as it was dubbed (Callahan, 1962; Welch, 1998) impoverished education. And not merely financially: the narrowing of the curriculum in the direction of vocational training was accomplished, along with a reduction in the ability of the education system to respond to the needs of African Americans (then called 'blacks'), rural dwellers, poor whites, and the growing proportion of American immigrants.

What was the basic rationale for the introduction of *scientific management* techniques into the schools and universities of the time? The argument:

…consisted of making unfavourable comparisons between the schools and business enterprise, of applying business–industrial criteria (e.g. economy and efficiency) to education, and of suggesting that business and industrial practices be adopted by educators (Callahan, 1962, p. 6).

In 1903, the *Atlantic Monthly* magazine argued the case strongly:

The management of school affairs is a large business involving in a city of 100,000 inhabitants an expenditure of probably $500,000 annually; the same business principles adopted in modern industry should be employed here (Callahan, 1962, p. 6).

Two years later, the National Education Association commenced its symposium on research directions with the topic of a 'Comparison of Modern Business Methods with Educational Methods'. By 1907 books on 'classroom management' were being published and widely read, arguing that 'classroom management may be looked upon as a "business problem"'. By 1910, it could be argued that:

Our universities are beginning to be run as business colleges. They advertise, they compete with one another, they pretend to give good value to their customers. They desire to increase their trade, they offer social advantages and business openings to their patrons (Callahan, 1962, p. 7).

School boards (the local unit of school government of in the United States) were cut in size, sometimes quite drastically, and came to be increasingly dominated by businessmen, whose major brief they saw as the renovation of school admin–istration along business lines. This represented a profound change from the practice of the nineteenth century, in which the best-known school administrators were people like William T. Harris, Horace Mann, and Henry Barnard, whose fame derived principally from their work as educational scholars and reformers.

One last important area of change provoked by the rising tide of business ideology in American education at this time was that of curriculum reform. One of the principal efforts engaged in by some of the more spectacularly successful businessmen of the time was to make the curriculum more practical. Well-known financiers and industrialists such as Andrew Carnegie, Cornelius Vanderbilt and John D. Rockefeller argued that their success had nothing to do with 'book learning' or 'mere scholastic learning', but was based on good old-fashioned common sense, together with the kind of business acumen that could not be taught in schools. Carnegie was particularly severe in condemning the wasteful, deleterious and impractical nature of college study:

In my own experience I can say that I have known few young men intended for business who were not injured by a collegiate education. Had they gone into active work during the years spent at college they would have been better-educated men in every sense of that term. The fire and energy have been stamped out of them, and how to so manage as to live a life of idleness and not a life of usefulness has become the chief question with them (Callahan, 1962, p. 9).

It was suggested that Business English could usefully be substituted for compo-sition, and that business principles, contracts and bookkeeping be instituted in schools, at least for those 70 per cent of pupils who did not proceed to high school.

At least for this group, and arguably for all pupils, the 'love of learning' should be subordinated to the 'love of earning' (Callahan, 1962, p. 10). This accommodation to the demands of business also led to the proliferation of more vocational courses in schools.

A teachers' union response to attempts to impose 'efficiency measures', USA, 1911

If efficiency means the demoralization of the school system;
dollars saved and human materials squandered;
discontent, drudgery and disillusion –
We'll have none of it!
If efficiency denotes low finance, bickering and neglect;
exploitation, suspicion and inhumanity;
larger classes, smaller pay and diminished joy –
We'll have none of it!
We'll espouse and exalt humane efficiency—efficiency that spells
felicity, loyalty, participation, and right conduct.
Give us honorable efficiency and we shall rally to the civic cause.

Quoted in Welch, 1998, p. 157

The historical examples of the implementation of 'efficiency' policies in education clearly show that the results of such exercises impoverished education in the following ways:

- a narrowing of the curriculum, especially in the direction of vocationalism
- poorer quality teaching, caused by cramming and 'teaching to the test'
- cost reductions, leading to much higher class sizes, and fewer recruits for teaching
- less capacity to respond effectively to cultural, gender and social class differences.

These results are not merely revealing in themselves, but serve as cautionary tales to those politicians, populists, and media hacks, who, ignoring the lessons of history, seek to reinstate such principles in modern guise. A potential example emerged when the federal Minister of Education in 2005 used the threat of withholding funding to state governments as a means to introduce compulsory reports on performance by schools across the country (*Sunday Telegraph*, 2005, 3 August). At the same time, the same federal Minister pushed strongly for teacher attendance and productivity records, and the return to an 'A, B, C, D, E' grading system.

Three billion dollars was at risk in NSW alone, until the state government finally relented, insisting that their schools 'tell it like it is' (*SMH*, 2005, 29 June). While parents may well appreciate more information from schools about their children's performance, the introduction of the machinery of testing and grading can end up distorting, rather than strengthening, the core education and mission of better quality teaching and learning, as was seen in the examples illustrated above.

As educators, we are entitled to ask at least three fundamental questions:

- What is the real purpose served by such reforms?
- How far will they assist in enhancing the quality of the teaching and learning processes?
- What are the most likely effects, and for whom?

In a sense, we can ask such questions of any proposed policy. But the lessons of those earlier episodes are that *payment by results* and *scientific management* reveal key weaknesses in attempts to impose business efficiency models in education. In practice, these often mask not only a reduction in both the quality of education provided, but also attempts to increase productivity levels in education, especially in the public sector. Notwithstanding these earlier examples, schools, TAFEs, and universities are once again in the grip of business efficiency fever. The latest terminology now speaks of total quality management (TQM), for example, or Balanced Scorecard (a management technology that, *inter alia*, displays green, red, and yellow flags as indicators of progress towards specific goals within the program, and depends on techniques of surveillance, in the form of regular, detailed reports from managers to their superiors, in order to operate), but the underpinning rationales and principles are much the same as earlier episodes.

The examples raised above show that arguments about efficiency, not least in the current era of worldwide economic stringency, often consist of little more than arguments about economics or, as in the above allusion to Pusey, the adoption of economism as the *leitmotiv* of reform. The particular form of economics that is appealed to, implicitly or explicitly, is of a *laissez-faire* form, in which government engages in only minimal regulation of the business cycle, and private enterprise is seen both as the prime engine of economic activity *and* the model for the operation of public sector institutions. In this model, social policy works best if run along pure forms of economic rationality such as the assumed 'laws of demand and supply', which should operate unfettered by interference in the form of controls upon monopoly, or by concerns with the environment or social welfare priorities.

The economic underpinnings

The incorporation of business efficiency practices and business management processes into contemporary education provides a vivid illustration of Pusey's argument, cited above. For such 'efficiency' movements in education are based upon economic assumptions—that both individual worth and the worth of education are ultimately measured in economic terms. That is, individuals have economic worth in much the same sense as other economic commodities, for example a natural resource. Just as natural resources can be sold in their raw state, or have more value added by further development of the product, so too human beings are seen as having more or less value by virtue of their level of education and skills. The value of individuals, and of education, is ultimately reduced to a form of accountancy.

Education, too, is seen in terms of its relative capacity to contribute to economic growth. Hence, individual and social involvement in education are each seen as an 'investment', to be weighed against other possible areas of return. (In economics, this is known as either individual or social rate-of-return analysis.) The elements of education that cannot be quantified easily are either discounted or assigned an (arbitrary) economic value. Within human capital theory, as this tradition is termed, individuals and societies are seen as 'rational' to the extent that they calculate how to maximise their return on their educational investment. Individuals and societies are also seen as rational in so far as they only invest in education to the extent that education delivers a better economic 'rate of return' (a technique within human capital theory) than other forms of investment (Blaug, 1972; Woodhall, 1972; World Bank, 1994; Carnoy, 1995).

Given the assumption that it is individuals who reap the reward of their 'investment' in education, the corollary is that they themselves should bear the costs. Effectively, then, such arguments assert the 'private good' function of education, rather than the 'public good' indicated above. That is, if someone is likely to gain a higher income as a result of additional training, they themselves should foot the bill for such additional education. The benefit to the employer, and more broadly to society in general, of having a more educated workforce and more reflective citizens is discounted. On the contrary, such arguments may legitimate the reduction of investment by the state, which, it is sometimes argued, should not have to invest (substantially) in the training of personnel, at least beyond the elementary level, since it is the individual who reaps the benefit (Marginson, 1989, p. 7).

Knowledge workers/knowledge economy

It has long been believed that education contributes to economic growth in society, perhaps even substantially—although it is fair to say that economists disagree sharply about how much and how soon the effects can be discerned. But it is clear that the rhetoric that construes education in economic terms has become even more fervent in recent years, in light of what is often called the 'knowledge economy'. We have heard for decades about a 'Learning Society' (Hutchins, 1968;

Husen, 1974), and in reports such as *Learning: The Treasure Within* (UNESCO, 1996), all of which celebrate the role of education as central to social development. Now, however, it is being argued that knowledge constitutes the basis of the new twenty-first-century economy. The old *Fordist* economy, it is argued, was based on models more appropriate to manufacturing industry, for which workers did not need much education, since the work they were required to do (paradigmatically, assembling cars at the Ford auto plant) demanded little initiative or thought. (This ignores, of course, the role of skilled tradesmen, such as toolmakers, who often needed to know how to solve technical problems on the shop floor.) Now, however, it is often argued, we inhabit a different, 'post-Fordist' universe, where workers are required to solve problems, individually and in teams. This calls for much higher levels of knowledge and skill.

Australia seems to have swallowed this new ideology whole (Frankel, 2004). Like many other developing and developed nations, it has invested considerable faith in the so-called knowledge economy, although it has been rather weaker in actually investing resources in it. Educational policies reflecting this new ideology drew on a twofold argument. First, it was argued, in the new knowledge economy it is jobs in the services sector of the economy (such as tourism, retail, education and health), rather than manufacturing, which form the basis of wealth creation and economic development. Second, Australia (like many other developed economies) can, in any event, no longer compete in manufacturing terms with low-wage economies such as China. Hence, for Australia it is all the more important to move towards a service-based economy, where it may have a comparative advantage, and where education and training form critical components of effective service delivery.

There are key problems, however, with an uncritical adoption of knowledge economy discourses, as well as problems in Australia's implementation. The first point is that, although the benefits of the knowledge economy are said to accrue to wider and wider sections of the population, in practice the results are much more mixed (Frankel, 2004). There are in fact fractures in the knowledge economy—many miss out on the much-touted benefits of higher wages and more job satisfaction and autonomy. In particular, less-skilled (less-educated) workers, and all those who cannot bargain for better benefits, because their skills are in less demand than others', tend to miss out. This includes many groups who are the focus of specific chapters in this book—recently arrived migrants, Indigenous communities, rural dwellers, part-time and contract workers (often women), and others at the base of the socio-economic pyramid. Indeed, many such individuals can in fact be de-skilled—stuck in dead-end, repetitive work, sometimes called 'Mc-jobs'. This cleft in Australian society is only likely to deepen, as the effects of the 2005 industrial relations reforms entrench differences between those who have more to bargain with and those who do not (*Australian*, 2005, 24 September, 28 January; *SMH*, 2005, 23 May, 30 January). 'It's not wages, stupid, it's skills' (*SMH*, 2005, 9 October). The journalist Elisabeth Wynhausen describes vividly the experience of herself and others in such low-skilled jobs in her book *Dirt Cheap* (2005), subtitled *Life at the Wrong End of the Job Market*:

> I tried to keep up. I couldn't. My body had stopped following orders. My hands hurt, my arm was bruised, my back ached. 'Don't panic,' Mandy had said more than once, but I was beset with panic. The contraption that pressed the cartons shut wasn't working properly. Suddenly a phalanx of open cartons came bouncing towards me, the whole lot going awry so that one carton levitated as the rest started bumping each other sideways. Eggs burst out of boxes and broke on the takeout chain. The sight filled me with terror. 'Mandyyyy,' I wailed. (Wynhausen, 2005, p. 55).

But some professionals, too, can become de-skilled in this context (Aronowitz & di Fazio, 1994).

The second problem is that, even if the knowledge economy thesis is accepted, Australia has committed inadequate resources to bring it about. One area where this failure can be seen quite readily is the amount invested in the crucial area of research and development (R &D) at a national level. Although the proportion of Gross Domestic Product devoted to R &D by Australia has risen appreciably over the past two decades or so, it is still modest by international standards. So is the amount devoted by the state to higher education, which actually fell from 1.7% of GDP to 1.5% from 1995–2000. OECD research that compares overall 'investment in knowledge' shows that Australia is below the OECD average, and well below that of many other comparable countries (Parliamentary Library, 2004)

In effect, the Australian state has reduced relative public sector effort in the area of education, particularly those areas of inquiry that are seen to have a less substantial, or less quantifiable, economic return. Moreover, the assumption that the private sector is (necessarily) more efficient than the public sector is often legitimated by the perceived greater conformity of the private sector to the canons of (business) efficiency, in particular the principle that the worth of activities should be measured, largely or wholly, in economic terms. Thus a simple correlation between efficiency and privatisation can occur at the core of so-called efficiency movements, which, under the guise of efficiency, are actually interested in pursuing a form of economism (measuring the worth of any program or policy using a supposedly 'scientific' form of economics that just narrowly calculates how much it will cost in financial terms, rather than factoring in social concerns). This may well have the effect of reducing quality (in education), rather than enhancing it.

Commodification of education

Another form of argument that links economism with efficiency movements in education is the way in which education may come to be characterised increasingly as a commodity (Apple, 1982; Lyotard, 1980; Welch, 1998; Peters, 1992) by both the state, and conservative pressure groups, who may often espouse a directly business ethic in respect of education. At the very least, such efficiency movements have tended to redefine the relation between the state and education, such that the role of the state is increasingly circumscribed (Yeatman, 1993; Cerny, 1990; Welch, 1996b). Indeed, privatisation may well be an associated feature of contemporary efficiency movements, on the assumed grounds that the public sector is inefficient. At the same time, however, the public sector is made increasingly captive to the argument that it must be run on business lines to be efficient. This 'efficiency', however, is promoted at the cost of other considerations such as equity, and the provision of service to the whole community, which thus means that the public sector in education is progressively disempowered, since it is now open to the charge that it is no longer fulfilling its charter adequately. Indeed, given efficiency arguments, it is harder to fulfil that charter, especially for marginal or disadvantaged groups, who have the most to lose at the hands of 'efficiency'.

5   Diverting risk

Part of the set of strategies used by the modern state is clearly evident in the Australian context: the shifting of risk from the state (as well as from banks and insurers), to third sector agencies and, ultimately, to families and individuals. In the past, the state as major provider of services such as education, health, transport and welfare bore the brunt of blame if there were faults in the system. In light of current trends that reflect the crisis of the state referred to above, this is no longer tenable. The response to this dilemma has been twofold.

Firstly, decentralisation of education has been introduced, with the strong endorsement of international agencies such as the World Bank (1994), the Organisation for Economic Cooperation and Development (OECD), and the Asian Development Bank (ADB). Partly as a result, it has become an enormously influential reform movement in governance, worldwide, over the past decade or more. Decentralisation has been justified both on the basis of democratisation, in particular promising the increased participation of local communities, and also on the basis of responsiveness, meaning that local communities know best how to tailor solutions to their own issues and problems.

Nonetheless, decentralisation has clearly been used by the state to divert the risk of failure. The strategy has strong potential advantages for the state, trying to balance demands for services on the part of the populace on one hand, and the incapacity to deliver these services, particularly in an equitable manner, on the other:

> Because the reproduction of class societies is based on the privileged appropriation of socially produced wealth, all such societies must resolve the problem of distributing the surplus social product inequitably, and yet legitimately (Habermas, 1976, p. 96).

The great advantage of decentralisation is that the risk, too, is decentralised. Now, when there is a problem with long hospital waiting lists, poor services in country regions, or inadequate maintenance of public schools, or unfunded superannuation schemes (*SMH*, 2005, 4, 12, 20, 23 May), the blame can be outsourced—to the hospital director, the regional administrator of services, the head of the local youth centre, or the headmaster (Welch, 1996b, pp. 7–11).

> I feel like we have been taken to the cleaners. When you go to the cleaners you get a note that says: 'All care but not responsibility'. With this devolution and self-management stuff, 'it's all responsibility and no power' (quoted in Welch, 1996b, p. 8).

But the story does not end there. The second strategy employed in recent years also involves shifting the burden from the state:

> As is occurring in Australia, governments are shifting more of the financial burden of healthcare and education directly to households—a trend that still has a long way to go. The shifting of risk to households is partly a result of global deregulation of financial markets and capital flows, and offers big benefits, as well as costs. But a lot of it is being driven by the impact of demographics—funding the retirement and other needs of the baby boomers. [Nonetheless] Most middle aged, middle income households in the West don't seem well prepared to either adequately fund their retirement, or manage the risks being transferred to their balance sheets. Governments need to help households manage this added risk (*Australian*, 2005, 30 April).

Often such strategies have been justified by appeals to a new form of governance, the so-called 'Third Way' (Giddens, 2000). This was heralded as a novel form of social compact that avoided both the statism of the left and the free-market ideology of the right. Many of its more substantial claims have since been heavily criticised. Nonetheless, debates about its merits or otherwise have done little to mask the real effects of contemporary education policies on the Australian social fabric. It is here that the question raised earlier in this chapter as to the role of the state in mitigating the effects of inequalities is again highlighted. The creation of innovative social and community coalitions involving government in new alliances to address problems of poverty and inequity in society may yield substantial results if the nett level of resources, financial as well as other, is increased. Tapping under-utilised community skills and resources also holds some clear potential benefits, especially perhaps in Australia, where such energy has not always been fully used or acknowledged. This, however, is very different from contemporary government strategies of using community agencies such as churches and others to staff and run government programs that have borne the brunt of budget cutting and staff losses. Such an agenda is consistent with global 'structural adjustment' ideologies (Welch & Mok, 2003) to reduce the roles and responsibilities of the state, especially for social programs. The effective 'outsourcing' of responsibilities for social success or failure to the community, family, or the individual has real benefits for the state, in reducing the extent to which it can be held responsible for equity and cohesion in society. It has far fewer demonstrable benefits to the community, however, or to churches and other community agencies, who risk being co-opted into tacitly supporting this social agenda. As churches have pointed out, their own autonomy becomes imperilled and they risk being transformed into quasi agencies of government. Equally the transfer of risk to families and individuals is only likely to entrench existing powerful differences in Australian society, between the 'haves' and the 'have nots'.

6 Diverting funds

The deepening of differences between rich and poor in Australian society has been further aided by specific funding policies of recent decades. The substantial shift of funds by both state and federal governments of both major parties to the private school sector is part of the wider reshaping of the Australian state described above, which has seen a similar trend towards privatisation occur in areas such as health, transport and welfare over the past two decades or so. Nonetheless, the process has accelerated since the accession of the Howard federal government in 1996. Finally, in 2000, the federal Minister of Education of the time, admitted the fundamental rationale for this diversion of funds to the private sector:

> We have to realise ... that parents who send their children to non-government schools are saving taxpayers a vast amount of money—about two billion dollars a year, more than that ... and that money is then available for the funding of government schools (Kemp, cited in Welch, 2003, p. 276).

While the money could in theory have been made available to the public sector, federal government policies ensured it was not. The introduction of two key schemes by the Howard federal government, the first in 1996, the second in 2000, oversaw the major diversion of funds from the public to the private sector. The first policy centred on the Enrolment Benchmark Adjustment (EBA), a formula that was based on the 'fact' that each child who moved from a government to a non-government school would save the relevant state government (constitutionally responsible for schooling) the sum of $3424. The Commonwealth therefore moved to end this 'anomaly', providing only half this amount to the states, per enrolment. In practice, what this meant was that each student's move from a public to a private school resulted in $1712 being withdrawn from the relevant state's budget available for schools. In addition, the Commonwealth moved to retain the sum of $406, which they paid to support each pupil in the government school system, in each state. Thus a total of some $2118 was to be withdrawn from Commonwealth funds to the state for every child that moved to a non-government school. For individual classroom teachers in public schools, the loss of one child meant little difference to their workload—but the loss of over $2100 dollars to the school in each such case was highly problematic. On the other hand, the scheme deregulated the establishment of private schools, allowing some 76 new private schools to open in New South Wales in the 4 years after the EBA policy was announced (*SMH*, 2000, 23 August, 29 September, 9, 17, 19 October).

The corrosive criticism of the inequities in the EBA formula led to its replacement by the so-called Socio Economic Status (SES) model, by the federal government in 2000, as a new means to finance some 30 per cent of 'independent' private schools. A separate deal was struck with the Catholic schools sector (*Australian*, 2000, 15 November). Under this model, the average SES (a composite index, comprising elements of income, occupation, and educational attainment of people in that region) was used as a basis for funding private schools in that region (*SMH*, 2000, 17 October). The fly in this smelly ointment was easily found—and has been pointed out by many (*SMH*, 2000, 29 September, 9, 17 October). The worst effects are perhaps most evident in country areas, where, although average incomes are often low, many wealthier farming families have long sent their children to elite and expensive boarding schools, either in major cities or in larger, regional educational centres. It is precisely these schools that benefit grossly from the new SES funding formula announced in 2000, which is based not on measures of actual wealth among those specific families whose children attend, but rather upon a statistical community average. This average—derived from the demographics of a region, in which the majority of lower incomes will yield an artificially low result—poorly reflects the actual wealth of the individual family whose child attends such elite schools, and hence their capacity to pay. This composite index is nonetheless preferred over a model based on the existing levels of resources available within the school, or on the actual income levels of parents whose children attend such schools. Not only is this a serious misuse of statistics under cover of promoting choice, it again reveals the socially regressive effects of the ideology of choice, promoted within an overall agenda of economic globalisation and structural adjustment (Welch, 2003).

The statistical problem was well highlighted by a prominent economic journalist, in an article that pilloried the logic that underpinned the move to subsidise private schools with public funds:

> The average Australian has fewer than two legs. Not many fewer but, as the number of one-legged people far exceeds the number of three-legged people, there is no doubt about the end result. Not surprisingly though, designers of products, from pants to staircases, don't focus on the average. Rather they tend to focus on the characteristics of the majority. Not so the Federal Government, though. Its attempt to explain why exclusive private schools are to receive millions of dollars in additional funding have relied squarely on the confusion that blind reference to averages can create (*SMH*, 2000, 17 October).

The duplicity of the federal government's reliance upon this composite index becomes even clearer when compared with other federal government programs: for almost all other recipients of federal government assistance, actual details of income are required. The socially regressive nature of the model is underlined in two further ways. First, private schools were promised that 'the new funding model is only applied if it would result in an increase over the old model' (*SMH*, 2000, 17 October), thus effectively guaranteeing the existing levels of resources available to already wealthy private schools. Second, when introducing the program, the federal Minister promised that not one cent would be lost to the public schooling system. In fact, this is highly unlikely. The additional $50 million supplied under the model to wealthy private schools needed to come from somewhere—in practice then, it would need to be financed via a rise in taxation (extremely unlikely, given that globalisation and structural adjustment agendas impose pressure to reduce taxation levels), or from spending cuts to public services, including public schools.

This diversion of funds by both state *and* federal governments from public to private schools has accompanied considerable expansion in the private sector over the past two decades (see Welch 2003; also chapter 9). The trend in one state is detailed in the following table, and describes a more general Australian pattern, although proportions differ among the different states.

As a direct result, (and also due to a parallel sentiment aroused by the media that state schools are failing or second-rate), state schools are becoming residualised (see chapter 9 on school choice for further details). Moreover, this residualisation of the local comprehensive high school (which a generation ago, was seen as a symbol of community integration and democratic opportunity) is being driven by an ethos of growing hostility towards the public sector (Painter, 1997;

Table 1.1 Enrolment share and change by school sector in New South Wales, 1985–2004 (%)

	1985	1990	1995	2000	2004	% change 1985–2004
Government	74.2	72.1	71.5	69.4	67.2	−9.4
Catholic	20.4	21.0	20.6	21.0	21.5	+4.9
'Independent'*	5.4	6.9	7.5	9.6	11.3	+109.2
Total (%)	100	100	100	100	100	

Source: Adapted from *SMH*, 2006, 6 February

*Quotation marks used around the term 'Independent' reflect the fact that such schools gain between 40 and 90 per cent of their income from government (Anderson, 1990a, 1990b). In this sense, they might be more accurately termed 'government-subsidised'.

Bamberry, 2005, p. 157), in which the private sector is always seen as the model to be aped by the public sector, whose employees are generally seen as lazy and/or incompetent. In practice, public schools are critically short of funds for all sorts of things and have become shabbier and less well maintained. As one example, the audit of public schools in New South Wales conducted by Vinson and Esson in 2005 identified some $180 million in repairs and maintenance as urgently needed by public schools, but the problem was ignored by a state government less and less able to deliver on the equity charter that was once fundamental to the sector.

In this, New South Wales is by no means alone. State governments around the country are not merely under-funding state schools (despite being constitutionally responsible for education), but are unable to fulfil their regulatory functions properly, and have even become hostage to the vagaries of the property market. Now, for example, if property prices falter, tax revenue falls, sometimes by hundreds of millions of dollars. The direct effect is that the most vulnerable in society suffer most, as a result of cuts to state government services:

> As the state government struggles to repair the holes in the budget caused by stagnant property revenue, the aftermath of the (property) boom could be painful for bystanders such as the old, the sick, the disabled and the poor. The suffering would occur if the Government were forced to cut services and lift charges for these groups as it covers the shortfall in property taxes (*SMH*, 2006, 7 February).

How has this parlous situation come about? It has been argued above that changes to the nature of the Australian state over the past two decades or so, accompanied by an ethos of managerialism, and obsession with tax cuts and debt aversion among state and federal governments have left them largely unable, and mostly unwilling, to act on the recommendations of expert committees or public inquiries that, after appropriate consultation, may propose significant investment, either in failing infrastructure (Vinson & Esson, 2005c; *SMH*, 2005, 4 May) or in key social justice areas of Aboriginal education, health, housing and employment. A letter writer to a major daily newspaper expressed it pungently, in the form of an open letter to the Prime Minister and Treasurer:

Letter to the Prime Minister and Treasurer

Please keep my and everyone else's tax cuts, and spend the money on the services they're collected to pay for, such as health, education and transport and providing the people of Australia with a better society. In case you've forgotten, it's what we pay you clowns to do. Declaring there is a 'budget surplus' when services are being run into the ground is like pretending your home is clean and well run, when in reality everything is rammed into the cupboards and swept under the rug. The government's language is misleading and its behaviour irresponsible, bordering on outright negligence. Declaring that you can give us back $21 billion when our health and education systems are in tatters is nothing short of obscene (*SMH*, 2005, 12 May).

Sadly, while this message was to John Howard and Peter Costello, it could just as well have been directed to any government, state or federal, of the past 20 years. A recent case in South Australia powerfully illustrates current government aversion to expenditure on public programs, no matter how urgent the demonstrated need. The South Australian government commissioned an inquiry into the 'atrocious' set of problems (*Australian*, 2005, 3 June) that beset the Anangu Pitjintjatjara peoples of the northernmost parts of the state. Aboriginal elder Lowitja O'Donohue, herself a Yankunytjatjara woman, was appointed as an adviser, but within months boiled over in frustration at what she described as 'window dressing … bullshit. Bread and circuses. That's what it's all about' (*Advertiser*, 2005, 16 July, 3 June). Complaining that she had 'never ever' been treated as shabbily as 'in the last twelve months by the [South Australian state] government', she pointed to many of the effects described above—procrastination and unwillingness to fund key positions identified as critical by the inquiry; attempts to denigrate her as a person, as a means to undermine the legitimacy of the recommendations; the impossibility of obtaining an interview with the state Premier (who was 'very busy'); the inexperience of the state bureaucrats involved 'with Aboriginal people, let alone the problems of remoteness and distance, and issues of cultural difference and language' (*Advertiser*, 2005, June 3); and that 'senior public servants had bullied her not to speak out' (*Australian*, 2005, June 3). The example, however powerful, is not limited to any one state or federal government, or any political party. Much the same 'egregious act(s) of hypocrisy' (*SMH*, 2005, 4 May) have occurred in other states at the same time, in both Aboriginal education policy and other equity areas. As the quotation above reveals, federal government is no less immune from the disease.

We should not overestimate the uniqueness of the Australian case. As chapter 12 on globalisation shows, parallel changes have occurred in many parts of the world, under the impact of structural adjustment regimes urged by international agencies such as those listed above. The impact in many countries on social and educational policies has been substantial, widening the gap between the 'haves' and the 'have nots'.

But it is equally important to acknowledge that national responses to the worldwide pressure for globalisation and structural adjustment do differ, even within the region (Welch & Mok, 2003). Not all countries have implemented its radical agenda so swiftly as Australia. In the Asia Pacific region, Malaysia, Singapore, and Vietnam have demurred in part, while in other regions several states in Latin America and Western Europe have also resisted. While globalisation effects can be powerful, we need also to remind ourselves of the persisting importance of the state, in political and policy terms (Weiss, 1998).

States can and do make a difference. And sadly, there is considerable evidence to show that the obsession by Australia's state and federal governments in the last decade or two with reducing tax and debt is leaving the education system, and more broadly the Australian state, impoverished and its infrastructure corroded. Until both state and federal governments turn aside from their damaging policies of under-funding both public infrastructure and social programs, and attempting to divert the risk to families and individuals, and until the faddish fever of managerialism fades once more, the main risk is to the quality of education. Whether we speak of the *learning society* or the *knowledge economy*, much more public investment is needed to fulfil the promise of a society based on knowledge, which all politicians so proudly proclaim. In order to achieve this new society, both policy settings and policy processes will need to change significantly.

Focus questions

1 How is policy made in the Australian context and how has the process changed over recent decades?
2 How has the role of the state changed, and what impact has this had on the policy process?
3 What does efficiency mean, and what impact has it had in the past on shaping education policies? Are there traces of this kind of thinking still at work in current policies?

4 How does policy work at school level, and how much control does a school or TAFE or a university have over implementation? How much input did they have to the development of the policy? Choose one state or federal policy in education (multicultural education, Aboriginal education, rural education, gender) as a test case.

5 What is the role of education in social change? Can schools make a difference?

Further reading

Ball, S. (1990). *Politics and Policy Making in Education*. London: Routledge.

Ball, S. (1998). 'Big policies, small world: An introduction to international perspectives in educational policy.' *Comparative Education*, *34*(2), 119–30.

Clarke, J., Gewirtz, S. & McLaughlin, E. (eds) (2000). *New Managerialism, New Welfare*. London: Sage.

Dale, R. (1997). 'The State and governance of education: An analysis of the re-structuring of the State-education relationship.' In A. Halsey, H. Lauder, P. Brown & A. Wells (eds), *Education, Culture, Economy and Society* (pp. 273–82). Oxford: Oxford University Press.

Frankel, B. (2004). 'False promises: Surviving the knowledge economy.' In *Zombies, Lilliputians and Sadists. The Power of the Living Dead and the Future of Australia* (pp. 108–35). Fremantle: Curtin University Press.

McKnight, D. (2005). 'The world made by markets." In *Beyond Left and Right. New Politics and the Culture Wars* (pp. 18–48). Sydney: Allen & Unwin.

Taylor, S., Rizvi, F., Lingard, B. & Arnold, M. (1997). *Educational Policy and the Politics of Change*. London: Routledge.

Vinson, A. & Esson, K. (2005). *Audit. Inquiry into the provision of public education in New South Wales*. Sydney: NSW Teachers' Federation, and Federation of Parents and Citizens Associations of NSW.

Welch, A. (1996). 'Reform or crisis in Australian education.' In A. Welch (ed.), *Australian Education: Reform or crisis?* (pp. 1–23). Sydney: Allen & Unwin.

Internet sources

The federal parliamentary library is a good source of short, relevant briefing notes, on areas of topical policy interest. For example, 'Investing in the economy's knowledge base'. Research Note 24, http://www.aph.gov.au/library/pubs/rn/2004-05/05rn24.htm.

A good source for federal government policy in education is www.dest.gov.au. You can also search state government Department of Education sites (www.det.nsw.gov.au, www.decs.sa.gov.au, etc.) for state government education policies.

2
Growing Up
Raewyn Connell

1 How children grow

We often think of children as pre-programmed for success or failure. 'Oh yes, another Hatfield,' we might say, 'comes from a bad family, bound to turn out badly.' Educational psychology used to be full of terrible stories of family taints, fixed hereditary intelligence (or stupidity), and fixed racial differences in learning.

These offensive tales have, with the growth of knowledge, vanished from the textbooks. But modern molecular biology has revived the idea, at least in the eyes of the mass media. We hear tales about the scientist who has found a gene for spatial perception, a gene for homosexuality, or a gene for intelligence. Few of these tales turn out to be true.

Biological growth is, of course, a vital part of human development. That is why educators are quite properly concerned with health, nutrition, and exercise for young people. Education is not just about reading and writing. It is about the growth of the whole person, and that includes the body. 'Physical education' is just as central to a balanced curriculum as academic learning is.

Physical needs

I once visited a primary school that had been built for a squatter settlement on the outskirts of the city of Porto Alegre in southern Brazil. This was a community of very poor people, mostly landless migrants from the countryside—part of the huge migration to the cities that has happened in Latin America in the past generation. Few had regular jobs, and most had built their own houses from scrap materials.

The Principal showed us the most important room in the building. It was the school kitchen. Here, the school's cooks produced the one solid meal that most of the children could rely on getting, any given day. The teachers here knew that hungry children don't learn much.

In the world as a whole, about one thousand million people are estimated to live below an absolute poverty line, where adequate nutrition is not guaranteed.

Biological growth is much more varied and interactive than simple 'unfolding' stories suggest. To a unique extent, compared with other species, many paths of development are possible for humans. Which of those paths is taken depends on a constant process of interaction with the child's environment, especially its social environment.

For *any* of the paths of development from human newborn to human adult to be successfully followed, continuous social support is essential. Children need society to supply food and shelter. Some homeless children as young as 10, a few even younger, support themselves in war zones and urban slums—but that is likely to be at terrible cost, and usually involves some adult support, for instance adult customers.

The need for social support is also a psychological matter, and can be seen in language learning. Structural linguistics suggests that there are some innate capacities that underlie the development of language in all humans. But for these capacities to be realised, the child must be part of a language-using community. Language, after all, is inherently about communication. Every child develops the technical capacities in language—learning to follow grammatical rules, to use relevant vocabulary, to find the right speech modality—by practising with people in their environment. Often the learning is speeded up by the other people in these interactions using them to steer the child's performance—'The dog *barks*, dear, not the dog bark.' In this sense the growth of the child's language competence is socially produced through a deliberate, though quite informal, educational process.

Social support is also essential for a child's emotional development. This point was first strongly made by researchers investigating 'maternal deprivation'. They studied children who had been orphaned or separated from their families (for instance by wartime evacuation) and found a common pattern of disrupted development. But the researchers who called this problem 'maternal deprivation' were trapped by their own stereotypes. They assumed that it had to be women, specifically mothers, who did the caring for young children. But this is not always how children are raised. Sometimes it is grandparents or older children who do most of the care work. This often happens in peasant societies where the middle generation, both men and women, provide the agricultural labour and are needed much of the time out on the farm.

Sometimes it is fathers who do the primary care, or share it. A later generation of researchers, influenced by feminism, asked the edgy question 'Can men mother?' and the answer is yes, men can (Risman, 1986). Men are perfectly capable of changing the nappy, giving the bottle, and providing the love, protection, and attention that young children need. Not only that—men *will* take an active role in early child care, if the social circumstances support them. This has been shown especially in the Nordic countries, where 'paternal leave' is supported by governments, employers, and public opinion, and a high proportion of fathers actually do become involved in caring for babies and young children (Holter, 2003). This is less common in Australia. However, there are about 76,000 lone fathers in Australia, caring for children under 18, so the issue is not a trivial one.

Social arrangements are reshaped from generation to generation, and sometimes within a single generation. Therefore the pathways of child development also change. The more complex and plural a society is, the more pathways of child development there will be within it. The multiplicity of life courses for young people will be seen again and again through this book.

One of the most striking examples of social change is in our very ideas about human development. We now take it for granted that young people move through infancy, childhood, and adolescence, and then move into adulthood. We assume these are very different stages of life, and we assume they form a natural sequence.

Yet a few centuries ago, in Western European cultures, these stages were not perceived at all. Historians have shown that the idea of 'childhood' as a distinct stage of life is relatively modern. Only after a cultural change extending through centuries—involving a reduction of infant mortality, the invention of schools, wider urbanisation and changes in the nature of work—did it become common belief that 'children' were a distinct category of humans, who should be kept out of the labour force in order to be nurtured and educated full-time. Indeed, this change was still going on after the creation of mass school systems. Public schooling was made compulsory in the Education Acts of the nineteenth century, in order to force rural and working-class families to take their young members out of the workforce and send them to be educated (Miller, 1998).

'Adolescence' appeared even later. The idea that there was a distinct stage of life between childhood and adulthood made no sense in societies where working people went straight from elementary school to be factory hands or servants, and where the rich could exercise their privilege at virtually any age. The theory of adolescence as a distinct psychological stage was proposed early in the twentieth century, and the popular idea of 'youth', 'adolescents', or 'teenagers' as a distinct group only became widespread after the growth of mass secondary schooling.

Though concepts such as 'childhood' are socially created, that does not mean they are artificial or unreal. Once such a category exists, it has very real effects. Family life was transformed when children could no longer be treated as domestic servants or additional labourers. Among other results, families became smaller when children became less of an economic asset and more of an economic cost. For young people, growing up became a matter of passing socially defined thresholds. Children grew up by entering specific institutions such as schools, being tested in various ways, and qualifying for the rights and duties of adulthood.

These institutions also reshaped the relationships in young people's lives. Going to school meant being separated, most of the day, from most adults. Schools also separated children from each other. Age-grading separated young children from older ones. School systems also very often separated boys from girls, rich from poor, and black from white. So instead of one 'world of childhood', multiple worlds developed, with differing resources, customs and cultures.

Rather than thinking of children's development as a programmed unfolding, it is helpful to think of growth as a series of *encounters*. Children meet their changed circumstances with changing capacities (mental, physical, emotional, social), which themselves are the products of previous encounters.

The changed circumstances that children encounter are sometimes dramatic, such as arriving at school for the first time, or going on a first date. More often they involve small changes, such as being confronted with a new arithmetic exercise in class or a demand to tidy their room at home. Responding to these encounters, children change both their environment and themselves.

This is an active process and, in that sense, children growing up are constantly making and remaking themselves. But they cannot do this just as they wish. They do it in circumstances that are given to them by the community they live in, by its history, and by the forces active in the community's life here and now. Understanding those circumstances, and the responses young people make to them, is a large part of what we attempt in this book.

2 Families and children

For most children, a family is their first educational institution, and other members of this family are their first teachers.

In societies where most families are economic production units—operating a farm, a trade or a small business—children are immediately seen as part of the labour force. In the longer term they are the people who will take over the family enterprise. In such circumstances a high birth rate is likely and the family does most of its educating in-house. Children are shown how to feed the hens, milk the cows, sew a quilt and plough a field. The family functions as a production unit and a vocational education centre at the same time.

With the social changes misnamed 'modernisation'—colonisation, industrialisation, migration to cities, the growth of a capitalist economy, a shift from communal property to individual property, and the growth of state regulation—the situation of families is likely to change. Many societies go through a 'demographic transition'. This means a shift from a high birth rate to a low birth rate; a fall in infant mortality, so that more and more newborns survive to grow up; and longer expectation of life for adults, so the average age of the population rises.

Such changes have enormous implications for families and the place of children in them. When fewer children are born, and more of them are likely to grow up, parents 'invest' more time and energy in the raising of each child. At the same time, the school system takes over much of the task of teaching from the family.

As the family loses some tasks, however, it gains others, especially in emotional life. The family becomes the site of more intense and elaborate emotional relations. The married couple is supposed to be linked by deep romantic love, not just by practical arrangements about work and property. Parents and children are supposed to have deep loyalties too.

When women's lives became less dominated by serial pregnancy and childbearing, while a male-dominated economy still barred them from most areas of employment, more and more women specialised in a social role called 'housewife'. This combined domestic work with intensive care and supervision of a small number of children, and emotional support of a husband who went out to do paid work in the market economy. The state may (and in Australia does) support this arrangement by tax concessions to married men. A small industry arose among psychiatrists, counsellors, ministers and journalists to reassure women that housewife–motherhood is their natural role in life and they are very happy in it (Oakley, 1976).

That is, in outline, where the 'traditional family' comes from. It is not traditional at all, but a product of quite recent history. What's really 'traditional' is serial pregnancy and high mortality among infants and mothers. (Anyone for the good old days?)

The housewife/breadwinner family has never, in fact, been the only form of the family or the household. In late nineteenth and early twentieth century Australia, there were significant numbers of women and men who never married or never had children. Households with children often had live-in servants. There were significant numbers of people who lived in 'extended family' households, involving a wider kinship group; and significant numbers who lived in non-family households such as boarding houses, bush workers' camps, etc. (Gilding, 1991).

If we look around contemporary Australia, it is clear that the Mum-Dad-and-the-kids idea of 'the family', always seen in washing powder advertisements, makes up only a minority of actual households. In the Australian Bureau of Statistics' 2003 'Family Characteristics Survey', it was found that out of 7.6 million households in Australia, there were 5.5 million family households, and among these were just 1.8 million intact-couple families with children under 18 (ABS, 2004b).

Contemporary sociological research recognises a great diversity of household and family forms. They include people who live alone, one-parent families, lesbian and gay couples with children or without, heterosexual couples without children, extended families, group households, blended families with children, and so on (Gilding, 1997).

These facts are not welcome to everyone. Conservative politicians and clergy are especially unhappy with this multiplicity, and insist that society should honour and support only one model, the 'traditional family'. But family plurality can't be pushed back into the bottle. It is important for teachers to recognise the sheer range of family situations from which the children in their classes are coming.

Some parents are able-bodied, some are disabled. Some parents are lesbian and gay; and lesbian and gay families also exist in different forms. Some parents are active members of religious groups, though most are not; some religious groups insist on a single pattern of family life and others are tolerant of diversity. Rural families face different economic problems from city families. Indigenous families often have the resource of strong kinship ties but at the same time have to deal with poverty and racism. Recent immigrant families often face severe language problems, in which their children become mediators between the parents and the English-speaking community. Increasing numbers of families blend different ethnic backgrounds, sometimes with conflicting ideas about how families should operate.

Even the heterosexual-couple-with-children family pattern is changing. With historically high rates of separation, divorce, and remarriage, many households that began as 'traditional families' have now been reorganised as 'blended families'. The 2003 ABS survey found 176,700 blended or step families with children under 18: about 7% of all families with children. Up to four parents may now be involved in the care of the group of children who live in a given household. Complex arrangements for access, sharing of decisions about children, and economic support have to be negotiated among separated parents.

As married women's workforce participation rates have risen, the two-income couple has become normal. Modern feminism made a withering criticism of the old 'motherhood' ideology as a trap for women, and there is now wider acceptance of gender equality. Young women in Australia now expect to do paid work for most of their lives. Most, however, still expect to take a period of time out of the workforce when they have young children.

This has also meant change for men. Fewer men are now the permanent sole wage-earner in a family. A re-thinking of men's role as fathers has begun, with more men valuing a close emotional attachment to children. 'Work/life balance' has become a hotly debated issue, with many men expressing a desire for a better quality of home life and less pressure from the workplace.

But economic trends are against them. In recent years the average hours in a working week have been *rising*, not falling, as a result of a more market-driven economy, the decline of union power, and the rise of capitalists' power in society. Family life is thus under contradictory pressures, and children's lives are shaped by the varying solutions and compromises that parents come up with (Pocock, 2003).

In one important respect, family relationships have failed to change. 'Time budget' studies and other research on families clearly show that, in Australia as in other developed economies, housework and child care remain overwhelmingly women's work. Families' massive reliance on women's wages has *not* been matched by a large rise in men's contribution to domestic work and child care. A great many women now do a double shift—one shift in the workplace, one shift at home. When supposedly 'family-friendly' policies in the workplace are available, it is overwhelmingly women, not men, who go on to part-time employment, or take leave, or use 'flexible' hours, in order to look after children (Baxter, 2002).

It is, therefore, women (sometimes grandmothers and aunts, but mainly mothers) who do most of the care of young children before they go to school. It is mostly women who do informal activities like reading stories, choosing TV programs, and taking young children out for new experiences at the beach, at the zoo, or in the mall. For the small number of families who undertake 'home schooling', it is likely to be women who carry most of the educational work through childhood and adolescence. For the majority of families, who do send their children to school, it is mainly mothers who establish early contact with teachers, bring young children to the school grounds, and negotiate the bumps as the child adjusts to the school environment. Fathers are more likely to come into the picture when the children get to secondary school. At this stage the children are closer to the labour market, and the school is less likely to be seen by men as a women's space.

Schools may or may not welcome parents on the premises. On the whole, school systems have become more conscious of this relationship and now generally have guidelines to encourage parent involvement. Schools may have programs where parents can turn up and help with 'reading recovery', sporting events, or excursions.

Yet this is still a problem area. With increasing concerns about security, and moral panics about 'paedophiles', it is increasingly difficult for parents (especially fathers) to just stroll in to the school and participate. The school–home relationship is, in that sense, increasingly formal. The institutional boundary between home and school established two centuries ago is still strong. In situations where there are important cultural differences too—for instance between Anglo teachers and Pacific Islander, Vietnamese Buddhist, or Lebanese Muslim parents—it may take a major, deliberate effort of community relations to establish useful contacts.

It is useful to think of all families as having *educational strategies* for their children. Such strategies are built up from the parents' own experiences of schooling—sometimes positive, sometimes bad—and are modified by parents' view of the future situations their children will face. They are very much influenced by what parents think schools and colleges can and cannot do for their children.

Family educational strategies are likely to vary between social groups. For instance, different immigrant communities have had very different experiences of education in their home countries, some coming from countries where school systems have been torn apart by civil war. Educational strategies also change over time. (See also chapters 3 and 9, section 5.)

Family strategies

The following quotations, from a recent study of vocational education in NSW (Connell, 2003), illustrate family educational strategies. Parents generally hope that children will pick up the parents' plans for them. Robyn, a student at Korana High, has certainly done so:

> (How much influence do you think your parents have had?) A lot. (Do you think that's good?) Yep. Because if they weren't behind me, I'd be a bum, and drop out of school in Year 10. (Really, why?) I don't want to be known as someone who dropped out of school. Knowing that I could have had more, if I had of stayed at school and finished Year 12. (Have all your friends stayed on too?) Yep. (Do you encourage each other?) Not really. Sometimes we bag each other out, but.

A family's educational strategy does not necessarily focus on academic learning. Yasmine, for instance, describes extended discussions about a trade for her son Malik. Malik's father had started this discussion when the boy was in Year 9:

> Basically to us he said 'I like wood', you know, he likes to do stuff with wood and that. I spoke to one of his teachers once, she goes, 'Your son doesn't like to sit in an office, you know. If you're going to choose a job for him, don't make him sit in an office because he doesn't like to be cramped in' … By the time he finished Year 10, I said to him, his Dad kept asking him, 'You still interested in construction and stuff like that?' He goes 'Yeah'. We started looking and that, we didn't push him, but. He was a bit undecided at the beginning. Should I leave school, shall I do that? You know. It was too confusing.

Malik in fact left school in Year 11 to start a carpentry apprenticeship—a positive educational outcome, though it was not high school 'completion'.

Engaged middle-class parents are likely to be focused on what post-school pathways their children will be launched into. This focuses their attention on choice of subjects, and maximising marks. Engaged working-class parents are more likely to be focused on simply keeping their children in school to the HSC. For instance Wynona, who regretted her own abandoned education ('I blew my chance at school'), fought to keep her son Mike going to school after finishing the School Certificate. She lost:

He was just sitting around bludging and he didn't want to get up. I'd just slap him around the head, and 'Get on with it!' And it drove me to nearly a nervous break-down. 'Cause you've got a husband on your back, 'Get him out and get a job!' And then you've got him, won't get moving. So, it was tough times. But he's turned out not a bad kid.

To everyone's astonishment, Mike brought himself back to school, after a traumatic period in the workforce. He is now doing well at Korana High, despite poverty and family breakdown in his immediate environment.

Children, then, do not come into the school environment as blank pages for the school to write on. They come bearing specific social experiences and learning, mainly from their families. Through their families, children's lives are shaped by strategies that relate to wider social horizons. The classroom is not a closed world; it is important to bear this whole network of connections in mind.

3   The many worlds of childhood

Back in the days when the Soviet Union still existed, the celebrated United States psychologist Urie Bronfenbrenner wrote a book called *Two Worlds of Childhood*, which contrasted growing up in the USA and the USSR. He argued that Russian children, though they did not have the material goods that American children enjoyed, grew up in a culture that was more interested in children and more sup-portive at an emotional and social level. Even earlier, the famous psychoanalyst Erik Erikson wrote a book called *Childhood and Society* in which he used the ex-amples of two North American Indigenous communities, the Sioux and the Yurok, to demonstrate different ways that societies managed children's growing up.

This research helped to demolish the idea of one fixed path of development. We now also recognise that there are important differences in childhood experience *within* a given country or culture. Indeed, in countries such as Australia that have experienced settler colonialism, waves of mass migration, elite migration, economic transformation, ethnic plurality and ethnic intermarriage, there are many worlds of childhood.

Different childhoods: growing up in Perth

Different worlds of childhood are vividly brought to life in writers' memoirs. Robert Drewe's *The Shark Net*, for instance, tells of growing up in a sandy Perth suburb in the 1950s, the son of anxious middle-class parents. After moving from Melbourne:

My mother had more rules than before. In the summer they were mostly to do with avoiding polio. Stay away from crowds. Don't swim in the river. Don't eat shop-handled pies, hamburgers, fish and chips or sandwiches. Don't touch things if you don't know where they've been … my father's behaviour was like a different person's. He was much more the boss. She told me he was now a big fish in a small pond. He seemed to me to be one of the people running Western Australia (Drewe, 2000, 76ff).

But the father did not get the rapid promotion he wanted, and Robert's mother had to deal with his anger and his drinking, while maintaining a facade of middle-class respectability. The marriage deteriorated into an emotional minefield that Robert learnt to negotiate with care, and eventually was glad to escape.

In another part of the same city, at the same time, Sally Morgan was growing up in poverty in public housing beside a swamp. In *My Place* she tells the story of her alcoholic, war-veteran father's struggle and death:

He had stopped even trying to get work, and was in hospital more than he was at home. Gone were the days when he used to bring fluffy baby chickens home for us to play with. There was a time when he couldn't go past a pet shop window without buying half a dozen little chickens for us. He still lived in his favourite blue overalls, but he never hid tiny Nestles milk chocolates in the deep pockets any more. He only hid himself, now. When he was home, he never came out of his room. The only thing he seemed interested in was the pub (Morgan, 1987, p. 27).

It was Sally's mother and grandmother who held the family together. Sally grew up in a disorganised, noisy household that was also close-knit and involving. She gradually discovered the Aboriginal heritage on her grandmother's side that had been for decades concealed from the children.

The character of relationships within families is generally the most important element of children's emotional worlds. Robert Drewe's repressed, prudish family was not a good environment for him to learn empathy and skill in human relations, but at least was not violent. Sally Morgan's family environment was more emotionally connected but, while her father was alive, was threatening.

A significant number of families are marked by violence between adults, and violence by adults towards children. It is very difficult to know exactly how many families experience domestic violence, but it is certain that most serious violence is by men; so some children grow up in fear of their father or stepfather. There is evidence that the more serious the violence, the greater the disruption in children's lives. Where family violence takes the form of sexual abuse of children, the long-term consequences may be especially severe (Gilding, 1997).

The neglect and abuse of children is endemic, and troubling, but fortunately it is not the main pattern of parent–child relations. Broad surveys in Australia find positive emotions for the most part, with a mixture of support and control by parents. Supportive adults, it seems, are central figures in most children's worlds. Despite economic pressures, the time that adults spend with children is not decreasing, and public opinion seems to support this. In a national survey conducted in 2005, one of the opinion questions ran 'Caring for children is the most important thing you can do in life'. To this, 84 per cent of women answered 'agree' or 'strongly agree', and so did 82 per cent of men.

One of the most important differences between worlds of childhood is the dimension of class. Growing up in poverty is very different from growing up in affluence. Families in poverty are often under significant stress. On average they have worse health and housing, they may be forced to move to look for work, they are more likely to experience pollution and violence in their environment, and they are more likely than middle-class families to be under scrutiny by police and welfare agencies. Children growing up in poverty are less likely to have good-quality meals and medical care, they have fewer of the consumer goods that their peer groups value, and they find it more difficult to form stable and constructive relationships with schools (see chapter 6).

Affluent families have the social authority and economic resources that poor families do not. Well-off parents often have a university education and, if they wish to, can buy an education for their children through the private school system. Their children grow up in a well-resourced environment full of plans and strategies that include being launched into professions, down the track. Order and control are an important part of what parents demand from private schools, and supply in their own children's lives. Emotional relationships, however, may be no closer than with families in poverty, because many middle-class parents are absorbed in business and professional careers that demand long hours.

Migration brings different experiences with education, and also different customs of child-rearing. In some immigrant communities, boys are treated with a great deal of indulgence while girls are closely controlled. In others, both boys and girls are expected to be focused on school achievement. The pattern of child rearing reflects current circumstances as well as tradition. Research with recent immigrants from China, for instance, shows that children often stay with one parent or with grandparents in China, or grandparents move from China to Australia, in order to make study and professional work by the parents possible (Da, 2003; see also chapter 7).

Children's worlds are being reshaped by the forces of globalisation. Among the corporate elite, a more globalised economy means that working parents—

usually fathers—may spend significant time travelling outside the country, and may sometimes have jobs overseas that require the whole family to move, or accept long separations. On the other hand, economic restructuring may abruptly destroy the industry on which a working-class community relied—for instance the closure of BHP's steelworks in Newcastle. Or it may cause a slow decline in employment and family incomes, which has happened in much of rural Australia (see chapters 4 and 12).

As children grow older they move more often out of the house, and their *neighbourhoods* become more important settings of their lives. Neighbourhoods differ from each other. Some are well established and some have a high turnover, some are all-residential, and some have factories and warehouses mixed in. Some wealthy 'gated communities' are practically homogeneous while some suburbs are rainbow-diverse. Community studies, such as the 'Australian Newtown' study of a working-class outer suburb of Melbourne, show that change over time is normal. Neighbourhoods evolve, industries rise and fall, ethnic groups move on, new generations take over. Recent research in California has shown how children are enmeshed in an intricate, and constantly changing, process of drawing social boundaries and making identities. In the United States context, ethnic boundaries tend to be emphasised while class boundaries tend to become invisible. This may also be happening in Australia (Bryson & Winter, 1999; Orellana et al., 2001).

The argument so far has emphasised differences among children's worlds. But there are also social forces that standardise children's lives. There is a framework of laws and regulations that govern adults' dealings with children. Compulsory education laws were among the earliest, alongside laws requiring vaccination. There is now a much wider network of regulation, for instance criminal laws against child sexual abuse and severe beating of children, laws requiring adequate health care and housing, reporting certain diseases, etc.

The other great standardising force is the corporate economy. Children and their parents are now seen as a significant market, and the result is a growth of advertising intended to manipulate children. This advertising is concentrated in children's TV shows, and increasingly 'product placement' has merged the advertising into the entertainment or the education. Some of the advertised products have become icons of consumer culture—for instance, Barbie dolls, Nintendo games and Big Macs. Periodic attempts to regulate this advertising, or to counter it by campaigns for healthier foods or non-stereotyped toys, have had little effect. Some critics feel that childhood itself is being destroyed by the tidal wave of commercial culture. This fear is exaggerated, yet there is no doubt that commercial culture is a powerful pressure on Australian childhoods and is probably narrowing, not expanding, children's experiences.

4 Adolescence

When the idea of 'adolescence' was first popularised a hundred years ago, it was seen as a period of transition and turbulence. This is still a very common view.

Anywhere between the ages of 9 and 15—there is a wide variation in timing—children go through the physical changes that bring them to biological adulthood. For girls this means the beginning of ovulation and the first menstruation; for boys, descent of the testicles and the first ejaculation. For a minority (between 1 and 2 per cent of children) the usual biological dichotomy does not apply and various *intersex* situations result. For the majority, sexual reproduction now becomes possible.

The reproductive changes are accompanied by secondary sexual characteristics that are often more visible. Girls develop breasts, pubic hair and an adult distribution of body fat. Boys develop beards and other body hair, and lower-pitched voices. Sometimes at the same time, sometimes before or after, there is usually another period of growth in height and mass, the adolescent 'growth spurt', which brings young people to their adult size.

These biological changes are often assumed to cause emotional upheavals and conflict. Journalists reporting teenage boys joy-riding in stolen cars will almost always mention 'testosterone'. Teen sex is often seen as the product of uncontrollable biological urges. Teenage moodiness may be given the same explanation. Adolescent revolt, the generation gap, rejection of parents, alienation from society, juvenile gangs, rejection of work, and political radicalism are all part of the popular image of adolescence as a period of natural turmoil.

Given the popularity of these ideas, it comes as a surprise to find that surveys of Australian teenagers carried out over the last 50 years have repeatedly found their relations with adults to be good, and the transitions not too stressful at all. This was true even in a Sydney survey conducted in 1969–70, at the height of student radicalism, when ideas of a 'generation gap' were widespread. Most teenagers in that survey reported positive relations with their parents, and broadly shared their parents' opinions about what behaviour was acceptable. At all ages from 12 to 20, when respondents were asked to nominate the most influential people in their lives, the commonest response was 'mother' (Connell et al., 1975).

Turbulence and conflict with the adult world are certainly part of the picture of growth. But it seems they are not the main experience in adolescence. Most teenagers, like most parents, value their family links, and try to repair them when tensions and disputes do arise.

If adolescence is not defined by inevitable turbulence, what are the sources of the shared identity of youth? Education itself may be the most important. The rise of secondary education was a major social change in its own right. To pioneering sociologists of youth, the high school appeared as a kind of incubator, where teenagers related to other teenagers rather than the wider culture, where peer pressures flourished, and a distinct youth culture could grow. The United States sociologist James Coleman (1961) called a famous book on high school peer group life *The Adolescent Society*, and he really wasn't joking.

In developed countries, high school life has now become an almost universal experience. At the start of the twentieth century, most Australian youth had no secondary schooling at all, and even among the minority who made it into public high schools, most left about the age of 15. At the start of the twenty-first century, the large majority of Australian youth complete the full course of high school. The statistical measure of this, the 'apparent retention rate' from Years 7 and 8 to Year 12, was 75.7 per cent nationally in 2004. The same process is underway around the world. As the recent *Growing Up Global* report says, in the developing countries today there are about 1.5 billion young people aged from 10 to 24. Their lives are currently being transformed by the growth of secondary education, which postpones their entry into the labour market, and results in later marriage and later child-bearing (Lloyd, 2005).

But whether this results in a separate 'adolescent society' is debatable. The Australian surveys mentioned above show that ties to families and the influence of parents usually remain strong throughout the teen years. There is also more governmental regulation of young people's lives as they approach adulthood. There are legal rules about the age for a driving licence, for getting married, for buying alcohol, for voting, the minimum age for legitimate sex, and so forth. There are rules about youth wages and conditions of employment. When young people get a job they have to pay income tax, and so enter the adult financial system. Some are given warnings by police, and some end up in juvenile court—in a ratio of about four young men to one young woman, and more often working-class and Aboriginal youth than middle-class white youth.

Teenagers' lives, too, are significantly affected by corporations. What is called 'youth culture' is often more accurately seen as 'commercial youth-targeted culture'. Corporations have defined youth as a market segment, and have created icons of consumption—the Nike shoe is perhaps the most famous. Compared with the child market, the youth market is bigger and has much more disposable income, and the consumers usually make their own buying decisions about fashion and entertainment, so there is no need for advertisers to bother with parents. The result is not just single advertising campaigns but a sustained marketing pressure on young people. You cannot watch television, listen to radio, open magazines, or walk through city streets without being confronted by images of beautiful young people defining themselves by the soft drink they buy, the cars they drive, the pants they pull on, and the fast food they eat.

Advertisers do not really create culture; they use it in order to manipulate consumers. In her famous book on corporate image-making, *No Logo*, Naomi

Klein tells of the United States advertising specialists who trawl the world of teenagers in the attempt to spot new trends, and the corporations that plant their products and advertising into youth culture (Klein, 2001).

So there is an interplay between young people's creativity and corporate marketing, rather than one-way causation. This is notably true of popular music. Hip-hop was not invented by corporate strategists. In fact hip-hop originated in very poor African–American communities, in the Bronx district of New York, with influences from poor Caribbean immigrants. Yet hip-hop has swept the world since its first hit, 'Rapper's Delight', in 1979. Corporations have made huge profits from it. At the same time, hip-hop has been troublesome for the establishment in the music industry. Gangsta rap was fiercely criticised and led to some boycotts, as well as some violence. Progressive hip-hop continues to operate as a social movement, not just a commercial product. There are many independent artists and promoters, and widespread use of electronic technology to circulate the music outside corporate networks.

To a significant extent, then, young people shape their own cultural worlds. The result is multiple youth subcultures, rather than a single youth culture. A variety of clothing styles, music, leisure interests, and sexual practices can be found in youth groups in any large city. Diversity is much less likely in rural settings. The high school is an important venue but it is far from the only one—the street, clubs and bars, private parties, the beach, sporting venues, video game arcades, are among the others (White, 1999).

At this stage of their lives young people are developing adult intellectual powers. They develop capacities to analyse, to criticise and to innovate. The great Swiss psychologist Jean Piaget referred to this as the growth of 'formal thought', by which he did not mean academic thinking, but the fundamental power to think beyond the given—to reason abstractly, to imagine alternatives, to reverse arguments, to think about sets of possibilities at once. Piaget saw this as a distinct 'stage' in cognitive development, a view now regarded as obsolete. Yet there is no doubt that for many young people, capacities for complex reasoning and abstraction do increase during the teen years (Inhelder & Piaget, 1958).

Prominent among the issues they are thinking about are sexuality and gender. Puberty is likely to mean a growth of sexual awareness, but does not mean automatic involvement in sexual relations—far from it. When, how, and with whom are often subjects of intense debate in teenage peer groups, as well as with parents and with potential partners.

During the teen years a proportion of young people find that their main sexual interest is in others of their own gender, and so begin to develop a sexual identity as lesbian or gay. For the majority in Australia, sexual interest follows a cross-gender path. For them, heterosexual interest easily becomes bound up with ideas of masculinity and femininity. In the mixed peer groups that are characteristic of the mid teen years, popularity is often closely linked with heterosexual attractiveness and conformity to gender conventions—the handsome sports star and the attractive socialite become stars in peer group life. Yet only a few people can become stars and their dominance is limited. Teenagers construct and inhabit multiple forms of femininity and masculinity (Martino & Pallotta-Chiarolli, 2003).

Young people do not suddenly pop out at the end of 'adolescence' and turn into adults overnight. Adult sexuality, cognitive powers, physical size, social skills and earning capacity may all appear at different times between about 15 and 25. These changes appear in a different order, and under different circumstances, for different people. Even governmental regulation is staggered, as legal thresholds for different activities are set at different ages. You can usually drive before you can vote, though nowadays the former is the more dangerous power.

Youth researchers now emphasise that the entry to adulthood changes in successive generations. The pattern of transition from school to work has changed greatly in the last generation. Marriage was once the almost universal requirement for setting up a heterosexual household and having children. But the rates of marriage in Australia are now falling significantly, and the number of children born to unmarried couples has risen sharply. More and more young people have redefined this transition through personal agreements about living together and bringing up children (Wyn & White, 2000).

5 Conclusion

Children and adolescents are not puppets, whether of biological programming or social forces. They are active in their own growth, in their own learning, in their encounters with the world, and in the creation of their own cultures and social relations. This is a tremendous asset for teachers, though it also makes teaching a demanding profession.

Young people and their situations are truly diverse. This is not a matter of random differentiation where 'every individual is different'. Often the diversity is strongly structured, for instance by family wealth or poverty, by social attitudes such as prejudice against homosexuality or ethnic minorities, or by the social geography that creates different environments for growth. Teachers cannot settle for a 'one size fits all' approach. To create effective educational strategies, we need to recognise the real diversity of children's circumstances and pathways of growth.

Focus questions

1 In a community you know, how is the child care socially organised? Who has control and responsibility? Who does the actual work?
2 What differences in 'worlds of childhood' can be found in a city you know?
3 What differences among family education strategies can be found among different social groups in Australia today?
4 Identify at least two 'youth subcultures' in the contemporary world. How different, and how similar, are the lives of young people in these different settings?
5 Identify historical differences in the experience of growing up, between the current generation and those who grew up 50 years ago (say, your parents or grandparents).

Further reading

Abbott-Chapman, J. (2001). 'Rural resilience: Youth "making a life" in regions of high unemployment.' *Youth Studies Australia*, *20*(3), 26–31.

Gilding, M. (1997). *Australian Families: A Comparative Perspective*. Melbourne: Longman.

Klein, N. (2001). *No Space, No Choice, No Jobs, No Logo*. London: Flamingo.

Lloyd, C.B. (2005). *Growing Up Global: The Changing Transitions to Adulthood in Developing Countries*. Washington: National Academies Press.

Martino, W. & Pallotta-Chiarolli, M. (2003). *So What's a Boy? Addressing Issues of Masculinity and Schooling*. Maidenhead: Open University Press.

Orellana, M.F., Thorne, B., Chee, A. & Lam, W.S.E. (2001). 'Transnational childhoods: the participation of children in processes of family migration.' *Social Problems, 48*(4), 572–91.

White, R. (ed.) (1999). *Australian Youth Subcultures: On the Margins and in the Mainstream*. Hobart: Australian Clearinghouse for Youth Studies.

3
Youth Transition

Margaret Vickers

1   New patterns of youth transition

Until relatively recently, the transition from school to work was thought of as a discrete stage in the pathway from childhood to adulthood. Young people were expected to attend school and while they were studying they mostly did not have 'adult' responsibilities. At a certain point, they left full-time schooling and entered the adult workforce. This progression is what Beck (1992) called the 'standard biography'. It assumed a linear progression from childhood dependency through youth to adulthood, which was associated with independence, full employment, and family formation. The standard biography belongs to a bygone era of full employment and rapid industrial development. This era, sometimes referred to as the 'long economic boom', began shortly after the Second World War and continued unabated for 30 years. It started to sputter during the 1970s, as the oil-price shocks exacerbated the effects of weaknesses in the global economy (Brenner, 1998). The end of the boom ushered in a series of structural adjustments, sometimes described as a shift from industrial to post-industrial production, but also described more loosely as economic globalisation. A major consequence of these shifts was that first-world governments colluded with global corporations, encouraging them to outsource manufacturing, reduce overall employment, replace secure jobs with casual work, increase working hours, and take over many public enterprises that then followed the established pattern of *downsizing* and *casualisation* (Hall, 1983; Bauman, 1998; Brenner, 1998).

2   'Learning to labour'

In the early 1970s the long economic boom was drawing to a close, but it was years before anyone realised what this might mean. It was during this bygone era of relative stability that Paul Willis carried out his classic ethnographic study of youth in transition, titled *Learning to Labour* (Willis, 1977). Between 1972 and 1975 he followed a small group of working class youth in 'Hammertown', an archetypal town in the British Midlands under conditions close to full employment. Willis's study has been enormously influential. It ran counter to the dominant theoretical paradigm of the day, which was perhaps best represented in the structural analysis of Bowles and Gintis. In *Schooling in Capitalist America* (1976), Bowles and Gintis argued that the function of schools was to teach working-class youth to take their place in the capitalist system, so that in the final analysis, the exploitative labour relations of capitalism would be reproduced. What Willis showed was that rather than being victims of blind forces, the boys in his study were active agents, complicit in their own class reproduction (Dolby & Dimitriadis, 2004). In effect, his boys actively created a culture of resistance and opposition to authority. He documented the emergence of an aggressive, white, working-class masculinity, making it clear that young people are active agents in inventing their own futures.

When Willis's boys left school early to join the labouring classes they did so with a sense of pride. They walked away, finally defeating the school's authority over them, and entered the heroic, masculine world of Hammertown's factories. It is important to remember, however, that Willis's work was carried out during an era of relative economic predictability and security in England, an era in which some semblance of the 'standard biography' was still alive and well (Currie, 1983, cited in Kenway & Kraack, 2004). The location of Willis's work in a specific historical context does not detracts from its significance. His most enduring legacy is his emphasis on the *agency* of youth. In later studies he continued to look at how young people make sense out of their lives in creative ways. As societies change, Willis sees young people as being at the forefront, negotiating new ways of being, developing new ways of negotiating technology and social relations. He describes them as 'responding in disorganized and chaotic ways, but to the best of their abilities and with relevance to the actual possibilities of their lives as they see, live and embody them' (Willis, 2003, p. 391). Many researchers around the world have continued to follow his lead, so that 25 years after the publication of *Learning to Labour* a group of scholars met with Willis in the United States, and held a seminar that led to a new volume titled *Learning to Labour in New Times* (Dolby & Dimitriadis, 2004). This text, which will be cited again later in this chapter, speaks of the importance of research that sustains close contact with young people's everyday lives, and explores the challenges of growing up in a global, post-industrial society.

3   The demise of the standard biography

The economic changes associated with globalisation and new technologies have consigned the so-called standard biography to the past. In reality the progression from school to work was never as simple and secure as the standard biography implied, and it was not universal. Even for urban youth such as those Willis described, full employment could be an elusive goal. Rural students have always been expected to work on the family farm, even if they were not paid. Combining study and work is no novelty in the bush. Nevertheless, the myth of an idealised standard biography persisted until at least the mid 1970s. Over the past 20 years, however, these taken-for-granted patterns have become less dominant and the transition to adulthood has become much less predictable. The boundaries between school and employment have become increasingly blurred, so that many young people now spend years juggling various combinations of study and part-time work before they are able to gain a secure foothold in the labour market. Alongside these economic changes, the lives of young people are also affected by other factors; for example, by reforms to the senior secondary curriculum, by new forms of income support, new forms of regulation that aim to keep young people at school, and, in some states, new arrangements that allow students to combine part-time work and school attendance.

Chapter 2 provided a discussion of the ways in which social processes change over time, leading to the possibility of new developmental pathways. Social and economic contexts change from generation to generation and sometimes within a single generation. As this happens, the pathways from school to work also change. New and more complex pathways become possible, disturbing the simpler patterns referred to above. Over time some of these possible pathways become actual pathways. Some examples of these 'new pathways' are described in this chapter. They are illustrated through the emerging biographies of four students: Steve, Mike, Trinh, and Jenny (see the boxed text).

Trinh, Mike, Steve, and Jenny [1]

Trinh

Trinh's mother, Phi Phuong, was only 13 years old when the Americans pulled out of Saigon. She arrived in Australia from a refugee camp in the Philippines in 1982, and met Thuy Nguyen at the East Hills refugee hostel, where they both lived for nine months before moving into a small apartment block in Marrickville. Although Phi came from an educated and literate family, she had only gone to school for a few years; then came the war and the refugee camps. Thuy's education had also been interrupted, so he started out driving a taxi while Phi became a nursing assistant at the St George hospital. Trinh was born in 1984 and her little brother Van two years later. Phi and Thuy always spoke English with their children. Phi sat with them at the kitchen table while they did their homework, and Thuy filled in on evenings when Phi was working late shifts. Phi heard that in NSW there were selective high schools that were free, so she made inquiries. She found a local coaching college that could help Trinh prepare for the Entrance Exam. From early in Grade 5, Trinh went there two nights a week after school. She sat for the entrance exam early in Grade 6, and a few months later learned she had won a place at North Sydney Girls High School. With her ambitious parents always behind her and long hours of travel every day, Trinh sometimes felt stressed. Phi had mixed feelings too. She would like to feel closer to her daughter, but Trinh seemed to be growing away from her, mixing with North Shore girls and becoming a 'real' Australian. In Year 11, Trinh chose science and her teachers encouraged her to think about doing medicine. With her meticulous study habits, she gained top marks in her Higher School Certificate (HSC). When the UAC placements finally came through, both mother and daughter were bursting with pride. Trinh accepted her place at Sydney University and entered the Medical School in 2002.

Mike

Mike is the second son of Patrick and Maureen Sullivan. The Sullivans have lived in the small coastal town of Shelly Beach on the south coast of NSW for generations. Paddy is a timber getter, and his father before him was a timber getter. He has been unemployed for two years now, and he blames the 'greenies': 'They've turned every bloody stand of spotted gum between Bateman's Bay and the Victorian border into a National Park,' he says. His oldest son, Jack, left school at age 15 to follow in the family tradition, but with the new emphasis on sustainable forest management, work in the timber industry is neither as secure nor as plentiful as it once was. Mike has come to the conclusion that there is no point following in the family tradition. Logging is over, as far as he can see. Yet he often thinks about leaving school, and he has no desire to do an HSC and go to the city, like some kids. What is grabbing his interest is the new vocational qualifications he can do at his local high school in Years 11 and 12. There's a marine studies course that covers safe boating, deck handling, and teaches you how to run tourist charter boats. Mike is also taking a hospitality course at school and he has a part-time job at the local restaurant. It is quite busy and lucrative on weekends when the Canberra types drive in. Mike thinks being a chef might be a good deal, but Paddy gets pretty worked up about it all. 'It's just not men's work,' he says. 'What's the use of a boy in an apron?'.

[Mike's story is based in part on Kenway and Kraack's (2004) study of 'Paradise', on the south coast of NSW.]

Steve

In 1978, Dave Morris and Pauline Peretti completed their Bachelor's degrees. They had grown up in Melbourne's north-western suburbs, attended local high schools, and were the first in their families to enter a university. In 1979, they got married while they were completing their teaching qualifications, then accepted a posting to Bendigo Senior Secondary College, where David joined the maths department and Pauline took over girls' physical education. Two years later their son Steve was born. He seemed to grow up so quickly, was smart at school, good at maths, and was crazy about computers. His parents used computers a lot for work and by the time Steve was 12, they acquired two computers, since Steve clearly needed one of his own. Steve was one of those boys who could solve any computer problem you threw at him. During high school he persuaded the local computer repair man to employ him part-time, and neither of them ever regretted it. It seemed only natural that Steve chose to do a computer science degree when he entered Melbourne University. He worked part-time at Hewlett-Packard while he studied, and became an associate consultant almost as soon as his final exams were over. On his 24th birthday, he told his parents that he had been selected for advanced training at the Palo Alto labs in California. Steve did not quite know where it would lead, but Dave was blown away, and just a little jealous. He had finally become a high school Principal, but Steve—who had only three years of work experience—was already earning more than he was.

Jenny

Jenny's mother Kate grew up in Penrith, at the north-western end of Sydney's great sprawl. Like most girls in her year, she left school at the end of Year 10, and picked up a retail sales job in a big department store at the Westfield shopping centre in Parramatta. In 1984 she married her boyfriend Shawn and they had two little girls—Jenny and Alice—in just three years. Shawn was a construction worker, mostly on the high-rise projects. Though the work he did was dangerous and demanding he usually earned good money. Late in 1987, Kate got the phone call that she had always dreaded. Shane had had a bad fall. He would not be able to work—maybe ever. The workers compensation claims took months to come through, and when they found out what they were entitled to, they gave up on their mortgage and turned in desperation to the public housing authorities. After some months on the waiting list, they were allocated to Mount Druitt, and that is where Jenny and Alice started school. Kate had to go back to work. Shaun did his best to care for the kids, do the shopping, and keep the family going. But he was often depressed and irritable. Jenny hated school. Kate wanted to help her with her homework, but she was usually too exhausted to do anything after she had got home from work and fixed the dinner. In fact, Jenny spent a lot of her time looking after Alice, and as she grew older she started to do the housework too. At school, Jenny could not make sense of maths, and her marks in most other subjects were not great either. She had worked out that if she sat very still in class and did not look up, teachers would not ask her any questions, so at least she would not be made to look stupid. She left school before the end of Year 10, believing that the supermarket where she was working part-time intended to offer her a permanent position. When the manager told her he had changed his mind, Jenny found herself out of school without a School Certificate, unable to enter Year 11, and unable to find a decent job. She has a boyfriend now, and is thinking that she might just get pregnant—at least having a baby would give her something to do.

4   Changes at school and at work

There are a number of ways in which the lives of Trinh, Mike, Steve, and Jenny are turning out to be different from those of their parents. Briefly stated, the contexts in which they are growing up are very different from those that existed during their parents' youth. The reasons for this include:

- the collapse of the full-time youth labour market since the mid 1970s
- the doubling of high school completion rates during the 1980s
- changes in government regulations, such as youth allowances
- the rapid rise of part-time employment among teenagers who are also studying
- the advent of mass tertiary education
- ongoing changes in the nature of work, including job losses in traditional areas, the creation of new occupations, casualisation, and increased labour mobility.

This list is far from complete. For example, there is no mention here of the way in which feminism has changed social expectations for girls, opening up new spaces for them in terms of careers and higher education. Social expectations have changed to a much a lesser extent for boys, and this means that Mike and his father are locked in an inter-generational conflict over what Mike should do. We will take this issue up later in the chapter. Another omitted factor is changes in family patterns, the emergence of more flexible modes of cohabitation, and a growth in the number of acknowledged gay and lesbian households. While other issues could be added, the ones listed above are already so complex that it will be difficult to do justice to each of them within this chapter.

What makes the task even more difficult is that each factor has different effects on different groups of students. For example, job losses in traditional areas are having significant effects on Mike and his relationship with his father. The casualisation of employment in the retail and service sectors and the disappearance of traditional 'female' factory work in textiles means that young women like Jenny who leave school early have great difficulty finding good jobs. These factors have almost no effect on Trinh, who is entering medicine, a traditional professional field. Even though she may not acknowledge it, Trinh has benefited from the second wave of feminism, which opened up new spaces for educationally successful women. On the other hand, feminism does not seem to have helped working-class girls like Jenny to the same extent. When Jenny's mother left school at the end of Year 10, she gained a permanent position in a department store in Parramatta within weeks. Today, with the casualisation of employment and increases in expected qualifications, positions like this are almost impossible to find for girls like Jenny. Since four out of five girls in each cohort now gain a Year 12 qualification, it's hard to win the race for a good job if you don't even have a School Certificate.

There are complex *interactions* among most of the factors listed above. The collapse of the full-time youth labour market was largely brought about through neo-conservative economic reforms such as the elimination of tariff barriers, globalisation and the outsourcing of labour, and the advent of cybernetic technologies. These same reforms are responsible for ongoing changes in the nature of work; changes that have fed into job losses in many traditional areas such as banking, mining, and manufacturing. This means that even if Mike did study accountancy and complete his Year 12 at Shelly Beach high school, there is no longer a bank in the town to give him a job. Environmental concerns and new levels of government regulation have also affected traditional male occupations, so that Mike knows there is no future in logging, even if his father does hope the 'greenies' might be forced to give up one day. While some industries are declining, others are emerging. Cybernetic technologies have led to the creation of new occupations, leading to global careers such as the one that Steve has so successfully penetrated.

These economic changes interact with young people's choices about schooling, with the nature of senior secondary provision, and with government regulations in areas such as youth allowances, job search allowances, and job training programs. One example of the *interaction* between economic and educational change is that the doubling of Australia's high school completion rates during the 1980s would probably not have occurred if the youth labour market had not collapsed at an almost equivalent rate over this same period (see the boxed text on 'Changes in the youth labour market and educational participation'). Australian economists Larum and Beggs (1989) found that the weakening youth labour market led to increases in the proportion of 15- to 19-year-olds attending school but, in addition, the level of household income and the provision of student allowances also made a difference. Students from families where household income was high were more likely to stay on at school than students from households with lower incomes, but students from poor families who received student allowances were also more likely to stay on at school than those who did not receive allowances.

Changes in the youth labour market and educational participation

Between 1975 and 2000

- more than half of all full-time jobs for teenage males disappeared
- more than two-thirds of all full-time jobs for teenage females disappeared
- the apparent retention rate to Year 12 increased from 34 per cent to 75 per cent.

In the year 2000

- over one-third of high school students were in part-time work; this figure is rising: it has increased by 10 per cent in the past decade
- approximately 80 per cent of girls and approximately 70 per cent of boys completed Year 12.

[Sources: Wooden, 1996; ABS; 2002c]

Economic factors such as those listed above have had a clear impact on young people's choices and on high school completion rates over time. Yet it is also possible that without the substantial curriculum reforms introduced by state and territory governments during the 1980s, high school completion rates might not have increased as quickly as they did (Vickers & Lamb, 2002). During the 1980s, all states and territories (except New South Wales) eliminated formal assessments at the Year 10 level, and most of them also did away with the Year 10 certificates. In fact, NSW is now the only state that still conducts formal external assessments and awards a School Certificate. During the late 1970s and 1980s most states also reformed the curriculum for Years 11 and 12. They introduced more flexible forms of school-based assessment and broadened the range of subjects offered, so that a substantial proportion of students were able complete Year 12 without seeking to qualify for a tertiary admission score. During the 1990s accredited vocational education (VET) courses were introduced into senior secondary curricula across Australia. Because of the VET reforms, schools like Shelly Beach can offer subjects at the Year 11 and 12 levels that interest students like Mike. The introduction of VET and the continuing reforms to the senior secondary curriculum are discussed in greater detail in chapter 10.

5   What are the consequences of early school leaving?

As more and more students stayed on at school the annual *Education and Work* statistics from the Australian Bureau of Statistics showed with increasing clarity that those who left school early were much more likely to be unemployed than those who completed Year 12. Each year's results follow a predictable pattern so that, for example, among 15- to 24-year-olds who left school in year 2000 without finishing Year 12, approximately 17.7 per cent were unemployed and not in training in May 2001. The rate for Year 12 completers was only 4.7 per cent (Australian Bureau of Statistics, 2002c). Teenagers like Jenny who leave school before Year 12 often face significant problems in finding work. Longitudinal research studies back up these findings. An important study by Lamb and McKenzie (2001) found that 10 years after they left school, 21 per cent of male Year 9 leavers were unemployed. Over the same time span—that is, 7 years after they were in Year 12—among those who had *completed* high school, only 9 per cent were unemployed. Over time, media commentary and official statistics such as these have constructed what is now viewed as a taken-for-granted fact: that if you don't finish Year 12, you are highly vulnerable in the labour market and you are taking a big risk with your life.

Yet early leaving is not always bad. One of the most common reasons teenagers give for early leaving is the desire for a job. If the job they gain leads to a contract of training (particularly an apprenticeship), parents and schools can rightly claim this as a successful outcome. Unfortunately many early leavers do not gain apprenticeships or enter equivalent forms of training. Those who do gain apprenticeships are less likely to find themselves unemployed than those who do not enter post-school training. However, with the exception of hairdressing, most apprenticeships are tied to 'traditionally male' jobs, so this does not help young women like Jenny. While the Lamb and McKenzie (2001) study cited above found that boys who left school early were significantly more likely to be unemployed than those who had finished Year 12, and that this was still true at age 23 or 24, they found that girls who left early were actually worse off. They found that well over half of the girls who left school early had *dropped out of the labour market altogether* by age 23 or 24. That is, by their early 20s these young women were not employed and were not even looking for jobs: they were either on welfare, or married and having children, or just hanging out.

The most startling aspect of the results from the Lamb and McKenzie study is the *degree of difference* between two groups of young women; early leavers like Jenny and Year 12 completers like Trinh. Among female early school leavers, 59 per cent had left the labour market by age 23 or 24. Among female Year 12 completers, this figure was only 7 per cent. If Jenny is like most other girls who leave school early, she will become a young mother before she has really had a career. If she tries to return to work when her kids are grown, she will have no qualifications and no experience to fall back on. In contrast, if Trinh continues to do well at university, by age 23 she will have her medical qualifications, she will start building up her career, and if she leaves work to have a baby she will always have a career to return to.

6 Why do students leave early and what can be done about it?

When students are asked *why* they are thinking about leaving school, two major themes emerge: essentially, their motives for leaving are either dominated by the desire for work, or by a lack of interest in (or a dislike of) school. Both the large-scale national longitudinal studies as well as local and state-based studies suggests that young people are making up their minds about when to leave early in their high school careers (Marks & Fleming, 1999; Lamb, Dwyer & Wynn, 2000; Marks, Fleming, Long & McMillan, 2000). International research provides similar findings. Several studies conducted in Canada and the United States also suggest that disengagement from school begins at an early age for many students (Ensminger & Slusarcick, 1992; Audas & Wilms, 2001).

Students like Mike's brother Jack say they are leaving because they have a job to go to, while others, like Jenny, tend to say they just hate school. There are also students who cite both reasons. There is a great deal of variation in the specific balance of student motives, depending on whether the student is an under-age leaver, leaves at the end of Year 10, during Year 11, or later. Reasons for leaving vary depending on where students come from (urban leavers tend to differ from early leavers in remote and rural areas). Gender plays a role too: boys like Jack are attracted to work and often succeed in getting it. However, the youth labour market offers few opportunities to girls who have not completed school. Girls who leave early often have nowhere to go, but just cannot stand school any more. Indigenous students, homeless students, and the very poor have a somewhat different balance of motives, yet across all groups, similar themes recur again and again.

The ABS survey on education and training experience in Australia reported that most early leavers cited *work-related reasons* for leaving school before completing Year 12 (ABS, 1997; see Table 3.1, p. 62). About 46 per cent of early leavers gave work and income-related reasons for quitting school. Most reported a desire to get a job or apprenticeship (42.5 per cent), while over 3 per cent reported that remaining at school would not necessarily help improve their chances of getting a job. This finding suggests that there are some young people who leave school because they do not believe that staying on would help them to get a job. For example, if Mike's school was not offering courses in marine studies and hospitality, it is unlikely that he would see any point in staying on through Years 11 and 12. A large amount of research has been done on young people's views about staying and leaving: this includes work by Lamb, Dwyer and Wyn (2000) who used longitudinal survey data, and by Pitman and Herschel (2002) and Hattam and Smyth (2000), who conducted substantial numbers of interviews. These studies found that many young people are conflicted about whether to stay or leave. They want to leave to get a job, but are concerned that this might damage their employment prospects. On the other hand, if the senior secondary curriculum in their school focuses entirely on tertiary admission, they cannot see the point in staying on.

The second most common reason students give for early leaving is directly related to their experiences of school. About 15 per cent of all leavers in the ABS study stated this explicitly, saying that they left school because they did not like it or did not like the teachers (see Table 3.1). If those who leave school because they are failing or do not do well are added to those who simply don't like school and those who claim to have lost interest or motivation, it appears that approximately one in three of all early leavers do not find school a happy or satisfying place to be. According to these findings, young people will not stay at school if they are having a miserable time, are failing academically, or are in trouble with teachers. These students will leave school even if they are not able to find work or do not have other education and training opportunities to go to (Fine, 1991; King, 1999; Spierings, 1999).

Some students leave school because of curriculum and program issues. Some drop out because school does not offer the course they want to do, and because the courses that are offered are not relevant or of interest to them. Lamb, Dwyer and Wynn (2000) found that up to 15 per cent of early leavers report that their main reason for leaving school was to do training or study not available at their school. A 2002 survey of 1125 Year 9 and 10 students in Queensland secondary schools found that a lack of curriculum choice in the lower secondary school leads some students to lose heart, believing that high school will not offer them the job training they want in order to prepare them for work (Pitman & Herschel, 2002). Taken together, approximately one-third of all early leavers say the main reason they left school was because they did not like it, they were not doing well, or that they had lost interest or motivation to continue (ABS, 1997; see Table 3.1).

Table 3.1   Main reason for leaving school before completing Year 12 [a], 1997

Reason[b]	%
Work-related reasons	**46.0**
Little difference to job prospects	3.5
Got (or wanted) a job or apprenticeship	42.5
Schooling-related reasons[c]	**36.8**
Did not do well or failed subjects	6.1
Did not like school or teachers	15.4
Lost interest or motivation	13.5
Unexplained	1.8
Personal, family or other reasons[d]	**17.2**
Own ill-health, injury, or disability	3.4
Other reasons	12.7
Unexplained	1.1
Total	**100.0**

(a) 15–24-year-olds only.
(b) Respondents nominated one reason only.
(c) Includes people who gave other schooling-related reasons.
(d) Includes people who gave other personal or family reasons.

Source: ABS, 1997

One conclusion drawn from the Queensland survey was that many young students were unaware that the senior curriculum included accredited-vocational-studies (VET). Interviews with these students suggested that they would remain in school if they could study 'something relevant'. The absence of VET from the *junior* curriculum led many of them to believe that school was only about academic study, and that it would never meet their needs in terms of preparation for the workforce (Pitman & Herschel, 2002). Queensland is now considering offering 'taster' VET in Year 9, and allowing students to accumulate credits toward a VET certificate from the beginning of Year 10. Some other states (South Australia and Western Australia particularly) are considering similar reforms.

The third major set of reasons for not continuing in school relate to family and personal factors. Table 3.1 suggests that approximately 16 per cent of early leavers tend to give 'other' reasons for leaving school. This should not be dismissed as a 'miscellaneous' group, for buried within it we find young people who are among the most disadvantaged in our society. So extreme are their disadvantages that many of them are homeless, some become habitual truants, some become juvenile offenders, and many leave the school system before reaching the legal leaving age. Early leaving occurs most frequently where there is poverty, transience and ill-health. Where a family is poor and affected by illness or mental health problems, older siblings often carry out parental roles. Jenny's domestic duties—minding Alice and looking after the housework—provide an example of this. And in Jenny's case, as with many students, her reasons for leaving school undoubtedly included a mixture of all three of the 'reasons for leaving' outlined above.

7   Family strategies

The discussion so far has focused on students' own reasons for leaving school. But young people do not act in a vacuum. They are tied into family relationships, so that their decisions are made in this context—sometimes in collaboration with their parents and sometimes in reaction against them. As we note in chapters 2, 7 and 9, one approach to explaining how families influence their children's lives is *family strategy theory*. Some families—like the Nguyens—systematically develop long-term plans. For example, Phi enrolled Trinh in a coaching program to pre-pare her for the selective entrance exam at least a year before she had to take this exam. Her family sat with her at the kitchen table night after night through primary school and through high school. In Trinh's mind there was no room for ambiguity; academic success was definitely central to her family's strategy. Steve Morris's family was similarly supportive. Dave bought him his own computer; he encouraged him to help with IT problems and to download new programs; he gave him control of online bookings for family travel, and built up his self-esteem in dozens of small ways.

These stories about the Morrises and the Nguyens are not isolated anecdotes. Based on extensive studies of families and their connections with schools, Melbourne sociologist Richard Teese argued that educational success needs to be seen as the outcome of an 'appeal' from the education system for behaviours of a certain kind (Teese & Polesel, 2003). Educated families are open to the appeal schools make, he says, and they have the capacity to respond to it. These families obsess over language development, favour standard 'educated' forms of speech, and encourage early reading. They select leisure activities aimed at cognitive growth and they consistently supervise their children's leisure time. Teese wrote: 'The interest and involvement of parents in the take-home tasks of their primary school children signals that school is central, not only to the children themselves, but to the family, and that the quality of a child's relationship to school critically affects the relationship between parent and child' (Teese & Polesel, 2003, p. 136). These behaviours are not so common in families where the parents are poorly educated. Thus, over time, a gulf opens up in the quality of school performance and in learner self-esteem, separating children from families of low socio-economic status from those whose parents are well educated.

As noted earlier, one problem with family strategy theory is that it tends to represent families as unified institutions implementing agreed-upon strategies. Parents' strategies, however, are not always aligned with the goals young people define for themselves. Family strategies can be a site for conflict and contention. For example, Mike Sullivan's father has a strategy for his family that makes a lot of sense to him, but Mike takes a different view. He thinks leaving school without an HSC is pretty risky. He is breaking with the traditions set by generations of Sullivan men who had left school and started timber felling at an early age. When they married they supported their families adequately on the modest but steady income this work provided. There really were no other decent jobs in Shelly Beach anyway. Staying on at school after Year 9 or 10 did not add to what you could earn in the logging business, and in any case it meant you lost two or three years of earnings. It made more sense, Paddy thought, to enter work early and to advance on the job, through experience. Paddy had seen kids from other families try to rise above themselves. They struggled through to the HSC and then did not make it into one of the city universities anyway. 'It was a waste of time and effort in a system that was not designed for people like us,' he said.

Paddy's views are much less common now among working-class families than they once were. As we read in chapter 2, Connell's (2004) study of working-class parents in New South Wales found that most of the parents interviewed thought that their children *should* stay in school to the HSC. Very few of these parents had done the HSC themselves. Among parents born in Australia during the 1960s—like the parents of Jenny, Steve, and Mike—fewer than one in three stayed on to Year 12. Unlike middle-class parents, the working-class parents that Connell interviewed did not imagine the HSC would launch their children into professional careers via higher education. Rather, it was because these parents considered that the HSC had now become the baseline labour market qualification that their children would need in order to stay in regular employment at all.

8 Reconfiguring work and reconstructing masculinities

This chapter began with a brief overview of the ways in which economic restructuring and globalisation have led to changes in the Australian workforce. The effects of these changes on rural Australia are discussed in chapter 4, where we learn that in some small towns and remote country areas the kinds of jobs that provided a pathway for young people leaving school early are now rapidly disappearing. The real growth in employment opportunities in Australia over the past 10 years has been in the service sector. Table 4.2 in chapter 4 shows that between 1996 and

2005, our economy created 340,000 new jobs for professionals but only 6000 new jobs for labourers and factory workers. That means that for every new job for a factory worker, the economy added almost 60 new jobs for professionals. At the same time, there were absolute *losses* in full-time employment in the transport industry and in skilled production, and the same is true for retail sales and elementary clerical work: in these areas there was a substitution of casual work for full-time employment. Employment also declined in environmentally sensitive areas such as logging and fishing, and there have been continuing declines over the past 75 years in the numbers of families supported through traditional agriculture.

With the disappearance of work that was traditionally defined as masculine, men are starting to penetrate and claim work that was traditionally considered feminine. This takes us back to Shelly Beach, to the story of the Sullivans, which is actually based on research by Kenway and Kraack (2004). These authors describe how some of the men in the south coast town they studied are redefining hospitality and catering work as 'masculine', even though the older residents continue to associate masculinity with heroic labour and find it difficult to respect 'feminised' work. Through their research, Kenway and Kraack are revisiting the ground that Willis explored 25 years ago. As Willis's boys defiantly marched out of school they walked straight into stable full-time labour. Today, this is no longer possible. Kenway and Kraack argue that what boys and their families now need to do is construct new definitions of masculinity that can accommodate what twenty-first century work is likely to entail.

Schools should be playing a key role in this transformation. A new focus on gender studies is needed to help young men get around the difficult identity issues that arise in what are seen as 'feminised' labour markets. The problem we now face is that *some* young working-class males are inventing themselves as 'new workers' while others are not. But it is equally important to remember that working-class girls have also lost ground as a result of globalisation and neoliberal economic practices. While half of all teenage full-time jobs vanished between 1975 and 1995, the figure for female jobs was two-thirds. Unskilled female work is now mostly casual, temporary, and poorly paid. There is a danger that by encouraging boys to take 'feminised' labour seriously, we will be increasing their willingness to compete with girls for the dwindling number of semi-skilled employment positions considered suitable for them. The traditional (and thriving) apprenticeship fields of construction, motor mechanics, and electrical and plumbing services remain tightly closed to women; there has been no change in the numbers of females admitted to these traditional apprenticeship fields over the past decade (Toner, 2005). Thus, as we encourage young men to enter traditionally female positions, we may in fact be placing young working-class women in double jeopardy.

9   Conclusions

We have seen in this chapter how the consequences of economic change have widely varying implications for young people and their families. Some young people, like Steve, have achieved positions in the new global economy that are beyond their parents' imaginings. Others, like Jenny, may find that they are actually worse off than their parents were. For her, the new 'downsized' economy with its casualisation of retail work had disastrous consequences. The social consequences of change are variably experienced according to class, gender, and ethnic differences. As Campbell (1993) notes, families differ from each other along these dimensions, and it follows that they develop different strategies over the short and long term to deal with the new demands associated with changing work structures, new industrial developments, the requirements of transformed markets, and new demands by the state.

With hindsight, it is possible to see how distinct patterns of youth transition emerge. Campbell (1993) conducted a study of the ways families responded to the substantial economic and social changes of the middle years of the twentieth century in South Australia. He showed how the sons of clergymen responded rapidly to the growing importance of formal educational qualifications, while the sons of farmers saw their futures in traditional terms, believing they would be secure on the land. The old middle class also sustained an ambivalent attitude to the extension of secondary schooling. Their expectations were conditioned by past patterns, and many of them planned on having their sons take over the family store, or run the family hotel, or take over a well-established building or contracting business. As Campbell (1993) notes, 'the old middle class ... often appeared to value formal secondary education, but not enough to impress on their children that their survival would depend on it' (p. 32). In contrast, the clergy, who owned neither land nor business, had a totally unambiguous attachment to higher education.

Now, in the early part of the twenty-first century, we once again face a period of rapid social and economic change, and once again families of all kinds are trying to plot courses that will lead to economically secure futures for their children. Young people are active participants in this process, and have their own ideas and strategies. There is a belief among some young people that uncertain labour market outcomes also threaten those who have completed school or gained post-school qualifications. As Wyn (2002) commented, 'There has never been such an emphasis on getting an education, and yet at the same time, there is a growing acceptance that an education alone will not secure people the job they want. Education has become one element in a very uncertain world' (Wyn & Rennie, 2002, p. 9). One of the other elements that many young people now see as essential is participation in part-time work. One in three Australian high school students have a part-time job in Year 11 or 12, and this figure has been increasing steadily. Having a job during high school makes very little difference to a student's academic success, provided that they work fewer than 6 to 10 hours per week. On the other hand, for those who go from school to work or from school to an apprenticeship, it has distinct advantages, since it appears to increase the likelihood of gaining a job or an apprenticeship position (Vickers, Lamb & Hinkley, 2003).

We are living through an uncertain period in which the boundaries between study and work are increasingly blurred. The period of transition has extended so that it often takes years before a young person arrives at a stable career. For some, such stability seems endlessly elusive. School leavers—especially those who leave without completing Year 12—are highly likely to be unemployed for a period, or spend some years in casual employment, or even return to study in order to qualify for employment in a new field (Spierings, 1999; Long, 2005). Schools need to become more flexible as young people and their families seek to respond to this new world. High school students who already have part-time jobs may need opportunities for flexible part-time participation in school. Others may need support as they develop the skills needed for employment, and look for their first job. Increasingly, schools will need to allow students to exercise greater agency over the activities they engage in as they navigate their way towards adulthood.

Focus questions

1 In 1977, Paul Willis described how working-class youth in 'Hammertown' chose to leave school early and enter working-class jobs. What were the social and economic conditions that formed the context for Willis's study, and how have these conditions changed today? What are the implications of these changes for youth transitions?

2 Young people exercise considerable autonomy and agency as they choose the paths they want to follow. At the same time, parents attempt to plot a path for their children, engaging in strategies that they hope will lead to secure economic futures. Yet parents' expectations are often conditioned by past patterns. Discuss some examples of the inter-generational conflicts that can arise in times of social change. You should include gender construction issues in the examples you review.

3 This chapter provided data from a number of studies of early school leavers. Discuss the factors that lead students to leave school early. What might schools do, now and in the future, to increase the proportions of young people who complete Year 12? Given the very substantial changes in the

social and economic context, should schools be changing radically? If so, what would schools of the future look like?

4 Why do you think young people today are taking longer (compared with their parents) to settle into permanent careers? What are some of the implications of this extended period of transition?

Notes

1. The biographical case studies presented in this chapter are fictionalised accounts based on multiple interviews.

Further reading

Dolby, N. & Dimitriadis, G. (eds) (2004). *Learning to Labour in New Times*. New York: RoutledgeFalmer.

Lamb, S., Walstab, A., Teese, R., Vickers, M. & Rumberger, R. (2004). *Staying on at School: Improving Student Retention in Australia*: Queensland Department of Education and the Arts on behalf of the MCEETYA National Fund for Educational Research.

Long, M. (2005). *How Young people are Faring*. Paper presented at the Dusseldorp Skills Forum, Sydney.

Teese, R. & Polesel, J. (2003). *Undemocratic Schooling: Equity and Quality in Mass Secondary Education in Australia*. Melbourne: Melbourne University Press.

Vickers, M., Lamb, S. & Hinkley, J. (2003). *Student workers in high school and beyond: The effects of part-time employment on participation in education, training, and work*. LSAY Research Report No. 30. Melbourne: ACER.

Internet sources

The government agencies that are responsible for youth affairs often have recent reports and statistics available. For the federal department see: www.dest.gov.au/. On this site for example is useful material on the Youth Pathways project.

The Australian Bureau of Statistics at www.abs.gov.au/ is worth exploring.

Many university libraries will have subscriptions to the material where it appears a payment must be made to download material.

4
The City and the Bush
Anthony Welch

We now have spatial locations which can be called 'global Sydney' or 'global Melbourne'—rich inner suburbs where there is full employment, well-paid workers, and which thrive because of the presence of knowledge-based economic activities. By contrast, many of Australia's rural-based regions are experiencing 'a vicious cycle of low and declining population growth, low investment, low incomes and high unemployment' (National Economics, 2000, p. i).

1   Introduction

From the very onset of British colonialism in the late eighteenth century, Australia was highly urbanised. The first small, fragile white communities clung to the coastal fringes, often apprehensive of a vast, unknown and potentially hostile interior. More than 200 years later, the island continent remains much more densely populated along its eastern and southern coastlines than in any other region. Despite a much more developed infrastructure at the beginning of the twenty-first century, in particular in areas such as transport and communications, all of Australia's largest cities, and the bulk of its population, continue to cling stubbornly to these same coastal fringes. Basic figures help to tell the story: in 2005, a nation of 7.6 million square kilometres contained a population of little over 20 million (slightly less than Taiwan), resulting in an overall population density of less than three persons per square kilometre (see Table 4.1). Western Australia, with a total land mass of just over 2.5 million square kilometres, has a total population of 2 million, of which Perth alone holds almost 1.5 million. The disproportion of city residents to country dwellers is similarly stark in South Australia, Northern Territory, and Queensland, and not much less so in most other states. Migration patterns continue to add to these disparities, with new migrants still preferring overwhelmingly to settle in Australia's larger, diverse, and more well-developed cities (for details see chapter 7 on ethnicity and multiculturalism in Australian education). This trend exacerbates ongoing difficulties in staffing rural hospitals, schools, and other public services, upon which families in country areas depend. Given this disproportionate settlement pattern, it would be a surprise if geographical factors, including the quality and equality of life-chances for regional, rural and remote communities, were not a longstanding concern (O'Connor et al., 2001).

Table 4.1 Australian population density, relative to other developed nations, 2005

	Land mass per square kilometre	Total population (millions)	Population density per square kilometre
Japan	377,835	127.5	337.3
UK	244,820	60.4	246.7
Germany	357,021	82.4	230.8
USA	9,629,091	295.7	30.7
Canada	9,984,670	32.8	3.3
Australia	7,686,850	20.3	2.7

Source: *Worldfacts*, Australian Bureau of Statistics, 2006

The data in Table 4.1 underline clearly that, Canada excepted, Australia's population density is very much lower than comparable developed nations, something that continues to pose particular problems for the provision of both the quantity and quality of services such as education in country areas.

But much more than just demographics is involved. Related to Australia's highly urbanised population pattern is the structure of the Australian economy, which has changed dramatically over the past century or so, in line with similar trends in developed nations elsewhere. Bamberry reports that whereas rural and mining industry comprised almost 30 per cent of the Australian economy in 1901, this had shrunk to less than 10 per cent by 2001. By contrast, the proportion contributed by the services sector increased from 59 per cent to 77 per cent over the same period (Bamberry, 2005, p. 71). Effectively, as Table 4.3, indicates, where once Australia proudly boasted that it 'rode on the sheep's back', agricultural industry now contributes a much smaller proportion to the gross national income. This, too, poses particular issues for country-dwelling Australians. Like other developed countries, Australia has now become a service economy: three quarters of Australian jobs are now in the service sector, which is heavily concentrated in our major capital cities. Exacerbating this concentration is the fact that tens of thousands of service sector jobs have been stripped from rural communities over the past two decades, largely by state and federal governments, in pursuit of 'small government' (Alston, 2004). Banks and financial services are another oft-reported loss.

As Table 4.2 reveals, the major growth in employment of recent years has been very much in the services sector, although not quite as simply as some have indicated. While 'the phenomenal growth in employment ... has overwhelmingly been driven by people with degrees and diplomas' (*Australian*, 2005, 24 September), the pattern has also been rather differential—more full-time jobs among the semi- and highly skilled, and more part-time for the elementary and mid-level service workers. A spectacular example of service sector growth lies within education. Australia's export of educational services, in particular the fact that around one in five of Australia's university students are now international, is estimated to yield a total of almost $6 billion annually to the Australian economy (this figure includes not merely fees paid by international students, but also the associated costs of living). This is about twice the amount for wool in 2003–04, and about the same as for wheat (ABS, 2005). Recent trends are towards fewer, but larger farms—from 150,000 to 130,000 nationally, over the past decade (*SMH*, 2005, 9 April)—and with an ageing workforce. Globalisation processes mean that Australian primary industries are now also far more open to decisions taken elsewhere: '... with the increasing internationalisation of industrial and finance capital, Australian agriculture has become quite vulnerable to decisions made in distant locations' (Gray & Lawrence, 2001, p. 9). Advances in agricultural technology also now mean that it is possible to farm large areas with far fewer workers, while another rural staple, mining, is also less and less labour-intensive. Combined with the relative lack of employment and training opportunities in country areas (Alston & Kent, 2001; Alston, 2004), and the ongoing effects of the rural recession and drought, this has led to the further depletion and greying of the rural populace as young people increasingly move to the coastal cities, in search of greater education and work opportunities, and a greater choice of social setting and lifestyle (*Australian*, 2005, 12 February).

> In regions like Bega Valley, Young, Murray Bridge, Burnett, and the Huon Valley, the kinds of jobs that provided a pathway for young people leaving school early are rapidly disappearing (Swan, 2005, p. 91).

Notwithstanding controversial tax breaks for farmers, introduced in 1999, which some seem to have abused (*Australian*, 2005, 28 May), poverty is increasing on many Australian farms, with more than one in four farms reporting negative income in 1995–96 (Gray & Lawrence, 2001, p. 65).

Although agricultural workers are not singled out in Table 4.2 (they would be included within the Labourers category), it clearly demonstrates that the recent full-time jobs growth in Australia, like in other developed economies, has been in the service sector category (particularly professionals, semi-professionals, and managers), rather than among workers involved in primary production. Part-time

Table 4.2 Employment growth in the Australian workforce, 1996–2005

Job category	New Full-time (thousands)	New Part-time (thousands)	Total New Jobs (thousands)	2005 Workforce (thousands)
Professionals	340.5	196.4	536.9	1926.6
Managers and Administrators	176.2	36.5	212.7	836.8
Semi-professional	264.5	115.8	380.3	1247.5
Tradespersons	67.0	43.9	111.0	1252.2
Advanced Clerical and Service Workers	−25.9	23.9	−2.0	401.2
Mid level Clerical and Service Workers	35.7	221.7	257.5	1652.3
Elementary Clerical and Sales and Service Workers	-9.5	133.9	124.4	986.7
Skilled Production and Transport Workers	−3.2	25.5	22.2	815.6
Labourers and Factory Workers	6.1	17.3	23.4	857.8
TOTAL	851.4	814.9	1666.4	9976.7

Source: ABS, 2005

jobs, too, have increased more in the service sector than in areas such as farms and mining. Indeed, the share of workers in primary industry as a proportion of the total workforce, and the relative contribution of the primary sector to the Australian economy, each declined markedly over the twentieth century. Tables 4.3 and 4.4 demonstrate respectively the changing contributions made by both agriculture and trade in services to the Australian economy, in recent decades.

Table 4.3 Changing contribution of agriculture to the total economy, selected OECD countries, 1980–2000

Country	1990 Exports (% of Total)	1990 Imports (% of Total)	1999 Exports (% of Total)	1999 Imports (% of Total)
Australia	**43**	**5**	**26**	**5**
France	17	12	11	8
Germany	5	14	4	8
Japan	1	13	0	11
New Zealand	66	6	45	9
UK	8	15	6	9
USA	20	8	8	4

Source: Tiffen & Gittens, 2004, p. 56

The Australian data reveal a steep decline in the proportion that agriculture contributed to the Australian economy over the last two decades of the twentieth century, of almost 40 per cent. By contrast, as the following table shows, the contribution that service sector trade has made to the Australian economy rose over the last decade of the twentieth century.

Table 4.4 Changing contribution of service sector to the total economy; selected OECD countries, 1990–2000

Country	1990 Exports (% of Total)	1990 Imports (% of Total)	1999 Exports (% of Total)	1999 Imports (% of Total)
Australia	**20.5**	**26.0**	**23.6**	**21.8**
France	26.4	21.3	21.9	18.8
Germany	13.4	19.4	13.3	22.2
Japan	12.8	28.4	13.2	29.2
New Zealand	21.3	28.6	25.5	25.9
UK	23.9	21.3	27.9	21.4
USA	27.3	19.0	24.6	4

Source: Tiffen & Gittins, 2004, p. 56

Table 4.4 shows that Australia's service sector exports increased by some 15 per cent over the 1990s, as a proportion of the total (while imports declined by 16 per cent). It can be hypothesised that a large part of the explanation for the rise in exports was the dramatic increase in education exports indicated above, which now occupy some 12 per cent of overall service sector export trade in this country (Welch, 2004, p. 4).

What does this say about our character as a nation? Does this mean that Australian identity itself is changing? Belying its self-image as a nation with strong roots in the land and 'country', the above sketch of key elements in Australian society reveals that most Australians are far removed from such roots, both geographically and (many country dwellers fear) empathically. Added to this, as we will see, our image of ourselves as an egalitarian, fair-go society, where anyone can succeed, is confronted by major cleavages between rural and urban Australia. These cracks in the Australian landscape have been deepened by perhaps two decades of economic rationalism, which has seen key services such as banking, telecommunications, health (*SMH*, 2005, 9 April), and education and training, stripped from country areas, contributing to their further marginalisation. It is no surprise that the further, full privatisation of Australia's national telecommunications giant, Telstra, planned for 2006, proved to be such an emotive issue, fuelling concerns by many country-dwellers that, once again, rural–urban inequalities would be further entrenched. As chapter 1 outlines, the increasing resort to market ideologies has become a key characteristic of the contemporary Australian state (as elsewhere to a greater or lesser extent—see chapter 12 on globalisation). While the effects of marketisation and privatisation have been felt in every area of the Australian state, it can be argued that they have had a more marked effect on rural, regional and remote communities, often already fringe-dwellers in more than the geographical sense. The very sense of community that is seen as a key feature of country life is under attack from such trends. And, as seen below, education can make a difference.

2   Background and history

Notwithstanding tens of thousands of years of continuous Indigenous education throughout the regions of Australia, the histories of the early British colonies of the late eighteenth and early nineteenth centuries did not accord education the highest priority—the sheer demands of existence usually took precedence. A shortage of skilled educators was a further problem that limited both the quality and quantity of schooling available. Even the early educational efforts that did occur, however, were very largely confined to the developing communities of Sydney, Melbourne and their equivalents in the other colonies. As colonial explorers began to push back the frontiers of the existing settlements, squatters, miners and others followed, creating a need for education in rural areas. Educational infrastructure such as denominational schools gradually grew up in rural communities, before the passage of the so-called free, compulsory and secular Acts in the various colonies in the 1870s and 1880s. Such educational provision as did develop was, like the majority of the Australian population, white, European, and Christian. As such, much of the education that was provided to Aboriginals could reasonably be described as a form of internal colonialism (Welch, 1996b, pp. 24–53). More than this, the prevailing racism of the time meant that Aboriginal Australians were mostly excluded from schools, often simply on the basis of their Aboriginality, although the 'Clean, Clad and Courteous' provisions were often invoked (Fletcher, 1989a, 1989b), in order to justify such exclusions (Burnswoods & Fletcher, 1980). Often, too, Aboriginal Australians were removed from their families, for education (Brady, 1993; Edwards & Read, 1989). Indeed, in many states, separate schools had to be established for Aboriginal pupils in rural communities, owing to opposition by the non-indigenous populace, to having Aboriginal children in mainstream local schools. Indian and Chinese Australians, some of whom provided much-needed services in rural areas, also suffered from the prevailing racism, and tended to be seen as of lower intellectual and moral calibre (Yarwood, 1964; Welch 1996b). See also chapter 7 on ethnicity and multiculturalism.

From the inception of the colonies, the Christian ethos underpinned educational provision. Sunday Schools were one of the early educational institutions of the colonial era, and provided some of the first forms of instruction in many rural areas. Stemming, like most antipodean educational innovations of the time, from England, colonial Sunday Schools were initially established by Methodists, Anglicans and Presbyterians, and provided the basics of literacy, if only, at times, the capacity to read selected passages from the Bible, which often formed the main teaching text. At least as important a reason for the growth of Sunday Schools in country settings, however, was that they suited the rhythms of rural life, at a time when at certain times of the year, 'many (children) are obliged to help their parents in the various operations of harvesting':

> In many respects, instruction in a Sunday school suited the educational needs of an agricultural district. Children were still able to help out on the farm during the week, and also attend school on a Sunday when all the family would be expected to attend Church and observe the Sabbath rest. The instruction at least provided basic literacy in a way that might have been more acceptable than full-time education (Mitchell & Sherington, 1984, p. 27).

Although child labour was still a common feature of colonial life, including in the developing cities, the particular need for the young in rural areas to lend a hand in the routines of agricultural production, especially at key times of the year, meant that enrolments in rural and regional schools fluctuated with the season: 'Many parents placed their children in school or took them out according to the seasons or the needs of the dairy' (Mitchell & Sherington, 1984, p. 27). Moreover, classes were not yet strictly age-segregated: youths of perhaps 17 or so might return to school, if time allowed, after several years of working on the land, to 'learn their letters', in the same classes as much younger pupils (Hyams et al., 1988). While the predominance of males among overall enrolments was common at the time, attrition rates were often higher for both boys and girls in rural areas than in the cities, with the numbers on the rolls at the end of the year often substantially lower than at the beginning.

While denominational schools provided the earliest educational response in rural areas, often wastefully competing against each other for a few pupils, 'National' schools had begun to replace them by the middle of the nineteenth century, a product of the widespread conviction that active state intervention was the only means by which general moral improvement in society could be achieved, especially for the 'poorer classes'. The principle of equal provision for all also lay behind the strong degree of centralisation that informed the development of colonial schooling systems. (This was very different, for example, from the tradition of local, community control that underpinned the spread of schooling to rural areas at much the same time in the United States.) The development of curricula, textbooks, teacher-training and educational administration, including quality assessment (by Inspectors), was all concentrated in the capital cities of the individual colonies, imparting a considerable degree of uniformity to schools in far-flung locations within each of the colonies.

Anti-Catholic sentiment was another common motivation, uniting disparate Protestant sects in support of national schools, and fuelling moves by some Protestants to end state aid to church schools altogether. But while the need to maintain enrolments at the fledgling National (state) schools in rural communities sometimes dictated that poor, working-class children attended the same classes as wealthier pupils, many wealthier supporters of such schools were by no means supportive of extending educational provision to the poor. In addition, there was still considerable attachment to the denominational schools, especially by those who did not wish to be tarred with the taint of pauperism by having their children attend a school for everyone, including the poor. Like their city cousins, wealthier rural dwellers were often just as concerned to preserve education as a mark of privilege or distinction (Bourdieu & Passeron, 1977; Bourdieu, 1983) for their otherwise undistinguishable sons and, less commonly, daughters. Hence, those who could afford to do so, often patronised girls' 'academies', or fledgling grammar schools for boys, at a time when education was still sex-segregated. Some of these institutions were boarding schools, with fees of perhaps £50 (a substantial sum in the mid nineteenth century) for basic board and curriculum. 'Accomplishments' such as piano, drawing and the like for girls, and extras for boys, were often available too, at additional cost. Such institutions did not always endure, at times because the head teacher came to prefer the attractions of a city school, and abandoned the rural institution. At the other end of the social scale, there were still those who, for reasons of poverty, remoteness, or because their parents kept them involved in agricultural work, did not attend school at all. As today, both educational participation and outcomes were weakest among Aboriginal students, who confronted both explicit racism, as well as an alien curriculum, in a foreign tongue.

Class relations in rural education did not provide the only axis of differentiation. Gender relations were as important. During the nineteenth century, respectable work for middle-class women was still restricted to very few professions: nurse, nun, or governess. In Ann Summers's classic history of Australian women, the pressure to institute teacher training programs, by around the mid nineteenth century, was as much associated with the need to provide cheap elementary school staff, as with moves towards greater status, wages, and respectability for professional women (Summers, 1994). Indeed, for much of the nineteenth century, women were seen as useful unpaid assistants to their rural teacher husbands. Male teachers' wives were expected to instruct girls in domestic skills (usually needlework); take charge of the discipline of the girls; be present at assembly and dismissal; and teach the infants:

> In effect, the male teacher's wife was viewed by the nineteenth century bureaucrats of state education as the least important cog in the wheels that turned the state teaching service. She was not counted as a teacher, nor was she paid a salary (Kyle, 1986, p. 132).

Indeed, the effrontery of one female teacher of the time, in writing to complain to the Board of National Education that, while she had been teaching in Kempsey National School for some 18 months, she had not been paid for this service, resulted in her husband (the *real* teacher) being dismissed, for 'frivolous conduct': 'The expectation and indeed the practice for most was that the wives of male teachers worked without pay' (Kyle, 1986, p. 132). By the end of the nineteenth century, however, young and often inexperienced women had become critical to educational provision in the bush, including in remote and difficult areas that men, who had greater choice, often refused: 'As the tentacles of free, compulsory and secular education spread over all states, it was women who provided its driving force' (Kyle, 1986, p. 139), despite persistent difficulties associated with sub-standard accommodation, loneliness, poor salaries and lack of promotion. In the face of such privations, some women left. Others were more fortunate and gained a transfer to a more bearable location. But many women remained, notwithstanding the harsh conditions, and isolation:

> Most children of European settlers in Australia attended little one-teacher, one-room shelters, often planted in a fenced corner of a farmer's paddock, or in a circle

of trees by road and creek. In the 1930s, 65 per cent of Australian schools were such as this, small and isolated (Mortimer, 1993).

But extending educational opportunity to small, scattered communities in far-flung locations necessitated more than opening a new school, whether denominational or the new and increasingly popular public schools. Necessity was often the mother of invention in early efforts to spread the benefits of education across the colonies' hinterlands. Innovations were of various kinds: creative curriculum and pedagogies (often the product of individual initiative, in the face of very restricted resources and facilities), new institutional forms, and technological innovations.

Itinerant teachers were one of the first innovations to be introduced, to bring at least half-time education to more remote locations, where enrolments could not justify a full-time school. Taught in private buildings, by mostly unqualified teachers, there were more than 100 of these in the colony of New South Wales by 1880. Small 'provisional' schools, built by local efforts, were another institutional form that operated in sparsely populated regions, where regular minimum enrolments of twenty-five for a public school, or thirty for a denominational school, could not be maintained (Whitehead, 1993; Burnswoods & Fletcher, 1980). As with itinerant teachers, most provisional teachers were untrained.

Significant technological innovations occurred with the application of radio, in particular the Traeger pedal wireless, developed in Adelaide in the years following the First World War (1914–1918). Alfred Traeger, a farmer's son, developed a pedal-powered radio, based on German military field radios. The pedal wireless was not merely adopted widely as the basis for communication in the new Royal Flying Doctor Service, but also became a key element in the development of distance education, via the new School of the Air. More than 3000 pedal wirelesses were built and Traeger travelled the outback, teaching radio operation and repair, and Morse Code, at least until he adapted a typewriter keyboard for use with the wireless set in 1933. For the first time, Traeger enabled remote families and communities to communicate with each other via wireless, and via the School of the Air, which, established in Port Augusta in 1958, pioneered a powerful alternative to the older correspondence school model of distance education. (The pedal wireless was widely adopted overseas, in countries as disparate as Canada and Nigeria, which also had remote and scattered populations.)

By the 1980s, many of the older one-teacher schools, which had sprinkled the far corners of most Australian states, had closed, with school buses making it easier for children to travel to larger schools. Even in the 1970s, however, teachers at such small and remote locations might still be allocated a (non-air-conditioned) caravan as school accommodation.

The above sketch underlines that the early development of schooling in rural areas within each of the Australian colonies was marked by several key features. Race, class, and gender cleavages were powerful within colonial systems, in rural schools as much as in city, and helped to sustain a social system based on privilege (Connell and Irving, 1992). (While Australians consider themselves as generally egalitarian, and much less marked by class and ethnic differences than the traditional systems of Europe, our history reveals that, from the very beginnings of the colonies, this was much less the case than we might like to think.) On the other hand, centralisation, based on the principle that everyone was entitled to efficient and good quality schooling, was another key motif to underpin the development of colonial systems, imparting considerable uniformity to scattered schools, in rural areas. Indeed, state intervention was fundamental to the development of a basic standard of educational infrastructure, throughout each of the colonies. In practice, the realities of colonial development dictated that small schools in rural, regional, and remote locations often struggled to provide the full range of curriculum to their pupils, while poorly trained teachers, many of them women, often endured harsh conditions, at least until a better post came along. Teacher turnover was a major problem, while for those who remained, privation, isolation, and loneliness were often the lot of the teacher, particularly at remote, one-teacher schools. This was all the more the case, since the earliest institutions of teacher training were also heavily concentrated in the capital cities, as were the first universities, which only grudgingly opened their doors to women in the late nineteenth century (Bowen, 1985).

Under such conditions, it is not surprising that the quality of rural schooling was more heavily dependent on community support, than in established urban environments. This went well beyond the fact that, for example, rural communities that wished to establish a National school in the nineteenth century were required to raise one-third of the cost of providing the school building. Community involvement and support made all the difference in terms of the relative success of rural schools. This may have included actual parental involvement, usually by rural women, for the teaching of, say, reading, within the school. Community support was also critical to build up curriculum resources, to help organise school concerts or other performances, to maintain or improve the school buildings, and perhaps provide rare trips to the city, to visit museums, or for related educational purposes.

3 Regional difference and educational opportunity in the current era

In response to the closure of such institutions as the Bourke School Hostel and other changes that effectively denied further schooling to children in remote areas, the Isolated Children's Parents Association (ICPA) was founded in 1971 to lobby for the continuation and improvement of existing correspondence schools and Schools of the Air, and for state and federal government support for living away from home allowances. Partly in response, the federal government instituted the Assistance for Isolated Children Scheme (AICS) in 1973. This provided an allowance, payable for children learning at home via distance education, as well as for children boarding away from home, and for establishing a second home to enable children to attend school regularly. State governments also established travel schemes, to enable isolated children to attend school. Evidence reveals however, that some families miss out on support, and funding is rather 'ad hoc' (Bourke, 2001; Alston, 2004).

Estimates are that between one quarter and one third of the approximately 1.8 million Australian elementary school pupils and 1.3 million secondary pupils attend schools in rural or remote areas (HREOC, 2000). Such schools are usually smaller, and can often only offer a restricted range of subject choices, compared with city schools:

> We have less teachers because we don't have so many students and then we don't have enough subject choices and then if we choose them we don't get them, and if we do get them we have problems with them anyway. We have to do them by ourselves (HREOC, 2000, response from Walgett NSW).

When classes are small and schools are stretched to support a range of subjects, especially at the senior secondary level, hours per week may be sacrificed:

> With the smaller classes, teachers can't be allocated a lot of time to spend with them. For geography in Year 11, we had four lessons a week and now we've got three, and with the timetable changes it's going to be cut down to two face to face lessons a week, which is just not enough for a two-unit subject (HREOC, 2000, response from Walgett NSW).

As seen below, rural pupils are less likely to complete Year 12 (which thus puts them at something of a disadvantage in terms of access to higher education), and have a narrower range of training offerings, at either local/regional TAFE, or in industry (Bourke, 2001; *SMH*, 2005, 1 October). As indicated above, higher poverty rates also characterise rural areas—the average poverty rate of inner metropolitan electorates was 7.6 per cent, compared with 8.2 per cent for outer metropolitan, 10.2 per cent for provincial, and 11.7 per cent for rural electorates (Parliament of Australia, 2004; see also Swan, 2005).

On the other hand, other than a commonly expressed preference for rural living (Bourke, 2001), advantages of rural schools cited by pupils include the smaller class sizes at the local school, and the personal interest that this allows, by teachers, in their progress:

Our school is small. There are only about 100 students at our school so we know everyone. We feel listened to at our school (HREOC, 2000, response from South Hedland WA).

I went to Darwin High before we came here and it was huge, and then we came here and it was much easier to learn. You might only have twenty kids in your class but there is more opportunity to learn and teachers do really care about if you pass or not (HREOC, 2000, response from Kununurra WA).

Another advantage often cited is the greater sense of community, and involve-ment in the local school.

4   Patterns of participation

Following longstanding concerns about the persistence of unequal participation and success rates between urban and rural populations, as well as schooling quality, the demands of travel, breadth of curricular offerings, high teacher turnover and staffing issues, the Human Rights and Equal Opportunity Commission (HREOC) produced a major report into rural and remote education (HREOC, 2000). A series of round-Australia bush talks identified access to appropriate, good-quality education as a significant concern in rural and remote areas. The HREOC inquiry received almost 300 written and emailed submissions, including from governments or education departments in every state, the Northern Territory and the Commonwealth. Hearings were held in over thirty-five locations and more than 3000 people responded to the survey.

The then Commissioner, Chris Sidoti, characterised the educational inequities found in the inquiry as:

...a human rights issue. Children in remote and rural Australia face substantial barriers that make it difficult to deliver the education they are entitled to expect. Are we as a nation prepared to do whatever is necessary to ensure adequate education for every child in rural and remote Australia? (HREOC, 2000)

Victoria's HREOC submission revealed 15 per cent of enrolments fell in rural areas and 8 per cent in remote parts of the state. In NSW 34.6 per cent of students attended rural and remote schools.

Country principals comment

June Rogan has taught in country schools all her working life. The Principal of Dorrigo High School, one of the smallest high schools in the state, she

is familiar with the picture of disadvantage in the bush setting. She says
Dorrigo, in northern NSW, may be only 70 kilometres away from a major
regional centre, but there are significant problems arising from isolation.
Many students, she says, are often bored with their local community and feel
they have exhausted all its possibilities in terms of education, entertainment,
and relationships.

Pam Ryan, the Principal of Orange High, a coeducational school of about 1100
students, is worried about a lack of school counselling and welfare services in
rural areas. The school's submission reveals that five students have attempted
suicide in the past 18 months, and the school counsellor reports that sixteen
more students suffer from depression and have had suicidal thoughts. Four
students had parents who had made attempts on their own lives as well.
Children at the school have access to a counsellor only four days a week
(HREOC 2000).

Only about 5 per cent of pupils nationally attend schools that qualify for
the Commonwealth's Country Areas Program (CAP) funding and only 12,243
received the Commonwealth's Assistance for Isolated Children, fewer than 1 per
cent of Australian students.

Notwithstanding decades of consolidation, many rural schools remain small.
The Queensland response to the HREOC inquiry revealed 121 government
schools with fewer than twenty pupils, while South Australia had thirty-four
schools with fewer than forty enrolments, and Tasmania's school on Cape Barren
Island had just six pupils. Western Australia reported one school with fewer than
ten students. Patterns of completion by rural and urban pupils also continue to
favour the latter (as also females in every category), as shown in Table 4.5.

Table 4.5   Year 12 completion rates by locality and sex: Australia, 1994–98 (%)

	Urban			**Rural**			**Remote**			**Total**		
Year	**M**	**F**	**Total**	**M**	**F**	**Total**	**M**	**F**	**Total**	**M**	**Fs**	**Total**
1994	66	76	71	57	71	64	51	65	58	63	74	68
1995	64	75	69	54	70	62	46	59	52	61	73	67
1996	62	72	67	55	72	63	46	65	55	59	71	65
1997	61	71	66	54	70	62	43	62	51	58	71	64
1998	62	73	67	55	71	63	48	61	54	60	72	66

Source: DETYA HREOC Submission; 2000, Schedule 5

Attendance rates also vary by region, with a strong bias evident towards urban settings. Indeed, as the following table reveals (Table 4.6), all five of the regions with the lowest attendance rates are rural, while at least two of them are areas of high Indigenous population.

Table 4.6 School attendance of 16-year-olds, top and bottom five regions (%)

Top 5 regions			Bottom 5 regions		
Mosman	NSW	97.3%	Kimberley	WA	40.4%
Ku-ring-gai	NSW	97.3%	Southern	TAS	46.9%
Camberwell	VIC	96.7%	Mersey-Lyell	TAS	48.3%
Brighton	VIC	96.5%	Balance (i.e. outside Darwin)	NT	51.1%
Woollahra	NSW	96.1%	South West and Central West	QLD	52.6%
Australia		80.2%	Australia		80.2%

Source: HREOC, 2000, citing ABS, 1996

Part of the problem of lower participation for rural families is travel, in terms of the additional costs involved (including those associated with participation in cultural excursions, technology activities, enrichment events, and sporting fixtures). The extra demands on time are especially difficult for smaller children, who may have to endure very long days, while the sometimes poor state of many rural roads leads insurance companies to deny insurance to rural communities who need to hire a self-drive bus (Vinson et al., 2002), and may make the roads impassable or dangerous at certain times of the year:

> One low-income family with several children said they could not afford the petrol money to travel each day to the nearest bus stop—20km, so their teenage son did not attend high school. He received distance education material, but his parents did not have sufficient education themselves to assist him. They had no phone, so he could not access phone support. The parents were attempting to educate the younger children themselves. A number of families with young children did not send them to school due to the bus travel time, and the condition of the roads. This would mean young children leaving home at 7am and getting home at 5, and they felt this was too much for their age (HREOC, 2000, Wide Bay Burnett Qld, submission).

In effect, education costs more to those in rural and remote settings than it does to city dwellers (Vinson et al., 2002), a problem exacerbated by increasing poverty among rural communities, the difficulty of obtaining part time-work for young people in rural areas, and their ineligibility for Youth Allowance, due to the asset-rich form of large properties (which however may not yield much income, because of drought, and uncertain commodity prices). For remote Indigenous communities, costs form a major barrier contributing to higher drop-out rates, (although by no means the only hurdle). It is still the case that in remote Indigenous communities, rates of literacy are particularly poor, and much progress beyond the primary level (which entails moving away from the community, something that most are very reluctant to do) still too uncommon. In 1994, over one-third of indigenous 15- to 24-year-olds had not completed Year 10, while in a more recent study, of the Mutitjili community (near Uluru), only 14 per cent of inhabitants were found to possess any kind of educational qualification (*Australian*, 2005, 15 October). See chapter 5, on Indigenous education, for more details.

Staffing difficulties are a longstanding problem in rural and remote schools, and constitute a significant barrier to higher retention and success rates, especially at senior secondary level. Longstanding difficulties in obtaining casual relief mean fewer rural teachers are able to gain experience as Year 12 markers (which again disadvantages rural senior secondary pupils, some of whom the Vinson Inquiry (Vinson et al., 2002) were already reported to have been allocated to 'time-killing' activities, because of the shortage of casual teachers). Difficulties with recruitment and retention mean that higher proportions of country teachers are inexperienced, while few choose to stay beyond the minimum period. Some subjects are particularly hard to staff, notably English as a Second Language (ESL), maths, science and information technology (IT). Obtaining specialist teachers in music and art can also be difficult.

Higher education and vocational education and training

Patterns of participation in higher education were also found to be stratified by geography. Despite comprising approximately one-third of all school pupils, the HREOC inquiry confirmed that rural and remote students still constituted only about half that proportion (17 per cent) of tertiary students in Australia. This was notwithstanding the fact that the number of rural students engaged in tertiary education had almost tripled over the past decade (to approximately 119,000 from around 40,000 in 1990) (HREOC, 2000). It was unclear how much of this significant increase was due to a rise in distance education, or how much of a barrier technology continued to be, particularly given the inadequate spread of broadband technology.

A further longstanding problem is the recruitment of teacher trainees and their preparation. Mainstream teacher training programs, peopled largely by young school leavers of urban background, do not provide the right type of teachers with experience of, and a commitment to making a difference in, rural areas. Programs such as 'Beyond the Line' in New South Wales, which attempt to give urban teacher trainees a taste of rural life, are sometimes very brief, and report withdrawal rates by participants of up to one-third (DET, 2005). Steps have been taken at rural universities such as James Cook (in Townsville), Notre Dame (Broome program), and Batchelor (Northern Territory) to target mature-age individuals from rural and remote backgrounds, including Indigenous trainees:

> While incentives are important, many studies (including overseas) have demonstrated that the most effective approach is to recruit trainee professionals from rural and remote areas. Accordingly, it is recommended that Universities be funded to provide for teacher education programs which would provide community-based training and target local mature-age entrants (HREOC, 2000, submission from James Cook University).

Options in vocational education and training (VET) are also often more limited in rural settings, and are a source of frustration for young people, causing high proportions to express intentions to leave the country for greener pastures (Alston & Kent, 2001; Bourke, 2001; *SMH*, 2005, 1 October; *Australian*, 2005, 12 February). This is particularly the case for girls: 'Young men can get apprenticeships in engineering, farm machinery, diesel mechanics or electrical contracting, but it's hard for girls to get apprenticeships in anything but hairdressing' (*Australian*, 2005, 12 February; see also Alston, 2004). Such departures then further drain the local school of much-needed resources, making it even harder to sustain a range of subject choices. Responses in one recent survey of several small towns in rural New South Wales revealed that as many as 85 per cent of girls and 71 per cent of boys intended leaving, largely due to the lack of employment and training options:

> We haven't really got very much subjects. When I was on a TAFE course I picked Building and Constructions. I really wanted to do it. But they put me in Office Skills and I've got to put up with it. They didn't even give me a reason (HREOC, 2000, response from Brewarrina NSW).

The composition of students in VET in schools programs and school-based apprentices and trainees is revealed in Table 4.7. The data reveal that more than one-third of all the VET in schools occurs in rural or remote locations, as do more than 40 per cent of school-based apprentices and trainees.

While the table tells us nothing about what rural students of VET actually study, patterns of enrolment for female students are more telling. While overall, about one-third of both female and male VET students live in rural and remote locations,

Table 4.7 Participation in school-based training programs, 2003 (%)

Region of students	VET in schools program students	School-based apprentices and trainees
Capital City	58.0	47.6
Other metro	8.1	9.7
Rural	31.0	36.6
Remote	2.7	5.5
Outside Australia	0.0	0.6
Unknown	0.2	0.1
Total	100.0	100.0

Source: NCVER, 2003

the fact that over half of all female TAFE graduates were employed in just three industries underlines not merely the narrower paths open to women graduates, but also reflects a macho culture in rural towns that leaves many young women feeling trapped (Alston, 2004). A major recent national survey of TAFE graduates showed that 27.7 per cent of females were employed in health and community services, another 14.6 per cent in retail trades, and a further 10.8 per cent in property and business services. While this trend is not unique to rural women, indeed is part of a wider trend of occupational segregation nationally, the fact that each of these industries is concentrated in larger towns and cities (NCVER, 2000) underscores the particular employment difficulties faced by female graduates of TAFE in rural areas (Alston, 2004; *Australian*, 2005, 12 February).

As we saw above, the faith in technology as a means to solve problems of isolation, lack of subject choice and related disadvantages, is also of longstanding concern. In practice, the results often fall short, and still do not compensate for the lack of face-to-face teaching. Despite Telstra's Universal Service Obligation, which requires it to provide a minimum of voice and digital cover to 96 per cent of the population, thus including many rural and remote regions, many rural dwellers are critical of the results. This inequity forms a considerable barrier to more and better quality distance education:

> The kids that are on distance education will always be at a technological disadvantage. They have the computers, they have the hardware, they have the software, and they have the teachers. We have the infrastructure at school but we do not have the telephone lines to support it. And that is an enormous disadvantage to the distance education kids. It is frustrating that the education infrastructure is there but the

technology infrastructure isn't. If you are on a radiophone—they have trialled this in South Australia—they can run on 320 bytes per minute. It would take you about three days to download a sentence (HREOC, 2000, response from Bourke NSW).

Current research is investigating the potential of satellite coverage to achieve what broadband has thus far failed to deliver. Experience suggests that country folk will await results with hope, rather than expectation (Swan, 2005).

5   Conclusion

While more cooperation and the enhanced use of clusters can assist rural schools, it is likely to be of less use to small and scattered remote institutions. The Commonwealth's Country Area Program (CAP) was widely appreciated, and some HREOC respondents felt it could be expanded. Indeed, the scheme's importance to rural education was underlined by the laments to the Vinson Inquiry (2002) of some rural communities regarding their loss of CAP funding, and their consequent inability to maintain school excursions and teacher professional development. Expanded coverage of IT, and its qualitative improvement, particularly via fast broadband or satellite, also offers some prospects for improvements in rural schools. The development of curriculum that is able to be implemented across the full range of institutions and settings, and adaptable for distance education, is also important, while the extension of VET opportunities in country areas would widen rural pupils' options, including for employment (DET, 2001). (At the same time, it would do little to address the lack of job opportunities in rural areas where, as was seen above, industry is sparser. This is particularly the case for remote Indigenous communities.) Broadening staff incentives such as rental subsidies, salary supplements to cover the additional costs of food and living, and travel allowances for professional development, would assist with staffing rural and remote schools. Indeed, a positive outcome of the Vinson Inquiry was the allocation of around $1000 per annum to each regional and remote teacher in New South Wales for professional development (Vinson & Esson, 2005a, 2005b), but it remains to be seen whether other states follow suit.

The development of more systematic induction programs and targeted recruitment for rural communities, including of local Indigenous trainees, is also a priority. Much more needs to be done to achieve anything like parity of participation and outcomes for rural and remote Indigenous communities, where schools are in short supply, teachers with cultural knowledge rare, and curriculum and pedagogic styles still inappropriate in many cases. The training of more Aboriginal and Islander Education Workers (AIEWs) would also assist with the provision of indigenous language, literacy and cultural awareness activities within rural and remote schools. Almost one-third of Indigenous students live in rural and remote Australia and up to one-third of those speak a language other than English as their first language. This figure excludes Aboriginal English, now only slowly being recognised as a distinct type. In the Northern Territory, for example, more than fifty Indigenous languages are spoken by its school pupils, while in Western Australia and South Australia language is still important in a number of rural and remote Indigenous communities, despite the loss of dozens of Aboriginal languages, over the last 200 years (Lo Bianco, 1987; Ozolins, 1993):

> [We need] identified Aboriginal teaching positions in all schools. [We also need to] enhance the pathways for Indigenous people wanting to be educators in their community (HREOC, 2000, Yipirinya School [NT] submission).

None of this will work, however, without political will. It is just this that is particularly problematic in the contemporary Australian state, however, in that, as Michael Pusey (1991) has argued, the earlier nation-building values that were fundamental to the establishment of health, welfare, transport and education systems throughout Australia, and that remain so vital to sustaining rural and remote communities, have been largely replaced over the past two decades or so by the ideology of economic rationalism, in which economistic values of efficiency and economy are used as the benchmark with which to assess the worth of any social initiatives or programs (Welch, 1996b, pp. 1–23; see also chapter 1 in this volume). That the relationship between the economy and society has now been inverted—where once the economy was there to serve society, now the relationship has been reversed—is of critical concern to rural communities, including in education. Over the past decade or two, this has had a telling effect on the sustainability of rural and remote communities:

> Of most direct effect on farmers, advice services which have been provided by state government agencies have been run down … Along with other rural dwellers, farmers have seen health, education and other services like language teaching for migrants move towards 'user pays'. In the hope of more efficient management of their systems when judged across the state, governments have reduced services and closed facilities where sparse populations do not meet a critical mass judged to provide sufficient demand (Gray & Lawrence, 2001, p. 62).

The re-centralisation of services evident throughout Australia over the past two decades or so has led not merely to a decline in levels of services in rural areas, but also to a loss of local knowledge and local expertise in policy matters (Gerritsen, 2000). It is here that the debate over social capital has some relevance. While still to some extent an elusive concept, social capital can be broadly described as the social glue that holds communities together—the institutions, relationships and networks, attitudes, and norms that operate among people, and that contribute to social and economic development (Putnam, 1993, 2000; Rothstein, 2002). Education is clearly a key component, not merely in building 'knowledge resources', but also in developing 'identity resources' such as self-confidence, self-esteem, trust, and celebrating success (DET, 2001; RIRDC, 2002; Vinson et al., 2002). Indeed, in rural communities:

> sorely challenged by current economic and social trends, schools are seen to be an appropriate hub of collaborative partnerships aimed at strengthening the skill base and associative bonds of their communities, thereby better enabling people to determine their futures (Vinson et al., 2002, p. 215).

The literature on social capital shows that it is capable of building just these norms, networks and trust in communities, including via education. It also shows that social capital is being eroded in contemporary society (in some more than others; see Putnam, 1993; see also Vinson, 1999, 2004), but that governments can at least develop policies and programs to support and enhance social cohesion and trust. The remorseless Australian trend, over the past decade or two, to 'small government', however, has eroded the viability of many rural towns. As Alston (2004) among others has shown, the reduction of much-needed services to rural families, and transferral of those that remain to a user-pays basis, is clearly eroding social capital in many parts of rural and regional Australia, particularly through the ongoing loss of young people, which has undermined the viability of all kinds of community organisations:

> A community's ability to deal with the challenges that are now characteristic of ... rural life is often adversely affected by a loss of individual and collective confidence, a diminished sense of shared identity and mutual trust, and a decline in the sharing of information that could facilitate joint action (Vinson et al., 2002, p. 214).

In the face of this erosion of rural community, as even a report by the Productivity Commission (2003) reveals, there is a clear and demonstrated need to preserve and enhance social capital in rural areas (see also Gerritsen, 2000; Swan, 2005; Alston, 2004). This includes state and federal support to communities, especially disadvantaged communities, to preserve social infrastructure, such as ICTs and telecommunications, libraries, banking services, health, education, transport, and family services (Alston, 2004; Wynhausen, 2005; Vinson et al., 2002).

Instead, the emphasis by state and federal governments on community capacity building activities 'locates the problem of rural decline at the feet of rural people themselves' and overlooks more collective strategies (Alston, 2004). The deliberate erosion of services and facilities, by both state and federal governments, and which is driving out-migration from country towns (Alston, 2004), has long been resisted by country folk, at times passively, at times more actively. The resistance is also translating into a degree of political resistance, including within the governing coalition's minor, traditionally rural-based partner:

> (The Nationals value) the bush as an ... important cultural and economic place that needs government intervention to prosper because it is more adversely affected by market forces due to its dispersed population, geography and narrower industrial base ... While the mode of delivery (of services) may change, the philosophy remains the same: government support where the market fails. Regional development requires government assistance and the economic growth of these regions cannot be left to the market alone (*SMH*, 2005, 1 October).

The development of effective, good quality education for rural and remote communities, including Indigenous, cannot be sustained by the communities alone. It is contingent upon outside support, including from state and federal governments, and related agencies. Cooperative policies and structures to support the enhancement of social capital in such communities, rather than economically rational policies that erode trust, and community infrastructure, are basic to any notion of quality and equality for the bush.

Focus questions

1 How has the particular population distribution in Australia shaped rural–urban differences, including in education?

2 Referring to the HREOC inquiry on rural and remote education (2000), how do the educational profiles of young people in rural and remote (note: these are not necessarily the same) locations differ from those in Australia's larger cities?

3 Which federal and state government programs are available to rural and remote communities to support their schools, and how effective are they, in your assessment?

4 How far can technology assist in overcoming disadvantage in rural and remote education? What are the limits of technology?

5 What is social capital, and what is its role in sustaining rural and remote communities, and their schools?

Further reading

Alston, M. (2004). ' "You don't want to be a check-out chick all your life". The out-migration of young people from Australia's small rural towns'. *Australian Journal of Social Issues, 39*(3), 299–313.

Alston, M. & Kent, J. (2001). *Young, Rural and Looking for Work*. Wagga Wagga: Centre for Rural Social Research, Charles Sturt University.

Brady, W. (1993). 'The education of Aboriginal women and girls in rural New South Wales.' In R. Petersen & G. Rodwell (eds), *Essays in the History of Rural Education in Australia and New Zealand* (pp. 129–49), Darwin: William Michael Press.

Department of Education and Training (DET) NSW (2001). *Vocational Education and training for NSW schools: Issues and Challenges for Distance and Rural Education*. Sydney: NSW DET.

Department of Education and Training (DET) NSW (2005). *Teaching in rural and remote schools and the Rural School Teacher Plan*. From www.det.nsw.gov.au/employment/teachnsw/rural_remote.htm.

Gerritsen, R. (2000). 'The management of government and its consequences for service delivery in rural Australia.' In B. Pritchard & P. McManus (eds), *Land of Discontent. The Dynamics of Change in Rural and Regional Australia*. Sydney: UNSW Press.

Gray, I. & Lawrence, G. (2001). *A Future for Regional Australia. Escaping Global Misfortune*. Cambridge: Cambridge University Press.

Higgins, M. & Vinson, T. (1998). *Social Disadvantage and Regional Youth Unemployment*. Melbourne: Jesuit Social Justice Centre.

Human Rights and Equal Opportunity Commission (HREOC) (2000). *'Emerging Themes.' National Inquiry into Rural and Remote Education*. Sydney: HREOC.

Lockie, S. & Bourke, L. (eds) (2001). *Rurality Bites: The Social and Environmental Transformation of Rural Australia*. Sydney: Pluto Press.

Mortimer, O. (1993). 'The Tasmanian area schools.' In R. Petersen & G. Rodwell (eds), *Essays in the History of Rural Education in Australia and New Zealand* (pp. 238–54). Darwin: William Michael Press.

Swan, W. (2005). *Postcode. The Splintering of a Nation*. Sydney: Pluto Press.

Vinson, A., Esson, K. & Johnston, K. (2002). *Inquiry into the Provision of Public Education in NSW. Report of the 'Vinson Inquiry'*. New South Wales Teachers' Federation and the Parents and Citizens Council.

Vinson, T. (2004). *Community Adversity and Resilience. The Distribution of Social Disadvantage in Victoria and New South Wales and the Mediating Role of Social Cohesion.* Melbourne: Ignatius Centre for Social Policy and Research.

Internet sources

Poverty rates by electorate. Research Note no. 49 2004–05. www.aph.gov.au/library/pubs/rn/2004-05/05rn49.htm.

Productivity Commission (1999) *Impact of Competition Policy Reforms on Rural and Regional Australia.* Report No. 8. www.pc.gov.au/inquiry/compol/finalreport/index.html.

Productivity Commission (2003) 'Social Capital: Reviewing the Concept and its Policy Implications.' www.pc.gov.au/research/comres/social capital/index.html.

National Centre for Vocational Education Research (NCVER) (2000) 'Women in VET 2000. At a Glance'. www.ncver.edu.au/students/publications/670.html.

Department of Education and Training (DET), NSW (2005) 'Teaching in Rural and Remote Schools and the Rural School Teacher Plan'. www.det.nsw.gov.au/employment/teachnsw/rural_remote.htm.

The ABS is an excellent source of data and analysis of many aspects of Australian society. For example, Australian Bureau of Statistics (2005) 'Value of Agricultural Commodities Produced, Australia'. www.abs.gov.au/Ausstats/abs@.nsf/0/48788628E4FD7A3FCA256D970021C495?Open.

5
Aboriginality and Pedagogy
Dennis Foley

1   Preamble

[The] conservative government of Prime Minister John Howard has pushed the needs of the Aborigines to the sidelines, with few complaints from his white constituency, analysts say. 'Aborigines are effectively off the white agenda,' said Hugh Mackay, a social researcher, '… many Australians carried a huge but unadmitted collective guilt about Aborigines that was reflected in the most appalling racist humour reserved for Aborigines. Australians embrace successful Aborigines … and some who really shine—like the Olympic medallist runner Cathy Freeman—are treated as national heroes. But if Aborigines are not glamorous and successful, we don't want to know about it.' [In] the 1970s and 80s successive governments made efforts to make amends to the Aborigines, but Mr. Howard rebuffed those policies. Aborigines may have numbered as many as a million in 1788 but had dwindled to 93,333 in 1901, according to the Australian Bureau of Statistics. They were forced off their land after British settlers began arriving in 1788 and then brutally suppressed … government statistics and reports of private groups show the perilous situation of Aborigines. The Ministerial Council on Education, Employment Training and Youth Affairs was told in 2000 by a special task force that only 20 per cent of Aboriginal students met reading standards. In some parts of Australia, criminal justice groups say, Aboriginal men are 25 times as likely to go to prison as whites … the health of the Aboriginal children was so poor that it affected their learning and communication skills. [An] Aborigine from a prominent Sydney clan [Dr Dennis Foley] said, '… we want our kids to have a chance in life … education, employment and healthy lifestyle—no more, no less than what white Australians desire' (Perlez, 2004, p. 3).

Sometimes it takes an international newspaper editorial such as that written by Jane Perlez in the *New York Times* to illustrate the stark reality of the problems that face Indigenous Australians. This chapter is an introduction for the reader into some Indigenous issues written from an Indigenous Australian viewpoint. There is no one person or government department responsible for the predicament that faces Indigenous Australian communities. Rather it is the responsibility (and in the interests) of all Australians, both Indigenous and non-indigenous, to share the burden and work together to remedy the concerns I discuss in the following paragraphs. It is also impossible for me to provide a history of the subjugation, discrimination, extirpation and genocide of Indigenous Australians (Moses, 2004, pp. xiii, xiv, 6) in one small chapter. You will have to read wider literature to achieve this.[1]

This chapter provides but a brief overview of the stark reality of Indigenous Australia in 2006. It is written mainly for students, no doubt mostly university students, many of whom may never meet, teach or interact at a personal level with Australia's Indigenous people. Other readers' understandings of Indigenous Australians will have been shaped largely by their prevailing cultural environment comprising the influences of family, media, education, professional associations and other affiliations. Another group of readers may be first, second or third generation immigrants or members of a minority group. A small percentage of readers will be Indigenous Australians who, together with immigrants or members of other minority groups, can identify with many or all of the issues raised in the chapter. Or perhaps you are one of the many Anglo-Celtic Australians who has a thirst for knowledge, is a critical thinker with an open mind and is prepared to listen, research, and then evaluate. To all readers who wish to become teachers, to become educators, it is hoped that this chapter will be of valuable assistance to you.

Those who become teachers may well be exposed to some of the concerns raised here. This will probably depend on the geographic location of their school, the demographics of the enrolled students and their socio-economic position. Chapters 4, 6, 7, and 9 expand on these issues. This chapter cannot help you deal with the social conditions and trauma faced by Indigenous Australians, but it can provide an introduction to the life experiences of many Aboriginal and Torres Strait Islander peoples that often thwart their limited chances to receive an education. This chapter's significance lies in its discussion of Aboriginal issues in education. It does not and cannot cover all the specific issues pertaining to diverse areas such as the Torres Strait or the Tiwi Islands, or specific cultural issues within the many hundreds of clan groups spread across the Australian continent.

If you think any of the content of this chapter is shocking, then you should research widely, familiarising yourself with the sobering truth regarding the mistreatment of Indigenous people and the ongoing destruction of Aboriginal societies. The chapter provides an insight into some of this material. It continues with an introduction to Indigenous identity and a discussion about whether there should be special treatment for Indigenous students. There is a brief outline of the history of Aboriginal education in Australia, then an introduction to Indigenous education, including the teacher's role. What teachers should know is the next topic. This provides an overview of some of the material that educators should familiarise themselves with. They include the early childhood patterns of learning of Indigenous children, the occurrence of Otitis media among Indigenous youth, and Aboriginal English. The final area discussed is classroom strategies for effective teaching with Indigenous students.

2 Indigenous identity

So who is an Indigenous Australian? The accepted 'common law' definition has three parts. An Aboriginal or Torres Strait Islander person:

- is of Aboriginal or Torres Islander descent,
- identifies as an Aboriginal or Torres Strait Islander person, and
- is accepted by the community in which they live (ATSIC, 1998, p. 60).

This three-part definition has been accepted and upheld by the High Court in the case, *The Commonwealth v Tasmania (1983)*, and was confirmed in *Gibbs v Capewell (1995)*. It has received general acceptance by governments and the Australian Indigenous community. Having established what is meant by identity, the question arises: 'Should there be special treatment for Indigenous students?'

There are three challenging questions that should be considered. First, and we aim these at our readers who are or intend to be teachers, do you think there is any need for teachers to identify students who are Aboriginal? Second, should we isolate the Indigenous students and give them special treatment? And third, should we promote Indigenous culture in the classroom?

The answer to the first two questions is simply 'No!' The answer to the third is an emphatic 'Yes!'

A child's 'race', creed or cultural background should not have anything to do with educational opportunities or outcomes. Previous research has shown that a system of auditing (linking cultural backgrounds to educational results) was implemented in northern New South Wales and south-east Queensland by some non-indigenous teachers. They sought to identify Indigenous students and then substantiate their findings by using discredited and racially discriminatory stereotypes of Aboriginal such as skin colour, brown eyes, dark hair, facial features and so on. This was practised in the classroom on an ongoing basis (Foley, 2000, p. 46). If the Indigenous child did not conform to these stereotypical body features the teaching staff questioned and/or denied the student's Aboriginality (Foley, 2000). A recent report on the New South Wales Aboriginal Education Policy has confirmed the ongoing presence of racism within schools (Lester & Hanlen, 2004, p. 29).

From outside, if the curriculum is satisfactory and students are performing at acceptable standards and do not identify as Aboriginal, then identity is the responsibility of the Aboriginal community, not that of the teachers. Public identification of students can often lead to racial intimidation by the students' non-Indigenous peers or, much worse, negative stereotyping by teaching staff as discussed above. The following story reveals the difficulties that Aboriginal people may experience as a result of institutional typecasting. In 1935 a fair-skinned Aboriginal man was ejected from a hotel for being Aboriginal. He returned to his home on the mission station to find himself refused entry because he was 'not Aboriginal'. He tried to remove his children but was told he could not because they were Aboriginal. He walked to the next town where he was arrested for being an Aboriginal vagrant and was placed on the local [Aboriginal] reserve. During World War II he tried to enlist but was told he could not because he was Aboriginal. He went interstate and joined up as a non-Aboriginal. After the war he could not acquire a passport without permission because he was an Aboriginal. He received exemption from the Aborigines Protection Act, and was told he could no longer visit his relations on the reserve because he was not Aboriginal. He was denied entry to the Returned Services Club because he was Aboriginal (ATSIC, 1998, p. 60).

Fair-skinned Indigenous Australians continue to suffer identity problems in the new millennium. They are not dissimilar to those experienced by the Indigenous soldier in 1935–45. Indeed, it can be ill-informed Indigenous people themselves who now raise identity issues about other Indigenous Australians. Given these complexities can Aboriginality be substantiated through a simple assessment of the colour of a person's skin, the shade of the eyes, the shape of the nose, the size of the brain, or by some other biological or physical term of reference? Can Aboriginality be determined biologically? You may be surprised to learn that many teachers have asked the author over the years if there is a blood test available to help them determine a student's Aboriginality!

The answer to all of these questions is 'No!'

The sad reality is that either many educators never teach or interact with Indig–enous Australians, or do so but remain unaware that students in their classrooms have had Indigenous upbringings (to varying degrees) and life experiences but do not publicly identify as Indigenous. Though the principle concern of this chapter is to look at Indigenous issues in education, any discussion about Aboriginal identity continues to flush amateur and professional race theorists out of the closet. It is important to state the obvious: an Indigenous Australian cannot be identified by the shape of their nose, colour of hair, shade of eyes, or the amount of melamine in their skin. Neither can Indigenous Australians be identified by the composition of their blood.[2]

You can begin to appreciate why Indigenous Australians find terminology such as 'half caste', 'quarter caste', and 'octoroon' extremely offensive. Consider how the idea of being 50 per cent, or 25 per cent or even 12.5 per cent Aboriginal could be translated into lived reality? Should, for example, our human bodies be divided into quarters? And if so, which organs or limbs should we identify as Aboriginal and which as Anglo-Celtic in origin? If this seems nonsensical to you, perhaps you could also consider why it is that so many non-indigenous Australians constantly ask Indigenous people to explain: 'What percentage are you?' Indigenous Australians do not by comparison ask settler Australians to identify their percentage of Britishness, Romanness, Normanness and Vikingness. The continued use of blood quantum as a tool of group identity is divisive and serves to reinforce long discredited racial beliefs. Teachers could do much to facilitate the disuse of these ideas and norms of identification by nipping them in the bud when they surface in class and the staffroom.

3   Since colonisation

Now that you have a basic understanding of Indigenous Australian identity, imagine yourself in the author's shoes. Try to perceive contemporary Australia from another perspective; view it from the standpoint of an Indigenous person and understand from the Indigenous perspective the many effects of 200 years of colonisation. This includes the loss of your ancestral homelands, your sense of homelessness and loss of identity, your domination by a foreign power, its disregard for your former way of life, and your diminished self-esteem. Perhaps you may then gain a more balanced appreciation of the historical forces that have shaped the contemporary experience of Australia's Indigenous people.

If you are well informed and exercise critical thinking you will be aware that the British invaded Australia without having received an invitation by any of the Indigenous groups to do so. They [the British] destroyed our traditional land-use management practices, over-fished our valuable marine food stocks until many became extinct, polluted our rivers, enclosed our lands with fences, exterminated our flora and fauna, starved us, gave us diseases that decimated our peoples to a fraction of what they once were, and made us suffer incredible hardships. The Australian Medical Association acknowledges that even in contemporary times:

> Indigenous Australians suffer a disproportionate burden of illness and social disadvantage compared to the general population, dying up to 20 years earlier than their non-indigenous brothers and sisters. This is a gap which has not lessened in the last 10 years … This is worse than in Nigeria, Nepal and Bangladesh (AMA, 2005, p. 1).

Another form of disease was imposed on our communities in the form of a Christian god. In his name we were penned in like sheep onto missions. Here we were abused. It seemed our women were ripe for household serfdom and our men for menial tasks. Both laboured in slavery-type conditions. The stolen wages cases in many states and especially in Queensland illustrate this horrific phase of our history. We were held prisoners under Aboriginal Protection Acts. After the invasion of our country, some colonists used our women for their sexual gratification; this continued as the frontier moved inland and in the mission system. The administrators, the bureaucrats, with the assistance of police, stole our children, starved us, fed us on meagre rations that resulted in debilitating health problems for generations. These same 'Protectors of Aborigines', however, did not educate us. Phillip Noyce's recent film entitled *Rabbit Proof Fence* depicts some of this disempowering and tortuous history. Molly tells of her life experiences at the conclusion of this film. As a frail old woman she reiterates how her youth was stolen by institutions, and how in time the same institutions stole both that of her sisters and of her children. It is suggested that you view this film if you have not done so already and read the *Bringing Them Home* report or at least a commentary on this dark chapter of our history by (Read, 2002, pp. 51–61).

Through time many—but importantly not all—Anglo-Celtic Australians have tried to exterminate us, breed us out, and absorb/assimilate us. Despite these attempts by settler society to generally make biological and cultural survival difficult for Indigenous Australians, it would seem a percentage of journalists, politicians, and non-indigenous community leaders still believe the causation of 'the Aboriginal problem' is best cast on those who have suffered the multiple dimensions of colonial violence. Chapters 6 and 7 survey some of the problems facing Australia as it grapples with widening class divisions, cultural difference and identity issues. Within this context, the plight of Indigenous Australians is deepening. In a radio broadcast made prior to the Sydney Olympics, John Pilger argued that the health of many Aboriginal children was a cause for national shame. He informed listeners that Aboriginal children were still suffering from illnesses that had already been eradicated from countries within the developing world (Neill, 2002, p. 34). Former Governor General Sir William Deane confirmed Aboriginal health remained a disgrace. After a visit to Maningrida in the Northern Territory, he noted the incidence of rheumatic heart disease was possibly the highest ever recorded in the world. It was six times higher than that recorded in the slums of Soweto in South Africa. Further, did you realise youth suicides within Indigenous communities are at epidemic proportions? Thirty years ago it was rare, almost unheard of, as were other indicators of social dysfunction, including domestic violence, alcoholism and petrol sniffing (Neill, 2002, p. 34).

Indigenous reformer Noel Pearson highlighted the prevalence of these concerns within the Cape York communities of northern Queensland. Pearson noted that if the life expectancy of Anglo-Celtic men in rural Australia was 50 years and sliding, if four in ten non-indigenous people aged between 15 and 40 years of age had a sexually transmitted disease, and if the non-indigenous population experienced the same rates of incarceration as Aboriginal people do, there would be nothing less than a state of emergency declared. This situation stands in stark comparison to the reality faced by Indigenous Australians. It seems that when these outrageous statistics are found in Aboriginal communities, they are greeted by the dominant culture with numb acceptance (Neill, 2002, p. 36). This is one of the driving forces in Pearson's vision of Indigenous communities taking control of their own future and the Cape York people struggling against the detrimental effects of a passive welfare system.

If newspapers ran headlines such as 'A national disgrace', 'A degree of violence and destruction that cannot be adequately described', 'Murder, rape and child sexual abuse in epidemic proportions', and 'Injuries resembling reports from war zones' (Neil, 2002, p. 76), you may be forgiven if you thought they were referring to massacres of Indigenous people during the eighteenth, nineteenth or early twentieth centuries. They were, however, drawn from the 1999 report of the Aboriginal and Torres Strait Islander Women's Task Force on Violence, which was tabled with the Queensland Beattie government. The report presents accounts of a 3-year-old girl in a remote community who was sexually assaulted by four males and a 14-year-old girl who when examined at a health clinic was so raw from being continuously raped since early childhood that she screamed throughout the examination. A policewoman who was in attendance was so distressed she needed counselling. The rape victim did not receive that opportunity. An Adelaide-based survey of Aboriginal rape victims showed that one in four was pack-raped. Non-indigenous men made up approximately 50 per cent of the perpetrators. One informant said that two of her daughters were killed by husbands through domestic violence. Estimates list that 90 per cent of Indigenous families in rural and remote areas were affected by violence. Nurses, police and ambulance staff working in these same areas were compared with United Nations peacekeepers delivering emergency services under dangerous and often violent conditions. From 1993 to 1998 in Queensland there were 76 homicides; more than one in three victims, and more than 50 per cent of offenders, were Indigenous, yet the Indigenous population comprises just 2.4 per cent of the population of that state. National homicide rates for Indigenous Australians are approximately ten times more than that for other Australians. Indigenous women were 45 times more likely than other women to suffer domestic violence (Neil, 2002, pp. 76–8).

Much of this violence has only surfaced within Aboriginal communities during the last five to ten years. This raises important questions. Why is this so? Why did this escalation occur during this period? These problems are a source of great pain to Indigenous people and are almost beyond our comprehension. Once again the reader is asked to try and imagine themself in the author's shoes. Is it surprising that Indigenous people wonder as to whether there is *justice* or *just us* when it comes to their struggle against the conditions operating within contemporary Australia?

> [If] female university students were being bashed at forty-five times the rate of other women, or murdered at fifteen times the rate of other women, the police, media, student unions, and women's groups would demand action. If one in six refugees settling here from a war-torn country had been pack-raped, all kinds of sophisticated trauma counselling would be offered. If a 3-year-old child was sexually violated by four different males, talkback hosts would demand to know what kind of society we were turning into … parliamentarians would call for a royal commission … but because, in this case, the victims and most of the perpetrators were [I]ndigenous, their plight went unheeded by the public at large … meanwhile the [then] Country-Liberal Party Northern Territory Government through its mandatory sentencing regime jailed Aboriginal people for crimes as trivial as stealing stationery or soft drink. The Howard Government refused to override these laws. Clearly, in some parts of Australia in the twenty-first century, property crimes committed by blacks against whites were taken more seriously than the murder of [I]ndigenous women and the rape of [I]ndigenous children (Neill, 2002, p. 79).

The frustration of Aboriginal people during the last 40 years has resulted in numerous cross-cultural conflicts. Examples include the peaceful Vincent Lingiari-led walk-off at Wave Hill Station in 1966, the 1972 Tent Embassy in Canberra, the 1982 Commonwealth Games protests in Brisbane, the Goondiwindi-Boggabilla race riots of the late 1980s, the December 1997 riot in Bourke, the so-called Redfern riots of 2004, and the recent locking down of the Gordon Estate in Dubbo on New Year's Day in January 2006. The Torres Strait people of northern Queensland also have a rich history of defiance that includes the strike of 1936 against the Queensland Government Protector and the brief military strike for better conditions during the Second World War (Ganter, 1994; Sharp, 1993).

Indigenous violence and conflict within the wider Australian society must not be condoned; neither should violence against Indigenous Australians be tolerated. Rather, Indigenous and non-indigenous people should be able to work together both to correct inequalities and ensure peaceful coexistence, and to critically examine the reasons for conflict so they can be remedied. This was the basis for my plea in the *New York Times*. Indigenous people 'want [their] kids to have a chance in life … education, employment and healthy lifestyle—no more, no less than what white [other] Australians desire' (Perlez, 2004, p. 3).

Within the post-colonisation period there has been a 'blame the victim' attitude by some commentators and bureaucrats.

4 Fallacies of blaming the victim

Consider how many times you have heard about 'the Aboriginal problem' or seen it discussed in the Australian media. There have been endless claims of wastage of taxpayers' money on Aboriginal programs, yet Minister Hand (Labor 1987–90) promised parliament the Aboriginal and Torres Strait Islander Commission (ATSIC) would be made accountable in all its actions (Bennett, 1999, p. 98). And it was. Even Mr Ruddock, when he was the government Minister in charge of ATSIC, could find no expenditure that was outside of the Audit Act. Despite this, however, ATSIC's funding was reduced and the commission subsequently dissolved. The alleged problem of wastage of money by Indigenous peoples is a difficult one to resolve. Numerous studies believe that substantial funding has in fact been wasted by the non-indigenous bureaucracies set up to administer Indigenous projects (Rowse, 2002, p. 223). The Commonwealth Grants Commission as recently as 2001 reconfirmed to the federal government that there was little or no accountability from the states to the Commonwealth for the billions earmarked each year to alleviate Aboriginal disadvantage (Tilmouth, 2005; Rowse, 2002, p. 229).

Building on Rowse it seems that the 'real' wastage occurs not at the Aboriginal organisation level but rather in the inflexibility of program delivery and the mismanagement of resources by government departments established to assist Aboriginal people. The hierarchical structure of government departments and the complexities of government funding systems ensure that program implementation is ineffective as much of the resources are consumed by bureaucrats and their governmental/departmental overheads. Little effective funding actually reaches the field (Bennett, 1999, pp. 137–44).

The Aboriginal activist Gary Foley stated to the author that if all the 'black-fellas' [Indigenous Australians] died overnight, there would be a million unemployed federal and state public servants. Where would the plush offices and huge salaries paid to a myriad Commonwealth and state public servants be? They have funding for their cars, their study leave, their holidays and their transport costs. They work in modern air-conditioned offices close to public amenities; they stay in good hotels and get lucrative daily travel allowances.

We need to reconsider the bad press espoused by the 'shock jocks' or 'the Anglo-Celtic male … pathological chauvinists' (Mickler, 1998, p. 251) on afternoon talk-back radio. Do you believe they provide a balanced understanding of the high incidence among Aboriginal people of alcohol and substance abuse, domestic violence, poverty, unemployment, lack of housing, lack of access to medical facilities, poor education attainment and so on? They do not; rather they opt for sensational topics that continue to entrench longstanding racial and social divisions within Australia.

Some of their critics argue they serve to keep alive two pernicious myths: the superiority of 'white' Anglo-Celtic civilisation and the myth that Indigenous Australians are a privileged group who receive welfare and other government assistance above and beyond that made available to non-indigenous peoples (Mickler, 1998). The latter claim of Aboriginal privilege was also popularised by Pauline Hanson of the former One Nation Party. The idea of Aboriginal privilege is remarkable 'in the face of prodigious counter-evidence that Aborigines are the most disadvantaged people in Australian society. We know ... that they are the poorest, least healthy, have the highest levels of unemployment, are the most under-housed, under-educated, over-jailed and youngest-dying social group on the continent ... how did it come to be that the same distinct population can be spoken of as a desperate social underclass in one breath, and akin to a neo-aristocracy in the next?' (Mickler, 1998, p. 13).

Despite this, it would appear that right-wing conservatives, in addition to talk-back radio sensationalists, still believe that Aboriginal people waste funds. The Northern Territory provides some clear examples of public-service-based wastage. These include the construction of a hospital and the establishment of a pastoral enterprise. Firstly, a hospital was built at Papunya (for a small desert community north-west of Alice Springs) during the Whitlam era (early to mid 1970s). It cost over $1 million. This was a significant sum at that time. Only one of its two fully equipped operating theatres has ever been used, and 'it stands like a monument of bureaucratic waste' (Neill, 2002, p. 37).

To highlight the extent of bureaucratic mismanagement of Indigenous affairs, I refer to Papunya yet again. Thirty years ago this was a showplace during the birth of Indigenous contemporary art. Between 1998 and 2000, however, end-stage renal disease doubled. So endemic was the illness and so desperate was the community for health assistance, the local artists auctioned off artwork to purchase their own dialysis unit as the available government resources could not be used to support renal disease sufferers. Further, during that same period there were approximately twenty non-government and church organisations providing essential services to a population of just 400 Indigenous people. Despite all this, the community continues to suffer from low life expectancy, high youth suicide, high infant mortality and low birth weight, and substance abuse. Petrol sniffing was endemic in 2000. Cars had to be locked in cages when not in use to protect their petrol tanks (Neill, 2002, pp. 38–9). The community has on average one NGO (Non Government Organisation) per twenty people without improvements to community education and health outcomes. It would seem this Indigenous community has been smothered in outside assistance. Or has it? This example begs many questions. Why are these programs not working? Why does a community have to buy its own medical support infrastructure (dialysis unit)? Who is responsible for this failure and why is there no coordination of services or accountability?

This lack of accountability by service organisations is undoubtedly one of the driving forces behind Noel Pearson's Cape York Project. The total number of Indigenous people living within the Cape York region would barely match that of a large suburb in Melbourne or Sydney. The region's many tiny communities, however, are being administered by as many as fifteen health programs, 200 educational programs, and a dozen economic development programs in what Pearson describes as 'a disparate, conflicting and overlapping way' (Neill, 2002, p. 39). Pearson is one of the first Indigenous leaders to acknowledge that responsibility ultimately lies with Indigenous people and that we must take responsibility for our own actions. This must not, however, be used as an excuse by service providers and governments for their record of poor achievement. Rather it should be viewed as an opportunity to work together to correct this imbalance of basic services that includes health, housing and education.

5 Introduction: Indigenous education

Education enables the individual access to a choice of lifestyle. As a nation that prides itself on its democratic egalitarianism, Australian governments have an obligation to provide education for all its citizens. The main responsibility for the provision of education, however, lies with state administrations. Over the past 40 years the federal government has made considerable financial contributions to the provision of education for Indigenous peoples. Despite improvement in some areas, many Indigenous Australian students continue to perform below their potential. Australian Bureau of Statistics (ABS) reports indicate that Indigenous Australians achieve at a level considerably less than other Australians, which in turn restricts their entry into university. Many of those who do achieve entry enrol in bridging or certificate courses before advancing into degree courses. If attendance at university is a measure of educational success, these statistics can be interpreted as an indicator that many primary and secondary education programs have failed.

Determinants of educational success include the school—its policy and developmental planning, staff and curriculum—the socio-economic status of the local community and their expectations, student abilities and interest, and funding bodies. Schools must provide for each student a quality education and be made accountable for this. This includes the provision of positive learning experiences, delivered by sensitive and informed staff, in an environment that enables each individual to reach their academic potential and develop socio-cultural skills that take into consideration the expectations of the local community. The inadequate delivery of a quality education for many Indigenous Australians has left them powerless and unable to free themselves from a life of poverty and diminished opportunity.

Readers who are prospective teachers should familiarise themselves with the local socio-cultural environment and the expectations of the local Indigenous community. The following two questions will provide a helpful starting point for their local orientation. You should ask yourself, 'How can policy and practice adequately provide for Aboriginal students?' and 'What can be learnt from academic literature regarding Aboriginal viewpoints, government policy, policy implementation processes and community experience?' to ensure you gain an understanding and appreciation of Indigenous Australian education issues.

Working with Aboriginal students as a teacher

To help you answer the questions of how policy can provide for Aboriginal students, and what can be learnt from the academic literature, some of the present author's and peers' own findings are discussed from p. 113. You, like us, may have your teaching affected by three diverse scenarios. First, you may work in a rural school with a large percentage of Indigenous students; second, you may work in a regional area or on the suburban fringe in a school that has a small number of Indigenous Australian students; or third, you may never teach Indigenous students, or perhaps you will but may never know it because they are not readily identifiable. There are common issues of which you should be aware to ensure your teaching of subject matter relating to Aboriginal history, culture, society and colonial race relations is presented in a knowledgeable, sensitive, and balanced way to both Indigenous and non-Indigenous students. To avoid negative preconceptions or stereotypes of Indigenous Australians shaping your attitudes and behaviour in the staff room and influencing your teaching and interaction with your students, you will need to think beyond your own cultural framework. It is acknowledged that you (the reader and potential educator) have been moulded, as we all have been, by your own cultural background. This may be very different from those of your students. It is important that you accept the right of the individual to respect the culture of their upbringing and moderate your own cultural assumptions. Even if you are an Indigenous person you will still need to modify your actions/decision making processes to make them comprehensible and acceptable to communities that are different to your own. This last point raises a vital issue, for contrary to popular opinion, not all 'blackfellas' are the same!

Indigenous Australian cultures, while having some similarities, are as diverse as those of Europe and western Asia. This can be best explained by the placement of a map of Australia over Europe whereby Perth is overlaid upon central Spain, Broome nearly atop Britain, Darwin near Norway, Melbourne in the Mediterranean Sea near Greece, and Brisbane adjacent to the Black Sea. While we sometimes loosely group all these peoples under the category of 'European' for specific purposes, we do not identify the Spanish, the British, the Norwegians, the Greeks and the Russians as the same peoples. They have different customs, languages, protocols, traditional foods, and so on. We recognise the ethnic and cultural diversity of Europe. The same is applicable to Aboriginal Australia. Many different protocols and socio-cultural complexities are practised by different clan groups situated right throughout Australian territory. We are many different peoples with diverse clan connections. Each has a distinct and separate cultural identity. Prior 'to the British invasion [of 1788], linguists estimated that there were approximately 230 languages, between 500 and 600 dialects' (Fesl, 1993, p. 8). As you can now appreciate, *we are not all the same*!

Social organisation

We are not **tribes** or **tribal**. Consult a dictionary, and understand the definition of a tribe. Indigenous Australians do not have chiefs or similar types of leadership structures.

Aboriginal people are a diverse group with differing needs and aspirations. As of 30 June 2001, the estimated Indigenous Australian population was 458,500. This represented 2.4 per cent of the nation's total population (Australian Institute of Health and Welfare, 2003). The geographical distribution of Indigenous Australians reveals that the majority (72.6 per cent) live in towns or cities on the eastern seaboard and in south-eastern Australia. Some 55.7 per cent of the Indigenous population lives in New South Wales and Queensland alone (ABS, 1999a, 1999b). Nearly 20 per cent reside in Brisbane and Sydney (Commonwealth of Australia, 2000). Urban or semi-urban living is typical of Indigenous Australian society as we know it today (Fisk, 1985).

6   History of Indigenous education

There is a serious disparity in educational levels in contemporary Australia between Indigenous and non-indigenous students and parents. The cause of the inequality is based on a history of denial of educational opportunities and, in more recent years, on attempts by government to assimilate or absorb Aboriginal people into mainstream society. Through this latter period, 'the education system … through its curriculum and teaching strategies has attempted to "de-Aboriginalise" Aboriginal people' (Heitmeyer, 1998, p. 198).

Arguably, earnest attempts to improve levels of Indigenous education began nearly 40 years ago after the 1967 referendum recognised all Indigenous Australians as citizens of the nation. In the early 1970s few Aboriginal students obtained a Year 11 or 12 grade schooling. Thirty years later, the Australian Bureau of Statistics (ABS) confirms that only 36 per cent of Indigenous students remain enrolled at high school until Year 12 (ABS, 2002a).

Between the 1880s and the 1930s there were introduced a new series of policies and practices relating to Aboriginal education. Each state had total responsibility for the management of Indigenous affairs until the late 1960s and, as a consequence, developed their own 'protection' acts. In general, however, it was agreed that Aboriginal children should be offered only minimal schooling. This was based on a contemporary Eurocentric perception that Indigenous peoples generally, and Aboriginal Australians specifically, had reduced intellectual capabilities and, as such, were a 'race' with limited potential for educational advancement. Operating within an historical context wherein racial thought informed social stratification practices, educators regarded Anglo-Celtic Australians as the most intellectually and socio-culturally advanced group and, by contrast, Indigenous Australians as the least evolved 'race' of people (Beresford, 2003, p. 43). The three major forces that shaped the development of Aboriginal educational policy were:

- theories of racial inferiority that were widely used to justify the limited provision of education
- segregation of Aboriginal people from the dominant settler society that underpinned the inadequate delivery of educational services to Aboriginal people
- the official policy of assimilation (Beresford, 2003, p. 43).

Racial inferiority

The myth of racial inferiority resulted in acts of racial prejudice towards Indigenous Australia. From the start, colonial educators were influenced by the theory of Indigenous intellectual inferiority. They had low expectations and aspirations for their Indigenous students, and routinely limited their access to schooling to only third or fourth grade. The anthropologist A.P. Elkin described the prevailing attitude in 1937 as follows:

> The only opportunity for employment available to [A]borigines is in labouring work and as shearers, stockmen and general hands on [cattle] stations. In Queensland for example … [A]borigines are handicapped in the fields of skilled labour beyond their own settlements. (Elkin, 1937, p. 481 cited in Beresford, 2003, p. 44).

The historical development of educational policy by the New South Wales Department of School Education provides a clear illustration of institutional and public attitudes towards Indigenous education. The *Public Instruction Act 1880* directed that all children, regardless of race or creed, must attend school if they lived within a 2-mile radius of a school. Many Aboriginal families saw this as an opportunity to provide their children with an education that was free of the Christianising zeal of missionaries (Heitmeyer, 1998, p. 198). This opportunity was opposed by a lobby group seeking to prevent the attendance at school by Aboriginal children based on racialised reasoning. The NSW Education Department replied in 1884 with the 'Clean, Clad and Courteous Policy'. This stated that as long as Aboriginal children were clean, clad, and courteous they would be permitted to attend school (Fletcher, 1989a). The anti-Aboriginal lobby group was not satisfied and opposed the Department's plan. In 1902 the 'Exclusion on Demand Policy' was enforced. This stated that Aboriginal children could not attend school if an objection was received from as little as one non-indigenous parent. This policy had devastating consequences for Indigenous youth. Various individuals and lobby groups within settler society, who held racially prejudicial/anti-Aboriginal attitudes, were able to ensure the majority of Indigenous children were denied basic education. This resulted in generations of uneducated and unskilled Indigenous Australians. The policy of 'Exclusion on Demand' was not removed from the New South Wales Teacher's Handbook until 1972. Equitable education was denied to Indigenous Australians throughout New South Wales for 70 years. This exclusionary practice was informed by ideas of racial superiority and inferiority. It emerged simultaneously with the formalisation of the White Australia 'policy' as the recently appointed federal leaders were beginning to contemplate the type of nation they wanted Australia to become. It is not surprising therefore that other states implemented similar frameworks that excluded Indigenous Australians.

This denial of educational opportunity led to reduced employment prospects and the relegation of Indigenous Australians to menial labour and transient existences. They were often forced to continuously relocate themselves in an attempt to find seasonal employment. These educational policies are seen as a major contributing factor to the enforced welfare dependence of Indigenous Australians. This may be understood through the use of a simple equation: *no education + poor employment prospects = poverty = dependence on welfare.*

A range of enduring negative stereotypes of Indigenous Australians have been in circulation at all levels of Australian society throughout the extended period of colonial settlement. These incorrectly equated skin colour with intellectual ability and socio-cultural inferiority. Many were categorised as vagrants as they were often forced to move from place to place in search of work. A vicious pattern often emerged whereby Aboriginal people were forced to become second-class people at the bottom of the social stratification ladder. Historically the educational system failed to meet the needs of Indigenous students. This history continues to contribute to socio-economic disadvantage (Beresford, 2003, p. 11).

Segregation

From the earliest days of British settlement, physical boundaries were established to keep Indigenous and non-Indigenous peoples separated from one another. Some argue that initial segregation was based on military needs. Debates continue as to whether subsequent attempts were motivated by a desire to protect Indigenous peoples or exclude them from the city limits due to their nakedness and 'savage-like ways'. Smith and Troy both suggest the bestowal of a gorget and the title of 'King' to Bungaree, in addition to the establishment of an Aboriginal camp along European settlement lines—including huts in neat rows, fences, gardens and an orchard—in 1815 at the then remote Georges Head in Sydney, as illustrating the desire to segregate Indigenous from non-indigenous peoples (Smith, 1992; Troy, 1993). The establishment of the La Perouse camp and the 'Black Town' (Blacktown) in Sydney are further examples of Indigenous people being relegated to peripheral sites by governing bodies.

Invariably Aboriginal camps and reserves were located adjacent to the rubbish dump, the cemetery, or the sanitation site. They were seen as slums; ghettos typified by flea-ridden humpies with unwashed clothing and unwashed bodies (Beresford, 2003, p. 48). The camps often lacked running water and the occupants experienced an inadequate diet that was further compounded by poor cooking facilities. These camps could still be found in most large country towns and on the edge of the urban sprawl until the early 1970s. The present lack of adequate housing opportunities for Indigenous Australians in Northern Queensland, Western Australia, and the Northern Territory means there are still many isolated segregated camps in existence today. The 'long-grassers' of Darwin and the camps on the eastern side of the Todd River in Alice Springs are highly publicised examples of Third-World living conditions. These are often associated with squalor, poor health, alcohol/substance abuse, and poor access to education. The reason for the existence of these camps in contemporary times is complex. Some people cannot find alternative housing so they are forced to live in humpies. Some people do not want to live in European-style housing and are demanding their right to live in a semi-traditional style of housing. The reasons become blurred when the health and education of the children and the general well-being of the women and aged are all jeopardised.

What we can determine is that decades of social segregation and generations of Indigenous people being denied access to education have had disastrous effects. Despite recent reforms to educational policy, high rates of non-attendance and early school drop-out are a tragic legacy of policies and attitudes that still segregate Indigenous people. This is because present programs offered within formal educational systems are still designed to 'serve white cultural and political needs' (Beresford, 2003, p. 51).

The East Kalgoorlie Primary School provides an example of a new way forward. It is attempting to break down the barriers of educational segregation by transforming itself into a specially designed *Systemic Aboriginal School*. A Systemic Aboriginal School is designed to incorporate Indigenous culture into lesson plans and teaching methods. If approved, East Kalgoorlie Primary will join Bunbury and Swan Valley schools as the third Systemic school in Western Australia (ABC Online, 2005).

Indigenous community schools

Another well-known example of a school that fulfils both the curriculum needs of the Australian educational system and the needs of Indigenous students is the independent Aboriginal and Islander Community school at Acacia Ridge in Brisbane's western suburbs. This is also fondly known as the Murri School. The school was established in 1986 with an aim to promote the development of Indigenous students as independent and skilled people who are culturally, morally, and socially responsible; employable, capable of self-fulfilment, and of contributing to society. Within the kindergarten, primary, and high schools, Aboriginal Elders occupy a high place of respect. Their knowledge and wisdom is valued by parents, students, and the community (The Aboriginal and Islander Independent Community School, 2005). The school has been widely recognised for its successes in literacy and numeracy education with primary-age students and is now extending its expertise into the secondary and adult education fields. It is also developing congruent and 'bridging' training strategies to more ably and fully serve communities. This can be seen in its successful implementation of the Department of Employment, Training and Industrial Relations' Community Literacy Program on campus over the past 2 years and the establishment of the Kulkathil Training Centre. The school enjoys an extremely high reputation among educators, funding agencies, and the various Indigenous communities it serves. It also enjoys a national reputation for excellence in Indigenous education (My Future, 2003). The school has a waiting list of non-Indigenous students who are keen to study within an environment that does not practise educational segregation.

The Murri School in Brisbane and like-minded schools scattered throughout Australia can be viewed as positive steps in the reduction of the long-term effects of formal segregation policies. But this is not enough. The destruction of the social interaction capabilities of groups of people (through segregation policies) requires more than a quick fix through the introduction of short-term government programs. This will not remediate the harm inflicted by generations of prejudice and neglect. However, there is hope, if those of you who are to be teachers are properly prepared to take up this challenge. The third phase in the history of Indigenous education will now be discussed.

Assimilation

The assimilation or absorption policy was devised in the mid 1930s in response to settler society's fears of racial miscegenation, Anglo-Celtic Australian degeneration, and a burgeoning population of Aboriginal people of mixed descent. The prevailing theory held that 'full-bloods' would eventually die out due to their inability to withstand the impact of modern civilisation. The first joint Commonwealth–State government conference on Aboriginal Affairs was held in Canberra in 1937. A commonly held opinion was expressed at the conference concerning the growing numbers of 'half-caste' people. They were identified as a national problem and a blight on the record of Australian race relations. The conference resolved that the only solution available was the eventual absorption of Indigenous Australians into the then dominant settler society. This plan for the biological and cultural absorption of Indigenous people led to the forced removal of children from their families and their institutionalisation in missions, government homes, and non-government organisations. Tens of thousands of children were removed by authorities through to the 1970s as the authorities believed that children of mixed descent should not be exposed to the cultural influences of their Aboriginal parents (Beresford, 2003, pp. 51–3).

> The terms 'full-blood' and 'half-caste' are legacies of the nineteenth and first half of the twentieth century and are deemed offensive to Indigenous persons.

There were many negative impacts of this child removal policy on generations of Indigenous children. These include: a focus on imparting Christian or moral doctrine rather than formal education; physical, sexual, and psychological abuse; poor living standards; the substitution of many years of hard physical labour for childhood innocence and curiosity; low expectations that destroyed any possibility of the attainment of self-esteem; and poorly trained individuals with low levels of knowledge of and respect for their Indigenous culture (Beresford, 2003, p. 53).

These conditions created severe educational limitations for children. The 1997 report on the 'stolen generations' by the Human Rights and Equal Opportunity Commission recognised the adverse psychological effects of the assimilation policy on both the children as individuals and as future parents. While the poor state of Aboriginal education was recognised in the late 1960s, and despite a growing body of research questioning the effectiveness of contemporary educational methods, cultural assimilation continued to be considered beneficial and was actively pursued until the mid 1970s (Beresford, 2003, p. 54–6).

Commissioner Wooten—when reporting in the Royal Commission into Aboriginal Deaths in Custody—noted that many Aboriginal parents had great difficulty in making their children attend school. This was particularly so during secondary schooling as their children were often the brunt of hurtful and insulting remarks from their settler society peers. These were often racially motivated. Parents also stated that many teachers also displayed a lack of understanding about their children's needs. The latter is a product of inappropriate and inadequate teacher training during the segregation and assimilation eras. In some instances this continued to be the case in universities until the 1990s. It is important to understand that most Aboriginal parents want their children to receive an education, but not at the expense of their child's Aboriginality, and not within a hostile learning environment (Heitmeyer, 1998, p. 210). Schwab (1999) highlights one of the many negative realities for Indigenous students within a society that discriminates between people on the basis of race and cultural background: 'racism, discrimination and forced assimilation most likely all come into play as Indigenous people make decisions about the degree to which they participate in what has been an imposed and foreign [education] system' (p. 21).

Teachers and potential teachers must realise that the Australian education system is an imposed structure of European rather than Indigenous Australian origin. It has the potential to be racially or culturally exclusive. Reflect for example on the outrage caused by federal MP Bronwyn Bishop in 2005 when she publicly advocated the prevention of Muslim girls wearing the *hijab* (headscarf) in Australian schools. The proposal could have denied the right of young Muslim women to attend Australian state schools in an attempt to maintain the values and dress codes of a predominantly Christian Anglo-Celtic Australian culture. Educational structures have long been similarly excluding towards Indigenous youth as they rarely allow for Indigenous ontology, pedagogy, and epistemology. Recent changes to funding for Indigenous education by the Commonwealth Government via the ASSPA (Aboriginal Student Support Parent Awareness) scheme (in addition to Abstudy, the Aboriginal Tutorial Assistance Scheme and other related education programs) may have the effect of further reducing the participation level of Indigenous parents in educational decision-making. This could impact negatively upon already alarming retention figures (Moyle, 2005, p. 32).

7   The teacher's role in Indigenous Australian education

The greatest fear held by Indigenous Australian educators is that Aboriginal or Indigenous Australian studies will continue to be taught begrudgingly and spasmodically. For example, many Australian students will only receive exposure to this subject matter once or twice during their combined primary and secondary education. Or it will only be discussed when tragic incidents occur, or only on national ceremonial occasions including Australia Day, National Aboriginal and Islander Day of Celebration (NAIDOC), or Sorry Day.

Aboriginal studies should not be tokenistic! It must be taught willingly, knowledgeably and consistently in all schools regardless of the composition of the student population. Failing to do so would deny a quality (and balanced) education to all Australian youth. Consider the pride with which New Zealanders regard their Maori heritage. This is made clearly visible when Maori and settler New Zealanders perform and observe a 'haka' at sporting functions. New Zealanders of European, Asian or Maori descent are proud of the courageous spirit of their Indigenous people and openly display this at public and private events. Maori history is an accepted part of New Zealand culture. The New Zealanders have embraced their Indigenous studies from K to 12. The teaching of Maori culture and history is not tokenistic within their education syllabus; it is kept alive and relevant for the total student population of today. As Australian educators we can learn from this. How, however, do we do this?

In Australia we seem to be ashamed of our Indigenous history. We do not teach our youth about the courage displayed by individual Indigenous Australians and groups during the extended period of first contact. This includes Pemulwey and the Eora of the Sydney basin between 1790 and 1802, Windradyn and the Wiradjuri in the early nineteenth century, Mosquito in Tasmania, or the Kalkadoons in Queensland. There are many more examples of the courageous spirit of Indigenous Australians as well as the hospitable spirit of Aboriginal people during British exploration and colonisation. We have much to be proud of.

8   What a teacher should know

There is much that teachers and intending teachers can do to ensure their teaching is educationally enriched through the inclusion of Indigenous culture and history, and at the same time made more rewarding and balanced for both Aboriginal and settler Australian students. Now we can discuss how you, if you are or are to be a teacher, may increase your understanding of Indigenous culture and history, approach interaction with local Aboriginal institutions and communities, incorporate Indigenous subject matter into your teaching, and provide some support to Aboriginal students and parents.

First, read a broad range of Indigenous literature. Learn about the colonial frontier from 1788 to the present time. For example, do you know the following Aboriginal Australians: Pemulwey, Mosquito, Bungaree, Windradyn, Sparrow, Jack Patten, William Cooper, David Unaipon, Mum Shirl, Vincent Lingiari, and 'Chicka' Dixon? Make it your business to discover the role they played in Australia's history and their contributions to Australian society. The talented athlete Cathy Freeman is an outstanding Indigenous Australian; there are and have been many more. Bring this information into your teaching. Australia also has a black history that deserves to be included within the curriculum. Should Indigenous history and cultural interaction not appear in your teaching, it will be incomplete and unbalanced. It will also be flawed and discriminatory. Create an environment in the classroom that enables the students to be proud of and willing to engage with the broader community. Do your own research and highlight notable Aboriginal identities from the local, state, and national Indigenous communities. An excellent starting point would be the extensive AIATSIS (Australian Institute of Aboriginal and Torres Strait Islander Studies) library in Canberra, which is accessible to the general public via their web site or in their reading room via their computer catalogue.

Second, and this is especially important if you are teaching in a rural school, find out who is the chair of the local Aboriginal Land Council. Make an appointment to meet them and share a cuppa. If there is a local Aboriginal Health Service, give them a call; talk to them, see what they can do to assist you and vice versa. For example, can they come to the school and give a talk to students and staff about the services they offer? This is very important, particularly if you suspect one of your students may suffer from Otitis media or another health problem. It is also important to be aware of the Language Group/s within the area. You can obtain this information from the Aboriginal Land Council or your Local Government Shire Council. It should be on both of their web sites. Find out about the catchment area of your school; research your local area. Who are the Aboriginal Elders? Get to know them; keep their telephone numbers handy as they are a wonderful resource as parents and speakers, co-educators, or reference points. Find out if there is an Indigenous parents' group. If not, and if the situation warrants it, then take steps to establish one (but let the Indigenous community run it). Get the old people into the school; make the school a welcoming and enjoyable place. If you are looking for best practice, research the Cherbourg Primary School (Queensland Education

Department). It has been successful in getting the Indigenous community involved. It has also improved student self-esteem.

Third, you can develop subject content that is inclusive of Indigenous studies. It is important that this be developed with your peers in an agreed and planned approach, based in sound pedagogy, and is evaluated and reviewed on an ongoing basis. This may not be easy to achieve. However, set it as a goal for your own self-development as it will provide you with opportunities to test and hone your interpersonal skills while you follow through these initiatives and establish joint ownership among all the school staff. Be inclusive of parents, community, and colleagues who may still hold fast to outdated attitudes and discriminatory behaviours. Such initiatives must have:

- clear, realistic and yet still challenging targets for improvement
- action plans that define tasks, assign responsibilities and establish timelines
- the resources (or have the means to procure them) necessary to support the change process.

Fourth, if your school does have Indigenous Australian students, assume a leadership role and seek to become actively involved in supporting and promoting Indigenous student success. Look beyond the school for assistance and sources of support. These may include parents, Indigenous support staff, community members and other Indigenous funding programs.

Be a proactive rather than a reluctant participant. Research. Interact. Network. Talk to Indigenous parents, make them welcome in your classroom, and respect all parents. The references in the side text provide outstanding resources for teachers who have Indigenous students.

Good references

- Craven, R. (1999). *Teaching Aboriginal Studies*. Sydney: Allen & Unwin.
- See also 'Improving outcomes for Indigenous students' at http://www.whatworks. edu.au. You will find these references are invaluable teaching resources even if you do not have Indigenous students in your class. They may assist you in subject content.
- *The Australian Journal of Indigenous Education*. While this is an academic journal, it is full of practical applications and helpful background information. Back issues are a rich resource to any teacher interested in this area.

Many teachers are, to varying degrees, aware that Aboriginal students have different backgrounds and needs from other students. You will need to modify your approaches so as to assist Indigenous Australian children reach their educational potential. There is, however, an unhelpful mindset that insists that Indigenous youth should not be treated any differently from other students. You will overcome these hurdles after you read and successfully implement 'strategies in the classroom' (included in this chapter).

It is also important that new teachers have a basic understanding of the early learning patterns of Indigenous children, Otitis media, and Aboriginal English, as well as an understanding of 'strategies in the classroom', which have been developed specifically for the teaching of Aboriginal students.

Early learning

Indigenous children are exposed to a range of early learning experiences. Some are fortunate and obtain their early education informally through kinship systems where a range of women (who are closely connected to them) nurture and care for the child. Some are not so fortunate. Many grow up within families that have suffered a range of traumas, leading to their involuntary relocation to urban areas. These children have often been exposed to serious social problems. In many cases they have reduced levels of closeness to their sisters, aunts, and even their own mothers. Where there are functional family structures, however, the children are taught informally in an environment that is conducive to their learning. This focuses primarily on their development of listening and observational skills (rather than reading and writing). This is a personalised mode of learning where the Elders are the educators. They convey the meaning of the subject matter and then reinforce this through repetition in story and real-life experience. Questioning is discouraged and it is not culturally appropriate for children to speak until they are asked to do so. This is discussed in further depth in the following section. Eye contact with the Elder is also discouraged. Where kinship structures have been maintained, these practices have continued unchanged in many communities.

When an Indigenous child commences attending kindergarten classes, it is often the first time they have been separated from their family and/or have had to deal with adults who did not belong to their family or community networks. Indigenous children statistically have very low records of kindergarten attendance. This is due to various reasons, including a lack of access to kindergarten, lack of funds, lack of available places, lack of transport, or a combination of factors. In many situations, while children may have had a nurturing family upbringing, their non-attendance at kindergarten means they commence school without the early educational training that establishes the essential building blocks for their educational future (Heitmeyer, 1998, p. 202). This is an area that requires further attention and greater understanding. Children who are deprived of opportunities to have elementary cognitive processes reinforced through kindergarten training begin primary school behind the 'eight ball' in a position of significant disadvantage. There is no doubt that this loss of basic skills widens as the children grow older. This is a major reason why the greater majority of Indigenous youth are always in 'catch up' mode.

Otitis media

There have been numerous studies undertaken across a diverse range of Indigenous communities that persistently indicate that a significant number of Indigenous Australian school children suffer some degree of hearing loss. The Royal Commission into Aboriginal Deaths in Custody estimated that between 25 and 50 per cent of Indigenous school children in the Northern Territory have a hearing loss caused by Otitis media (Heitmeyer, 1998, p. 203).

Hearing

When I was doing some work in a suburban Brisbane school in 1999, I enquired about a reluctant Grade 9 class member who was Indigenous. I noticed that when he was not looking at me he did not appear to understand. It seemed as though he could be lip-reading. The teacher had allowed him to sit at the back of the class, a position in which the student felt comfortable. The teacher thought he did not want to participate. In her defence she was overworked in an overcrowded classroom in a poorly resourced school. When I spoke to the child at recess he had the customary symptoms of a nasal discharge and a stale odour emitting from his ears. In one ear I found a live fly, in the other I found numerous maggots. It is no wonder he did not participate. Upon his return from the hospital and after subsequent visits to the health clinic, it was confirmed that his hearing had been permanently damaged. If only that teacher had referred him to the school nurse when she first saw him becoming inattentive, rubbing his ears, and having a runny nose. I ask you to consider who the victim is in this case? Both the child and the teacher are now statistics. However, statistically this young man will now have little prospect of finishing school and little possibility of finding suitable employment. A future of welfare and long-term unemployment, low self-esteem and poor self-worth are the all too common futures for youth such as this.

Incidents of Otitis media are not restricted to the bush. You do not have to live in rural and remote areas to suffer from ear infection (and you do not have to be Indigenous). The Australian Government has acknowledged that middle ear infections are very common in Indigenous populations and represent the most common cause of conductive hearing loss among them. Effective clinical management of the condition is essential. The risks of neglect include reduced levels of language development, educational participation, and socialisation in general. Indigenous students are often isolated within the education system and suffer alienation as a result. Can you imagine the added trauma the child will encounter if they also have to deal with impaired hearing?

Effective teachers talk to their children's faces (always remember, however, when doing so to Aboriginal children, do not demand eye contact). If you have to continuously repeat statements to an Indigenous student, this can be a warning sign. If a student talks in a class on a regular basis, this may be another sign. He or she may simply be asking the person next to them what you had just said. Take care not to scold Indigenous students for both these forms of behaviour before you confirm or rule out the signs of Otitis media. If you chide without checking first, the student may withdraw into a silent shell and you will extinguish the flame of learning. These students will inevitably drift to the back row where they cannot hear and cannot learn. Indigenous students who occupy the back row and do not interact should be of concern to you.

Effective teachers also put directions on the board or on prepared overhead transparencies. In a well-equipped school they may have the luxury of PowerPoint. Make sure the slides are not cluttered and the print is large. This keeps students on track and eliminates the constant question: 'What are we doing, Miss or Sir?' Commence your lesson with a summary, perhaps a mind map, and conclude with another summary. This will not prevent or remediate hearing problems, but you, as a qualified educator, will maximise your professional effectiveness.

In conclusion, speaking to student's faces can be a valuable way for you to appraise their level of understanding and/or enthusiasm. Learning to read the facial language of students can serve many functions. Importantly this includes the early detection of Otitis media.

Aboriginal English

The next topic to be discussed is Langwij or Aboriginal English. This is difficult to define as it can change with geographical location. It is recognised as a legitimate dialect of English and is the result of a mixture of various Aboriginal languages, which are rich in their traditions of communicative behaviour. If you are unfamiliar with Aboriginal English, you will miss many of the subtle meanings conveyed by both the words and their accompanying body language (Heitmeyer, 1998, p. 204). Many of the words in Aboriginal English do not retain the same meanings they have in Standard English. One example is the word 'deadly'. It has nothing to do with death. It refers instead to something that is fortuitous or good! I suggest you obtain copies of the following:

- A booklet published by the Department of Employment, Education and Training (DEET) entitled *Langwij comes to school: Promoting literacy among speakers of Aboriginal English and Australian Creoles*. A copy was sent to every school in Australia by DEET. It is an excellent resource with many examples and strategies.
- *English and the Aboriginal Child*, published by Eagleson, Kaldor & Malcolm in 1982. Some argue this is outdated because it was published 20 years ago, however it still remains a useful reference for young teachers who are going into the rural 'unknown'.

In areas where Aboriginal English is spoken, Indigenous students will regard the classroom with less trepidation if teachers respect their use of Aboriginal English and value such signs of Aboriginal cultural innovation. You will find the most constructive educational approach will be to delay the introduction of teaching in Standard English until after students have gained a degree of writing skills and developed some levels of confidence. The student will then effectively become bilingual. I suggest you prepare yourself for an enlightening experience because Aboriginal English is recognised as being both colourful and very direct!

Language in the classroom

An amusing story was told to me by a young teacher many years ago who was trying to get a group of Grade 6 students to expand their sentence structure beyond the following Creole statement:'dhat viikl wee you bin boroim lastaim I brokdaun' (the car which you borrowed last time has broken down). The teacher tried to develop this sentence, expecting a response something like 'the truck was unable to deliver the material as the differential was broken', or such like. One young gentleman however, proudly read out to the class 'no delivery cause the truck was fucked'. Be aware that the honesty of young students can be surprising. You never know what they are going to say.

It is also important to understand that Indigenous Australian behaviour and speech (in some areas) is ruled by a kinship system. This is structured according to how you are related to other people. This determines the type of speech you can use. For example, there are certain people to whom you are not permitted to speak. Others must be spoken to in formal language, others in familiar language. You may note that 'Please' and 'Thank you' are in some cases absent. Within a kinship group, there is no need to use these words as you already have obligations to that person and/or family. You are expected to give and to do things for others. Thanks are therefore not necessary. Unfortunately, Western concepts of politeness are enforced on Indigenous students by teachers who remain unaware of these complexities. You will need to take the time to become 'educated' in the local ways in rural schools. In some rural schools, English may be the second, third, or fourth language. It is important to understand that the absence of a child's polite speech may not necessarily be an indication of a child's bad manners or disrespect.

The lack of eye contact given to Elders is another sign of respect. This is often perceived by teachers as being the opposite: rude. This is one of the important cultural underpinnings of Indigenous adolescent behaviour. You will therefore need to modify your thinking so as to become receptive to these cross-cultural differences. This may include introducing non-Indigenous children to Indigenous cultural norms and also, for the sake of classroom cohesion and balance, introduce Indigenous students to the corresponding behaviour of settler culture. This will allow the Indigenous child to maintain their kinship beliefs and at the same time extend their cross-cultural awareness. Teaching the Indigenous child settler society concepts of eye contact and other mannerisms in a culturally sensitive manner can prove invaluable in later life when the Indigenous student graduates with vocational aspirations as they will need these cross-cultural skills to survive in the dominant culture.

Another concern young teachers often raise is the issue of questioning. Within Indigenous education systems questioning is discouraged and the challenging of ideas is not accepted. Aboriginal knowledge is imparted by telling and showing, students observe, then imitate and refine until they have mastered either the technique or the knowledge. If you are teaching within a rural area, be aware of these issues and talk to the appropriate Indigenous groups.

Awareness of kinship groups

Several years ago, a young teacher in a remote school caused a furore when she made some disruptive boys sit next to a group of girls as a punishment. Next day all the Indigenous students were withdrawn from the school by their angry parents. The teacher had unknowingly placed together a small group of children who could potentially marry each other in adult life. Under their Indigenous law they were not allowed to look at each other or talk to each other. Placing them together resulted in the children making contact and breaking the law. She foolishly refused to listen to the pleas of the students at the time.

There is so much to discuss and the space to do so within this chapter is very limited. Aboriginal and Torres Strait Islander cultures are rich. Teachers have much to learn. If you display respect and empathy to Indigenous people, you will be enriched by pedagogy, ontologies, and epistemologies as old as time. This leads us onto teaching strategies within the classroom.

9   Strategies in the classroom for teaching Aboriginal students

We now move on to some strategies for the classroom should you be or become a teacher and be sent to a rural school. Previously we have discussed the concepts and significance of student identity, and touched on self-esteem. This section outlines steps you can take to facilitate the development of a classroom environment in which student identity and self-esteem are enhanced. There are five major goals that are vital for your success:

- ensure a safe and predictable environment
- relate home and community experiences to school activities
- build positive relationships with students
- facilitate positive relationships between students
- facilitate congruence of student/teacher goals to ensure achievement is recognised by the student, the teacher, the parents, and the school.

Within each of these five major goals there are activities and processes that are important to students. They assist students to strengthen their identity and provide alternatives to stereotypes. A simplified version of the teacher's process of how to approach these goals is outlined below.

Ensure a safe and predictable environment

- Negotiate some rules/sequences with the group, and make group rules and consequences explicit using group talk, role plays, drama, and modelling.
- Complement positive behaviour and encourage raised expectations through means that prevent spotlighting, sarcasm, and shaming. Be positive and use praise.
- Be a leader in your personal explanation of and response to stereotyping; explain where individuals and the group are going and why.
- Be an advocate of students' recognising the achievements of other students, as well as the value of these students to the school, the staff, and parents.

Relate home and community experiences to school activities

- Be informed on students' backgrounds and life experiences.
- Involve Aboriginal parents and community in classroom life.
- Present and critically discuss diverse models of Aboriginality.
- Legitimise and value Aboriginal history, culture, and everyday social experiences.
- Meet racism head on through discussion, role play, and literature. Implement a social literacy program. Use your own personal library, the school council

and university libraries, watch the web, and look at publications by authors in cross-cultural studies and/or Aboriginal history. Some well known Indigenous publishers include Aboriginal Studies Press, Aboriginal History Inc., IAD Press (Institute for Aboriginal Development), the University of Queensland Press, Magabala Books, Keeaira Press and more.

- Familiarise yourself and engage with home sociolinguistic etiquette (use of silence, questioning techniques, access to conversational 'floor') in the classroom, but also train Indigenous students in the appropriate use of speaking and listening techniques that are used by the dominant settler society.

Build positive relationships with students

- Listen to students and provide positive feedback.
- Recognise that we do not know everything; allow yourself to be taught by your students.
- Highlight student strengths both privately and publicly (there is a fine line between the two that comes with experience).
- Use touch (when appropriate) to reinforce affirmation.
- Use humour positively.
- Share some of your personal experiences with students.
- Accept and value students while acknowledging their potential for change.
- View mistakes and failure positively; see them as necessary steps in the process of learning. Ensure that the students understand and respect this.
- Never give up on students; maintain high expectations. (My primary school teacher never gave up on me, neither did my Year 10 maths teacher. They are wonderful memories that in later life spurred me on to achieve goals like obtain a PhD.)

Facilitate positive relationships between students

- Teach students to listen attentively and give feedback to each other. Use games, directed activities, and teacher modelling.
- Encourage students to touch appropriately (through games and discussion).
- Develop empathy among students (use discussion, games, role play, drama, stories, or poetry).
- Teach students the necessary skills to enable them to resolve conflict between one another (use games, daily routines, art and writing).
- Elicit the universality of some childhood experiences and needs (for example, fun, humour, play, friends, freedom and relationships with some adults).

Facilitate congruence of student/teacher goals to ensure achievement is recognised by the student, the teacher, the parents, and the school

- Negotiate goals with all parties.
- Highlight skills and achievements.
- Provide opportunities for success.
- Deal positively with mistakes.
- Inform parents and other school staff regularly of the process and outcomes (Hudspith & Williams, 1994, pp. 34–5).

We live in an increasingly mechanised and computerised society that impacts on teachers and schools. The same society demands that we teach cognitive skills and knowledge to students so they can become active participants in industry and commerce, both of which operate primarily to serve the interests of the dominant settler society. Reflect on the applicability of all this to a rural or remote school teaching Indigenous youth who will have few, if any, local job prospects. Perhaps you can now start to understand the difficulties teachers and parents face when they attempt to improve school retention levels. The demands of an unrealistic and often irrelevant curriculum can lead to an overemphasis on teaching and learning to the detriment of the social and emotional life of Indigenous students. The creation of a classroom environment in which all children can increase their feelings of self-worth may be a necessary prerequisite to effective cognitive learning for each Indigenous child. The wider the cultural differences between teachers and students, the greater need for teacher sensitivity and awareness (Hudspith & Williams, 1994, pp. 34–5).

10 Conclusion

It is often stated by practitioners that nursing and teaching are two of the most satisfying vocations. Yet one repairs and, for the Indigenous student, the other can destroy.

Indigenous education, Indigenous health, housing, and social reform have been political footballs for decades. Many of us agonise over whether anything will ever change for the better. However, change can happen in education when teachers review the curriculum, the pedagogical application, and epistemological processes. Have you ever thought about using an Aboriginal guide to inform students about local Aboriginal sites, having an Indigenous artist in residence producing art with the children, inviting an Indigenous poet or Elder to the school to workshop life stories and interact with students about a dream we call reconciliation, or organising lessons on bush tucker, survival, and traditional land-use management practices that are ecologically sustainable?

Do not let your students and yourself become tourists looking on Aboriginal culture with romantic visions, or viewing it as if it were a prehistoric relic, something lifeless that should be stored in a museum. Embrace it, enjoy it, and let it become a vital part of the life of your classroom and the national culture more generally through its incorporation into the Australian educational process.

Do not let Aboriginal or Indigenous studies remain tokenistic. Help us destroy the eighteenth and nineteenth century myths and stereotypes that still plague the thoughts of many settler Australians. Indigenous studies are equally as important as Gallipoli, ANZAC, and the explorer stories. They are alive and exciting if you, as a teacher, let them be so.

Focus questions

1 Who is an Indigenous Australian? What are the common stereotypes that are used against them?

2 Has the education system failed the Indigenous people of Australia? Explain your answer.

3 Racial discrimination and negative views of minority groups are often a product of the upbringing of the student within the family. How might teachers assist their students to learn to recognise their cultural assumptions before they enter the workforce?

4 How important is the making and implementing of policies regarding Aboriginal education to improving what happens in schools and classrooms?

5 How can reconciliation be achieved in the present and future generations? State the required resources and action plans and/or changes of attitude that will be needed? If you do not think it can be achieved, explain why not.

Notes

1. Neill, R. (2002). *White Out. How Politics is Killing Black Australia*. Sydney: Allen & Unwin; Trudgen, R. (2000). *Why Warriors Lie Down and Die*. Darwin: Aboriginal Resource and Development Services; Broome, R. (1994). *Aboriginal Australians*. Sydney: Allen & Unwin; Mickler, S. (1998). *The Myth of Privilege*. Perth: Fremantle Arts Centre Press; Bennett, S. (1999). *White Politics and Black Australians*. Sydney: Allen & Unwin; Moses, D. (ed.) (2004). *Genocide and Settler Society. Frontier Violence and Stolen Indigenous Children in Australian History*. New York: Berghahn Books; Sharp, N. (1993). *Stars of Tagai: The Torres Strait Islanders*. Canberra: Aboriginal Studies Press.

2. Blood quantum was a measure used to support a biological concept of race. This revolved around notions of racial purity, ancestry, and origin rather than the cultural concept of ethnicity, which focused on cultural beliefs, practices, and affiliations (Clark, 2004). The definition of Indigenous Australians on the basis of their blood content was informed by nineteenth century models of biogenetics. These included the now discredited fields of eugenics and phrenology. Blood quantum principles assumed the race of a given group of people was a fundamental genetic characteristic that determined a person's identity. The practice was 'inherently racist' (Clark, 2004, p. 41). Blood quantum was first used for official identification purposes in the *Dawes Severalty Act* 1887. This piece of American legislation sought to establish a scientific basis upon which to identify who was and was not a Native American. It is interesting to note American legislation has historically defined and redefined 'Indianness' in thirty-three different ways (Brownell, 2000).

Further reading

Australian Journal of Indigenous Education. While this is an academic journal, it is full of practical applications and helpful background information. Back issues are a rich resource to any teacher interested in this area.

Bennett, Scott. (1999). *White Politics and Black Australians.* Sydney: Allen & Unwin.

Beresford, B. & Partington, G. (eds) (2003). *Reform and Resistance in Aboriginal Education, The Australian Experience* (pp. 10–40). Perth: University of Western Australia Press.

Craven, R. (1999). *Teaching Aboriginal Studies.* Sydney: Allen & Unwin; see also 'Improving outcomes for Indigenous students' at www. whatworks.edu.au. You will find these references are invaluable teaching resources even if you do not have Indigenous students in your class. They may assist you in subject content.

Heitmeyer, D. (1998). 'The Issue is Not Black and White. Aboriginality and Education'. In J. Allen (ed.), *Sociology of Education: Possibilities and Practice* (pp. 195–214). Katoomba (NSW): Social Science Press.

Hudspith, S. & Williams, A. (1994). 'Enhancing Aboriginal identity and self-esteem in the classroom.' In S. Harris & M. Mallin (eds.), *Aboriginal Kids in Urban Classrooms.* Wentworth Falls: Social Science Press.

Schwab, R.G. (1999). *Why Only One in Three? The Complex Reasons for Low Indigenous School Retention.* Centre for Aboriginal Economic Policy Research. Research Monograph 16. Canberra: Australian National University.

Internet sources

This site provides advice for teachers of Aboriginal children and others: www.whatworks.edu.au/.

Australian Journal of Indigenous Education can be found at www.uq.edu.au/ATSIS/ajie/.

6
Class and Competition
Craig Campbell

1   The class question in education

People often feel discomfort when they talk about social class. Somehow the idea of class presents in too raw a form the idea and reality of social difference and hierarchy, the idea and reality that large groups of people are routinely more powerful and wealthy than others, and that very often it is difficult for people to escape the groups that they have been born into—even if they wanted to. The idea and existence of social classes is also disturbing for some other reasons.

Many Australians resist identifying themselves as belonging to a social class, especially if it is a 'lower' class. Others who are clearly in the class of the wealthy and powerful can resist classification too. Sometimes it does not do to trumpet one's advantages—one's wealth and power in a society that has often prided itself as being either classless or egalitarian. Like similar societies of mainly European settlers, there has been a historical resistance to class-based societies. This derived from the idea that 'new' societies such as Australia, New Zealand, Canada, and the USA could escape the rigidities of the feudally based divisions of old Europe, where aristocracy and peasantry were defined by blood (birth into certain families) and law (fixed privileges and obligations).

In Australia there were early victories over the rigidifying of class divisions by blood and law. Membership of legislative councils would not be restricted to a few families of pastoral wealth. All men, and eventually women—and even later Aboriginal people—regardless of their social class would be able to vote in elections for lower houses of parliament. Even jobs in the public service by the end of the nineteenth century were opened to *talent* or *merit* (fitness to do the work and the production of qualifications) rather than patronage (appointment resulting from one's membership of a network, perhaps family or class-based—or having attended certain schools or universities).[1]

Nevertheless, avoidance of one kind of class system did not rule out the development of another. Even in Europe where elements of the old class system linger on to the present day (monarchies, aristocracies, a House of Lords), new social classes associated with post-feudalism, the rise of modern nation states, modern trading economies, urbanisation and industrialisation, emerged. In the world of Western Europe, North America, and Australia and New Zealand, modern *working, middle* and *ruling classes* came into being through the nineteenth century. This new system of social classes continued to emerge, adapt and evolve through the twentieth and into the twenty-first centuries.[2]

As modern classes were not to be defined so rigidly by birth or law, the ways that a person ended up in one class or another changed. One of the ways that this could occur was through schooling. Education had once played virtually no role— especially in determining whether one was an aristocrat or a peasant—although an appropriate education for either was certainly useful in the assumption of social responsibilities, or an ability to scratch out a living. For modern social classes, school and higher education have played an increasingly important role in the processes of determining a person's occupation, their levels of potential wealth and power—and their potential membership of a social class.

Therefore it is the argument of this chapter that schools have often played an important role in social *class formation*. At the same time, the ways schools work in relation to class formation is not always predictable. Individuals and families from different social classes and different sections within classes use schools differently, and more or less effectively. Where it is possible to detect common approaches to schooling among individuals and families who share similar occupations, wealth, and social influence, it is then that we are likely to detect distinctive relationships between the social classes and schooling and education.

There is a strong tradition in sociology that regards social class as a fundamental determinant of school participation and success. In the second half of the twentieth century in both the United Kingdom and Australia, important books were published that not only connected schooling to social classes, but also showed pretty convincingly that the different kinds of schooling the social classes received helped maintain social class divisions (Banks, 1955; Floud, Halsey & Martin, 1957; Jackson & Marsden, 1986 [1966]; Encel, 1970; Connell, Ashenden, Kessler & Dowsett, 1982). The consequence of those divisions, it was argued, led to very great inequalities. Access to higher education, the professions, well or poorly paid jobs, white collar or blue collar work, different working-class jobs, in the trades or unskilled labouring jobs, all were responsive to the class origins of young people, and the kind of schooling they received as a result. In Australia in as early as the 1940s, an economist, J.A. La Nauze had demonstrated not only the social class bias of university entrance, but also the monopoly over the professional degrees such as law and medicine by students from non-government, fee-paying secondary schools, which were more likely to be attended by students from middle-class families (La Nauze, 1940).

The early arguments about the link between social class and unequal schooling opportunities and life-chances were not as simple as they seemed, however. There was much more to it than a straightforward description of a social system that produced social injustice.

In this chapter we look at some of these complexities. That there are many more social phenomena than social *class relations* that produce inequality in society is certainly one complicating factor. Just as important is the necessity to understand a little better what social classes are, how they operate, and how they change over time. This is especially important in the early twenty-first century, a period in which much traditional class-based politics and organisations are in retreat; especially those associated with the working class. Nevertheless, thinking about the relationship between social class, schooling, and the kinds of post-school adult lives that Australians live remains a crucial issue.

In the cities of Australia, there are distinctive working-, middle- and ruling-class areas. Mark Peel (2003) has written about some of the poorest working-class areas in Australia. The suburbs of Broadmeadows (Melbourne), Inala (Brisbane), and Mount Druitt (Sydney) are extraordinarily different from those of Toorak (Melbourne), Vaucluse (Sydney), and Hamilton or Ascot (Brisbane). People have different lives in these places; they tend to send their children to very different kinds of schools. They likely belong to very different social classes, and sometimes the social class differences can be reinforced by ethnic differences as well. But these suburbs represent the extremes. There are plenty of gradations between, as can be seen by looking at official indexes of social advantage (for example, Australian Bureau of Statistics, 2004a). Focusing on the extremes, however, points to the continuing relevance of the material effect of social class on the lives that Australian people lead. In this chapter we explore the role of schooling and education in the continuing production of a class-based society. In using that phrase, the 'production of a class-based society', however, the actual role of schools is not necessarily presumed to be the crucial factor. There are usually many. Societies and the relationships between the groups within them are built by a very large number of social forces along with class, and they wax and wane, like class, in their importance (see Best, 2005).

2   Social classes and the way they work

In the middle of the nineteenth century, Karl Marx decided on the basis of his historical research and observation of economic and social developments in Europe that a new class-based society was being born. He argued that the way in which industrial production occurred brought two modern classes into being.

The workers in factories, working for low wages, with no power other than their labour-power, produced not only the goods of the factories, but also profits for the owners of the factories. This profit was the *capital*, which gave rise to the description of society as a whole as *capitalist*. According to Marx it was a fundamentally unfair and unstable society. There were two classes, working and capitalist, whose interests were so opposed, which were so fundamentally in the roles of exploited and exploiter, that social revolution was a predictable outcome (Marx & Engels, 1988 [1848]).

Since the mid nineteenth century the brutality of early industrialism has been much ameliorated, at least in Europe, North America, and Australia and New Zealand. Some of the conditions that led to heightened class conflict have improved—to the point that early in the twenty-first century, for very large numbers of people, social class is no longer a primary point of reference for the way they describe themselves and the way they operate in society; that is, the way they define their identity. Nevertheless the legacy of the Marxist idea of class is to make the asking of certain questions of continuing importance: 'How does our society work?', 'How is wealth produced?' and 'Who benefits the most from how it is produced?', and then:

- Who owns the great corporations, and how do they treat their workers?
- What relationships exists between those who have great economic power and those who govern?
- What social and economic processes lead to the continuing production of rich and poor, working and ruling class, advantaged and disadvantaged?
- What power do working-class people have over their own lives?
- How are social ideas generated that sustain social inequality or division?

And where might schools and schooling fit in to any answer to these questions?

This theory of class and the sorts of questions that arise from it tend to presume a society that is strongly polarised and often conflict-ridden. Such a theory belongs to a group of theories described as *conflict theory*. It is easy enough to discern some of the problems with it and them. They tend not to be so useful in describing how complex societies work and where there is fair social stability. They can also, in their crudest form, suggest that most human lives are very much determined by their economic and labour circumstances. Marxist-derived theories of class are by no means obsolete, but since Marx the theories have been radically developed, often to explain the unexpected stability of capitalism and the role of culture in explaining the character of social relations and social change.

The second important thinker, also a German, of the late nineteenth and early twentieth centuries, who made an enduring contribution to the way that social classes are understood, is Max Weber. His contributions are less easily summarised since his theoretical models of how society operated were more complex, reflecting the importance of other factors as well as the mainly economic in explaining human social behaviour. Nevertheless, Weber maintained the significance of economic relations to social class formations. But there were other issues to be understood as well. In his conception of class, the kinds of property, commerce, or labour that engaged people helped determine class membership and association. Instead of there being a basic two-class structure, Weber's theory leads us to the idea that there can be many more than the basic two. Where Marx's theory provided an explanation for the existence of a ruling class and a working class, Weber provided an understanding of an often fragmented and stratified middle class. The idea of *stratification* was important to Weber as he found many reasons for classes and class groupings to *differentiate* themselves one from another. In this theory there is much more room for associations or institutions such as schools to assist in the understanding of how classes are maintained and operate.

Also of significance are the importance of *occupations* in social class making. Different occupational groups are able to position themselves in the economy in ways that give them distinctive class characteristics—and advantages or disadvantages. An example of this might be the differences between teachers and doctors, both of which are thought of as middle class, and both of which are dependent on prolonged higher education for their training, employment, and class positioning. The differences in their work, the way they are employed, and the valuing of their work often produce different class characteristics and strategies; for example, in relation to attitudes to public and private employment, taxation policy or trade union and professional membership and activity. For Weber, class was not the sole or even a necessarily dominant determinant of social structures. There was also *status* and *association* or *party*. In the discussion of teachers and doctors we can immediately see that status is potentially a crucial disrupter of class unity, as are the associations through which different occupational groups define and seek to achieve their interests. Associations can be based on any number of interests, characteristics, or circumstances. Religion produces one such set of associations. In Australia, Catholics and Protestants often had different interests. It is no accident that religion as much as class helped determine the character of Australian school systems. Working-class Catholics have usually sent their children to non-government Catholic schools. Working-class Protestants have usually sent their children to government schools. The status accorded to individuals and groups deriving from having attended either set of schools changed from the early twentieth to the early twenty-first century. Religious, ethnic, gender, occupational, and other characteristics and associations produced by them routinely disrupt simple class-based explanations of the way that societies work.

As is the case for Marxist-inspired class theories, there have been many developments from Weber (see Best, 2005; Giddens, 2001.) The main points we take from these developing sets of theories about classes is that the probability that social classes not only exist but also continue to produce social hierarchies and inequality is very high, but that class and class relations are not nearly the only phenomena that help us explain social relations, structures, practices, and institutions. One of the effects of more recent postmodern social theory has been to further fragment straightforward explanations of the way individuals and groups operate socially. It is now possible to think of persons or groups as containing or expressing multiple and often contradictory characteristics. One person may operate in class solidarity in one environment, say if their job is being threatened by new industrial relations laws, but act in un-stereotypical ways in other contexts, for example in his or her patterns of consumption of material or 'cultural' goods. Their gender, sexuality, ethnicity, nationality, and religion may be but a few of the more obvious places to look in explaining diverse social behaviour (see chapters 7 and 8).

This has been a necessary discussion as we get closer to looking at social classes, education, and schools. To conclude this section, there are number of propositions we put forward:

- Classes are in a constant process of formation and dissolution, with schools contributing to that process.
- Classes exist in relation to one another, to varying degrees competing for wealth and power, and schools are often caught up in that process.
- Classes are constituted by real people in families and other collectivities who develop distinctive ways of thinking and acting in relation to their interests, and the way they operate in education is responsive to this process.
- Schools and their educational processes occur differently, and have different meanings in the context of different and dynamic class cultures.
- The practices and cultures of classes and class relations can be both empowering and disempowering for individuals and their families depending on the social context. Schools and teachers are often active agents in this process, for better or worse, and sometimes both.

Traditionally, education has been seen as really important in the discussion of the following class-related phenomena. First is the idea that through education, individuals and groups may be given the *opportunity* to better themselves. The poor, girls, Aborigines, recently arrived migrants—and working-class children and youth—at various stages in Australian history have through education been offered opportunities to improve their lives. That is, education and schooling have often been seen as a crucial element in the process of *social mobility*, hopefully upward movement into better work, a more comfortable life, into another social class. Second is the idea that schooling can be about *social control*; that is, a means of controlling social classes and groups thought by sections of the ruling and middle class as 'unruly', potentially a threat to property and social order. Third is the idea that education and schooling may contribute to the *reproduction of social inequality*. This biologically based metaphor attempts to explain how the children of people in particular social classes tend to stay in the same social classes as their parents. Somehow schooling can be implicated in the process by which social classes are reproduced across the generations. We discuss some of these ideas in the following sections.

> ### Earl Bathurst explains the need for government-funded Anglican schools for children from the labouring classes in New South Wales and Tasmania:
>
> … securing to the rising Generation … the Advantages of all necessary Instruction, but also in bringing them up in Habits of Industry and Regularity, and for implanting in their Minds the Principles of the Established Church … (Bathurst to Macquarie, 1820, in Austin, 1963).

3   Schooling and social classes in history

There was often a clear separation of the social classes in the schools of nineteenth century Australia. Most working-class children were lucky to have more than a few years in an elementary school. It was not until the 1870s that school attendance became compulsory, and even then there was wide latitude for irregular attendance (Miller, 1986; Theobald & Selleck, 1990).

It was only in the second half of the nineteenth century that governments really began to assume responsibility for the schooling of rural and urban working-class children. Before then, the various churches had provided elementary schools, usually with government subsidies. There were also, throughout the nineteenth century, small private schools, usually run by women who, for a very small fee, taught working-class children their letters. Often working-class families were more comfortable in such schools since they were spared over-zealous religious teaching in the denominational schools, or the sharp criticisms of their children's dress, speech, punctuality, attention, achievement and even cleanliness by the government school teachers and inspectors (Miller & Davey, 1988).

The Education Acts of the 1870s in nearly all the Australian colonies had similar features. Besides making school *compulsory*, they mainly made education *free*, and to a fair degree attempted to establish a *secular* curriculum. Just as important, they mostly cut off funding (taxation-supported *state aid*) to denominational (church) schools. It was the last two of these decisions that confronted the Roman Catholic bishops in particular, and allowed school arrangements to contribute to the ethnic and religious divisions in the Australian working class. Of all the larger churches, it was only the Roman Catholic and Lutheran that decided to maintain their networks of parochial (local) primary schools.

The churches of the dominant Protestant denominations—in particular the Anglicans, Methodists, and Presbyterians—decided instead to focus their educational efforts on providing secondary grammar schools and colleges for the middle- and ruling-class families of their denominations. Some Roman Catholic orders of brothers and nuns also established such schools, including the Jesuits and Sisters of the Sacred Heart of Jesus, for example.[3] From the mid nineteenth century in particular, the curricula of these church and private schools in each colony were closely tied to meeting the public examination board syllabuses controlled by the emerging colonial universities (Musgrave, 1992).

Because of this, two enduring social class patterns in Australian schooling emerged. First was that non-government schools developed a strong control over the character of secondary education, and that secondary education served the interests of middle- and ruling-class families (Campbell, 1999b). Second was that elementary or primary education, mainly provided by government and Roman Catholic schools, served working-class families in particular, though not exclusively. Most children who attended these schools were expected to leave as soon as they were able. The curriculum in such schools was based on 'practical' skills and subjects: reading, writing, and arithmetic, with at various times some attention paid to citizen-building including the fostering of British Empire loyalty through English, history, and eventually social studies. Also there were subjects such as cooking and cleaning for girls and woodwork for boys. This pattern was modified through the twentieth century, but elements of it remained. Retention rates for working-class children were and are substantially lower than for middle-class children. Working-class youth, though now remaining in secondary school for several years, tend to take up the VET (vocational education and training) subjects rather than the more abstract mathematics, sciences and foreign languages. Working-class children are much more likely to be found in government and Roman Catholic schools, while middle-class children are more likely to be found in government selective and non-government schools.

By the late nineteenth century, there were social and economic developments that would disrupt clear class divisions in schooling. The growing need in modern industry and the economy for technical and managerial expertise based on educational levels above that of the primary school meant that the pressure for government schools also to offer secondary education became irresistible. The government high schools of the very early twentieth century offered new opportunities for upward social mobility to new groups of working- and lower-middle-class students. Some of these schools in the larger cities, such as Melbourne High, Hobart High, Adelaide High, Perth Modern and Sydney Girls' and Boys' quickly adopted many of the cultural practices (such as prefects, Saturday sports, school uniforms, and songs) that marked out increasing numbers of middle- and ruling-class church and private schools. They also sought distinction in teaching the curriculum that the universities demanded for its entrants. These new high schools, though close to being free schools, tended to be used best by young people from one part of the middle class in particular. These were the children from parents of the 'new' middle class, the middle class that was growing rapidly based on clerical and other 'white-collar' employment in businesses and the public service (Bessant, 1984; Campbell, Hooper & Fearnley-Sander, 1999).

Increasing numbers of employers required qualifications in the form of *credentials* from their new employees. These credentials, whether they were the Junior or Senior, Intermediate or Leaving, School Certificate or Higher School Certificate, were disproportionately gained by the children of the middle class. As a recent history of the middle class in England stated: 'Education is absolutely central to the English middle classes: they are the people who pass exams' (Gunn & Bell, 2003, p. 147). This was equally true for Australia. Unlike segments of the 'old' middle class that depended on their ownership of small businesses, including farms in rural areas, the new middle class had little property that could be handed on to children in order to guarantee their future living. The main thing that they could hand on was an attitude towards education. By doing everything in their power to encourage their children to succeed at school, a new kind of 'property' could be gained. With an educational credential, young people became qualified for desirable white-collar work, or even entrance to tertiary institutions such as technical, agricultural and teachers' colleges, or universities, where the next level of credentials could be gained, perhaps opening access to the professions.

The sociologist, Pierre Bourdieu, calls this process by which families pass on to their children an attitude towards education, and the skill in exploiting what the school and its teachers may have to offer, *habitus*. Through the combined effects of habitus and the ability to use what the school has to offer, *cultural capital* is accumulated. In the *field* of education, the middle class are much more likely to have the appropriate habitus, and are much more likely to accumulate forms of cultural capital that are useful in gaining useful credentials and winning middle-class jobs (See Bourdieu, 1997; Bourdieu & Passeron, 1990).

From a 'professional' journal of an undergraduate aiming to become a teacher: reflections on social class and teaching practice placement:

The school I am in is located in the southern suburbs [Adelaide] but it is quite a good school. All the students are well behaved and easy to get along with. The school is a real community where most students live in close proximity to the school. The school would be classed as a 'middle-class school' as many parents have professional/working lifestyles. I am quite pleased with this and it would be in the same 'class' as myself. (Quoted in Whitehead, 2005b.)

Old and new professions were particularly attractive to many middle-class families. Some of the professions, especially law and medicine, were very prestigious indeed and could lead to great wealth. Others such as dentistry, engineering, teaching, architecture, and eventually nursing were respectable enough, and usually better paid than the working-class trades such as carpentry, plumbing, and bricklaying. Members of the middle-class professions were often organised by professional associations that maintained a close surveillance over professional education and the value of the credentials providing entry. They often sought to restrict entry to the professions, thereby maintaining shortages and higher salary levels (Perkin, 1989). Some professions such as teachers were not particularly successful in this. Their sheer numbers and the presence of so many women, routinely paid lower rates than men, told against their bargaining power. Most government school teachers formed organisations that eventually looked more like trade unions than professional associations and, as was the case in New South Wales in 1942, some joined the working class Trades and Labour Councils (Mitchell, 1975). They even adopted working-class tactics such as stop-work meetings and strikes from the 1960s to advance their claims. The case of teachers as part of the middle class shows the importance of Weber's development of class theory. Associational and status issues are essential in developing an understanding of teachers and their work (see also chapter 11).

In the twentieth century, some forms of secondary education were systematically extended to working-class youth. Often this occurred from the 1920s in central, home science and junior technical schools. Rarely was the university-controlled academic curriculum offered. State education departments usually developed alternative credentials that allowed subjects such as social studies, domestic science, technical drawing, woodwork, arithmetic—and typing and shorthand, which were increasingly taken by girls. It became more difficult in the twentieth century for the controllers of school systems to channel students into the different kinds of schools simply on the basis of a student's social class, or general perception of what was good for them. New management technologies (ways of sorting and selecting) were developed, often at the point of transition from a primary to a secondary school. *Intelligence tests* and *vocational guidance* were used to measure and describe a student's ability, intelligence, interests, and potential or aptitude. Not only were students in Australia routinely sent to different schools as a result of such procedures, but they were differentiated within schools. They could be *streamed*, *tracked*, and *set* in different courses, subjects, and subject levels of varying difficulty and content.

All these technologies seemed to promise some scientific certainty, even a child-centred education of sorts. The new discipline of psychology and its sub-discipline, educational psychology, played a crucial role. Initially funded by the Carnegie Corporation, the Australian Council for Educational Research (ACER) cooperated with the teachers' colleges and universities to develop a large range of tests to assist this work.[4] It took until well into the 1960s for a clear understanding to develop that many of these practices failed to deliver scientific certainty about young people's educational and employment potential. In fact, many of the practices reinforced not only class, but also gender-, race- and ethnicity-based inequalities; often they assisted in the reproduction of the classes and class difference. (See McCallum, 1990; Miller, 1986; Simon, 1971.) Another social theorist of great influence in education, Basil Bernstein, developed an explanation for part of what was going on. He argued that the tests and educational practices developed for schools rewarded the language usages of middle-class families. The cultural and language practices of working-class and non-dominant ethnic groups tended neither to be recognised nor valued by most schools (Bernstein, 1997). In Australia, the team of researchers that worked with R.W. Connell in the early 1980s used the term *competitive academic curriculum* to describe some of the practices that favoured middle-class children and youth in schools (Connell et al., 1982).

From the 1960s and 1970s there was increasing recognition, even at the government level, that working-class children were not getting a fair deal from Australian schools. The Whitlam Labor Government established the Schools Commission with a brief to fund schools with large numbers of 'disadvantaged' children (Karmel, 1973). Most of the disadvantaged were from the working class, unemployed, recent migrant and Aboriginal families. Very significantly, the schools that could receive additional funds to assist disadvantaged children included non-government schools and, in particular, the parochial and non-elite Roman Catholic primary and secondary schools. On one level, this activity was of enormous significance in the recognition at government level of social class differences in schooling, participation and success. However, the relative absence of class terminology from government policy would eventually allow the possibility of middle-class disadvantage to be argued as well. This could be seen in the discussion about the disadvantage endured by 'gifted and talented' students stuck in classrooms with 'ordinary' children. Though advocates of gifted and talented programs argued that class background was irrelevant in the identification of such students, some of the selection practices involved were similar to those of an earlier era of testing and selection. Middle-class families often had the advantage in making schools and teachers work in the interests of their children.

This brief discussion of schooling and social classes in Australian history has attempted to show the importance of social class in the development of Australia's educational practice. Schools have been deliberately structured at various times to cater to the needs of the different social classes. Curriculum has often been differentiated between various mixes of abstract and practical, liberal and vocational subjects. These have formed the basis of different subjects of study for children from different social classes. Families in the various elements of the working, middle, and ruling classes have sometimes chosen different schools for their children, often in the expectation that a certain curriculum and social mix of students would best meet their class-related family aspirations. Though there was an attempt to create a classless government secondary school, the comprehensive high school, in nearly all states in Australia in the second half of the twentieth century, they were not always successful. Non-government schools survived, and within the government high schools, the technologies of streaming, tracking, and setting continued to have the effect of differentiating students, sometimes on class and ethnic lines (Campbell & Sherington, 2006).

4   Working-class families and contemporary schooling

Working-class families rarely have a great deal of money left over from the effort to provide the basics in housing, food, and transport. The demands of compulsory schooling in the late nineteenth century and well into the twentieth were often resisted. Sending children to school, clothing them, and buying books was expensive enough. Resented rather more was the loss of earnings. A child who left school at 13 or 14 could contribute to the household by paying some board. He or she had some money left over for personal use. And best of all, the grind and discipline of the school, often with a curriculum that appeared difficult and pretty useless, was put aside forever. Working-class youth advanced towards adulthood more rapidly than middle-class youth. Though wages were often low, they were not too low, especially after the introduction of the basic wage in Australia (1907). Working-class youth could often afford to marry and have their own children reasonably early. There were plenty of labouring and factory jobs for boys in the economic boom periods, and where the skilled trades were sought, apprenticeship models of training dominated. Unlike much school education, there was a recognisable link between 'theory and practice' and 'mental and manual labour'. An extended secondary education, concentrating on the academic curriculum, was only for unusual working-class families and youth, at least until the 1960s and 1970s.

The problematic relations between schools and working-class families was not only centred on economics. Even though the modern industrial working class arrived reasonably late in history, social and cultural traditions developed quickly enough. In sports, rugby league and Australian Rules football were favoured. The hotels in working-class districts accommodated other leisure activities. Trade unions and the Labor party helped organise political activity. Friends were made and met at work and in the neighbourhood. Housing affordability usually meant there were distinctly working- and middle-class suburbs in the cities. In rural areas the class divisions were often more visible—country towns rarely had suburbs by which rich and poor could be separated. For some working-class people, schools were seen as culturally alien. School teachers could be seen as unbearably superior in their attitudes, and critical of working-class life and culture. Parents were often seen by teachers as problems for the mission of the school. Parents might be held responsible for poor English usage, be uncooperative in making sure homework was done, and be unimpressed by the description of their kids having a day or two off from time to time as 'truancy'. Their own experience of schooling might have been that of failure. In the days of corporal punishment, which lasted in most Australian states through to the 1970s, no doubt it was working-class children and youth who had the worst of it. Being called to the school for an interview about their children could be a nightmare. Most working-class parents wanted their children to succeed at school, but most also understood when they declared they had 'had enough' (Connell et al., 1982).

From a 'professional' journal of an undergraduate aiming to become a teacher: reflections on social class and teaching practice placement in a 'working class' school:

My initial impressions are that it is actually a nice little school, and not the type of school that I imagined it to be. I kind of thought that because it is in a low socio-economic area, that most of the kids would be mean and angry, and unable to control. (Quoted in Whitehead, 2005b.)

Early school-leaving was seen as a problem right through the twentieth century. The vision of ill-disciplined and ill-educated working-class larrikins, and later on, delinquents, and later on again, homeless youth and gangs, confronted respectable society. Being 'up to no good' could include substance abuse, including tobacco and alcohol in earlier days to the illegal drugs of the present, and loitering in the streets. Such behaviour had long presented a challenge for the respectable middle class, which included the builders of government schools and school systems. Sexual promiscuity was also seen as part of the problem. Girls in particular came in for criticism as they were considered 'at risk' of early pregnancy and in all likelihood unable to raise children in an orderly, healthy, and respectable manner. Schools had multiple purposes in mind for working-class children and youth. They were to receive a basic education, making them workers and/or mothers who were educated enough. They were to receive training in certain values, including self-discipline. Such values and training included punctuality, respect for their betters, honesty, making an effort, and developing loyalty to the nation. Young people were to be kept off the streets, as well as being provided with basic preparation for employment and home-making. These were all part of the purposes of public schools. The Roman Catholic schools added the making of religious subjects to such purposes, the inculcation of 'faithfulness' in its original sense.

Working-class delinquency (early twentieth century)

Groups of boys of ages varying from 7 to 15 roam the streets and parks, smoking cigarettes, playing pitch and toss, garden robbing, and haunting the back entrances of business establishments. These boys and youth ought either to be at school or in some useful occupation. Their condition is one of moral peril, and graduation from these nurseries of vice too frequently takes place (1903).

Young girls from 12 to 16 are permitted to parade the streets at late hours, aping the worst manners of their elders, forming very undesirable companionships, hearing conversations anything but edifying, and witnessing and participating in conduct calculated to blunt finer feelings (1901).

(From reports of the South Australian Children's Council, 1903, 1901, SA Parliamentary Papers.)

The purposes of working-class families and students did not always align with the intentions of the schools towards them. Depending on the ambitions of students or their parents, the schools could be useful enough in gaining various qualifications, especially if skilled working-class jobs or white collar employment was intended. The new state academic high schools of the twentieth century were especially valued by a minority of upwardly mobile working-class youth (Campbell, 1999a). Most non-government schools and universities with their fees remained very difficult to access. While the junior technical and home science schools were often popular with working-class families into the 1970s in South Australia and Victoria, they were increasingly criticised. They were increasingly seen as trapping working-class children in an inferior curriculum, with structural lack of access to more prestigious school credentials and the opportunity to go on to tertiary education. In the 1970s, Labor parties, federally and in the individual states, adopted these criticisms. *Access and equity* became dominant themes of educational policy through to the late 1980s (see Connell, 1993; Lingard, 2000; Marginson, 1993; Welch, 1996b).

> ### From a 'professional' journal of an undergraduate aiming to become a teacher; teaching as upward social class mobility:
>
> Probably the most significant way I was influenced by my peers was that if I wanted to do something with my life I had to break out of the blue-collar mentality most of my peers shared. (Quoted in Whitehead, 2005b.)

Where earlier sociologists had concentrated on the ways that schools, school structures, intelligence testing, and school assessment regimes had discriminated against working-class children and youth, ensuring higher levels of failure and *dropout* than for middle-class children, new *ethnographically* inspired research from the 1970s added a major insight into the relationships between schooling and working-class youth. In his book *Learning to Labour*, Paul Willis (1977) discovered that for many working-class male youth, compliance with the school and its practices led to a diminution of their status within their peer groups and the communities that mattered to them. (See also Dolby & Dimitriadis, 2004.) Making trouble for teachers, not doing well at school, and early school-leaving, rather than leading to low status led to the opposite. This research conducted in a working-class area in England pioneered later efforts in linking the idea that successful working-class masculinities were linked to school resistance. In Australia, Walker (1988) and Connell (2000) showed there were important similarities between what Willis had written about, and how working-class boys often operated in Australian schools. For working-class girls the issues were often different (Kenway & Willis, 1990). Historically, they, with Aboriginal children, usually had even younger school-leaving ages than their brothers.

By the 1990s and early twenty-first century, the issues facing working-class youth in schools had changed again. Where working-class girls and boys in the early 1970s still had fair access to unskilled factory or other semi-skilled and unskilled jobs, the recession of the mid 1970s, the rise of high youth unemployment, and the contraction of traditional working-class jobs in industry led to new problems. In most states of Australia the school leaving age remained at 15 years, but the difficult youth labour market demanded a raising of retention rates. More than ever, successful completion of school through to Year 12 was seen as essential if youth, and working-class youth in particular, were to have any chance at all in making a successful transition to employed adulthood. (See also pp. 59–60.)

In all the Australian states, new senior high school curricula were invented and adapted in the attempt to keep working-class youth interested in school (Schools Commission, 1980; see also chapter 10). These were young people who would in earlier times have left school early for apprenticeships in the trades and basic-wage jobs in industry. The pressure on working class youth and their schools was also related to pressure on the working-class itself. With factories closing in many parts of Australia, in the cities as well as country towns, and with the move towards transforming workers from award-regulated wage earners into semi-independent contractors, many working-class families experienced levels of unemployment and/or insecurity not seen since the Depression of the 1930s (Thomson, 2002).

Schooling had become more important than ever to working-class youth as good employment opportunities began to slip away. Casual and part-time jobs became more available, but the possibility that they would lead to better paid and permanent jobs was very uncertain. At the very moment that such youth urgently needed effective schools, government policies towards public schooling in particular began to change. Federal governments from the late 1990s began to invest proportionately less in public schools, and in areas of high unemployment and factory closures, such schools found it increasingly difficult to operate. Pat Thomson has illuminated this phenomenon for South Australia in *Schooling the Rust-belt Kids* (2002). In New South Wales the problems of young people and schools in the area of Mount Druitt in western Sydney received dramatic attention in 1999 when a page 1 newspaper headline and article published the news that no student from one school had passed the Higher School Certificate or received a tertiary-ranked score entitling them to university entrance. The furore that followed led to a government enquiry that detailed the disabilities under which the working-class public schools laboured (Laughlin, 1997; see also Vickers, 2004).

The Melbourne-based educational sociologist Richard Teese argued strongly that there was a continuing link between the socio-economic background of students, and their propensity to school failure. Based on research in Melbourne, he argued that the curriculum remained a crucial factor in producing failure for students from unemployed and working-class families: 'School subjects are codified, authoritative systems of cognitive and cultural demands' (Teese, 2000, p. 3). He went on to argue that because some schools, especially non-government and selective public schools, specialised in the academic subjects, this had the effect of 'exporting failure' to many government schools, which were either located in areas of high unemployment, or were failing to compete in a vigorous school market:

> In comprehensive high schools, residential segregation brings together many students with multiple disadvantages—low self-esteem, poor basic learning, language handicaps, poverty and family breakdown. Instead of a mass of cultural and economic resources being concentrated on one advantageous site and applied to the high end of the curriculum—as happens in private schools—there is an accumulation of liabilities at the one site. This weakens the instructional effort and risks severe retribution against those students who stray into the more academic subjects (p. 189).

There have always been problems for working-class families in extracting benefit from modern forms of schooling. Some families have been able to use schools with success. Some students have, through educational opportunities, left their working-class origins behind. In later times, and as the working class and its institutions have come under pressure, and traditional working class jobs have contracted in number, education and extended school attendance has become more important in the struggle for access to employment. Where structures of class intersect with those of ethnicity, in particular recent immigrancy combined with non-English speaking background, the problems in schools and employment are exacerbated (Jamrozik, Boland & Urquhart, 1995, pp. 120–31). There is plenty of evidence of curriculum reform in the attempt to keep young people at school, but there is also evidence to show that in some areas the difficulties are too great, and that substantial numbers of schools and working-class students in them are failing (Teese et al., 1995). There remains a disjunction between what working-class parents often want from schooling, and what the schools think they should want (see Connell, 2003, 2004). Even when working-class children do well at school there are still times that produce discomfort: the problem of being 'found out' (Reay, 2004).[5]

5   Middle-class families and contemporary schooling

In recent times, the Australian middle class has become much less dependent than it had been before the 1990s on employment in the public or government sector. This has resulted from the tendency to smaller government and the out-sourcing of government functions to business. Under the influence of neoliberalism and with a remarkable period of economic growth since the 1980s, business corporations have employed much greater numbers of white-collar and professional workers

(Martin, 1998; Connell, 2003, 2004). Employment security in the corporations is usually less than in the public sector; it is often less well protected by union membership and interventions by professional associations. Patterns of work have emerged that would distress the older Australian middle class. There is more frequent mobility between jobs, employees can expect short and long periods of unemployment, and the hours of work involved are usually much greater than the old 35 to 40 hours per week. Under these circumstances a number of sociologists and commentators have detected the phenomenon of 'middle class anxiety'. In Australia, the most perceptive analyst has been Michael Pusey. His book *The Experience of Middle Australia: The Dark Side of Economic Reform* (2003) tells a story of many in the middle class feeling betrayed or anxious in a more dangerous world, where governments cannot be relied on to maintain decent public services in health, transport—and education. In this world, individuals and families are forced to look to their private interests, to organise their affairs carefully, and to become players in the developing markets of private employment, private health, and private education. Other scholars have linked these changes to changes in the character of Australian liberalism, where the public interest has retreated before that of the private (see Brett, 2003; Sawer, 2003; and chapter 1 of this book).

These changes have only intensified the interest of most middle-class families in securing a good education for their children. Scholars in the United Kingdom have analysed the characteristics of this intensification of interest. Stephen Ball (2003), for example, has written about the retreat of middle-class families from government comprehensive schools. (See also work by Brantlinger, 2003; Devine, 2004; Gewirtz, Ball & Bowe, 1995; Power, Edwards, Whitty & Wigfall, 2003.) The social context of schooling is a crucial issue. Too many students from ethnically diverse or poor suburbs represent a threat to middle-class strategies. Middle-class parents feel a need to influence if not control the practices of schools in the interests of their children. In Australia, the same pressures and strategies occur (Campbell, 2005). In the desire to find a suitable school, not only good performances in publicly reported examination results and standardised testing are looked to. The capacity of a school to convince parents that it is a well-disciplined school, has excellent educational facilities and teachers, has an exciting extra-curriculum and dynamic school leadership—all these are weighed up by middle-class parents. The symbolic importance of school uniforms and the manner in which they are worn is also taken note of. The Australian film *Looking for Alibrandi* (Woods, 2000) can be interpreted with some of these issues in mind. Increasingly some schools rather than others, despite relative equivalence in the student–teacher ratios, and the qualifications of their teachers, attract middle-class families more than others. Some selective and specialist state high schools are attractive, some comprehensive high schools in relatively uniform middle-class suburbs are attractive, but absorbing the strongest growth are non-government, fee-charging schools (especially those with low fees). School choice and social class is further explored in chapter 9, pp. 226–36.

It is difficult to find clear statistics about the behaviour of different social classes in relation to the schools their children attend. In the Australian census, for example, there is a strong reluctance to use classes as a basis of categorisation; nor is there a fine enough distinction between different kinds of schools. Nevertheless, if we contrast changes from 1976 to 2001 in the kinds of secondary schools to which parents (in this case fathers) send their children, we get some understanding of the forces at work (see Tables 6.1 and 6.2).

Table 6.1 Type of secondary school attended by youth with fathers whose occupations are described as 'professional', 1976 and 2001: New South Wales (%)

Type of school	1976	2001	% change
Government school	68	51	−17
Catholic school	19	25	+6
Other non-government	13	24	+11
Total (%)	100	100*	
Total (N)	30,492	66,146	

Source: Australian Bureau of Statistics, censuses 1976, 2001 (commissioned table)

* Error in total only apparent, due to 'rounding' of percentages.

Table 6.2 Type of secondary school attended by youth with fathers whose occupations are described as 'managerial', 1976 and 2001: New South Wales (%)

Type of school	1976	2001	% change
Government school	68	51	−17
Catholic school	21	28	+7
Other non-government	11	22	+11
Total (%)	100	100	
Total (N)	38,397	57,868	

Source: Australian Bureau of Statistics, censuses 1976, 2001 (commissioned table)

We contrast the kinds of schools to which middle-class families are increasingly sending their children with those of working-class families in 2001. In this case the fathers are categorised as being skilled workers; that is, having a trade (Table 6.3).

Table 6.3 Type of secondary school attended by youth with fathers whose occupations are described as 'skilled worker', 2001: New South Wales (%)

Type of school	%
Government school	65
Catholic school	27
Other non-government	8
Total (%)	100
Total (N)	62,377

Source: Australian Bureau of Statistics, Census 2001 (commissioned table)

As we would expect, there are very different patterns of school attendance shown in Table 6.3. These working-class families in 2001 send their children overwhelmingly to government and Catholic schools. In 2001 the middle-class families with fathers who were in the professions or worked as managers supported the non-government sector at very much higher rates. These patterns would not be markedly different for other states in Australia since much of the new patterns of school choice are subject to federal policy and funding rather than the education policies of individual states.

A very deliberate approach to the education of young people has been a longstanding practice of middle-class families. This involved the deferral of the pleasures or gratifications associated with early transition to the workforce and adulthood, to ensure that middle-class children were properly set up for respectable and well-paid careers. 'Stay at school', 'work hard for your exams', 'we'll pay for extra coaching in the subjects you find hard', 'aim for marks high enough to get into your preferred uni course'—all of this can be demanding on young people who are increasingly tempted by high-cost leisure activities and the consumer goods marketed to their age group. The compromise is often that part-time jobs are taken at the same time that full-time education is pursued. Nevertheless, middle-class families have been consistent for over a century in believing that education is one of the most important keys to success. The proving of *merit*, and the idea that the meritorious should get the best and most influential jobs (*meritocracy*) is crucial to this thinking. (See the pioneering book by Michael Young (1958).) The issues associated with youth transition are further explored in chapter 3.

Ball (2003) and others have pointed out a new factor in this process, however. With middle-class anxiety in the neoliberal age comes a reluctance to trust merit alone. 'Positionality' becomes important: *which* school and *which* university being attended become factors in the competition for secure and well-paid middle class employment, as well as the basic need to acquire a good qualification or credential.

Finally, in this discussion of the middle class, we refer to a debate that has developed from the late 1990s to the early years of this century. A new class, the *aspirational class,* is occasionally detected as being active in the cities of Australia (Morton, 2001). This class, arguably found in higher mortgage-belt areas of the cities, sometimes including people without well-paid jobs but hungry for the security of their children, were thought to be the voters that were increasingly lost to the Labor Party in the post-Hawke/Keating-era series of Liberal electoral victories. These were sometimes identified as the new *battlers*—and those susceptible to the new low-fee non-government school options. In class terms they were very likely the group traditionally identified as upper working and lower middle class, a group that across the twentieth century had always been alert to the possibilities of upward social mobility. The increasing attachment of this group to the new low-fee schools of the Anglicans, Catholics, and the various 'Christian' schools was another factor in the splintering of attachments of some middle- and working-class groups to government schools.

6   The other classes: the underclass and the ruling class

It is by no means accepted by all, or even many, that there is either an underclass or a ruling class in Australia. Part of the problem is with the naming of them. More people are prepared to accept that there is a growing disparity in Australia between the very wealthy and powerful, and the very poor and disempowered.

The idea of an underclass has stronger support in Europe and the United States where the existence of urban poverty deriving from endemic unemployment, and associated with racial discrimination against recent immigrants, or in the case of the United States, Black Americans, is all too easily measured and observed (see Best, 2005, pp. 40–2). Some Australian scholars argue that the idea of an underclass is especially problematic; those most likely to use the term appear to regard the underclass as morally or intellectually deficient, unable or unwilling to change irresponsible lifestyles and being welfare-dependent not through circumstance but moral failings (Peel, 2003, pp. 21–3; Jamrozik et al., 1995, p. 60).

In Australia, this group of urban poor, as in Europe and the United States, was produced and characterised by many of the same phenomena: very high rates of unemployment, high rates of single parent, usually single female-headed, families (which are usually poorer than those with two parents), high dependence on rental and public housing, and often including large groups of recent migrants or ethnic groups also with high unemployment rates. The declining support from governments through welfare, public health, and other social services, including education, exacerbate, and perhaps in some cases, cause the problems. The growing

Table 6.4 SEIFA Index of Advantage/Disadvantage: lowest, lowest in postcode areas with population > 5000, highest in postcode areas population > 2000 for each Australian state and territory, 2001 Census

(i) Lowest indexes for each state or territory

Postcode	District	Index
6646	Lake Carnegie & Wiluna (WA)	703.44
5421	Terowie (SA)	723.04
2306	Windale (NSW)	741.92
7305	Merseylea & Railton (Tas)	789.76
3520	Kinypanial & Koring Vale (V)	797.12
4620	Aramara & Glenbar (Q)	802.32
0870	Alice Springs (NT)	869.84
2609	Fyshwick & Majura (ACT)	963.28

(ii) Lowest indexes for each state or territory where postcode populations are > 5000

Postcode	District	Index
5113	Elizabeth West (SA)	798.80
3019	Braybrook & Robinson (V)	825.68
7030	Bridgewater & Brighton (T)	835.12
4114	Kingston & Logan City (Q)	842.08
2502	Cringila & Warrawong (NSW)	853.68
6167	Casuarina & Kwinana (WA)	884.64
0822	Annie River & Bathurst Is (NT)	910.24
2906	Banks & Conder (ACT)	1081.84

(iii) Highest indexes for each state or territory where postcode populations are > 2000

Postcode	District	Index
2061	Kirribilli & Milsons Point (NSW)	1248.48
3002	East Melbourne (V)	1217.12
2603	Forrest & Manuka (ACT)	1207.92
6015	City Beach (WA)	1207.36
4069	Chapel Hill & Kenmore (Q)	1181.76
5066	Beaumont & Burnside (SA)	1166.08
7053	Bonnett Hill & Taroona (T)	1146.96
0820	Darwin & East Point (NT)	1097.84

Source: Australian Bureau of Statistics, SEIFA Indexes, Census 2001

de-industrialisation of Australia is the other major contributor. If General Motors or Mitsubishi close factories in Adelaide, associated businesses also close, and new jobs for low-paid, semi-skilled, and 'unskilled' industrial workers can be very difficult to find.

The dimensions of the problem can be seen by comparing the characteristics of some of the poorest and wealthiest areas within Australia. There are two sets of SEIFA (Socio-Economic Indexes for Areas) reported here. The first (Table 6.4) is the Index of Advantage/Disadvantage. This index takes into account variables such as the income of families, people with a tertiary education, and people employed in a skilled occupation. Here, select districts are reported according to postcode. The lowest, then the lowest of postcode areas with more than 5000 inhabitants, and the highest of postcode areas with more than 2000 inhabitants are reported.

Besides revealing extreme differences in advantage and disadvantage—concepts closely related to class—the indices also point to the problems for people living in isolated rural districts as discussed in chapters 4 and 5. A very large number of those in isolated districts are, of course, Aborigines.

For children from families where poverty and endemic unemployment are rife, the local government schools are also likely to be in trouble—although not always. With few students surviving long enough at school to do Year 12, the chances of a broad curriculum being offered are low. In some states, the least experienced teachers, and some with a weak command of English, often end up in such schools (Vickers, 2004; Thomson, 2002). Existing disadvantages are often consolidated as the local government schools find it difficult to pay for additional specialist teachers and other resources. In schools with wealthier parent populations, there are often sufficient funds from voluntary school fees to pay for such services. It is sometimes difficult to see where the breakthrough will come in terms of achieving common social justice outcomes for an increasing number of Australian families. Schools and teachers have often been at the forefront in assisting here, but the early twenty-first century has seen more than the usual difficulties. Decisions of governments can be crucial in these processes. Writing about Broadmeadows High School, Peel (2003) shows the effect of the education policy of the Kennett Liberal government in Victoria on producing a diminished capacity of schools to work creatively in a very poor working class community (pp. 142–3). The authors of *Running Twice as Hard* demonstrated the problems after the closing of the federally funded Disadvantaged Schools Program (Connell, White & Johnston, 1991).

For children from the other end of the spectrum, the world is a different place. By using the term 'ruling class' we do not deny the democratic political system that exists in Australia, nor the fact that many people in ruling-class families choose not to exert the power that their wealth, status and potential control over business, politics, and industry might bring. Nevertheless, to be born into the wealthiest and most powerful families brings a very different experience of education from what other Australians might experience. Janet McCalman (1993) and Peter Gronn (1992) have written important historical analyses of these experiences. Peel and McCalman have shown that there are differences between Melbourne and Sydney. For example, where in Melbourne the graduates of the church or corporate schools predominated in the professional, business, and government elite, in Sydney, the equivalent group was more likely to come from the older selective government schools (Peel & McCalman, 1992). For the most part the wealthiest and most powerful families in Australia send their children to a limited range of non-government schools. They include Scotch College, Geelong Grammar and Presbyterian Ladies College in Victoria, St Peters in Adelaide, Hale in Perth, Church of England Grammar in Brisbane, and The King's School and Abbotsleigh in Sydney. But there is also a long tradition of sending young people interstate and even to England for secondary education, and increasingly to substantially private universities such as Harvard in the United States or Oxford and Cambridge in England.

The mission of a ruling-class school (Hale) in Perth

Hale School exists to develop in its students:
- a lifelong love of learning
- a life-enhancing sense of self that engenders self-belief, confidence and humility
- the will and the skills to meet intellectual, physical, spiritual and emotional challenges
- an appreciation of and the opportunity to be involved in a range of cultural experiences
- an understanding of the spiritual dimension of their lives
- leadership through service at the School and in the wider community
- tolerance, understanding and compassion in their relationships with others
- an appreciation of the human and physical environment in a changing world.

(From Hale website, retrieved February 7, 2006)

If anything, the importance of education has increased over the years for ruling-class families. The new conditions of globalised capitalism have led to a more dangerous world for many of the older ruling-class families. The threat of corporate takeover, from international sources as well as local, perhaps based on the successful monopolisation of new technologies or the ability to manipulate government and trade relations more successfully, have meant a greater dependence on well-educated corporate executive officers and senior management. A narrow group of schools and universities serve the interests of the ruling class, and continue to inculcate the habitus and cultural capital required for class maintenance. The conditions of neoliberalism have transformed Australia's ruling class, but the demand for exclusive schooling for its children remains. (On the transformation, see Connell, 2002b.)

The impacts of globalisation and more recent economic developments in relation to education are discussed in chapter 12. Nevertheless, education and schooling are not diminished in the present period in their ability either to alleviate or consolidate class differences.

7   Assessing the significance of class

Being born into a particular social class in contemporary Australia does not necessarily determine the kind of life a person is likely to lead. Nevertheless, a person's social class origin usually has a great deal to do with how easy it is to do certain things in the making of a life. For some in the social classes marked by poverty and unemployment the chances of escaping such conditions are difficult. Schooling can be crucial in creating opportunities. At the same time, schooling can consolidate disadvantage. Middle-class families historically have been the most dependent on schooling opportunities for securing career-based employment, especially those elements that have not been able to sustain small business ownership. They have been the most strategic users of schools in the struggle for the credentials that schools can deliver. Those credentials are not easily exhausted. They can continue producing employment and other opportunities into the future, although the pressure increases to re-educate and gain new credentials over a working lifetime.

Other social classes historically have not been so dependent on schooling. A great proportion of traditional working-class jobs did not require much schooling. Traditionally upper, middle, and ruling class families valued education, but not necessarily for the direct vocational opportunities it provided. In the nineteenth century, an education based on the higher accomplishments for girls and classics for boys produced, to use Bourdieu's terms, cultural capital and distinction, useful for class networking, class consolidation, and social status. In the contemporary era, with so many areas in the production of wealth linked to advanced scientific, technological, and managerial education, it is fair to say that education is more closely linked to employment and the processes of class formation than ever (Jamrozik et al., 1995, pp. 54–63).

This then leads to the most important class-related question of all in education: to what degree are the resources and processes associated with education, and their life-transforming potentials, equally or unequally made available to different social classes, and how well are they able to be used by families from the different social classes? Some hypothetical answers to these questions are available for speculation when asking the following questions. Who goes to which schools? Which schools have wonderful or barely adequate facilities? Which families from which suburbs are far more likely to achieve university entrance? Which students from which suburbs are more likely to end up leaving school early, and likely to end up in low-paid and casual jobs, if not experience prolonged unemployment? Some of the answers to these questions can be graphically explored in the 'social atlas' publications for the main Australian cities produced by the Australian Bureau of Statistics and various geographers.[6]

And a final question for this and other chapters: what is the actual and potential role of teachers in a school in all of this process?

From a 'professional' journal of an undergraduate aiming to become a teacher:

I want to create a better educated society. I want to empower children with the skills to make a difference in the world … I want to work with disadvantaged students (low socio-economic areas …) to improve their opportunities in life. Empower them with the skills to change their circumstances. (Quoted in Whitehead, 2005b.)

Focus questions

1 To what degree does social class remain a significant factor in explaining the way that Australian society works, and who gets what in terms of opportunity, wealth, and social power?
2 Clearly, children and youth from different social classes go to different kinds of schools. Why does this happen?
3 What might the effects be on young people of different social classes if it is true that schools tend to value middle-class children, with their language and behaviours, to a greater degree than others?
4 How should teachers in a school develop strategies to work with children from working-class families or families marked by endemic poverty and unemployment?

5 In answering Question 4, are there dangers in working from the belief that such children are in 'deficit', culturally and in other ways? What might working-class people feel about being thought of as being in 'cultural deficit' and how might a school work from a different analysis?

6 How do schools adapt or work differently in terms of curriculum, teaching methods, and extracurricular opportunities for children and youth from different social classes?

7 Can individual teachers, or teachers working together, positively affect the way that students from different social classes have traditionally tended to experience school?

Notes

1. See McGregor (2001) for a general discussion on the working of class in Australia.
2. On the emergence of modern social classes and class systems in Australia, see Connell & Irving (1992).
3. On the development of the church schools, see Sherington, Petersen & Brice (1987).
4. This organisation continues to do so in the present day. Schools and teachers routinely use their 'reading age' tests, for example. The ACER is very much involved in the development of standardised, nationwide tests of numeracy and literacy. See www.acer.edu.au/.
5. Another way of saying this in Bourdieurian terms would be that the habitus of working-class children and youth, even those doing well, occasionally exposes them as not understanding, or not knowing how to respond to certain situations. This can produce discomfort, and even shame. Early school leaving or university dropout sometimes results.
6. The Australian Bureau of Statistics catalogue number for the social atlases of all main cities for the Australian census (2001) is 2030.0.

Further reading

Ball, S.J. (2003). *Class Strategies and the Education Market: The Middle Classes and Social Advantage.* London: RoutledgeFalmer.

Connell, R.W. (2003). 'Working-class families and the new secondary education.' *Australian Journal of Education, 47*(3), 237–52.

Connell, R.W., Ashenden, D.J., Kessler, S. & Dowsett, G.W. (1982). *Making the Difference: Schools, Families and Social Division.* Sydney: George Allen & Unwin.

Dolby, N. & Dimitriadis, G. (eds) (2004). *Learning to Labour in New Times*. New York: RoutledgeFalmer.

Miller, P. & Davey, I. (1988). 'The common denominator: Schooling the people.' In V. Burgmann & J. Lee (eds), *Constructing a Culture*. Melbourne: McPhee Gribble/Penguin.

Power, S., Edwards, T., Whitty, G. & Wigfall, V. (2003). *Education and the Middle Class*. Buckingham: Open University Press.

Reay, D. (2004). 'Finding or losing yourself? Working-class relationships to education'. In S.J. Ball (ed.), *The RoutledgeFalmer Reader in Sociology of Education* (pp. 30–44). London: RoutledgeFalmer.

Teese, R. (2000). *Academic Success and Social Power: Examinations and Inequity*. Melbourne: Melbourne University Press.

Teese, R. et al. (1995). *Who Wins At School? Boys and Girls in Australian Secondary Education*. Melbourne: Department of Education Policy and Management, University of Melbourne.

Thomson, P. (2002). *Schooling the Rustbelt Kids: Making the Difference in Changing Times*. Sydney: Allen & Unwin.

Internet sources

Take into account that some organisations' sites have a particular interest in making an argument one way or another.

www.abc.net.au/rn/bigidea/stories/s599782.htm
www.det.nsw.edu.au/reviews/index.htm
www.abs.gov.au/
www.aare.edu.au/confpap.htm
www.dest.gov.au/
www.aeufederal.org.au/Publications/index2.html#PAP

7
Cultural Difference and Identity
Anthony Welch

1 Multicultural Australia?

'For those who come across the seas, we've boundless plains to share'—a refrain from Australia's national anthem, *Advance Australia Fair*, sung regularly at school assemblies by children across the country. And indeed with around 24 per cent of Australians born overseas, and a reputation worldwide as a prototype of a modern, diverse society (*SMH*, 2005, 10 December), Australia can fairly be deemed multicultural. Yet many teachers, students, and their parents may wonder what the above refrain really means, in the face of recent, and apparently contradictory, events. These include efforts in recent years to demonise asylum seekers and prevent their landing on Australian shores, the widespread, cross-cultural support for Australia's football victory over Uruguay in late 2005, and the violent, racist clashes at Cronulla, and elsewhere, in December of that year. Victimisation of Australian Muslims has led to counter-demonstrations, including by a group, Sisters of the Muslim Community, asserting the right by women to wear the hijab (*SMH*, 2005, 31 August, 3 December). How does Australian society respond to difference, and what is the role of education in fostering diversity, and building and sustaining identity?

As with chapter 5 on Indigenous education, this chapter further underscores the point that cultural differences have long been a critical element in Australian education and society. Indeed, it can fairly be claimed that with the exception of Indigenous groups, Australians are all migrants. This key feature of Australian society has become all the more marked since 1945, in the context of its vigorous postwar migration program, a comparatively bold piece of social engineering that sets it apart to an extent from other countries of migration, such as Canada, Argentina, or the United States, where immigration was not as persistently planned (Jupp, 2002).

The fact that Australia is a country of migration, however, and that its history and identity is inseparable from that fact, does not mean that it has always been a bed of roses for migrant groups, nor that the education that was received in the new country was always well suited to diverse migrant cultures and aspirations.

As is evident in some of the examples below, while Australia can fairly be said to be one of the more successful multicultural nations, its history is replete with racism, so that it can be said that each generation must renew the commitment to diversity and multiculturalism, including in education. Throughout the last two centuries or more, it has often been the case that first-generation migrants have had to struggle for acceptance, while the second generation has more commonly enjoyed the fruits of their parents' labour, including in education. As we shall see, education has often been a powerful incentive for immigration, with parents aspiring to better educational options for their children in the new country, and the social mobility that more and better education can confer. At the same time, some groups have been more successful than others in negotiating associated processes of adaptation, integration, and cultural maintenance, as seen in the case studies of different communities below.

2 Culture, language, and identity in Australian education

Key concepts raised in this chapter are about identity, difference, and culture. These are all the more important within the education arena, given that education is such an important and powerful site of cultural transmission. What an education system transmits is ultimately the result of a concrete process of cultural selection and omission (Williams, 1961, 1977): it represents a powerful statement about what is deemed valuable and important in that culture. Indeed, education can reasonably be understood as always being an induction into culture: the question is whose, and on which terms? (Chapters 5 on Aboriginal education, 6 on social class, and 8 on gender could also be read in such terms.)

So what is culture, and how important is it in understanding education? The term has been defined in various ways, but is clearly a key concept in understanding both society and education. Part of the problem in coming to an overall understanding of this key term stems from the different ways in which it has been used: 'Culture is one of the two or three most complicated terms in the English language' (Williams, 1983, p. 87). The term cult, in the religious sense, is one of the older meanings, as is (agri)culture, in the sense of working or tilling the soil. We also use the word in the sense of attempting to confirm a sense of social superiority (as with the term high culture), to put down or denigrate someone else's culture (pop culture, gang culture, gangsta culture), or to apply to the way of doing things associated with a particular place or people (Japanese culture, for example). The notion of tending or cultivating something (a crop, a mind, or a way of behaving) is fundamental to these accounts, which also serve to remind us that there is no single version of culture. We must always speak of cultures in the plural sense:

The specific and variable cultures of different natures and periods, but also the specific and variable cultures of social and economic groups within a nation (Williams, 1983, p. 89).

This also underlines that culture is not static, but changes according to socio-historical circumstances. Necessarily, then, culture is not abstract (restricted to the world of ideas, remote from people's day-to-day lives and practices), but also includes the material (ways of making things, such as art, houses, or implements).

This understanding also embraces education; indeed education, whether in tribal settings, or in modern schooling systems, is one of the most powerful ways of inducting young people into a given culture. Curriculum, too, can be understood as a cultural construct, a particular selection from available cultures (Welch, 1981; Apple, 1990a, 1990b). But what if that culture is not felt to be 'our' culture? What if the curriculum is experienced as 'other' by young people who feel that their cultures are not (adequately) acknowledged by the schooling system that they experience daily?

This has often been the perception of many children from other cultures in Australian schools. Not merely are their languages often not available from among those taught in school, but the official knowledge that is codified in the school curriculum does not embrace their cultures, their values, or their knowledges. Given that not all cultures are equal, that in fact culture has power, it is no surprise that immigrant parents and children have long lamented the absence of their cultural knowledge in the official school curriculum. What this makes problematic, then, is the relationship between 'what knowledge is considered high status, and some of the relations of power we need to consider ... (in society)' (Apple, 1997). As indicated above, problematising the relations between culture and power in society and education can also be a useful way of understanding class, and gender relations in education, as also can Aboriginal education (see chapters 5, 6, and 8, in this volume). The following diagram represents a useful way of understanding the interplay of culture and power, in relation to key elements of society.

Figure 7.1

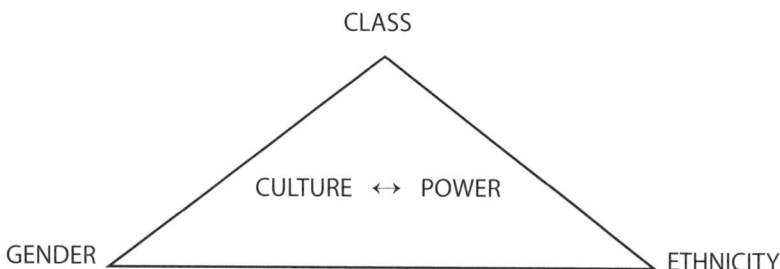

For much of Australia's history, it was often assumed that people who came to this country should simply abandon the culture of their homeland, in order to fit into the Anglo cultural norms of majority Australian society. This included children who were faced with the official school curriculum, based on much the same set of assumptions. Only in recent decades has this ideology of assimilation given way to the policy of multiculturalism.

In practice, identity is nothing like as simple as the assumptions that the assimilation era implied. Certainly, identity is multifaceted—an individual may identify primarily as a woman, a Buddhist, or an Australian, and it has been argued that in an era of globalisation, national identity is being reshaped, and is perhaps declining in importance (see chapter 12 for more on the impact of globalisation). The experience of many migrants, bicultural, and many also bilingual, is complex and contradictory, leading many to feel in-between, neither one nor the other (Cohen, 1998; see also the boxed text about Zheng He, towards the end of this chapter). Certainly, many children, and their parents, had no wish to cut themselves off from their cultural roots—they wished to maintain cultural relations with the homeland, and to keep their language. Indeed, in a vibrant, poly-ethnic society, the rich blend of diasporic communities, and their links to their homelands and to other parts of the diaspora, are often now seen as an important cultural and economic resource, rather than a liability (Cohen, 1998; Hugo, 2005b; Welch & Zhang, 2005; see also the section on highly skilled Chinese, later in this chapter).

Given that language is clearly one of the most important bearers of culture, it is clearly important for Australia to foster its community languages, and knowledge of relevant cultures. This will enhance its social, cultural, and economic relations both with its neighbours—including for example, China, Vietnam, and the world's most populous Islamic country, Indonesia—as well as European nations from which Australian migrants have long been drawn (Germany, Italy, Greece, Eastern Europe) and the Arab world. Yet, a recent analysis concluded that '...there was far more bilingual education in Australia in the 19th century than at present' (Clyne, 2005, p. 2), and while both of Australia's largest cities have populations of which at least 25 per cent speak another language at home, far too little is being done to nurture this store of cultural knowledge and expertise:

> Like some other English-speaking countries, such as the United Kingdom, the United States and New Zealand, Australia is treating languages at best as a luxury and not a necessity, at worst as a diversion from more important things, which are defined in monolingual terms (Clyne, 2005, p. 22).

In defiance of an acknowledgement that in a multicultural society many languages need to be fostered, two policies over the 1990s selected certain key languages as national priorities. The *Australian Language and Literacy Policy*, or ALLP (1991) listed a range of priority languages (European, Aboriginal, and Asian), and promised $300 to each school in which a pupil successfully completed Year 12 in one of eight languages to be specified by each state, from the overall national list. The second policy, the *National Asian Languages and Studies in Australian Schools* (NALSAS) of 1994, was based on the economistic premise (see chapter 1) that certain key Asian languages were of critical importance to Australia's future, and was part of a larger move to integrate Australia more into the region. This instrumental approach to the learning of languages and cultures intended that 60 per cent of Australian school pupils would take one of the priority Asian languages (Mandarin Chinese, Japanese, Indonesian, and Korean). While significant funding was committed to support the program, which was generally seen as successful in fostering the study of Asian languages, the federal government axed it in 2003, despite widespread protests.

Table 7.1, following, shows the main community languages spoken in Australia, and their degree of growth, or decline.

Table 7.1   Selected community languages spoken in Australia, 2001, with percentage change from 1991

Language	No. of speakers in 2001	Percentage change since 1991
Italian	353,606	−15.6
Greek	263,718	−7.7
Cantonese	225,307	38.9
Arabic	209,371	28.6
Vietnamese	174,236	58.1
Mandarin	139,288	155.9
Spanish	93,595	3.4
Tagalog (Filipino)*	78,879	33.4
German	76,444	−32.6
Macedonian	71,994	11.7
Serbian	49,202	102.2
Hindi	47,817	110.4
Korean	39,528	100.1
Indonesian	38,724	42.4

Source: Clyne, 2005

* Tagalog, the main language of the Philippines, cannot be distinguished in the Census from Filipino, the national language.

The growth and decline of specific linguistic communities evident in Table 7.1 reflect the changing patterns of Australian migration, over recent decades (see Tables 7.3 and 7.4, below). But these patterns differ substantially, by state. Below in Table 7.2, you can see the ten principal community languages in five major capital cities.

Table 7.2   Top ten community languages in five Australian capital cities, 2001

Sydney	Melbourne	Adelaide	Brisbane	Perth
Arabic (142,467)	Italian (134,675)	Italian (37,803)	Cantonese (13,796)	Italian (32,893)
Cantonese (116,384)	Greek (118,755)	Greek (25,119)	Vietnamese (13,374)	Cantonese (14,889)
Greek (83,926)	Vietnamese (63,033)	Vietnamese (12,355)	Mandarin (13,244)	Vietnamese (11,587)
Italian (79,683)	Cantonese (59,303)	Polish (7454)	Italian (11,368)	Mandarin (10,882)
Vietnamese (65,923)	Arabic (45,736)	German (7103)	Greek (8239)	Indonesian (6322)
Mandarin (63,716)	Mandarin (37,994)	Cantonese (6609)	Spanish (6874)	Croatian (6313)
Spanish (44,672)	Macedonian (30,859)	Arabic (4252)	Samoan (6788)	Polish (6161)
Tagalog (40,139)	Turkish (26,598)	Serbian (3862)	German (5763)	Macedonian (5782)
Korean (29,538)	Spanish (21,852)	Mandarin (3825)	Tagalog (5288)	German (5724)
Hindi (27,283)	Croatian (21,690)	Croatian (3457)	Hindi (4669)	Arabic (5293)

Source: Clyne, 2005

Table 7.2 shows very different patterns of language concentrations in the five capital cities. Sydney has by far the largest group of Arabic and Cantonese speakers, while speakers of Italian and Greek are far more numerous in Melbourne. But both cities share their top five languages. German speakers are among the top ten in the three smaller cities, but not in the larger two. Hindi speakers are among the top ten in only Brisbane and Sydney. The proximity of both Brisbane and Perth to Asia seems to be reflected in their list of language communities to a degree. Adelaide's language communities, by contrast, still reflect a somewhat more European pattern, with Polish, German, and Yugoslav languages still among the top ten. In Sydney, only three European languages figure among the top ten, and the Spanish-speaking group is in fact mainly composed of Latin Americans. In Hobart, only Greek has more than 1000 speakers, while Italian and German are the next largest. In Darwin, there are, 2716 speakers of Greek, followed by 939 speakers of Filipino, and 736 speakers of Cantonese. Canberra has 3690 home users of Italian, 2854 of Croatian, and 2,801 of Greek (but both Mandarin and Hindi are rising swiftly) (Clyne, 2005, p. 10). The overall pattern of languages taught in Australian schools is compared with their national rank throughout Australian society, and their significance among 0–14 year olds, in the following table (7.3).

Table 7.3 Top ten community languages in Australian schools, 2001

Language Rank (Schools)	No. of Students	Language Rank (National)	Top 20 rank, among 0–14 age group (national)
Japanese	402,882	Not among top 20	17
Italian	394,770	1	5
Indonesian	310,363	20	13
French	247,001	18	20
German	158,076	9	15
Mandarin Chinese	111,464	6	6
Arabic	31,844	4	1
Greek	28,188	2	4
Spanish	24,807	7	7
Vietnamese	22,428	5	2

Source: Clyne, 2005

The data show that patterns of language use, and the cultures that they support, are closely related to waves of migration. Migration is certainly a key element in Australian society, but how has it affected Australian society, and changing constructions of national identity, including in education?

3   Australia's migration history

In 2002, Australia welcomed its six millionth immigrant—a Filipina information technology specialist. Paradoxically perhaps, at the very same time, Australia was establishing internment camps in remote desert locations (Woomera, Port Hedland), and offshore in places such as Nauru and Manus Island, to incarcerate asylum seekers from countries such as Afghanistan, Pakistan, Iraq, and Iran. The latter camps were deliberately established overseas, as part of what Prime Minister Howard dubbed euphemistically the 'Pacific Solution', in order to prevent asylum seekers from landing on Australian shores. (It was not the first time that Australia had behaved similarly—in the mid 1970s, similar hysteria was whipped up in the face of attempts by an equally small number of Vietnamese 'boat people' to come to Australia, after the end of that war.) While poor nations like Nauru welcomed the additional resources provided by Australia to set up the internment camps, there were others who criticised the venture as an exercise in neo-colonialism. Why was Australia warmly welcoming some immigrants, while at the same time desperately seeking to prevent other aspirants from settling in the country? How does an understanding of Australia's history of migration, and the schooling made available to migrant groups, help us understand such apparent contradictions?

Perhaps the first point to make derives from the fact that it was the British that colonised Australia, at the end of the eighteenth century. It could have been otherwise: it has been argued that the Chinese discoverer Hong Bao sailed to Australia around 1422, as part of voyages of discovery commissioned early in the Ming dynasty (Hu, 2003; Menzies, 2002), while Portuguese and Dutch sailors arrived in the sixteenth century. Later, at the end of the eighteenth century, La Perouse, the French explorer, arrived in Australia shortly after Captain Cook.

But in the end it was not the Chinese nor the Dutch, nor the Portuguese nor French that colonised the Australian continent in 1788 (it is an interesting exercise to speculate how different its development would have been if they had). Indeed, as James Jupp (2002) has argued: 'Australia was not settled by the "Europeans", but by the "British", partly to keep "Europeans" out! Its subsequent history was determined by that fact' (p. 3).

Other key features of Australian immigration are also related to the fact of British colonialism. By the time of federation (1901), some 20 per cent of Australia's populace was overseas-born, including significant Chinese and German minorities, and smaller populations of Pacific islanders and Afghans (see below). Nonetheless, from the very beginning of the Australian colonies, Australia's population intake was planned, and reflected its British heritage:

> Australian immigration policy over the past 150 years has rested on three pillars: the maintenance of British hegemony and 'white' domination; the strengthening of Australia economically and militarily by selective mass immigration; and the state control of these processes (Jupp, 2002, p. 6).

As Jupp goes on to point out, while the first two pillars have been challenged in recent decades, the third continues to reign supreme. State control over immigration was an early and insistent feature of the Australian colonies, and still is.

Arguably, part of the contradictions of Australian immigration history derives from the tension between place, and dominant cultural heritage. On the one hand, the continent's location at the heel of South East Asia, in the South Pacific, with all of its nearest neighbours being non-European (the single exception being, then as now, New Zealand), suggests an Asian–Pacific influence. Indeed, while emigration from the population centres of Indonesia and India was relatively rare in the nineteenth century (and mainly to plantation economies, such as Fiji), Chinese emigration dated from the 1840s, when that country was forcibly opened up by the British, during the so-called 'Opium Wars'. But even at that time, when China's population was estimated at around 300 million, the arrival of a few thousand indentured labourers in the late 1840s (and a few hundred Indian and Melanesian settlers) and tens of thousands of Chinese migrants (largely from southern Fujien and Guangdong provinces) in the aftermath of the discovery of gold in Victoria (where, by 1859, Chinese comprised almost 20 per cent of the male population (Sherington, 1990, p. 66)) and the other colonies from the 1850s was met with racist outbursts, and riots, among elements of the dominant ethnic group, largely of British extraction (Jupp, 2001, p. 45). Largely as a result, many of the Chinese settlers who migrated as a result of the gold discoveries, in the hope of making their fortune, eventually returned home (Sherington, 1990). As a result, China-born settlers declined from 38,142 in 1861 to 6404 in 1947 (Hugo, 2005a).

These intemperate outbursts by local whites, however, underlined that place was much less important than perceived racial purity and notions of dominant culture. Australia's cultural referent was unmistakably British: the colonial ruling class during the nineteenth century (sometimes pilloried as the 'bunyip aristocracy') still looked to 'Mother England' for cultural inspiration, values, and the design of legal, parliamentary, and social institutions, including education. This singular dependence was reinforced by the dominant ideology of social Darwinism, which held that a hierarchy of races existed, with white British culture at the apex (Welch, 1996b, pp. 29–30; Jupp, 2002, p. 7). While the worst effects of this pernicious ideology were reserved for Aboriginal groups, whose dispossession, rape, murder, and marginalisation it licensed, it also underpinned the belief that non-Caucasian immigrants (sometimes seen as occupying an intervening status position, between whites and Indigenous minorities) should be non-permanent, ineligible to inter-marry, and restricted to relatively menial occupations. Legislation in the various colonies embodied these prejudices, using devices such as poll taxes and residence fees to effectively proscribe immigration by Chinese settlers, and subsequently by Indians. (Much the same occurred in Canada and the USA at much the same time.) Some non-whites were even deported from Queensland in the 1880s, after race riots by white settlers. Small wonder that such racist views, a by-product of European imperialism of the nineteenth century, viewed Indian and Chinese migrants to Australia as dangerous. The Chinese minority was depicted as devious, lascivious, and evil, while Indians were blamed for frightening lonely women, depressing wages, and contaminating milk (Tavan, 2005; Welch, 1996b, p. 107; Yarwood, 1964, pp. 124–5). 'Asiatics' and other non-Caucasians were seen as only legitimately able to exist in the colonies if employed in menial jobs, a view supported both by owners of capital and by the labour movement (and the new political party to which it gave rise, in 1891: the Australian Labor Party). Popular periodicals of the time such as *The Bulletin* reinforced such prejudices.

Such views underpinned what came to be known from the 1880s onwards (at a time when the total of Chinese and Indigenous population would have reached no more than 5 per cent of the national figure) as the 'White Australia' policy, enshrined in the infamous Immigration Restriction Act of the new national parliament in 1901, and effectively in place until the 1960s (Sherington, 1990). The decades-long use of a dictation test, invariably in a language not known to the immigrant, determined that in 1947 the proportion of the Australian populace that was neither Caucasian, nor Aboriginal, stood at a mere 0.25 per cent (1 in 400). 'Australia had become one of the whitest countries in the world, outside northwestern Europe' (Jupp, 2002, p. 9). In the late 1930s, such exclusionary ideology was used to prevent many Jewish refugees fleeing Nazi Europe from being accepted in Australia, with a 3-year cap of 15,000 being set (Tavan, 2005, p. 28; see also Bartrop, 1994). Even some of those who did gain entry were promptly interned because their language was German, despite being refugees from Nazi persecution (Norst, in Jupp, 2001, p. 179).

Assimilation—the view that migrants should seek to be as much like the locals as possible, in terms of language, dress, and culture—was the spirit of the age, and remained official policy well into the post–World War II era, including in education. Nonetheless, it was arguably a step forward from the racial determinism of earlier eras, which held that environment did not shape people's perceptions and behaviour. Migrants were now advised 'not to behave in any way that would attract attention. Assimilation would be complete when nobody noticed the newcomer' (Jupp, 2002, p. 22).

Nonetheless, by the late 1940s, and in the face of increasing acknowledgement of the sensitivity by Australia's Asian neighbours to the continuation of the White Australia policy, the thinking had begun to change. A proposal in 1947, by Arthur Calwell, Australia's first Immigration Minister (who himself spoke a little Mandarin, and had numerous Chinese friends), to allow naturalisation of Chinese residents was defeated in federal Cabinet, but the same Minister managed to change the administrative category of Middle East from 'Asia' to 'Europe', thereby allowing many Lebanese to immigrate to Australia. By 1950, the incoming Menzies government, while confirming the existing discriminatory policy, indicated that this did not mean that 'the Minister could not exercise a reasonable discretion to meet particular circumstances' (Tarvan, 2005, p. 65). At a time when the proportion of the Australian population that was overseas-born was a mere 9.8 per cent, 'White Australia had been struck a small blow' (Tarvan, 2005, p. 66).

A further initiative, which embraced persons displaced by war from refugee camps in Europe, brought 70,000 immigrants per year to Australia, a figure that grew to 150,000 in later years (Calwell, in Jupp, 2001, p. 71). Nonetheless, it was only from the mid 1960s that the policy of policing entry, with only 'white' and preferably British migrants being sought, effectively ended. The Australian Labor Party (ALP) deleted reference to the White Australia policy at its national conference in 1965, a fact that was heralded by newspapers of the time as 'a decisive blow to the White Australia policy' (Tavan, 2005, p. 156). In fact, British migrants formed half of Australia's annual intake until the 1960s, and the UK was only replaced (by New Zealand!) as the largest source country in 1966. Nonetheless, the 1961 Census revealed a dramatic rise in non-British, non-indigenous elements of the Australian population (Jupp, 2001, p. 67), as indicated in Table 7.4. While the ideology underpinning White Australia was being challenged by the 1940s, official policy still differentiated between 'British' and 'aliens' until 1983—at various times, Germans, Austrians, and Turks were classed as enemies and denied entry, while poor southern Europeans were also excluded for a period (Jupp, 2002, p. 15). Equally, the use of assisted passage (a form of subsidy to intending migrants) to encourage those of particular backgrounds was more common than in other countries of migration such as the United States or Canada. But British and northern European migrants were much more likely to gain an assisted passage than Greeks, Italians, or Portuguese, for example. While the 1960s saw 875,000 come to Australia under this scheme, no Turks gained assistance prior to 1964 (Jupp, 2003, p. 16; see also Tavan, 2005, p. 181). The election of the Whitlam Labor government saw the discriminatory migration scheme formally abandoned, and replaced (as Canada had already done) with a points system, based on both 'desirable' personal and social qualities, and occupational status (Jupp, 2001, p. 68).

The peak migration years for several of the European ethnic groups was in the 1970s, and thereafter a degree of cultural ossification often occurred, as new groups from the home country no longer entered to refresh the cultures of immigrant communities. This was by no means the first time that Australian migrants' cultures had become fossilised, as immigrant communities became cut off from changes in their homeland—much the same was true for Germans who migrated to Australia in the nineteenth century, and for East Europeans and Scandinavians before the Second World War. Education played a role in this phenomenon of cultural ossification, as schools often used outdated textbooks from the homeland, embodying a culture that had long since changed, while language teachers (rarely native speakers themselves) were often unfamiliar with recent developments in the source culture.

Table 7.4 Major non-British, non-indigenous ethnic groups, by birthplace, and total, Australia 1947, 1961, 1996

Ethnic Group	Number 1947 (by birth place)	% total populace 1947 (by birth-place)	Number 1961 (by birth place)	% total populace 1961 (by birth-place	Number 1996 (by birth-place)	% total populace 1996 (by birth-place)	Total number, 1996*	Overall % populace, 1996*
Italian	34,000	0.45	228,000	2.10	274,000	1.50	600,000	3.28
Greek	12,000	0.16	77,000	0.72	167,000	0.91	348,000	1.90
German	14,000	0.18	109,000	1.00	141,000	0.77	675,000	3.69
Polish	6,573	0.09	60,000	0.56	72,000	0.39	164,000	0.89
Chinese	12,000	0.16	14,395	0.14	293,000	1.60	369,000	2.02
Vietnamese	715	0.0	2,747	0.03	176,000	0.96	176,000	0.96
Lebanese	1,886	0.02	7,245	0.07	158,000	0.86	224,000	1.22
Total Aust. Population	7,579,358	1.06	10,634,267	4.62	18,310,700	6.99		13.96

(Jupp et al 2001, Sherington 1990, Official Census 1947, 1961)

Note:
1. The use of birthplace as the principal measure in the above table, based on Census measures, significantly underestimates total numbers and proportions of longstanding ethnic groups, such as Italians and Germans. Hence, the final two columns (marked with an *) incorporate second and other generations.
2. Chinese also includes ethnic Chinese from SE Asia, and elsewhere.
3. In 1947 Census Lebanese includes Syria, Vietnamese were included in category: 'Other Countries in Asia'
4. In 1961, Census, Vietnamese were included in category: 'Other Countries in Asia'

Notwithstanding moves to end racially determined migration, and towards skill and family reunion as the two basic planks in Australia's migration platform, based on a points system introduced in 1979, migration from countries within the region grew relatively slowly, at least in absolute terms. By 1981, of a total population total of some 14.5 million, 'there were only about 300,000 Australians of Asian origin' (Sherington, 1990, p. 166). There were, of course, significant differences among Asian migrants. The India-born population, some of whom had been students in Australia, had risen to 42,000, principally Anglo-Indian (Sherington, 1990, p. 167). While Australia's Korean population had grown to around 9000 by 1986, the Chinese population had grown to between 150,000 and, 200,000 by that same year (from around 12,000 in 1947, after decades of discriminatory migration programs). As also confirmed in Table 7.4, China-born now greatly outnumbered Chinese who were born in Australia. The significance of the shift in source countries is seen in the fact that whereas in 1982–83, UK-born settler arrivals comprised 28 per cent and China-born 1 per cent, by 2002–03, UK-born settlers had declined to 13 per cent, while China-born arrivals now comprised 7 per cent of the total (Parliamentary Library, 2005). 'By 1996, around 41 per cent of Australians were either immigrants or children of immigrants, one in five was not of British … descent, and one in twenty was not of European descent' (Jupp, 2001, p. 70). Many of the former are international students.

The balance between permanent and temporary migration is another area of significant change, in recent decades. Whereas in 1982–83, the numbers of permanent arrivals outstripped that of long-term temporary arrivals (83,010, compared to 79,730), by 2002–03 the picture was very different—long term arrivals had risen to 279,879, while permanent arrivals had risen only slightly, to 93,914 (Parliamentary Library, 2005). Many of the former are international students.

Overall migration from South-East Asia rose from 10 per cent of the total intake in 1982–83 to 20 per cent in 2002–03 (Australia's Migration Program, 2005), while Asian migrants now form around 40 per cent of Australia's annual intake of settlers (Jupp, 2003, p. 15). Significant numbers of ethnic Chinese migrated to Australia from South-East Asia, but here too there were differences. Chinese-Malaysian migrants were often highly qualified and, upon settling in Australia (after having been discriminated against in Malaysia, in both education and society), entered the professions, while ethnic Chinese from Vietnam (about 40,000 of whom came to Australia in the decade after the fall of Saigon in 1975) were generally less educated, but with a strong entrepreneurial spirit (Sherington, 1990, p. 167). Mainland Chinese figured large among both business migrants and the highly skilled, recent figures for which are seen in Table 7.5. In many cases, Asian migrants were more highly educated than the general Australian population, as is also often the case for Asian migrants to Canada and the United States.

But more than the composition of settlers has changed. Table 7.6 shows that Australia's overall migration intake has increased substantially over the past decade (as it has on other occasions in the past). This is particularly since the turn of the century, partly in response to shortages in key labour force areas, such as skilled manufacturing and seasonal agricultural work in rural areas. The Regional Sponsored Migration Scheme (RSMS) is one measure introduced to respond to difficulties in obtaining skilled workers in rural areas, who, if they are prepared

Table 7.5 Settler arrivals by birthplace 1993–94 and 2003–04: leading countries

Birthplace	1993–94	2003–04	% Change
UK & Ireland	9563	19,214	100.9
New Zealand	7772	14,418	85.5
China	2740	8784	220.6
India	2643	8135	207.8
South Africa	1654	5849	253.6
Sudan	340	4591	1250.3
Philippines	4179	4111	−1.6
Malaysia	1252	3718	196.9
Indonesia	622	2584	390.8
Singapore	502	2224	343.0
Vietnam	5434	2212	−59.3
Zimbabwe	143	1620	1032.9

Source: DIMIA, cited in *SMH*, 2005, 29 October

Note: Just as in Table 7.4, it is likely that some of the migrants from Vietnam, Indonesia, and Malaysia are of Chinese ethnicity. See Jupp, 2001, p. 81.

Table 7.6 Settler arrivals 1996–2005

Year	Total	Year	Total
1996–97	74,000	2001–02	85,000
1997–98	68,000	2002–03	110,000
1998–99	68,000	2003–04	110,000
1999–2000	70,000	2004–05	120,000
2000–01	76,000	2005–06	140,000

Source: Parliamentary Library, 2005

to settle in the regions, are enabled to migrate permanently (New Faces, 2001). Just as in the immediate postwar years, migration is still seen as a solution to domestic labour shortages, skilled and unskilled. The changing totals of both family (reunion) and skilled migrants are shown in table 7.8.

As indicated in earlier tables, the current situation is still very mixed. Rather like Canada, and other such countries of migration, Australia can claim to have had open, non-discriminatory migration for close to 40 years. By the late 1970s, this meant that something like 30 per cent of Australian migrants stemmed from the Asian region, a pattern that has, if anything, strengthened slightly since. A decade later, some 37 per cent of Australia's annual settler intake was from Asia (Sherington, 1990, p. 168), while current estimates are that some 39 per cent of Australia's current annual intake of migrants stem from the Asia-Pacific region (Tavan, 2005, p. 1). By the mid 1980s, those who could claim direct maternal and paternal descent from British and Irish descent comprised less than half the population (Sherington 1990, p. 170), while of the total overseas-born among the Australian population, the proportion that were UK-born declined over the century 1901–2001 from 58 per cent to 25.4 per cent (Parliamentary Library, 2005). Other aspects have remained more stable—since 1971, the proportion of the overseas born in the Australian population has ranged from 20 to 24 per cent (Parliamentary Library, 2005).

The spread of migrant communities is also very mixed. By far the greatest density of migrants is to be found in the capital cities, most particularly the two largest cities of Melbourne and Sydney. Melbourne's suburb of Richmond that in the 1960s was largely peopled by working-class Anglo-Australians, and some European migrants, is now a vibrant centre of Vietnamese culture, as is Sydney's Cabramatta, peopled largely by Vietnamese from the south of the country, and Marrickville (once solidly working class Anglo-Australian, later settled by many Greeks), which has a greater concentration of Vietnamese from the north of the country, as well as significant numbers of Lebanese, Chinese, and others. Although smaller pockets exist elsewhere, such as the longstanding German communities that settled in South Australia's Barossa Valley and the Western District and Wimmera in Victoria in the nineteenth century, Scandinavians in Queensland, and Italians in northern New South Wales and Griffith, many Australians outside the metropolitan areas still lack much direct experience of living, working, and studying with people from other cultures. On the other hand, some migrant groups have intermarried more than others, with more recent migrant groups such as Indo-Chinese and some Lebanese having had little time to do so, while some more long-term minorities such as Greeks, Italians, and those from the former Yugoslavia have displayed relatively low rates of inter-marriage. Equally diverse are patterns of English language usage at home (Clyne, 2005; Cruickshank, 2003).

4 Implications for education

The far-reaching changes in Australian society sketched above have not left education untouched, and illustrate the complex role of education in social change. While education is often a key agent of change, including by fostering values of multiculturalism among the young in recent decades, it is not usually an initiator of change. More commonly, education responds to changes elsewhere in society, sometimes slowly and incompletely, with vestiges of older values, and showing signs of institutional inertia. Education is not alone in this regard, being an instance of what was termed social lag by the American sociologist William Ogburn (1923, 1964). He argued that social change is often asynchronous, with some parts of society changing more rapidly than others. Has Australian education always kept pace with other dimensions of social change, in particularly the increasing levels of ethnic diversity?

Nineteenth century education in Australia was no less susceptible to the prevailing ideologies of race and religion than other aspects of society. Indeed, religion and racism were often mixed. Even the (largely Irish) Catholics, who represented a significant element of the Australian populace, were commonly seen as different, and discrimination was common. How much more so for Chinese and Indians in Australia, who were not merely non-Christians, but who were also non-Caucasian? Christianity itself was not unsullied by racist doctrines (Evans et al., 1975, p. 102), while newspapers, magazines, and anthropological journals commonly paraded spurious assumptions about the characters and physical appearances of non-whites (Evans et al., 1975, p. 6; De Lepervanche, 1980, p. 28; Welch, 1996b, pp. 28–33, 107).

While Aboriginal Australians suffered most from such assumptions, Asian settlers also suffered. The rising tide of evolutionary theory, epitomised in the publication of Charles Darwin's famous *On the Origin of Species* in 1859, was popularly held to give scientific support to the view that a racial hierarchy existed, with Aboriginal Australians at the base, and white European society at the apex. Asian races fell somewhere in between, it was commonly held. Hence, with very few exceptions, little or no provision was made in schools for the cultures of Aboriginal children. A severe and unyielding mix of science, Christianity, and capitalism was the basis for the white curriculum, to which all others were also subjected. As indicated above, many of the colonies had passed legislation severely restricting Asian immigration in the 1880s, and since Indians and Chinese were prohibited from settling in Australia, and Asian men were prohibited from bringing their wives and children with them, appropriate schooling for them was largely irrelevant. Even for those 'Asiatic' women who did give birth, federal legislation was soon passed, in 1912, that specifically denied them the Commonwealth maternity bonus, of £5, for every live birth (Tavan, 2005, p. 8).

5   The cultures of Australian education

The above sketch shows that, for the entire period since the British colonised Australia at the end of the eighteenth century, Australia has had significant numbers of settlers from key non-UK sources. At the onset of the new millennium, this diversity is even more evident. But what forms of education have been provided, and what has been the experience of migrant Australians in education? The following two sketches, of the education of Muslim Australians and of highly skilled Chinese migrants, illustrate dimensions of the changing face of education and immigration.

Muslim Australians and education

Like Jews, Christians, and Buddhists, Muslims stem from many cultures. But in the story of Islam in Australia, the Afghan and Lebanese communities figure strongly. In each case, acceptance has not been automatic, nor has appropriate education always been forthcoming.

Chinese settlers bore the brunt of anti-Asian sentiment in the nineteenth century, perhaps because they were more numerous (the New South Wales census of 1891 revealed that there were 10,120 Buddhists, for example, who were mainly Chinese). But Muslim settlers were often tarred with the same brush. The same New South Wales census revealed that there were a mere 528 Muslims—mainly Afghans. Overall numbers in Australia in 1891 confirmed this disparity: Buddhists numbered 22,717, as compared with an estimated 3000 Muslims, who were mostly employed as camel drivers; for example, in the 1870s on the construction of the Adelaide to Darwin telegraph line. The Afghan camel drivers met with discrimination and occasional violence, including from trade unions of (white) carriers, who refused to allow them to join and, in 1879, passed a motion to disallow Asian immigration at the first International Trade Union Congress, held in Sydney in 1879 (Kabir, 2004). Just as Chinese workers were pilloried as 'filth-eating and disgusting Tartars, idolatrous pagans, yellow and beastly strangers, cut-throats and barbarians', so too Afghans were described, with their camels, as 'the filthiest lot' and 'saddle-coloured aliens' (Kabir, 2004, pp. 52–4). Such sentiments were not merely licensed by pseudo-scientific ethnographies, and early anthropologies, including practices such as craniometry, but were widely believed by the wider population, and not merely by Australian residents. With few exceptions, whites everywhere held similar views.

Afghans in Australia, as elsewhere, followed Islamic practice, such as offering prayers (*salat*) five times daily, fasting (*sawm*), following the *Halal* dietary code, and acts of charity (*zakat*). Such practices were enough to single them out for unwanted and unwarranted attention as 'Asiatics', as evident in the following extract from a rural Western Australia newspaper of the time:

> We calmly arise to protest in language simple and unadorned against the opening of our doors to aliens of Asiatic extraction … We see the shadow of a great evil at our doors at the presence of a large number of Afghans upon this field. Afghans are not all bad men … but their presence here is an infringement of the spirit of the Act passed by Parliament prohibiting Asiatics flocking into our fields to compete with the men of our own race and blood (*Coolgardie Miner*, 1894, cited Kabir, 2004, p. 51.)

Many Afghans were forced to live on the margins of society, both figuratively and literally, occupying Ghantowns on the fringes of small villages and towns. The passage of the *Immigration Restriction Act 1901* effectively limited the number of

Afghans to several hundred (although then, as now, a few hardy souls probably continued to enter illegally), while agitation by whites against the camel industry was common in colonies such as South Australia and New South Wales. This was despite the importance of Afghans and their camels to both the pastoral and mining industries, especially in rural and regional areas. Common charges (also used against Chinese and Aborigines at the time) of criminality, and importing diseases such as syphilis, led one Afghan to respond in 1903: ' If Afghans in some few cases suffer, they have to thank your people for it'. The charge of criminality provoked the following retort:

> Your so-called authorities are as much prejudiced against the Afghans and as ignorant of their general habits and true character as yourself … Can anyone guarantee that the percentage of white criminals is always lower than that of the Afghan law-breakers in proportion to their population? No; certainly not. Your people are quite blind to their own faults when they condemn others' (Musakhan, Letter to the Editor, *Barrier Truth*, 1903, cited Kabir, 2004, p. 60).

The imposition of camel taxes in Western Australia, and other discriminatory measures, only added to the woes of Afghans, some of whom formed associations and threatened to withdraw their labour, until the offensive regulations were withdrawn. Some Afghan males did marry, usually Aboriginal women or Europeans 'of the lowest socio-economic levels' (Kabir, 2004, p. 65), but little is known of the education of their children. Only in larger population centres, such as Broken Hill and Marree (in South Australia), were mosques of significance established, and Imams available, for teaching purposes. The mobile lifestyle of the camel-drivers also made stable education for their children more difficult. The formalisation of a discriminatory immigration policy in 1901 meant that many Afghans were returned to their homeland, while the onset of the car also made camel driving less viable. (See also Theobald, 2001.)

Lebanese migrants date from the 1880s, in the aftermath of the gold rushes. Mainly Maronite Christians, immigration patterns were often based on specific villages in Lebanon, with an individual, often the father, being the first to immigrate, and the immediate and extended family thereafter. Sydney contains by far the largest Lebanese community, with 114,491 registered at the 2001 Census. Currently, of those born in Lebanon, almost half are *Maronite* Christian, while 20 per cent are *Sunni* Muslim and a further 16 per cent are *Shia* Muslim (Cruickshank, 2003, p. 56). Many identify principally in terms of religion, or village, rather than language (see also Asmar, 2001, p. 149). Codes of honour and patriarchy are significant traditional cultural motifs, but have often changed to a degree after settling in Australia (as has occurred elsewhere). Nonetheless, according to some, 'There are different rules for boys and girls, especially when it comes to discipline.

Anyone who denies this is kidding themselves' (Jamal & Chandab, 2005; see also *SMH*, 2005, 3 December). The Arab-Israeli wars of 1967 and 1973 provoked further immigration, but levels of literacy (including in Arabic), education, and qualifications remain low for many, as do employment and income levels. Most speak Arabic at home, and rates of language shift to English are low, often under 10 per cent. This can cause difficulties, including of communication, between older and younger generations. The overall picture remains one of disadvantage for many, but particularly for Muslim Lebanese, including its youth. As evident in Table 7.2 above, the biggest Arabic-speaking community, by far, remains in Sydney.

In the post-Second World War era, Muslim communities expanded, with the introduction of an immigration treaty with Turkey in 1967 resulting in the arrival of some 10,000 Turkish settlers. Islamic communities in Melbourne and Sydney established 'weekend schools', where their children could be instructed in the tenets of Islam, learn the Koran (in Arabic), and perhaps also learn the language of their parents (Arabic, Urdu, Pashto, Turkish, Farsi, or other). As was not uncommon among other migrant groups of the time, qualified teachers were very scarce, and few parents had sufficient knowledge to act as effective teachers. In this context, sending children for a few hours to the local mosque, or to the local school, on Saturday or Sunday, was usually the most that could be done (Saeed, 2003, pp. 149–50). Studies of Turkish young people showed that levels of qualification were well below that of the overall Australian population, while 'the disparity for men and women was greater than for the general population' (Inglis, Elley & Manderson, 1992, p. 59). As had occurred with earlier migration communities, non-Anglo educational qualifications were often not accepted in the Australian system (Iredale, 1997). The third wave of Lebanese migrants to Australia, who came during and after Lebanon's disastrous civil war, were predominantly Muslim, forming almost 40 per cent of all Lebanese-born migrants, and 13.3 per cent of all Muslims (Humphrey, 2001, p. 564).

Given the larger numbers of Lebanese and other Islamic migrants, Islamic education has understandably grown. The growth of Arabic speakers has been commensurate, from 50,000 in 1976, to 120,000 in 1986, and 163,000 in 1991. Of these, 40 per cent are Australian-born, while another 40 per cent are Lebanese-born (Cruickshank, 2003, p. 54). Community schools are currently responsible for the teaching of about 50,000 students of Arabic language, but retention rates are poor, while in primary and secondary schools only a small proportion of Arabic speakers learn their language. Teachers of Arabic are often untrained as language teachers, and some have 'uncertain proficiency in MSA (Modern Standard Arabic)' (Cruickshank, 2003, p. 66). Currently, there are Islamic schools in almost all states with a total of perhaps 12,000 to 15,000 enrolments (Saeed,

2003, p. 151). As can be seen from Table 7.7 below, the two decades of the 1980s and 1990s were when most of the schools were established, reflecting the patterns of migration from Lebanon and neighbouring countries, as well as from other regions. By 1986, there were more than 109,000 Muslims in Australia, from the Middle East, Cyprus, Yugoslavia, Malaysia, Indonesia, Egypt, Fiji, Pakistan, and Bangladesh (Kabir, 2004, p. 152). Asmar cites 200,805 individuals who identified themselves as Muslim in the 1996 Census (Asmar, 2001, p. 140). The profound disruptions to employment and education experienced during the Lebanese Civil War by many third-wave migrants to Australia meant that, according to the 1986 census, although a higher per cent of Muslims possessed higher degrees than the general Australian populace, and almost as many had Bachelors degrees, far fewer held vocational qualifications than the Australian population (Kabir, 2004, p. 168). Young Turkish Australians were generally less well educated than the overall Australian population (Kabir, 2004, p. 172), although significant progress had been made compared to a decade or two earlier. By the 1996 census, Muslim Australians were shown to be as educated as the Australian-born population, and in the categories of Bachelor and higher degrees, more so (Kabir, 2004, p. 273). Overall, at least 10,498 Muslim students were reported as studying at Australian universities in the 1996 census, yielding a rate of attendance higher than that for the general population. (It should be noted, however, that some of these Muslim students were likely to have been international students.) Nonetheless, the rate of higher education participation is very differential: some have pointed to a significant polarisation among Lebanon-born in Australia, with some gaining the higher educational qualifications needed to access professional and managerial jobs, 'while others experience inter-generational unemployment and poverty' (Batrouney, 2001, p. 568).

The same census showed that the unemployment rate for Muslims was 25 per cent, relative to 9 per cent for Australia-born and the total population (Kabir, 2004, p. 272), a disparity that persists in parts of both Melbourne and Sydney. This rate was also significantly higher than that of their Christian Middle East–born counterparts (Kabir, 2004, p. 275; see also Humphreys, 1998). Language issues were partly to blame for higher levels of unemployment: 'Some Arabic-speaking children dropped out of school early, especially if they had an inadequate command of English … for them employment would be difficult. Some also left school because they could not relate to the school's dominant culture' (Kabir, 2004, p. 275).

The schools vary greatly in size, with King Khalid Islamic College in Melbourne and Malek Fahd Islamic School in Sydney being among the largest, with enrolments of over 1000 each. Many schools enrol both primary and secondary

Table 7.7   Islamic schools in Australia by state, suburb, and year of foundation

Name of School	State	Suburb	Founded in
Al Noori Muslim Primary	NSW	Greenacre	1983
Arkana College	NSW	Beverly Hills	1986
Malek Fahd Islamic School	NSW	Greenacre	1989
Noor al Houda Islamic College (Girls)	NSW	Condell Park	1995
Sule College	NSW	Prestons	1996
Al-Amanah College	NSW	Bankstown	1997
King Abdul Aziz College	NSW	Rooty Hill	1997
Risalah Islamic College	NSW	Lakemba	1997
Al-Zahra College	NSW	Arncliffe	1998
Al-Faisal College	NSW	Auburn	1998
King Khalid Islamic College of Victoria	VIC	Coburg	1983
Islamic Schools of Victoria (Werribee College)	VIC	Hoppers Crossing	1986
Minaret College	VIC	Springvale	1993
Islamic College	VIC	Broadmeadows	1995
Darul Uloom Islamic College	VIC	Fawkner	1997
Isik College	VIC	Broadmeadows	1997
East Preston Islamic College	VIC	Preston	1998
Australian Islamic College	WA	Dianella	1986
Australian Islamic College	WA	Thornleigh	1990
Al Hidayah Islamic School Inc	WA	Bentley	1994
Australian Islamic College	WA	Kewdale	2000
Islamic College	SA	Croydon	1998
Islamic School of Brisbane	QLD	Karawatha	1995

Source: Saeed, 2003

students, and although many were able to obtain support for their establishment from both local Islamic communities, and from overseas sources, all now depend heavily on government support. This is no different from other religious schools, such as Christian, or Jewish: 'In most cases, around 80 per cent of the funding for the running of the school comes from the government. Fees vary from as low as $600 to around $2000 per annum' (Saeed, 2003, p. 150). Some Islamic schools have already become very successful in the high-stakes Year 12 results race, which determines not merely university entry, but also functions as a powerful recruitment tool for parents deciding which school to choose for their children. (For more on this, see chapter 9, on school choice.) Malek Fahd, in Sydney's western suburb of Greenacre, for example, has been unapologetic about weeding out less academic students, whom it feels are less likely to bring it credit by gaining high HSC scores in the increasingly competitive and status-ridden New South Wales school system (*SMH*, 2004, 7 October). Largely as a result, it was ranked within the top twenty-four schools across the state, when the New South Wales HSC results were announced in late 2005. KKIC and the Australian Islamic College in Perth are also very successful, having each produced students rated among the best in the state. Other schools are located in poorer suburbs, such as Broadmeadows in Melbourne's north, and working-class areas of Sydney, and thus qualify for heavy subsidies from government. Overall performance of the sector varies greatly.

As for all schools, curriculum is governed by state Education Departments and boards of studies. With the exception of religious teachers, who are generally required to be fellow Muslims, 'the teaching staff and curriculum are much like other public schools' (Saeed, 2003, p. 155), although perhaps more diverse, stemming from the Middle East, South-East Asia, and Turkey among others. Just as with other faith-based schools whether Coptic, Catholic, or Lutheran, religious instruction is emphasised—several hours a week are devoted to the study of Islam, including midday prayers (*Zuhr*) and Friday prayers (*Jum'ah*). But, as with other minorities, finding qualified teachers can be a problem, while difficulties are also experienced with textbooks for religious education, which are almost always imported and hence often do not reflect the Australian context adequately (Saeed, 2003, p. 154). Attention is also paid to the observance of key religious festivals, while food supplied at the school must conform to halal standards. Modesty is deemed important, hence Islamic dress codes dictate long pants for boys (shorts are not thought proper), and long-sleeved blouses, and slacks or long skirts, for girls. Headdresses are common. Some schools are mixed, others single-sex.

Even before the first Gulf War (1991) instances of 'name-calling, ridicule, harassment and physical threats' against Muslim students were reported (Kabir, 2004, pp. 175–6). Incidents of such harassment only increased in the aftermath of the war, especially against Muslim women, some of whom were often more conspicuous due to wearing the *hijab*. One New South Wales parliamentarian, the conservative Christian Fred Nile, even called for Muslim women to be banned from wearing the *chador* in public (Kabir, 2004, p. 283), as have one or two other federal parliamentarians since. There are also charges by some who 'see Islamic schools as divisive, preventing full participation of their female students in Australian society' (Saeed, 2003, p. 151). Interestingly, much the same critique was made of schooling for Greek girls in Australia, as late as the 1970s and 1980s (Welch, 1996b, pp. 126–8; Strintzos, 1984). Clearly, there are different gender regimes within branches of Islam, including its educational institutions. Some recent scholars have attempted to disinter a form of Islam that is less patriarchal (Barlas, 2002).

An Islamic teacher (Imam)

Sheik Fehmi Naji al-Imam migrated to Melbourne from Lebanon in 1951, at the age of 23. An active member of Melbourne's Islamic community, he was instrumental in establishing its first Islamic Society in 1957, the same year in which he organised the first Islamic Weekend School. Initial enrolments numbered 15, and the curriculum consisted of the Koran and Arabic language. Gathering donations from the local community, as well as from overseas, he went on to establish a mosque and Islamic centre in Preston, where he remained Imam for the next 25 years. Although now in his late 70s he remains active, including as a religious teacher at the mosque, and with refugee groups (From Saeed, 2003).

Although not all Muslim women choose to wear the *hijab*, calls to ban the headdress reflect either ignorance of the importance of wearing the *hijab* for some Muslim women's sense of identity (Barlas, 2002; Bennett, 2004; see also Internet sources listed at the end of the chapter), or a rejection of cultural difference. Such attitudes only add to the sense that some Muslim Australians have, that they are singled out for discriminatory treatment, and add to the alienation that some young Muslims have voiced.

Certainly, Muslim Australians confront a range of complex problems. The social and economic problems evident in suburbs such as Sydney's Bankstown and Lakemba, for example, are multi-faceted and complex, but are clearly related both to unemployment and low levels of education. (As chapter 1 in this book makes clear, the two increasingly go hand-in-hand, especially in a 'knowledge economy' era, when credentialism is rife.)

Investigations in 2005 confirmed that literacy levels especially among young Islamic males are still well below average, a fact that of itself denies them access to many job opportunities: 'Literacy … is a huge issue. And with that comes low or no qualifications and high levels of unemployment' (*SMH*, 2005, 19 December). Analysis of the 2001 Census data for males aged between 15 and, 24, living in Bankstown and Lakemba and who identified themselves as Islamic, pointed to 'a pattern of underachievement among young Islamic men' (*SMH*, 2005, 19 December):

Among 15–24 year olds, only 39 per cent of Islamic males in Bankstown said they had reached year 12 (some were still at school). But 46.5 per cent of Islamic females and 45.4 per cent of males across Sydney said year 12. Unemployment among this group was higher at 16.3 per cent in Bankstown and 15.4 per cent in Lakemba compared with 7.7% for young men across Sydney. Employment (many are still in education at this age) was also significantly lower, at 35 per cent in Lakemba compared with 54 per cent of young men across Sydney. This data does not bode well for this group of young men, following in the footsteps of other waves of migrants, who worked hard, whose children went on to uni., started their own businesses and prospered. Iemma [the Premier of NSW] is testament to that story, but he cannot assume it will be repeated this time. The NSW government needs to address how the education system is failing this group of boys, because illiteracy, poverty and unemployment are surefire ways to produce angry young men (*SMH*, 2005, 19 December).

These figures also need to be seen in the context of average rates of Year 12 completion, in New South Wales and nationally, currently at 70 per cent or higher. What they confirm is that unemployment rates for young Islamic men in Bankstown and Lakemba are around twice that of the average for young males in Sydney, while Year 12 completion rates are less than two-thirds of the average for New South Wales, or nationally. These are part of a worrying pattern of a 'lack of understanding of community and authority' (*SMH*, 2005, 19 December) among a small section of the Muslim community, mostly males, leading to feelings of anger, frustration, and alienation: 'They feel they don't owe any allegiances to anyone' (*SMH*, 2005, 19 December). These problems, when allied to racism in the wider society, particularly against Muslims (Collins et al., 2000; Poynting et al., 2004), fuel an explosive mix of alienation on the part of some young Muslims, and resentment on the part of some white Australians.

6   Highly skilled migrants—recent Chinese migration and education patterns

But there are also other migration and settlement patterns, some of which involve attracting highly skilled migrants. As was indicated above, patterns of Australian migration have shifted substantially in recent decades, from a concentration on filling labouring and manufacturing jobs, to those with high levels of skill, and appropriate work experience, who now form around half of all settlers, annually (Table 7.8).

Over much the same period, the policy of non-discriminatory migration has led to a significant increase in the numbers and proportions of Asian migrants to Australia. Table 7.8 shows that, while family-reunion visas became a smaller proportion of the total over the period, the skilled visa category has grown significantly, as a proportion of the total intake. The ongoing loss of expensive, high-skilled labour from the Asia-Pacific region to Australia is contributing to charges of 'brain drain' from some of Australia's neighbours, although as

Table 7.8 Family and Skilled Migrant totals, 1990–91 & 2003–04

Eligibility Category	1990–91 Total	1990–91 %	1996–97 Total	1996–97 %	2003–04 Total	2003–04 %
Family	53,934	44.3	36,490	42.6	29,548	26.6
Skilled	48,421	39.8	19,697	22.9	51,529	46.8
Gross annual intake	121,690		85,752		110,000	

Source: Parliamentary Library, 2005; Jupp, 2002

is evident from the case study below, 'brain circulation' is sometimes a better descriptor, as the loss to developing countries is not always permanent, and even when it does result in more permanent resettlement, modern communications technology allows sophisticated trans-national networks to be built up and sustained (Welch & Zhang, 2005).

One of the more prominent groups to have been part of these changes has been that of China-born migrants, who in 2004 totalled 181,987, making them the third-largest overseas-born group in the country, and the largest Asia-born (Hugo, 2005b). While, as we saw above, earlier generations of Chinese settlers were more likely to have been engaged in small business, gold-prospecting, and the like, the current pattern is for highly qualified China-born to migrate, often after initially studying at an Australian university. Currently, skilled migrants make up more than half of the total of the China-born settler intake, annually (Hugo, 2005b), while tens of thousands of Chinese students are now enrolled at Australian universities. Overall, Australia's university system is highly internationalised, with more than one in five of all enrolments being international (Welch, 2002).

A significant proportion of international students at Australian universities now go on to apply for Permanent Residence (the first step towards Australian citizenship). Chinese students are prominent among such cases, accounting for almost 20 per cent of the total in 2004–05. Long-term migrants from China are very highly skilled (Hugo, 2005b), with almost 80 per cent falling into the top three occupational categories (manager/admin; professional; associate professional). Significant numbers of Chinese migrants have moved to take up posts at Australian universities in recent years, as either lecturers and tutors, or researchers. This is only likely to increase, for a range of reasons. Firstly, as in other developed nations, the Australian academic profession is ageing, which means that over the next decade or so, many will retire (around 20 per cent of Australian academics are aged 55 or over). On the other hand, the Chinese university system is huge, producing over 2 million graduates each year. Many Chinese students dream of

Zheng He

Zheng He was born in the southern province of Fujien, China in the early 1960s. Coming from an academic family was enough, during the Cultural Revolution, for his father to be sent to the countryside, where the family endured years of painful privation. Despite these difficulties, all three children in the family worked hard to educate themselves. Zheng He gained his BA and MA in China, then worked for years in a local hospital. Keen to study further, he went to Hong Kong, and finally Melbourne to gain his PhD. After graduating some years ago, he gained an academic post at an Australian university, and has since moved to another. His sister works in Hong Kong, and his brother in California. He maintains strong connections with China, visiting to teach or research each year, but is sometimes frustrated that his efforts to build relationships with colleagues there do not always succeed. When in China, he is welcomed, but no longer accepted as a full Chinese. In Australia, too, he also sometimes feels not entirely accepted.

studying abroad, both because they want to take advantage of the many strong, research-oriented departments and universities that exist in the more developed Western nations, and because they want to experience living abroad. Indeed, it has long been the case that some of China's best and brightest study abroad, of whom only a minority return, commonly only around 20 per cent (Welch & Zhang, 2005). Overall, since 1978 (when China opened up again, after the decade of isolation of the Cultural Revolution), some 580,000 Chinese students studied abroad, but only 160,000 have returned (Zweig & Fung, 2004).

A common pattern is for such individuals to gain at least their Bachelor's degree, and perhaps their Masters degree in China, but to pursue a PhD in Australia, and secure their academic job either during or after their doctoral degree. Several hundred China-born academic staff now work as tutors or lecturers, or occupy research-only positions. Pursuing doctoral qualifications in another language, and working in another culture is difficult. However, being bilingual and knowledgeable in both cultures affords opportunities to collaborate with colleagues in China, or in other parts of the Chinese-speaking world (Taiwan, Singapore, or Hong Kong), or with the substantial Chinese knowledge diaspora in Europe and North America (Welch & Zhang, 2005). This important knowledge network often brings invitations to teach in China, or engage in research collaboration, but can bring its own frustrations when attempts to build bridges and establish joint projects do not always succeed. Despite this, the desire to maintain and build up relations with colleagues in China remains strong, and it is common for such individuals to teach in China regularly, on behalf of their Australian university, and to conduct joint research with Chinese colleagues. Good quality PhD students from China may also be sought out. Negotiating different cultural expectations, however, can be problematic—when in China, food and sometimes accommodation are often provided to guests, but when Chinese colleagues visit Australian universities, such hospitality is mostly paid for personally, by the Australian host. This can be quite costly. Reports of discriminatory or racist attitudes and behaviour on the part of local students, colleagues, or administrators within universities and government agencies, have also been reported by some Chinese-Australian academics (as also in Canada and the USA), the large majority of whom are Australian citizens, have lived in the country for more than 10 years, and often have family in Australia.

The trend towards highly skilled migration adds another dimension to older understandings of multiculturalism in Australian education, which have often been based on less highly skilled migration patterns. There is no doubt that such knowledge diasporas will become more important in the coming years, particularly for those who can teach in English. Australia's developing relations with Asia gives added impetus to the trend towards highly skilled migration, as does the age structure of the Australian academic profession, and ongoing skills shortages in other key professions such as nursing, teaching, and engineering.

7   Barriers to effective multiculturalism in education

While Australia is rightly regarded as a successful example of a modern, multicultural nation, and has had multicultural education policies for some 30 years, this is no cause for complacency, nor does it mitigate racist legacies, such as the events at Cronulla in late 2005 demonstrated. What are the barriers to more effective multicultural education?

Some have been pointed to above and in earlier literature (Welch, 1996b, pp. 105–131; Kalantzis, 1990). Difficulties in securing good-quality teachers of community languages, and appropriate curriculum resources, are not unique to contemporary Muslim communities, but were reported by supporters of Greek (and other community) schools and languages in the 1970s. Textbooks in the humanities and social sciences have improved, so as to be more culturally inclusive, but more needs to be done on this front also. School participation rates of several of the more successful migrant communities, notably East and some South-East Asian, Greek, and Jewish, have now surpassed that of the overall population, but other immigrant communities (such as Maltese, Arabic, Turkish, and Pacific Islander) have been less successful (Cruickshank, 2003):

The Lebanese have been left behind compared with other groups such as the Chinese, Vietnamese, Greeks and Jews. Their level of education and therefore their level of employment and employability are lower than average … So there is a lot of resentment there (Jupp, 2005).

This is made all the worse by the cutbacks to migrant English programs, which have been savaged for more than 20 years (Welch, 1996b). The demise of the Adult Migrant English Service, and its replacement by private providers, has withdrawn from public service one of the key means to effective citizenship in Australia. The closing or mainstreaming of specialist agencies such as the Australian Institute for Multicultural Affairs and the Bureau for Immigration and Population Research further softened the focus on migration and resettlement, while cutbacks to public schooling systems in all states have effectively reduced specialist services such as English-language support programs for NESB students. Services to refugee children, too, are stretched. The hidden curriculum still often perpetuates monocultural values and practices, while school organisation could often still do more to respect and promote difference. Assessment procedures, too, need to be re-examined to see whether a variety of cultural responses are considered legitimate, or legacies of monocultural practices persist.

A good start would be to give more support to the teaching of languages. The growing sense of English as a global language has only weakened further the already lamentable failure of native English language speakers to study other languages, while community languages still languish in the school curriculum. As Clyne argues, although languages are designated a Key Learning Area (KLA) within the school curriculum, implementation often falls far short of ideal, and in some cases students are advised to take higher levels of English, rather than persist with a community language. The hidden curriculum of the school values such subjects as mathematics, the sciences, and English well above that of languages. Yet well beyond the economic benefits that are usually cited in an economically rational era as the defence for learning a language, there is the important move away from what has been termed a monolingual mindset. Learning another language provides another window onto the world, with all the benefits of increased flexibility and understanding that goes with it. Australia has a rich mix of languages and cultures, which needs work to be preserved, yet too often children grow up without the benefit of their parents' language, which cuts them off from that culture, and often results in barriers being erected between parents and children. As a recent Governor General lamented:

The thing that distresses me most is how little most children and grandchildren of overseas-born Australians retain of the cultures and languages of their lands of origin. The loss of ancestral languages is grievous for the individual and the nation. We should be a nation of great linguists (Clyne, 2005, p. 65).

But the longstanding failure of many Australians to learn languages other than English (LOTE) is but a proxy for the wider problems of understanding cultural difference. The German theorist Hans-Georg Gadamer (1975; see also Snodgrass, 1992; Welch, 1993) has provided a typology of relations between self and other, which, if extended to the arena of intercultural relations, can offer a means of analysing different modes (see below).

Multiculturalism can also not flourish in education if children do not mix with those of other cultures, and there are some worrying signs that show that certain schools are becoming more culturally concentrated, with a corresponding reduction in the opportunity to mix on a daily basis with those from cultures that are significantly different. For example, some schools in Sydney have now become heavily peopled with students of Arabic background, with a major decline in students of English language background. In high schools such as Bossley Park, Condell Park, Chester Hill, Beverly Hills Girls, Moorefield Girls', and Birrong Girls' (and Boys'), numbers of Arabic background pupils have grown by close to 300 per cent or more, over the decade 1990–2001, and this has been paralleled by, in most cases, a significant decline in English language background pupils (Cruickshank, 2003, p. 48).

8   Ourselves and the 'other'—types of intercultural relations

From our earliest months of life, we come to appreciate that we are not alone in the world, and hence we learn to understand the 'other'—first our immediate family, then a widening network of families, friends, and acquaintances. Schooling further widens this circle of 'others'. But not all these relations are built on equality and reciprocity. Inevitably, our parents are some of the more powerful 'others' in the first years of our life, and often speak for us, and tell us what to do. In large part, they help shape our world, hopefully in ways that help us grow in understanding and enlarge our sympathies. But how do grown-ups relate to each other, including in intercultural settings?

Much thought has been given to such questions by social theorists. The case studies and analysis above have provided important insights into the developing nature of Australian multiculturalism in Australian education. But how can progress towards this goal be measured? Are there frameworks of understanding that allow us to establish benchmarks?

The following typology of relations between I and Thou (self and other), by the German theorist Hans-Georg Gadamer, may be one useful way to think about this issue, particularly if we extend his analysis into the world of intercultural relations.

For real understanding to occur, Gadamer argued, other cultures must not simply be seen as objects, to be 'known', controlled, and manipulated. This form of interest in control corresponds to the first of Gadamer's 'I–Thou' relationships that can characterise an attempt to know or understand.

In this first type of relationship, one consciously avoids any presuppositions in regard to the 'other', in order to discover its essence: 'what it contains' (1986, p. 322). The 'other' in this sense is seen as an impersonal object, in just the same manner as a scientist views an object of experimentation (say; an insect under a microscope). A proper scientist, according to this view, neither has, nor should have, any feelings for the insect she studies so carefully under the microscope. The spurious claims to racial science that pervaded nineteenth century anthropology, and did so much violence to both Aboriginal cultures, and pilloried Chinese and Afghan minorities in this country, can be seen as examples of this type of inter-cultural relation. Clearly such an approach leaves no room for the expression of the 'other' culture in its own terms. In this, a supposedly scientific or objective attitude takes precedence, as part of a belief in the power of method and a general attempt to explain the world in technical, and preferably lawlike, terms. This is the realm of pure theory (usually based on a form of science derived from mathematics or physics) in which morality plays no role. The other culture is simply objectified.

The second form of relationship begins to acknowledge the other (Thou) as an entity, or person, but only in a rather limited sense whereby the 'I' still feels in a superior position. In this second form of relationship, for example, the 'I' still feels able to express the feelings or thoughts of the 'Thou' better than they might do themselves:

> One claims to express the other's claim and even to understand the other better than the other understands himself. In this way the 'Thou' loses the immediacy with which it makes its claim. It is understood, but this means that it is anticipated and intercepted reflectively from the standpoint of the other person (Gadamer, 1986, p. 322).

In cultural terms this amounts to the student of another culture putting words into its mouth; that is, taking licence to speak on behalf of another. The claim to understand can operate here as a means to distance oneself from the claim of the other. It can also clearly operate as a form of control. Not only is the culture interpreted through one's own terms, but mutuality and reciprocity are absent— the 'other' is still unable to speak for themselves. The 'I' undergoes no change as a result of this interaction and does not gain any new perspective on his/her own culture. The 'give—and take of true dialogue' is absent (Snodgrass, 1992, p. 37). This second type of intercultural relationship can reasonably be seen to have characterised the assimilationist era in Australian society, including its education system, when migrants were simply expected to shed their culture, rather like an overcoat that could be discarded, and assume the (white, Anglo) culture of the mainstream in the new country. The same assumptions informed curriculum, textbooks, teacher training, and school organisation.

The final form of relationship is by far the most reciprocal, indeed characterised by what Gadamer terms a 'fusion of horizons' (Gadamer, 1986, pp. 273, 337; Bernstein, 1983, pp. 143–4). Just as we cannot form the horizon of the present without the past, so too does our understanding of another culture begin from an understanding of our own. But this final form of intercultural relation is based on an open-ended dialogue, where neither party is in control. This is where we 'risk and test our own prejudices' (Bernstein, 1983, p. 144). In this form of interaction, there are no privileged epistemological or cultural positions.

Here, Gadamer argues, the 'I' must go beyond the world of his/her taken-for-granted cultural and epistemic realities, and proceed with genuine openness and respect, to engage with the Lifeworld (*Lebenswelt*) of the other ('Thou'). This is in many senses similar to the way another German social theorist, Jürgen Habermas, describes the 'ideal speech situation', a mode of communication that excludes domination of one party over another (Habermas, 1971, 1976, 1981, 1990; Thompson & Held, 1982; Hesse, 1976).

> The goal of coming to an understanding is to bring about an agreement that terminates in the intersubjective mutuality of reciprocal understanding, shared knowledge, mutual trust, and accord with one another. Agreement is based on recognition of the corresponding validity claims of comprehensibility, truth, truthfulness [or sincerity], and rightness (Habermas, 1979, p. 3).

In this final form of relationship between self and other, the interest is in freedom from coercion, in egalitarian social relations. Mutual recognition is thus seen as the basis for human communication, but this is understood in relation to a critical conception of society. The question that remains for a critical social science is still that of what kinds of social, political, and economic conditions need to be realised in order to sustain an open society, without one group dominating, or speaking for, another.

The implications for cultural interaction, and the connections between ethnicity, class and culture, can be clearly derived from all three modes of cultural interaction. The first mode objectifies another culture, and sees any notion of sympathy for the 'other' as misleading and inappropriate. By still speaking for the 'Other' and interpreting their thoughts, feelings, and aspirations for them, the second mode also fails to provide a base for mutual, reciprocal relations between cultures, whether of class, gender, or ethnic groups. The third model, however, meets both these objections. For the model of an ideal speech situation is one in which neither party has an interest in anything other than the reaching of agreement. This occurs via an open dialogue, in which each protagonist accepts that their understanding of the other is open and changeable. It resists, however, situating that dialogue within current relations of power in society, which have the capacity to deform open dialogue.

Even with its widespread support, can multiculturalism in Australian education fulfil such lofty ambitions? Not on its own, certainly, but it has an important role to play. And the notion of fusion of horizons, or the ideal speech situation, each provides a useful empirical and ethical benchmark, against which to measure programs and policies. Given such a benchmark, the persistence of masculinist cultures among some Anglo and non-Anglo Australians; racism, including in our schools (*SMH*, 2005, 23 December); efforts by the federal government in recent years to demonise asylum seekers, and to create a climate of fear regarding the other (Marr & Wilkinson, 2004); populist law and order ('zero tolerance') campaigns by state politicians that result in higher rates of imprisonment without addressing the root of the problem; and sensationalist reporting of both international and domestic affairs (*Australian*, 2005, 14, 17 December; *SMH*, 2005, 21 December) that has the effect of stereotyping Muslims (Poynting et al., 2004) are a poor base for mutual intercultural relations, including in education.

Focus questions

1 How has Australia's history of migration helped to shape contemporary Australia? How has the pattern of migration to this country changed?

2 How far should ethnic groups be able to control their own schools and curriculum? What is the role of ethnic schools in a diverse, democratic society?

3 What are the main barriers to effective multicultural education, and how do these relate to the overall character and structure of Australian society?

4 What are the principal features of the multicultural education policy in your state? How well is it known and understood, and how well implemented is it at school level?

5 How should we understand 'difference' in education, and how do we relate to the 'other'? What can you do in the classroom context to counter racism and discriminatory treatment?

Further reading

Asmar, C. (2001).'Muslim students in Australian universities'. In A. Saeed & S. Abkarzadeh (eds), *Muslim Communities in Australia*. Sydney: UNSW Press.

Hugo, G. (2005).'Australia's international migration transformed.' *Australian Mosaic, 9*(1).

Iredale, R. (1997). *Skills Transfer*. Wollongong: Wollongong University Press.

Jamal, N. & Chandab, T. (2005). *The Glory Garage. Growing up Lebanese Muslim in Australia*. Sydney: Allen & Unwin.

Jupp, J. (2001). *The Australian People. An Encyclopedia of the Nation, its Peoples and their Origins*. Cambridge: Cambridge University Press.

Kalantzis, M. (1990). *Cultures of Schooling*. London: Falmer.

Lopez, M. (2000). *The Origins of Multiculturalism in Australian Politics*. Melbourne: Melbourne University Press.

Saeed, A. (2003). *Islam in Australia*. Sydney: Allen & Unwin.

Welch, A. (1996).'The politics of cultural interaction: multicultural education in Australia'. In A. Welch (ed.), *Australian Education: Reform or Crisis?* (pp. 105–131). Sydney: Allen & Unwin.

Internet sources

The following sites give insight into some of the issues raised in this chapter.

www.aph.gov.au/library/pubs/rn/2004-05/05rn48.htm
www.Islamworld.net

The following site requires a subscription:

www.islamfortoday.com
www.islam21.net
www.cctr.ust.hk
www.dest.gov.au/sectors/school_education/publications_resources/profiles/ archives/advancing_australias_languages.htm#publication

See also your state government multicultural education policy statement at the respective government department's site; for example, www.det.nsw.gov. au, www.decs.sa.gov.au, etc.

8
Gender
Margaret Vickers

1   Introduction: the boys' education crisis

In Australia and in other industrialised countries, the education of boys is seen to be in crisis. Beginning around the mid 1990s, policy and research on gender issues shifted decisively away from girls and girls' issues to examine what was going wrong with the boys (Weaver-Hightower, 2003). In Britain and Australia especially, the media furore about the plight of our boys has continued for almost a decade. Over this same period politicians have announced substantial funds for new educational programs and the attention of researchers has increasingly turned towards examining boys' issues (Arnot, David & Weiner, 1999; Rowan et al., 2002). The boy-advocates have presented their case so passionately that those whose reading does not go beyond media sources and popular literature could be forgiven for believing that our schools are organisations specifically designed to help girls rather than boys. Writers such as Biddulph (1998) and Sommers (2000), for example, argue that our schools are 'feminised' institutions that actually disadvantage boys and harm our young men.

In this chapter, these assertions are examined and alternative arguments about gender, educational practice, and the role of gender policies are developed. First, we take an historical view, and find when we go back to the origins of our high school and university systems that these were designed as men's domains. During the twentieth century, feminists fought to give girls the right to assimilate themselves into these predominantly masculine institutions. During the years following the Second World War, the gender gap in terms of educational performance gradually closed (Arnot, David & Weiner, 1999). Although media commentary tends to suggest that girls now regularly out-perform boys, the evidence for this claim is patchy and often exaggerated (Vickers, 2005). Furthermore, moral panic about boys' failure has tended to encourage dangerously simplistic representations of gender relations, in which boys and girls are represented as homogeneous groups in opposition to each other. Boys are portrayed as uniformly failing (which they are not) and girls as uniformly winning (also untrue). As Collins, Kenway, and McLeod (2000) argued, a more useful approach involves asking *which* boys are disengaging from school, and why, and which boys and which girls are succeeding, and what can we learn from the differences among these groups?

The chapter also examines the relationship between schooling, gender, and work. It appears that although many girls are doing better than boys at school, many of them are not doing better at work. On the contrary, it appears that girls who leave school early are far more likely than early-leaving boys to drop out of the labour market altogether (Collins, 2000). Yet at the same time, working-class boys are also facing problems as they think about their future careers. Technological and structural changes in the workforce have led to a dwindling supply of the kinds of traditional jobs that mostly depended on heroic 'macho' labour (Dolby & Dimitriadis, 2004). It is becoming important in this context to help boys think about what kind of men they might become and to encourage them to consider what Connell (2005) calls 'alternative masculinities'.

2 The origins of public education and the status of girls

By the end of the twentieth century, most Australian families took it for granted that our education system provides opportunities and expectations that lead most young people to move routinely through 12 years of schooling and complete a high school qualification. While there are substantial differences in the quality of the education provided for students from different family backgrounds (as discussed in chapters 6 and 9), in terms of male–female performance, the overall statistics suggest that girls are now doing better than boys in terms of high school completion rates and admission to university as well. Currently, eight out of every ten girls complete high school while only seven out of ten boys do and, on average, young women take 55 per cent of the new places available at the point of admission to our universities. At least two things about this picture are extraordinary. First, it is just over 150 years since Australia's first universities were established, yet it has only been in the past 15 years that university admission statistics have placed girls ahead of boys. Second, the achievements of young women have occurred *not* because our secondary education and university systems were designed to be girl-friendly, but because young women worked out ways of doing boys' subjects and succeeding in fields that are traditionally considered to be male, fields of study that were originally constructed in terms of masculine skills and knowledges.

The University of Sydney was founded in 1850 and the University of Melbourne was proclaimed less than three years later, yet neither of these universities produced a single female graduate for the first 30 years. Bella Guerin, the first woman to graduate from an Australian university, gained a Bachelor of Arts degree from the University of Melbourne in 1883 (Selleck, 2003). Her admission to the University was possible following a long struggle that culminated, in 1879, in a reversal of the ban on women. Following a similar reversal in Sydney, a tiny trickle of women started passing through both universities. They attended classes taught only by males, and totally lacked female company on campus. Although a few women were employed as laboratory assistants and lecturers in the early twentieth century, it was not until 1959 that the Queensland geologist Dorothy Hill became Australia's first female professor (Campbell & Jell, 1998). A decade later Sydney appointed Leonie Kramer to a professorial chair, making her the first of her sex to gain this status at Sydney, a university that had been operating for 106 years.

The masculinist ambience of Australia's universities was not merely a local expression of male domination in a young and brash colonial society. Older universities in the United States and in Britain also excluded women students for at least the first few decades of their existence, and in the case of the oldest universities, women were excluded for the first few hundred years (Purvis, 1991). In Western civilisation the conception of a university arose out of an Enlightenment vision of modernity. In keeping with Enlightenment philosophy, the purpose of the universities was to promote *rational* knowledge, or as Seidler (2006) explains, they were to promote a vision of modernity in which 'culture' was to dominate 'nature' and human reason was to control the body and its desires. One of the most deep-seated assumptions of European philosophy, one that is widespread in popular culture too, is that men are rational while women are emotional (Connell, 2005). The case for the exclusion of women from universities was that they were 'naturally' intuitive rather than objective, and they were expressive rather then instrumental, so their presence would detract from rather than improve the academic community. As Connell (2005, p. 164) put it, 'Hegemonic masculinity establishes its hegemony partly by its claim to embody the power of reason, and thus represent the interests of the whole society …'. Seidler's (2006) account of masculine authority in a patriarchal culture also emphasises the way male authority is connected with disembodied reason.

One of the ideas that has dominated the participation of women in secondary and higher education is the Doctrine of Separate Spheres (Degan, 1986). According to this doctrine (which still emerges in popular culture images today) the role of women is to *manage* the home, emotions, culture, morality and children. Men, on the other hand, are expected to *govern* the economy and large-scale social and political institutions. In Australia and the United States, much public policy surrounding education, employment, and working conditions was built on this model. Thus, even when women were admitted to universities, they were not expected to enter the same courses or study the same subjects as men. What was deemed to be 'women's knowledge' in the late nineteenth and early twentieth centuries focused strongly on domesticity, the care of children, nutrition, and hygiene.

In the United States, higher education programs composed of these offerings were put in place to accommodate women (Degan, 1986). Nevertheless, the courageous women who were the first to enter our universities ignored this doctrine and successfully completed degrees in the sciences, medicine, dentistry, or law. Women who sought a profession were often encouraged to become elementary school teachers or nurses. Based on her analyses of the politics of pedagogy and gender in the United States, Conway (1987) argues that this policy was not pursued for reasons of equity, but rather because it was believed that the costs of staffing elementary schools would be prohibitive if the most of the teachers were men. A similar policy was followed in Australia: this meant that primary teachers were educated separately, outside of university settings, until the late 1970s.

While the doctrine of separate spheres permeated many aspects of public policy, its application to the provision of secondary education was exceedingly thorough. Throughout the nineteenth century secondary education in Australia was primarily offered though fee-paying schools run by the churches. These single-sex schools provided quite different offerings for the two sexes: mathematics, science, history, literature, and languages were on the curriculum for boys, and while the girls might study literature, the subjects on their curriculum were essentially designed to prepare them for duties at home (Hayes, 1996). The first government secondary schools were also segregated: Sydney Boys' High and Fort Street Girls', Bathurst Boys' and Bathurst Girls'. During the early twentieth century as the systems of secondary education took hold in New South Wales and in Victoria, a complex and differentiated pattern emerged. While in these early years girls at MacRobertson GHS in Melbourne or at Fort Street GHS in Sydney might have been required to take needlework, they were also able to pursue a serious program of academic study leading to university admission. Other girls were less fortunate: those who attended the Schools of Domestic Arts had no access to courses of study that led to a matriculating examination.

After 1961, the Wyndham scheme led to the closure, absorption, or conversion of most of the state's Domestic Arts schools and Technical schools into new comprehensive high schools. The academic high school that had been originally designed for boys now became the blueprint for *all* schools in the New South Wales public secondary system. As Collins (1988) suggested, what had been designed for boys was seen as normative and neutral, desirable for all. Girls could now study the same subjects as boys, and while some did, many did not. At the beginning of the 1970s, boys outnumbered girls two-to-one in Australia's universities and only a tiny proportion of girls studied the difficult mathematics subjects or physics at the Year 12 level. As it happened, the feminist movement took off about a decade after the introduction of the Wyndham scheme and this meant that feminist leaders fought to have girls assimilated into what boys did. Girls were encouraged to take maths and science, to go to university, and to take on serious academic studies in literature, languages and history. In effect, girls have learned to walk the double track, taking on more and more boys' subjects, while at the same time sustaining a feminine identity (Collins, 1988).

In the not-too-distant past, literature, languages, and history were academic fields in which males had the upper hand (remember that until 1960 Australia had no female professors). Women's success in these fields over the past 50 years has tipped these subjects from the male to the female side of the gender divide. Thus, boys have felt the need to move into narrower fields of endeavour to demonstrate their masculinity. As Martino (1998) found, boys will do anything to avoid self-expression and the exploration of their emotions in literature classes. The problem boys face is that in a masculinist culture, gender is a zero-sum game. If girls are really good at something, it can't be a boy thing. As Collins (1988) suggested, the danger we face is that if girls are seen as really successful at school, boys may feel they have to move out of taking school seriously altogether. If this is the case then we do have a crisis with boys' education, but it needs to be broadly rather than narrowly defined. In the next section of this chapter we examine some of the evidence on boys' and girls' performance in school and review the kinds of policy responses that this has provoked.

3   A review of the evidence on gender score gaps

In October 2005 Brendan Nelson announced a commitment of $19.4 million to schools for the *Success for Boys* program (DEST, 2005). The Minister claimed that these expenditures were justified by *overwhelming* evidence that boys are falling behind girls in terms of educational performance. These media releases place great stress on the (slight) superiority of females in literacy, while ignoring the (again slight) superiority of males in numeracy (MCEETYA, 2005). A balanced and cautious examination of the available data suggests that for both literacy and numeracy results, the gender-based score gaps are small relative to the gaps between the literacy and numeracy scores achieved by the children of professionals and the children of process workers.

Four sources of data are commonly cited in relation to this issue:

- Longitudinal Surveys of Australian Youth
- literacy and numeracy benchmarks from the *National Reports on Schooling*
- international surveys conducted as part of the OECD's PISA program
- final year 12 results.

For each of these data sources, it is possible to compare the scores obtained by boys and girls, but the interpretation of these comparisons is not always straightforward. For example, it is important to ask whether the observed differences in male and female scores lies within the margins of sampling error, or whether it is large enough, relative to the sampling variation, to demand attention. Second, it is useful to compare the magnitude of gender-based differences in scores with the magnitude of differences based on certain other variables, such as family background or ethnicity. Third, if a particular data source is *not* based on a random sample of students, then a comparison of the scores obtained by girls and boys (or any other subgroup) can be fraught with difficulty. This is a particular concern when comparisons of Year 12 results are used to make inferences about the academic achievements of boys relative to girls. The remainder of this section reviews current data from these diverse sources and discusses the nature of the evidence these sources provide in relation to gender differences in academic performance.

Longitudinal Surveys of Australian Youth (LSAY)

The LSAY studies provide a series of comparable measures of junior secondary students' literacy and numeracy scores over a 23-year period, from 1975 to 1998. Each LSAY study involved a national sample of over 5000 students. In some years the sample was defined in terms of year of birth (sampling 14-year-old students) and in other years it was based on grade (students in Year 9). Individual-level data was collected on reading comprehension, mathematics, gender, language spoken at home, geographical location, and family occupational status. In 2002, Rothman analysed data based on five studies from this series, using data that was collected in 1975, 1980, 1989, 1995 and 1998. An interesting feature of this study is that it allows for comparisons of differences in performance over time as well as differences by gender, parents' occupational background, and other factors.

Rothman (2002) found small but consistent gender-based differences in student performance for both males and females over the 1975 to 1998 period. First, data from the LSAY series seems to suggest that males have marginally higher levels of numeracy than females. The magnitude of the gender gap between the mean scores for males and females was found to be *one scaled score point* in 1975. This gap in numeracy scores neither increased nor decreased over the period studied. However, the magnitude of this gap is quite small, and as an earlier study by Ainley & Marks (1997) suggested, such differences may be indistinguishable from sampling variation.

Table 8.1 Longitudinal Surveys of Australian Youth

The data	Five national longitudinal samples of over 5000 made up students in Year 9* in 1975, 1980, 1989, 1995 & 1998: each cohort was followed for 6+ years
Measures	Year 9 numeracy test Year 9 reading comprehension test
Gender effects	Small but consistent differences in mean scores for *each* cohort studied: Numeracy: males are superior to females by one scaled score point Reading: females are superior to males by one scaled score point (this increased to two scaled score points in 1995 and 1998)
Family background effects	Large, consistent differences in mean scores by family background in each cohort studied. On numeracy scores, students whose parents were professionals were *five* scaled score points ahead of students whose parents were labourers, across all five cohorts. For most cohorts# family background was also associated with a five-point gap in reading comprehension

Source: LSAY

* in some years the sample was defined in terms of year of birth (age 14)

the exception was the 1995 cohort, where the family background gap was 3.8 scaled score points

This gap is also small when it is compared, for example, with the performance gap between students whose parents are labourers or process workers and students whose parents are professionals. Having well-educated parents makes a huge difference in mathematical performance; when students from these two social categories were compared using the 1998 data, there was a mean difference in numeracy performance of *five scaled score points*. This five-point gap was consistent across the 23-year period of the study. This means that family background factors account for much greater differences in performance scores than does gender. In relation to reading comprehension scores, Rothman again found small but consistent gender-based differences, this time favouring girls. On average, girls were ahead of boys by one scaled score point in 1975, but by 1998 this gap had increased to two points. Again, the magnitude of this gap is relatively small if it is compared with performance gaps based on family background.

Rothman and McMillan (2003) conducted additional analyses of the 1995 and 1998 LSAY performance score data, using multi-level modelling to explore the possibility that *school attended* might be contributing systematically to student outcomes. They found that once *school attended* and *school sector* were included in the models, the impact of socio-economic status was diminished at the individual level. However, the socio-economic background influences re-emerged mediated through the school variable. Thus, while there had been some speculation that performance differences associated with socio-economic status (SES) had declined systematically from five scaled score points in 1980 to 3.8 scaled score points in 1995, by 1998 the SES effect was re-established. This time, however, it was mediated through the segregation of Australia's schools, reflecting the effects of increased private school attendance over the past 10 to 15 years.

National literacy and numeracy benchmarks

In Australia, the state and territory Ministers and the federal Minister engage in joint policy development exercises through the Ministerial Council on Education, Training, Employment, and Youth Affairs (MCEETYA). In 1997, MCEETYA established the National Literacy and Numeracy plan. This led to the development of national benchmarks for reading, writing, and numeracy; and proposed that these should be used to assess students in all states and territories at grade levels 3, 5, 7 and 9. Thus, while data from the LSAY series provides an indication of levels of student performance at the junior secondary stage, the *benchmarks* now provide nationally comparable data for students in Years 3, 5 and 7. The *National Reports on Schooling* for 1999 and 2000 provided data for students in Years 3 and 5, indicating what percentage of students in each state and territory had achieved the reading and numeracy benchmarks. These reports also indicate what percentages of students achieved the benchmarks by gender, by language background other than English, and by Indigeneity. As a guide to the accuracy of the estimates, 95 per cent confidence intervals are also reported. For example, in 2000, the percentage of Year 3 girls achieving the benchmark was reported as 94.3 ± 1.8, which means that a difference of up to 3.6 percentage points could be attributed to sampling variation. The best we can do is to say we are 95 per cent sure that between 92.5 per cent and 96.1 per cent of Year 3 girls achieved the national reading benchmark in 2000. For Year 3 boys the mean was 90.9 and the corresponding confidence interval was 88.2 to 93.6 per cent. Since in this case the ranges or the confidence intervals for boys and girls overlap, we have no grounds for concluding that Year 3 girls are doing better than Year 3 boys in terms of the national reading benchmarks.

Table 8.2 Literacy and numeracy benchmarks

The data	Benchmark assessments are conducted annually in each jurisdiction at the Year 3, 5, and 7 levels. Years 3 and 5 were tested in 1999–2000. Students in Years 3, 5, and 7 have been tested since 2001.
Measures	States and territories report the percentage of students achieving reading, writing, and numeracy benchmarks, as well as the confidence intervals. Typically, 92 to 96 per cent of all students achieve the benchmark level.
Gender effects	There are no significant differences by gender in the percentages achieving the reading benchmark at Year 3 level. Small, significant differences in reading emerge at the Year 5 and 7 levels and there are small, significant differences in the percentages achieving the writing benchmark at all levels; these differences favour girls. There are no significant gender differences at any level in numeracy.
Comment	Even where *mean* literacy scores are *equal,* LSAY data indicate there are more boys than girls in the lowest performance bands on literacy tests. This finding is consistent with the *benchmarks* data, indicating that more boys than girls are located in the bottom 5 per cent nationally on literacy test performance.

Source: *National Reports on Schooling*

While the *National Reports* for 1999 and 2000 provided data for students in Years 3 and 5, from 2001 onwards the *National Reports* also included data for students in Year 7 (MCEETYA, 2005). There are now five consecutive years of data for Years 3 and 5 and three years of data for Year 7. Across all these data, no significant differences have emerged between boys and girls in terms of achieving the numeracy benchmarks. From 1999 to 2002, there were no significant differences between Year 3 boys and girls in achievement of the national reading literacy benchmark, but a small difference in favour of girls emerged in 2003. In all years, however, there were significant differences between boys and girls in achievement of the national reading benchmarks at the Year 5 and Year 7 levels. The more recent *National Reports* also include data on writing benchmarks and on these more girls than boys achieve the benchmarks, at all grade levels. Rothman and McMillan (2003) note several earlier Australian studies that also documented gender differences in literacy among primary school students. It appears, however, that these differences are weak during the early grades, that girls gain a slight edge in reading and writing by Year 5, and that they maintain this small gap in literacy performance throughout their high school years.

International surveys

Since 2000, Australia has been a participant in the Organization for Economic Cooperation and Development's (OECD) Program for International Student Assessment (PISA). This program involves measurements of the literacy, numeracy, scientific literacy, and problem-solving skills of samples of 15-year-olds in forty industrialised countries.

Table 8.3 International surveys conducted as part of the OECD's Program for International Student Assessment (PISA)

The data	Large nationally representative samples of 15-year-old students completed PISA tests in forty participating countries that are affiliated with the OECD.
Measures	Mathematical literacy measure—results available for 2000 and 2003. Reading literacy measure—results available for year 2000.
Gender effects (Australia)	Mathematics: no differences in mean scores for *either* cohort, but twice as many males as females achieved the highest proficiency level. Reading: the mean score for females is superior to that of males, and twice as many males as females performed below proficiency level 2.
International comparisons of gender effects	Australia's overall scores place us among the best-performing OECD nations on the PISA tests. Our gender gap in mean reading scores is equal to the average gender gap in reading across the OECD, but the degree of inequality in Australia's scores on this test is greater, with more males performing poorly in Australia than in comparable OECD countries.

International comparative results for both the 2000 and 2003 rounds of PISA indicated that there were no significant differences by gender in mean scores for mathematical literacy in Australia. However, while the mean scores achieved by boys and girls were equivalent, almost twice as many Australian males as females achieved the highest PISA proficiency level. This is consistent with the cross-national pattern; in twenty-seven of the forty countries participating in PISA, males out-performed females on the mathematics tests (Thomson, Cresswell & De Bortoli, 2003).

Literacy results have not yet been published for PISA 2003, but the results for PISA 2000 indicate that there is a gender difference in favour of Australian females in terms of reading literacy. However, a similar gender gap in reading literacy was noted across most of the countries participating in PISA. Overall, the mean gender gap in reading literacy for Australian 15-year-olds is the same as the OECD average. What is a cause for concern is the wide spread of scores on reading literacy for Australian students, since this suggests that we need to focus more on our poorest performers, and 'bring up the tail' (as Doherty, McGaw and O'Loghlin (2004) suggested). This may include a focus on improving the literacy levels of males who are performing poorly. In the 2000 round of PISA, more than twice as many Australian males as females performed below PISA proficiency level 2 on the reading literacy assessments (Lokan, Greenwood & Cresswell, 2000).

Student performance at the Year 12 level

Sometimes Year 12 examination results are also enlisted to support the case that boys are lagging behind the girls in educational achievements. On the face of it, there may be some cause for concern. Following changes in assessment practices in senior secondary science and mathematics subjects, females are now often out-performing males, particularly on school-based assessments that depend on a written component. However, gender comparisons need to be based on 'like' groups of males and females. This is clearly not the case in relation to Year 12 subjects in which the proportions of male and females studying the subject are grossly unequal. For example, as NSW Board of Studies data show, the ratio of males to females enrolled in Year 12 Physics is usually approximately three to one, and in Software Development and Design the ratio is typically nine to one. As a result, girls who take such subjects tend to be a highly motivated, self-selected group. Because of this selectivity bias, it might be expected that their mean scores would be higher than those of the males who also enrol in this subject.

A recent study by Cox, Leder, and Forgasz (2004) examined the apparent performance gap between male and female candidates in science taking the Victorian Certificate of Education (VCE) examinations in 1999, 2000, and 2001. While the scores obtained by females taking VCE science subjects suggested that on the whole they were indeed out-performing males, further analysis suggested that these differences may be attributable to selectivity bias. One component of the VCE assessment system that is compulsory for all students is the General Achievement Test (GAT). The GAT comprises three components. When the researchers examined male and female scores on each of these, they found small differences in stereotypical directions. Males had better scores on the maths/science/technology component, females had better scores on the written component, and on the arts/humanities component males and females performed equally. When these three measures were combined, male and female performance was found to be equal in each of the three years covered by the study. Since the GAT is compulsory it is not subject to selectivity bias. Thus, when GAT scores are used to explore whether there is a gender gap in student performance, the supposed gap disappears.

Table 8.4 Student performance at the Year 12 level

Evidence	Media sources have drawn attention to the exemplary performance of some females in science and mathematics at Year 12 level (in the NSW Higher School Certificate and the Victorian Certificate of Education). In one study, Forgasz and Leder (2004) collated the scores obtained by females taking VCE science subjects in 1999, 2000, and 2001 and found that on the whole they were out-performing males
Do such comparisons indicate a bias in the curriculum in favour of girls?	No. In most of the subjects in question, males outnumber females at least three to one, so females who take these subjects are a self-selected and highly motivated group. The samples being compared are not comparable because there is selectivity bias. It is to be expected that the mean scores of females taking advanced science subjects would be higher than those of males who enrol in these subjects.
A common measure—the GAT	The General Achievement Test (GAT) is compulsory for all VCE students, so it is not subject to selectivity bias. Overall, when the three components of the GAT were combined, male and female performance was found to be equal in each of the three years covered by the study.

To summarise, it appears that while there is no consistent difference between boys and girls on numeracy tests, girls have a small but consistent advantage over boys in terms of achievement on literacy tests. However, this gender gap in literacy for Australians is entirely consistent with international trends recorded in the OECD PISA studies.

4 The gender gap in high school completion rates

What does seem to be a specifically Australian problem, however, is that for the past 15 years female high school completion rates (or more precisely, apparent retention rates) have remained ten percentage points higher than those of male high school completion rates. It was not always so. In 1975 when Jean Blackburn and her committee were drafting *Girls Schools and Society,* all the data available to them suggested that the boys had always outstripped the girls in terms of high school completion rates (Commonwealth Schools Commission, 1975). Soon after their report was released it became apparent that girls' rates of retention to Year 12 had started to exceed those of boys.

Much of this can be attributed to the impact of labour market changes on the levels of post-compulsory participation of teenage males and females. Between 1977 and 1997, the number of full-time jobs available to Australian teenagers fell sharply. Labour market data assembled by Wooden (1996) indicates that over these 20 years:

- more than half of all full-time jobs for teenage males disappeared
- more than two-thirds of all full-time jobs for teenage females also disappeared
- by the mid 1990s, one-third of high school students were in part-time work.

Looking back 30 years to the mid 1960s, the nature of the changes that have occurred in the teenage labour market become even more obvious (see also chapter 3). In 1966, only one-third of each teenage cohort completed high school and two-thirds of all teenagers were in the labour force, most of them working full time. Teenage unemployment was negligible. The mid 1970s was a turbulent period that signalled the end of the great postwar boom, the end of tariff barriers, and a new era of economic competition. During the 1980s, high school completion rates doubled. By 1991, over 70 per cent of all teenagers were completing high school, and fewer than 20 per cent of 15–19-year-olds had full-time jobs (Wooden, 1996; Lewis & Koshy, 1999). Ever since 1991 the overall national high school completion rate has remained above 70 per cent and it is now considered normal to expect that three-quarters of all students in each cohort will complete Year 12. The gender gap is also a stable feature of the current pattern of retention rates: while male retention rates tend to hover around 70 per cent, female retention rates typically hover at around 80 per cent and, as a result, the overall retention rate generally lies between 74 and 76 per cent.

It is possible that one of the factors contributing to the completion rate gender gap is that girls are outperforming boys academically. Research studies by Lamb and others confirm that the rate of early leaving is indeed greater among young people with weak Year 10 results. However, there is a *gender gap* in this phenomenon. *Girls who perform poorly* in Year 10 are more likely to stay on at school than *boys who perform poorly* (Lamb, Hogan & Johnson, 2001). One of the most plausible explanations for this difference between the behaviour of poorly performing boys and poorly performing girls is that boys who don't enjoy school are more likely to find a job to go to than are the girls. In part, this is because of the gender bias in traditional apprenticeships. The electrical trades, construction, motor mechanics and so on remain overwhelmingly male-dominated, reflecting the continuing gender segregation of the labour market. Males traditionally entered these occupations immediately after reaching minimum school leaving age, and a majority of new apprenticeship commencements still go to males who have not completed Year 12 (NCVER, 2001; Toner, 2005). Although girls can take up traineeship positions, only a small percentage of them enter traditional apprenticeships. Unlike their brothers, most girls cannot leave school and enter a secure pathway that combines training with employment. As the study cited above suggests, low-performing girls tend to battle on at school, while boys with similar levels of ability leave.

Males who leave school without completing Year 12 have much better labour market options than girls, as the table below indicates. In terms of full-time employment 7 years after school, males who completed school were only marginally better off than those who did not (a 4 per cent improvement) while females who finished school were 20 per cent ahead of those who did not. As already noted, Australia's segmented labour market offers privileged ports of entry for males who have not completed high school through the apprenticeship system.

Table 8.5 Percentage of students who were in full-time employment in their seventh year post Year 12 (at age 23–24)

	Completed Year 12	Early Leavers
Males	79	75
Females	69	49

Source: Data derived from LSAY-95; see Collins (2000)

Long-term declines in full-time teenage job opportunities have affected both males and females. As already noted, over two-thirds of full-time jobs for females disappeared over the 20 years from 1977 to 1997 (Wooden, 1996). Labour market opportunities for young women have continued to decline since then. In the latest edition of its annual series titled *How Young People are Faring*, the Dusseldorp skills forum reported that over half a million 15–24-year-olds are *not in full time work and not studying*, and that whereas 40 per cent of these are young men, 60 per cent of them are young women (Long, 2005).

Among 15–24-year-olds who are not enrolled in full-time TAFE or university study and who are, therefore, eager to find secure employment, it is the boys who appear to be winning. The figures from the Dusseldorp skills forum cited above suggest that girls have fallen further behind over the past decade. The 60–40 gap cited above is the largest male–female gap in the labour market and educational participation since 1989 (Long, 2005). As Richard Teese (2002) points out, young people have been squeezed out of the full-time labour market and have had to seek opportunities by remaining in school. This pressure, Teese suggests, has been felt more by girls than boys.

5 Gender gaps and youth opportunities: comparing the US and Australia

Further evidence that labour market factors may make a substantial contribution to the gender gap in high school completion rates comes from a cross-national study by Lamb and Vickers (2003). Using data from the Longitudinal Surveys of Australian Youth (LSAY-95) and an equivalent large-scale longitudinal data set from the United States (NELS:88), they analysed high school completion data and related these data to students' post-school destinations. They found that 76 per cent of the Australian participants in the LSAY-95 sample completed Year 12 in 1998. The expected gender gap was evident in that 82 per cent of the girls and 70 per cent of the boys completed high school. The NELS:88 data represent a similar sample of US students: these students were in Year 8 in 1988, and graduated from high school in 1992. Official statistical data for the US indicate that males and females typically have comparable Year 12 completion rates. Overall, 79 per cent of the students in the NELS:88 sample completed Year 12 without ever leaving school; for males the figure was 78.4 per cent and for females it was 79.6 per cent. The difference between male and female completion rates in the US sample is, therefore, very small.

Table 8.6 Australia and the USA: high school completion rates, participation in apprenticeships, and teenage fertility rates

Australia	USA
76% complete Year 12	79% graduate, never drop out
18% become apprentices or trainees	1.7% become apprentices
1.5% become pregnant during high school	5% become pregnant during high school

Source: Vickers & Lamb (2003): data derived from LSAY-95 and NELS: 88

In both the US and Australia, most students continue in full-time study after leaving school. Between 49 and 52 per cent of students in both the Australian LSAY sample and the US NELS sample entered a tertiary education institution. One way in which the two countries differ, however, is that Australia appears to offer more egalitarian labour market training opportunities than does the US. This is mainly because the US apprenticeship system is very small and, therefore, highly selective (see Table 8.6). Only 1.7 per cent of America's young people entered an apprenticeship or traineeship, while in Australia the proportion of the LSAY-95 sample who entered an apprenticeship or a traineeship was ten times this figure (17.8 per cent). In the US, apprenticeships are the gateway to well-paid jobs that are mostly in construction, and they tend to be taken up by students who are from families of high socio-economic status. In Australia, the bias is in the opposite direction, with apprenticeships being a more common destination for students from families of lower socio-economic status (Vickers, Lamb & Hinkley, 2003). The Australian system covers a wide range of occupations including apprenticeships in the licensed trades and traineeships in clerical and retail occupations; however, the more rewarding apprenticeships mostly go to males, as already noted. For the LSAY-95 sample, Lamb and Vickers (2003) found that an apprenticeship or traineeship was the main post-school activity for 25.7 per cent of Australian males while for females the equivalent figure was 10.6 per cent (see Table 8.7).

Table 8.7 Australia and the USA: high school completion rates, participation in apprenticeships, by sex, and teenage fertility rates

Australia		USA	
Male	**Female**	**Male**	**Female**
Completed year 12 (%)		Graduated without dropping out (%)	
70.0	82.0	78.4	79.6
Became apprentices/trainees (%)		Became apprentices (%)	
25.7	10.6	2.6	1.7
Became pregnant during high school (%)		Became pregnant during high school (%)	
	1.5		5

Source: Data derived from LSAY-95 and NELS: 88

Another US–Australian difference that these data point to is that the proportion of teenage girls who become pregnant during high school is much higher in the US than in Australia. (Demographers refer to proportion of females in a defined category who actually become pregnant as the *fertility rate.*) As the NELS:88 data indicate, a substantial proportion of girls who drop out of American high schools state that their reason for leaving school is that they are pregnant or want to have a family. Boys more frequently then girls state that they left school because they got a job, and this is evident in both the Australian and the US survey data. At the same time, a large proportion of early leavers in both countries state that they left school because did not like it and could not get along with their teachers. Thus, two factors tend to exacerbate the gender gap in high school completion rates in Australia: these are the low rates of fertility among teenage girls and the high rate of uptake of apprenticeships by young males who secure an apprenticeship and leave school to take it up without completing Year 12.

6 The role of the school in the construction of gender

As Collins (1988) succinctly put it, 'being a boy or being a girl is a personal identification process imposed from the beginning of first awareness. It is there in the very nouns by which the child is first addressed … we are labeled boy or girl, he or she, and treated according to that label from birth … [yet at the same time] … much of what it means to be a boy or a girl happens at school' (p. 22).

Since the school is the social space in which much gender development occurs, it is important to think carefully about what schools are like as settings for the making of masculinities and femininities. An important strand of organisation studies that assists us here is the development of the idea of gendered organisations (Acker, 1990). This research suggests that organisations themselves are gendered; that gender is not just a property of individuals, something that enters into a neutral organisational context when men and women arrive. Rather, gender relations are embedded in the very nature of organisations themselves. Connell (2002a) proposed that the arrangement of gender relations that is characteristic of a given organisation may be called its 'gender regime'. Gender regimes are multi-dimensional, embracing the four dimensions noted below. They are liable to have internal unevennesses and tensions, and they are always subject to change, though specific features of gender arrangements may persist for a surprisingly long time.

Organisations are gendered through:

- the division of labour—e.g. there are gendered jobs in the organisation's structure
- power relations—e.g. men and women exercise authority differently
- emotional relationships—e.g. patterns of antagonism and solidarity are gendered
- organisational cultures—e.g. beliefs about gender difference, equal opportunity, are gendered.

For a more complete discussion of the gender regimes of organisations, see Connell (2002).

Schools and education systems are gendered organisations in this sense. Gender patterns in the work of schools and in their effects on children are not accidental, are not an aberration, but are deeply embedded in the histories of schools and school systems and their current modes of operation. For example, in recent years the federal government has made a number of declarations about what it considers to be the negative effects of the 'lack of male role models' in primary schools (Nelson, 2004). But this situation is not new: there is a longstanding gender imbalance in primary teaching, and even more in early childhood teaching. Even if people thought it was a good idea to have more male teachers, this is not going to be fixed by asking more men to show up for primary teaching programs. This is because the gender imbalance in primary teaching is part of a larger gender division of labour in the education system as a whole—the under-representation of men in kindergartens is matched by the under-representation of women as professors in universities. While most people agree that it would be an excellent thing to have a more even gender balance in this part of the workforce, the economic and cultural forces shaping teacher recruitment into primary and early childhood education are overwhelming and make this highly unlikely. (In passing, it is worth noting that at least one recent research study suggests that boys at the primary and middle levels do not fare any better with male teachers compared with female teachers (Martin & Marsh, 2005).)

The gender regimes of schools and education systems not only involve multiple dimensions of gender, they also involve significant unevenness. There are some parts of a school's life, commonly, where gender is strongly marked, and other parts where gender is very muted. This is important for understanding the school's role in the construction of masculinities.

The role of the school in the construction of masculinities

In an essay on 'teaching the boys', Connell (1996) suggested the possibility of identifying 'masculinity vortices' in schools. This means areas of school life where processes of masculinity formation are intensely active. Three are particularly noticeable:

- 'Boys' subjects', such as manual arts and technical drawing, which are historically connected with gender-segregated occupations and often taught by men with a background in those occupations.
- School sport, especially competitive team sports such as football, which are important in the wider culture as symbols of masculinity—this inevitably filters through into school life.
- The discipline system, especially given the tendency of conflictual discipline to produce hierarchies and exclusions in school life.

At the same time as recognising areas of school life that are gender-saturated, we should also recognise other areas of school life that are relatively gender-neutral. Teachers may deliberately play down gender in classroom management; for instance, by arranging mixed-group seating, or by treating all children in a mixed classroom in common ways. (A familiar example: addressing a class as 'children' rather than 'boys and girls'.) There are occasions when the children themselves will ignore gender boundaries and gender solidarities. The de-gendering strategy is not unique to schools. Indeed, it is now a familiar strategy in organisational life, used for instance by public sector managers as a way of implementing equal opportunity rules (Connell, 2005). Whenever teachers say 'I treat them all as individuals' or 'I don't treat boys and girls differently', they are implicitly adopting a de-gendering approach and may be creating a de-gendered zone of school life. This is not always the best thing to do from an educational point of view, since there are times when we do want to make gender an explicit theme of discussion and learning. But it is now a familiar and widespread strategy.

The gender regimes of schools may be deliberately constructed to produce effects on masculinity. Such masculinity-making agendas are familiar in educational history. Matthew Arnold's reforms in English ruling-class schools were intended as an agenda of moral education, forming Christian gentlemen, and the later widespread introduction of formalised school sport was also intended to foster a specific pattern of manliness. Studies of colonial education, most notably Morrell's (2001) brilliant study of settler schools in Natal, in South Africa, show how a whole school system could be constructed around such an agenda. The specific pattern of masculinity these schools installed as hegemonic was the one necessary to sustain the dominance of an elite of white, propertied, patriarchal families in the rough and often violent context of colonialism. But the logic of masculinity-making agendas can be turned in more democratic directions, as brilliantly shown in Denborough's (1996) imaginative program for working with boys to reduce violence.

The organisational patterns of schools and education systems may also have unintended educational consequences. Earlier in this chapter we referred to the different pathways that open up in secondary and post-secondary education, as electives replace the common curriculum that prevailed in primary schooling. These pathways tend to be gendered in a number of ways. They have gendered histories, they are often tied to gender symbols, they are linked to gender divisions in the economy, they are taught predominantly by men or by women, and so on. It is not surprising then that there are growing gender differences in subject enrolments through secondary school, and actual gender segregation in some areas of vocational education. As we saw earlier in this chapter, during the late nineteenth and early twentieth centuries, the doctrine of separate spheres dictated that women should not be in the same classes or study the same subjects as men. It is a mistake, therefore, to attribute gender patterns in 'subject choice' to the magic influence of genetic differences between males and females. Rather, these differences are historically produced patterns, they can change over time, and they are connected with the wider patterns in gender relations.

At an even more basic level, the school as an institution shapes patterns of masculinity by constituting a social milieu in which hundreds of children or youths are thrown together over long periods. A peer forum is created in which relations between patterns of masculinity are highlighted. In such a setting the issue of hegemony—relations between the dominant pattern of masculinity and subordinate or marginalised patterns—is very likely to become an issue of concern in boys' lives and a source of turbulence in gender relations. For instance, boys in school may struggle for dominance in the local peer group, in the course of which bullying and exclusion can arise. Bullying of boys who are thought to be effeminate or homosexual is a very common source of tension and violence in schools.

The struggle for dominance in gender terms among boys and men can also be an important source of educational problems. For instance, especially in working-class communities, there are groups of boys who attempt to claim masculine honour, attempt to claim a leading position in gender terms, but do not have the cultural and institutional resources to do so through academic competition. Such boys are more likely to fall into conflict with the school and sometimes become violent towards other boys or towards teachers. What Connell (2005) called 'protest masculinity' is a likely result. Poynting, Noble and Tabar's (1998) important study of Lebanese youth in Sydney shows such a pattern arising, in part, as a response to being a target of racism and experiencing social exclusion. Boys following such trajectories may abruptly end their educational careers and go onto the labour market without qualifications and with very weak employment prospects.

In the mid 1970s, Paul Willis wrote a classic study that asked why working-class youth left school to enter working-class jobs, through their own apparent choice. Recently, Kenway and Kraack (2004) revisited this question in the very different economic context of the early twenty-first century, where much blue-collar work has vanished. They examined the effects on families of the closures of mines and mills, bans on fishing and logging, and the automation of manual labour. In one part of this study they provide a compelling account of social and economic change in a traditional fishing town on the south coast of New South Wales. Working men are grappling with the near collapse of the local fishing and logging industries, and among many families there is a loss of heart. Many of the timber men and fishermen disparage the fledgling tourist industry. One long-term resident commented: '... this town is made up of hard-working types ...

they work with their hands and can't be turned into office boys' (p. 105). Yet it is tourism—being a chef or running cruise boats for visitors from the city, for example—that particular teenage males have decided will be the best bet for their futures. Not all families support this cultural shift in the nature of men's work. As one father asked, 'What future is there for boys with aprons?' (p. 103).

Through this research, Kenway and Kraack have identified one of the central issues that gender policy should concern itself with. What boys and their families now need to do is construct new definitions of masculinity that can accommodate what twenty-first century work is likely to entail. As Kenway and Kraack note, the problem we face is that *some* young working-class males are inventing themselves as 'new workers' while others are not. These young men are negotiating the difficult problem of getting around the identity issues that arise in what are seen as 'feminised' labour markets. The term *feminisation of work* refers to the trend for an increasing number of workplaces to take on characteristics formerly associated with the 'female' retail and service sectors.

The challenge for teachers and schools is to work out how to deal with resistance to this trend among young men who subscribe to working class 'macho' masculinities. The young men and women whose futures are most compromised by these social and economic changes have the most to gain if they move beyond the constraints gender stereotypes impose on their imaginations and ambitions. They are the ones who will benefit most if our schools and our teachers can find a way to develop and deliver educational programs that encourage boys and girls to think flexibly about the kinds of men and women they would like to become.

Focus questions

1 For over a decade, eight out of ten Australian females who started high school completed Year 12, while only seven out of ten males have done so. Some media commentators promote the view that this means schools have become 'feminised'. What evidence is there to support this view? Are there other factors that might contribute to the male–female difference in completion rates observed in Australia? What are these? How would you evaluate the evidence available in relation to these factors?

2 Evaluate the evidence provided in this chapter regarding the male–female differences in literacy outcomes. In which groups of males and females are these differences most evident? Why do you think this is so?

3 The feminist movement led to changes in girls' aspirations: young women who went through school in the 1980s and 1990s went on to university in

unprecedented numbers and many of them took on what had previously been thought of as 'boys' subjects' (for example, mathematics and physical sciences). This chapter argued that many girls have learned to walk a double track, succeeding at 'boy things' while at the same time sustaining feminine identities. Imagine a situation in which boys decided to walk a double track. What might this look like? How could it be achieved?

4 If you were to design a *Success for Boys* policy, what would it look like and what would it aim to achieve? Is there, in this new millennium, any need for a policy to help girls succeed? Which girls would this policy target, and how might it work?

5 Schools are gendered organisations that provide particular contexts for the making of masculinities and femininities. Explore this idea. Illustrate it by choosing a school you know, and describing some of the ways in which the power relations, emotional relationships, organisational cultures, and/or job structures were gendered. Provide an example that illustrates how a setting like this might influence young people as they construct their own understandings of what it might mean to be 'masculine' or 'feminine'.

Further reading

Arnot, M., David, M. & Weiner, G. (1999). *Closing the Gender Gap: Post-war Education and Social Change*. Cambridge: Polity Press.

Collins, C., Kenway, J. & McLeod, J. (2000). *Factors Influencing the Educational Performance of Males and Females in School and Their Initial Destinations After Leaving School*. Canberra: Commonwealth Department of Education, Training and Youth Affairs.

Connell, R.W. (1996). 'Teaching the boys: New research on masculinity, and gender strategies for schools.' *Teachers College Record, 98*(2), 206–35.

Connell, R.W. (2005). *Masculinities* (2nd edn). Sydney: Allen & Unwin.

Rowan, L., Knobel, M., Bigum, C. & Lankshear, C. (2002). *Boys, Literacies, and Schooling*. Philadelphia: Open University Press.

Internet sources

The following sites have interesting material. The first belongs to the Victorian department of education: www.sofweb.vic.edu.au/gender/index.htm.

The next site is the report *How Far Have We Come?*, which looks at gender disparities in Australian higher education: www.avcc.edu.au/documents/policies_programs/women/Gender_Disparities_20Report_Jun03.pdf.

The government report, 'Boys: Getting it Right' is available as follows: www.aph.gov.au/house/committee/edt/eofb/index.htm.

9
Schools and School Choice
Craig Campbell

1   The retreat from the idea of a common school

The Australian education system is peculiar. It has a much weaker *public* (or *government* or *state*) system of education than most parts of Europe and North America. Why this is so, and its consequences for families, children, and youth, is a main focus of this chapter. Since the 1980s the government sector has generally declined, not always in absolute terms (that is, in the actual numbers of students who are educated within it) but in the proportions of students who go to government and *non-government* schools. At the beginning of the twenty-first century Australian youth are enrolled in a diverse range of schools. That diversity occurs within as well as between each of the broad sectors defined as government and non-government. The second main focus of the chapter is how young people get to be students in the different kinds of schools; that is, we have a look at *school choice* and the conditions under which it occurs in Australia.

For much of the twentieth century, the policy of governments was not to encourage diverse schools, nor was it to encourage active choice-making by parents between schools. Until the 1960s, nearly all tax-raised government funding went solely to government schools. Moreover, there was district zoning; families had the right to send their children to only one government school in a network of many. The major effort of government was that of adequate provision; that is, simply to make sure that all communities, rural and urban, had easily accessible government schools—in particular, primary schools. The picture was not quite so clear at the secondary school level, where for considerable periods the idea was that there should be different schools for different students. Such schools could be formally or informally based on students' social characteristics and the curricula they wished to experience. In the first half of the twentieth century school discriminators included a student's ability or intelligence, or probable vocational destiny. The secondary level was also more contested by the non-government sector, especially by the various church-owned colleges, which traditionally had produced a very high proportion of the university students in each of the Australian colonies and states.

The main effort of government through the early twentieth century was to provide a *system* of schools and schooling opportunities. The dominant metaphor that described the connections between the elements of the emerging system was that of an *educational ladder*. Successful completion at one level of schools should provide right of entry to the next level. Such a system would be marked by opportunity, and the reduction of 'dead ends': institutions and qualifications that could lead to nothing further. State education departments were fond of drawing elaborate flow-charts demonstrating the connecting links between the most isolated rural schools and infant classes with the pinnacle of the system—the universities and the various institutes of technology or technical colleges. (For example, Barcan, 1980, p. 243.)

While it was occasionally a concern, more emphasised was the provision of a structure of opportunity, rather than the numbers of young people who actually achieved ascension from one layer to the next. Needless to say, for much of the twentieth century, and especially before the 1960s, the proportion of students making it to the pinnacles of the system was very low.

Eventually each Australian state produced a common or comprehensive secondary school as well as a common primary school (Campbell & Sherington, 2006). Western Australia was the first state to move in favour of comprehensive government schools in the 1950s, with New South Wales doing so a decade later. Victoria and South Australia waited longer. There the tradition of junior technical and technical secondary schools, with a rather different educational mission to the academically oriented high schools, held on through the 1970s.

By the early 1970s it appeared that common primary and secondary schools, overwhelmingly government schools, would be the dominant providers of school education in Australia. Problems with the rising cost of teacher salaries and education in general brought a period of difficulty to the non-government sector. By the end of the 1970s, however, this trend had begun a radical reversal, and from the 1980s an emergent uniform school system dominated by common government schools had begun to fragment. A new era of diversity, and the encouragement of school choice within the government sector and between government and non-government, quickly developed. (See Anderson, 1992; Marginson, 1993; Sherington, 2004.)

In trying to understand the peculiarities of the Australian system of education, there are many issues requiring our attention. But at least two require close attention. The first is the peculiar approach that the Australian colonies and states developed towards educating their large numbers of working-class Catholic children, and second is the Australian federal system of government. The Australian Constitution (1901) left education as a residual power to the states, but also created the conditions whereby it was all too easy for the federal government to produce a parallel set of educational policies if it wished. From the 1960s, it wished.

2 The historical emergence of different schools for different groups

New South Wales and the other colonies, as they were established, understandably adapted British approaches to schooling. In the late eighteenth and early nineteenth centuries, the initial expectation was that education would be a private affair for most, and especially the wealthier classes. If there were to be sets of institutions beyond the private, then the Church, and in particular the Anglican Church, was the intended provider. After all, the Anglican Church was the established Church of England.

In so far as government took any responsibility at all for providing some education to the children of convicts and the labouring class, it was Richard Johnson as the first Anglican clergyman who had the job. We do not know what proportion of children attended any of the classes he was responsible for, but we do have an indication of the reading curriculum. Substantial numbers of pamphlets or tracts were brought to the colony by Johnson. As some of their titles indicate, the link between government-sponsored, church-organised education for the lower orders, and the creation of honest, hard-working 'subjects' was made early. Tracts included: 'Cautions to Swearers', 'Religion Made Easy', 'Exhortations of Chastity', and 'Exercises against Lying' (Barcan, 1980, p. 9).

The first directly funded and controlled government schools appear to have been specifically devoted to social control and the reformation of the most unruly groups in society. So there were schools for orphans (1795), girls (1801), and natives (1815). In each case, these were schools for children whose parents had either disappeared or, in many cases, were simply considered unsatisfactory, ignorant, or vicious. The first government schools were in fact the predecessors of reformatories and reformatory schools. It is possible that such origins biased some of the wealthier and powerful families against government schooling on a long-term basis.

In the first half of the nineteenth century, most colonies subsidised some church schools and individual teachers who established schools in different localities. An early difficulty was the range of different religious denominations present in the colonies, all with fair numbers of children to educate. Unlike the United Kingdom where there tended to be a dominant church in each of England, Wales, Scotland, and Ireland, the Australian colonies had contesting denominations in each individual colony. Catholics, Presbyterians, Wesleyans (Methodists),

Lutherans, and others could not accept that only Church of England schools would get government subsidies. Government subsidies went to each of the main denominations, and so emerged the first of a series of colonial settlements in terms of *systems and funding*. (It is not possible here to explore the differences in timing and approach in each separate colony.)

This settlement, which left most schooling in the hands of entrepreneurial teacher families and churches, had problems. Each colony was sparsely populated, and the system of denominational subsidy could lead in some districts to several schools being established, each of which might have very small numbers of students. Increasingly numbers of influential people began to argue that such a system was not only economically and educationally inefficient, but that it was also socially divisive. So from the 1830s a new debate began over the question of how governments might economically and efficiently assist in the provision of schooling.

In order to get any new answers to such a question, one very important intellectual and cultural shift needed to occur. This was to conceive of the possibility of separating religion and education. The invention of a government school with no attachment to any particular church, and which might attract students from any Christian church, and maybe even enrol non-Christian pupils, was a large step for colonial Australia. Nevertheless there were intellectual movements from the seventeenth and eighteenth centuries that allowed the possibility of such a separation. (It occurred relatively early in the United States where its late eighteenth century constitution rigidly separated church and state.) The movements that helped define modern approaches to 'reason' and 'science' were at the core of this, as well as the breakdown in the unity of Christendom in Western Europe from the sixteenth century. Arguments were increasingly heard by the late eighteenth and through the nineteenth century that churches were untrustworthy in relation to the provision of education. In the end, 'faith' or 'superstition' would defeat 'science' and 'reason' if education was left in the hands of the churches. (We see the continuing debate on such matters in the controversy over the place of 'intelligent design' in the school science curriculum.)

In the Australian colonies there were increasing numbers of public leaders who, though Christian themselves, were ever more confident that governments rather than churches could provide better forms of schools and education—and save money while so doing. Of all places, Ireland provided the possible model for a new kind of government school. There, 'National' schools, with their 'national curriculum' based on a series of school readers, had been invented. In Ireland, the occupying power was English and Protestant, with most people being Irish and Catholic. The British government was not prepared to allow government-funded Catholic schools to educate the population. Instead there would be National schools with a curriculum based on readers that were 'Christian' rather than specifically 'Catholic' in message. It was such National schools with a generally Christian-oriented curriculum that would be the basis of the first government schools open to any child in the colonies of eastern Australia.

Initially, the Church of England and the Roman Catholics strenuously objected. Polymorphous Christianity was not good enough and for a time a parallel system was run. There were two systems in eastern Australia, controlled by the Denominational and the National Boards of education from 1848. They were rival systems, and as time went on, governments in each colony with this dual system began to view more favourably the efficiencies and accountability of the National schools over the denominational. Not long ago, this period in Australian educational history was seen as uninteresting. It is no longer the case. At the beginning of the twenty-first century there are recognisable similarities visible with these educational settlements of the mid nineteenth century. There is a major difference, however. Where the denominational or church schools fell into increasing disfavour in the nineteenth century, in the current period it is the government schools to which this is happening.

These National schools, the predecessors of modern government schools, were very popular in rural and urban areas—among middle-class people in particular, but also with those working-class people who were happy to send their children regularly to school. From Sydney, George Rusden was appointed agent of the Board of National Education in 1849. He set out on several epic journeys, the major one being southward. From Yass he rode his horse to Albury and then Melbourne, and across to Portland. He also went north to Grafton and Brisbane, and the Hunter Valley. All the way in large and small villages and towns he held meetings of parents and citizens, seeking local support to get National schools started. He discovered that most Australian colonists were not as alarmed by the possibility of national schools as the Catholic and Church of England bishops (Austin, 1958). In many rural areas the choice was a National school, or no school at all. So we have the second settlement: the foundation of government schools, National schools with a generally Christian outlook (admittedly rather more Protestant in spirit than Catholic), and a continuing, but increasingly marginalised, government-funded set of denominational or church schools. Schooling in the 1860s was neither compulsory, free, nor secular. In South Australia with its lower proportion of Catholics and Anglicans, there were no separate boards. There was a strong feeling among the most influential South Australian colonists that no government money should go to any church schools, and that came into effect as early as 1851.

Young people who were most likely to be schooled for a long period of time, to get more than a basic education, were usually in denominational (church), and private schools, which had developed a *superior*, *higher* or what would be eventually known as a *secondary* curriculum. National schools were mainly *elementary* schools, beyond which very few children would go.

In the second part of the nineteenth century the forces in favour of building up the government schools at the expense of the church and private schools had a series of massive victories. They led to the great Public Instruction and Education Acts passed in nearly all of the colonies in this period. Besides consolidating the *National* schools into *public* or *government* school systems, the Acts cut off all state aid to non-government schools. Henceforth revenues from public taxation would only go to public schools. At this point in history, the Australian colonies set out in a direction quite different from Canada and Britain, where church schools continued to receive either central or local government funding. A chart of the timing of the different Acts in the colonies follows.

Table 9.1 Achieving mainly free, compulsory, and secular government schools through the great Education Acts of the nineteenth and early twentieth century in the Australian colonies and states

	'Free'	'Compulsory'	'Secular'
Victoria	1872	1872	1872
New South Wales	1906	1880	1880–82
South Australia	1892	1875	1852
Tasmania	1908	1868	1854
Queensland	1870	1900	1875–80
Western Australia	1901	1871	1895

Source: Barcan, 1980, p. 151

We cannot go into detail as to why these Acts were passed except to say that in this period the Catholic Church grew more conservative, less willing to make any compromise towards joining in the movement towards government schools. In the colonies there was also strong anti-Catholic and anti-Irish prejudice. At the same time, the idea that the proper basis of good and efficient education could be secular, or at the least based on common Christianity, continued to grow. But there were newer ideas as well. One was that by providing schools with the right curriculum, efficiently taught, and by forcing all children to attend such schools, this could lead to greater economic prosperity and industrial advance. There was also the resurgence of an old idea: that compulsory attendance, especially for poor children, could improve on the lax discipline and unsatisfactory influence of their families. The possibility that government elementary schools could become universal and paternalistic institutions, compensating for the perceived failures of families and even churches, was increasingly popular among the colonial governing elites. Economic advance and increased social order could both be achieved. Each of these arguments contributed to the passing of the Acts, although some of the longest arguments in parliaments as the bills were discussed were over when and how Bible-reading might be allowed, and whether or when clergy should have visiting rights to government schools (Austin, 1961; Austin & Selleck, 1975; Miller & Davey, 1988).

The most outraged at this, the third settlement, was the Roman Catholic Church. The bishops instructed the faithful that to attend a government school was to attend a godless school, filled with Protestant heresy. Without government aid, the Church was not wealthy enough to continue paying reasonable salaries to lay Catholic teachers in the Catholic schools. Such teachers were usually replaced by 'religious' teachers, mainly sisters (nuns) and brothers who took vows of chastity and poverty. An age of heroism set in that paralleled that of the development of the National schools. For example, characters such as Mary McKillop and Tennyson Woods founded and organised schools of the Sisters of St Joseph, especially in the more remote and poorer districts across the colonies. The Catholic Church thus built their own parochial (local) school systems, mainly resourced from the unpaid labour of the 'religious', and the fundraising of parish churches (Foale, 1989; Fogarty, 1959; O'Donoghue, 2001). Catholic education was thus alienated from what was developed as 'public' schooling in Australia. This alienation lasted 100 years, and its effects are still perceptible in Australia today.

> ### The Catholic Church rejects public education:
>
> They boldly and defiantly tell you it is their determination to do away with your schools, and substitute for them Godless schools, to which they will compel you, under penalty (or imprisonment) to send your children … they threaten the Catholics of this Colony … with religious persecution in the shape of a Godless and compulsory system of education (Bishop J. A. Goold, Bishop of Melbourne, 1872, in Austin, 1963, p. 220).
>
> ### A case for secular public schools:
>
> The temples are still full of worshippers, the offerings still tinkle in the plates, the confessionals are still thronged with breast-beating penitents … But go out in the world. Where is your religion then? Does it inspire the politician, assist the man of science, or aid the physician? No, it embarrasses them all … The measure of the people's knowledge is the measure of the people's religion. Educate your children to understand the discoveries of Tyndall, Huxley, and Darwin, and you will find them pleasantly laughing at the old fables of Jonah, Balaam, and Lazarus (Marcus Clarke, 1879, in Austin, 1963, p. 220).

So, by the beginning of the twentieth century there was a strong and rapidly growing set of government schools and systems, which was especially strong for the years of compulsory attendance. Large, centralised bureaucracies increasingly ran them, with thousands of trained primary teachers, mainly young and unmarried women, as teachers (Theobald, 1996; Whitehead, 2003). The schools were controlled by regulations, central syllabus prescription, inspectors, and elaborate systems of teacher transfer and promotion. There was a much weaker group of church schools, most of them elementary and Catholic. The Protestant churches, with the exception of the Lutherans, departed from elementary education and concentrated on providing a few colleges, mainly for the middle class and the wealthy. Some of the Catholic orders concentrated on this market also. Finally there was still a group of genuine private schools run for profit. Without government or church help, increasing numbers closed their doors. Today there are virtually none of this old group left, except for the odd private coaching college.[1]

The beginning of the twentieth century also saw Australian federation (1901). As has been noted, the Constitution left education as a residual power of the states. Except for occasional interest at the university level, the federal government showed every sign of respecting the intent of the Constitution. During the Second World War, however, the federal government gained the sole power to collect income tax, and thus achieved financial dominance in the Australian political system. It now had the financial power, if not strictly the constitutional power, to interfere in all levels and areas of government. The problem for the states was that the Commonwealth or federal government would often grant the money *with conditions on how it was to be spent*. So it was that one of the prime characteristics of the present era—activist federal governments attempting to set policy in all areas of school education, and often being resisted by state governments—came about. (There is a significant literature on this topic; for example, see Harman & Smart, 1982; Lingard, 2000; Marginson, 1997a; Smart, 1982.)

The state aid settlement; that is, the decision that no non-government schools would get government funding, mainly held through to the 1960s. The Liberal Party (founded in 1944), very much a Protestant party to the 1960s and beyond, had been very happy with the status quo. The Labor Party founded in the 1890s, somewhat less believably given the proportion of Catholics who voted for it, also held to a 'no state aid' policy.

In the first half of the twentieth century, the major change in terms of institutions was that state governments decided to get involved systematically in secondary education. First came academic high schools, providing opportunities and an educational ladder for a minority of clever children. Also came a lifting of the school leaving age to 14, and later 15 years, which required upward extensions to the primary schools. Such schools included central, intermediate, junior technical, and domestic science schools among others (Cleverley & Lawry, 1972).

The new government academic high schools challenged the older church colleges for public examination successes. Melbourne High, Fort St High, Hobart High, Adelaide High, Sydney Boys' and Sydney Girls', Perth Modern and Brisbane Boys' and Brisbane Girls' became popular with middle-class families (Campbell, 1999a, 1999b). Parents asked themselves: 'Why pay college fees if you can get an academic education that might get you into university or a good white-collar job in the city—for free?'

So, by the end of the Second World War the government school system remained in the ascendant. It was powerful and extensive. It provided a mainly free, solid education to all sectors of the community, except a large group of Catholics whose schools were in the main desperately poor. Even the elite church college sector was under pressure as the academic high schools won the loyalty of significant sections of the middle class. In New South Wales, for example, the emerging political, business, and social elite was increasingly educated at what we now call government selective high schools. Labor leaders Herbert Evatt and Neville Wran were educated at such schools, as were a smaller group of future Liberal leaders including John Howard.

In the second half of the twentieth century this settlement began to collapse; slowly at first, then from the late 1970s, quite rapidly. At least four factors can be identified that led to this. The last was common across Australia, Canada, the United States, and the United Kingdom. The first was peculiarly Australian:

- the reintroduction of state aid to non-government schools
- the financial pressures on the states to provide enough schools for children of the postwar 'baby-boom'
- pressures towards multiculturalism arising from an increasingly multi-ethnic society
- severe loss of faith in government action in favour of neoliberal approaches, in the economy but also in education.

This emergent Australian educational settlement eventually left public education stalled and, for the first time in over a century, in relative decline in comparison with the non-government sector.

The end of the denial of state aid to non-government schools was in the main a consequence of the Cold War. With the successful expansion of communist regimes in Eastern Europe and East Asia from the mid 1940s, anxiety grew among governments in the West, including Australia, that communism was the new threat to world peace. The Catholic Church was an important participant in the struggles of the Cold War. While the Australian Catholic Church had been sympathetic to Labor, and had little time for the worst of capitalism, its aggressive opposition to communism affected the relationship. Communism was atheistic and the direct enemy of the Church in countries such as Poland and elsewhere.

In Australia the labour movement was increasingly seen by some as communist-influenced—indeed some of the powerful trade unions had communist leaderships. An internecine struggle broke out between anti-communist and Catholic-associated organisations and the left of the labour movement. This conflict was especially bitter in Victoria. It was there that the Labor Party split in the mid 1950s (see Fitzgerald, 2003). In many states of Australia Labor governments lost office. The Liberals could only celebrate because former Catholic Labor votes were directed towards them through the preferential voting system. The task for the Liberals was to secure this new vote permanently. Certainly a strong anti-communist defence policy would help, but there was also the old Catholic grievance: no state aid to Catholic schools in a period when such schools were in trouble. By the early 1960s, the trend was clear: the baby-boom would dramatically increase the number of Catholic children to be sent to Catholic schools, and the numbers of Catholic religious who were teachers had entered a period of decline.

One of the things that might be done, at state and federal level, was to offer state aid to Catholic schools. Other Cold War circumstances added to the argument. After the war, the Soviet Union rapidly developed its own atomic bombs and missile delivery systems, and put the first satellite and human into space. Anxiety over these developments led to a panic about the adequacy of science and technology education in the West. In Australia the science curriculum was backward and science laboratories were both few and poorly equipped; nor did many secondary schools have useful libraries.

It was under these circumstances that the federal government made its move, offering huge grants to government and non-government schools, including Catholic, in order to provide science laboratories (1964) and later libraries (1968) and scholarships to clever students. State governments also began offering grants to non-government schools or their students at much the same time. These offers were mainly accepted with joy by the non-government sector and the old settlement was overturned.[2] Once Liberal-Country Party governments had begun offering state aid to non-government schools, the Labor Party and Labor governments could hardly afford not to do the same (Connell, W.F., 1993).

After 1972 at the federal level, following the election of the Whitlam Labor government and through the Karmel-led Schools Commission, the old settlement was finally ended. Federal government funding for all schools would occur on the basis of *need* rather than their religious or ownership status. That a very large number of the poorest schools were Catholic meant that through one scheme or another, government funding rapidly became the primary source of all funds for Catholic systemic schools. How the need of schools is calculated changes with successive federal governments; the main point is that it is no longer possible to imagine that any government in Australia would withdraw aid to non-government schools. An organisation of supporters of the old settlement, DOGS (Defend Our Government Schools) mounted a High Court challenge. There was, after all, fair evidence that the Constitution never envisaged that federal governments had a role to play in school education, and that, like the American constitution, federal government funding of churches, and therefore church schools, was also contrary to its intent. The DOGS challenge was rejected by the High Court in 1981 (Australian Council for the Defence of Government Schools, 2005).

The truth also was that by the 1960s, the state governments could barely afford the necessary expansion of their public school systems. The children of the post-Second World War baby-boom and the new suburbs in which their parents were building houses demanded an extraordinarily rapid increase in the numbers of schools and teachers. They needed federal aid, regardless of the conditions that might be placed on it.

Another factor that eventually contributed to the stalling of the public education system was the fact of an increasingly multi-ethnic Australia. At first strong attempts were made to contain the diverse cultural pressures by adopting multicultural policies and curricula within government schools, but eventually the collapse of the old state aid settlement meant that Greek Orthodox or Jewish schools, or new low-fee Anglican, Uniting Church, or various 'Christian' or Muslim schools, could just as easily demand their share of state aid. The number of new non-government schools targeting specific ethnic-religious populations rapidly expanded. (See also chapter 7.)

Finally there was from the late 1970s the growth of neoliberalism, or 'economic rationalism' as it was described in Australia. Public policy increasingly argued for the benefits of diverse institutions being encouraged to compete for customers in a market. Among such institutions would be schools, both government and non-government.

3   Public and private schools

As a result of the previous discussion, we can see the origins of Australia's current system of government and non-government schools. In fact, nearly all schools in Australia are funded to some degree by governments. There is virtually no such thing as a genuinely 'private' sector of schools. The terminology survives as a shorthand, but inaccurate, way of describing the diverse range of non-government schools. Government schools are usually run by large departments of education and training, with varying degrees of local control devolved to area directorates, school principals, and school councils. Non-government schools are very diverse in the way they are owned, governed, and run. Most Catholic schools are organised as systems of schools; their central bureaucracies are the various Catholic Education Offices. A smaller number of Catholic, usually secondary, colleges, are *independent* schools, run by what is left of the originating religious orders and the school trusts and councils they established for the purpose. Other independent schools are sometimes known as *corporate* schools; that is, they are governed by incorporated trusts or councils, and are often ultimately owned by churches. But there are also schools not owned by churches such as the various progressive schools following community, Steiner, Montessorian, or other educational approaches and philosophies.

Another important issue in discussing the differences between government and non-government schools relates to the ways that non-government schools are also regulated by authorities ultimately established by governments. Probably the most important of these is the authority in each state that controls publicly recognised school credentials (certificates of achievement) and the production of the senior school curricula. Nearly all government and non-government schools enrol their students for the various examinations and assessment exercises that produce credentials such as the Higher School Certificate, SSABSA Certificate, Victorian Certificate of Education, and so on. Many states insist that persons employed as teachers hold certain minimal qualifications regardless of government or non-government sector. Some state governments only allow non-government schools to operate if they are registered, with their registration being dependent on meeting various requirements relating to curriculum and facilities. Another factor that tends to allow the idea that there is in fact a unitary system of Australian education is that most federal government specific purpose programs, in the encouragement of literacy objectives for example, are equally available to government and non-government schools. There is also a regular meeting and secretariat of state and federal Ministers of education that seeks to establish common approaches to educational issues across Australia. The Australian Council of Educational Research (ACER) provides research, policy advice, and testing services to each sector as well.

This evidence of a unitary system cannot be taken too far, however. The radical difference between the government and non-government school sectors can be reduced to the issue of *inclusivity*. Most government schools are open to all children and youth regardless of their background. Most non-government schools discriminate against children, youth, and families on the basis of their ability to pay fees, practise a certain religion, or meet certain less definable standards: perhaps behavioural, or if they are poor, the inability to win a scholarship. While government schools also have some powers to exclude students on the basis of behaviour standards for example (suspension and expulsion), they are not nearly as easy to effect as those in the non-government sector.

To conclude this discussion of public and private schools in Australia, we look at some recent and basic statistics related to the size of the school systems (Tables 9.2 and 9.3).

Table 9.2 Number of schools in Australia by category of school and percentage increase from the previous 10 years, 1984, 1994, 2004 (N, %)

Year	Government N	Government % growth	Catholic N	Catholic % growth	Independent N	Independent % growth
1984	7544		1705		776	
1994	7159	-5.3	1699	-0.4	821	+5.5
2004	6938	-3.2	1695	-0.2	982	+16.4

Source: Australian Bureau of Statistics, *Schools* (Series no. 4221.0)

Table 9.3 Full-time school students in Australia by category of school, 1984, 1994, 2004 (N, %)

Year	Government N	Government %	Non-government N	Non-government %	Total N	Total %
1984	2,260,551	74.9	757,052	25.1	3,017,603	100.0
1994	2,214,938	71.5	884,442	28.5	3,099,380	100.0
2004	2,249,724	67.5	1,082,240	32.5	3,331,964	100.0

Source: Australian Bureau of Statistics, *Schools 2003* (Reissue) (Series no. 4221.0) Table 6, p. 12.

Table 9.4a Full-time primary school students in Australia, by state and category of school, 2004 (N, %)

State	Government N	Government %	Catholic N	Catholic %	Independent N	Independent %	Total N	Total %
NSW	440,309	70.6	125,440	20.1	58,230	9.3	623,979	100
Vic	316,143	69.4	99,002	21.7	40,277	8.8	455,422	100
Qld	287,406	74.4	60,839	15.8	37,899	9.8	386,144	100
SA	108,786	69.1	27,573	17.5	21,091	13.4	157,450	100
WA	150,222	72.9	35,180	17.1	20,675	10.0	206,077	100
Tas	35,918	77.4	6797	14.6	3694	8.0	46,409	100
NT	19,801	79.5	3123	12.5	1991	8.0	24,915	100
ACT	19,788	63.0	8721	27.8	2886	9.2	31,395	100
Total	1,378,373	71.4	366,675	19.0	186,743	9.7	1,931,791	100

Table 9.4b Full-time secondary school students in Australia, by state and category of school, 2004 (N, %)

State	Government N	%	Catholic N	%	Independent N	%	Total N	%
NSW	303,920	62.9	112,770	23.3	66,380	13.7	483,070	100
Vic	220,073	60.0	80,974	22.1	65,831	17.9	366,878	100
Qld	161,400	63.8	46,121	18.2	45,290	17.9	252,811	100
SA	57,080	62.7	17,591	19.3	16,401	18.0	91,072	100
WAS	79,544	61.2	25,787	19.8	24,658	19.0	129,989	100
Tas	24,767	69.1	6,250	17.4	4,836	13.5	35,853	100
NT	8,534	70.4	1,490	12.3	2,091	17.3	12,115	100
ACT	16,033	56.5	8,467	29.8	3,885	13.7	28,385	100
Total	871,351	62.2	299,450	21.4	229,372	16.4	1,400,173	100

Source: Australian Bureau of Statistics, *Schools 2004* (Series no. 4221.0)

These tables (9.4a and 9.4b) show that the fastest rising school sector is the independent; that is, the non-government, non-Catholic sector. It shows that both the percentage share of enrolments and the number of schools is declining steadily for the government sector in comparison with non-government schools, although the actual numbers in government schools are declining much less rapidly than the share. One can also see from these tables that the states and territories with smaller, less centralised populations remain more dependent on government schooling than the others. The decline of enrolments in the government secondary schools is greater than that in the primary. It is possible that within another decade (2014) in some states the percentage of students in government schools, at least in secondary, will be less than half. In some parts of Australia's larger cities, that is already the case.

4 Creating a school market

From the late 1970s new theories of government and economy, resurrecting some of the ideas of classic liberalism, advocated reduced government activity in the provision of services and a new encouragement of the market economy. Such policies were supported from a number of different perspectives. In general the belief was that entrepreneurial activity had been stifled by overbearing government activity, that citizens had become over-dependent on the 'nanny state', that potential economic growth had been held back by disproportionate levels of state intervention in labour markets and the provision of services, and that the best way to ensure reform, including new efficiencies in production, was to trust market forces to weed out the weaker or conservative elements, in favour of the entrepreneurial and progressive. Neoliberalism has been adopted to some degree by all governments, federal and state, Labor and Liberal–National, from the beginning of the 1980s.

For education, this has meant an ideological withdrawal of trust in centralised and bureaucratically organised government school systems. Simon Marginson (1993, 1997a, 1997b) has developed the most comprehensive of the analyses of this process in Australia, but see also the international literature on the development of school markets, or *quasi-markets* (Whitty, 1997; Whitty & Power, 2002). The term 'quasi-market' is useful since it points to the fact that in most of the Northern American and Western European countries, as well as Australia and New Zealand, where neoliberalism has taken hold, the markets are not *free* markets. In fact they are usually dependent on government support. In Australia the encouragement of non-government schools, and parental choice of schools, could only have occurred with the introduction of extensive state aid to non-government schools. Some scholars have even argued that parents are increasingly being *forced* into the role of being *consumers* of private services that were formerly and satisfactorily provided by the government direct. A parallel process can be observed in relation to the *privatisation* not only of education, but also of health, welfare, and transport (Pusey, 1991).

As Tables 9.2–9.4 above demonstrate, the growth of diverse schools, creating an educational market, has proceeded quite rapidly since the 1980s. This process occurs not only between the government and non-government sectors, but also very importantly, within them as well.

Non-government schools can be secular or church schools, progressive in their approaches to the curriculum or conservative. They can provide for specific ethno-religious communities—Maronite Christian, orthodox or progressive Jewish, Lebanese Muslim, Greek Orthodox, fundamentalist Christian—and there are also the very high-fee schools with church or secular foundations reaching back into the nineteenth century. Some of them charge fees approaching $20,000 per year, and in so doing promise social exclusivity and extraordinary educational facilities and probably advantages.

Government schools are also encouraged to enter the market, competing against each other as well as the low-fee non-government schools in particular. The encouragement of such competition was dependent on the end of school zoning, and the development of specialist schools, some of which had the right to discriminate in favour of some students rather than others (that is, they were *selective* or *semi-selective* schools). These developments have led to a greater diversity within the government sector: specialist schools, senior colleges, junior schools, selective schools, mixed selective and comprehensive schools and so on. Specialist schools have often developed curricula focused around the performing arts, sport, or technology. Often it has been in the interest of schools to publicise special programs, maybe for the gifted and talented, or to develop special services for disabled students. All schools are increasingly engaged with the advertising and public relations industry to maximise their enrolments (Whitehead, 2005a).

One of the problems with the creation of markets in schooling is that the probability is heightened that large gaps will develop between schools that succeed and those that do not. Families and students who attend schools that are failing are likely to be disadvantaged. Not all families have the skills and resources to compete equally effectively in the emergent markets of education. Some government schools in particular, especially those in areas with high unemployment and high concentrations of recently arrived non-English speaking immigrants, face the possibility and fact of becoming 'safety net' schools with poor retention rates, restricted subject offerings in the senior years and inexperienced teaching staff. (See Thomson, 2002; Vickers, 2004.)

5   The process of choosing a school

Choosing schools for children has become one of the key moments in the histories of many families. The consequences of the act not only affect the education and life of the young person in a very direct way, but also have great symbolic value as well. It can be a means of a family saying: 'We are this kind of people, and we have these values and ambitions.' So school choice is a phenomenon that potentially gives us great insight into the sociology and politics of the way our education systems both operate and interact with the rest of society.

In asking the question of how families make their choices (or deliberately refuse to, or simply fail to participate in the choosing process), we need to be systematic in our approach. There are many approaches to school choice that can provide insights. We choose to discuss three: family strategy theory, social reproduction theory, and liberal economic and political theory.

Family strategy theory

In this approach we view the family a little like a ship upon a stormy sea. Decisions are constantly being made about how the family is to operate, how the family is to survive, and how it is to be advantaged. Sometimes there is long term planning—'I put my child's name down for such and such a school when he or she was born'—and sometimes there appears to be a distinct lack of planning—'He or she wanted to go to such and such a school because friends were going there'. Sometimes research goes into it—'We went to all the open days, read all the brochures carefully, interviewed the Principal of each school'—and sometimes not—'It was the closest school so that's where we sent her'.

This approach has the advantage of seeing families as powerful makers of their own histories, but it has defects as well. It can overemphasise the capacity of family members to make significant decisions, when there is often very little room to move. It can present the family as a united decision-making institution, when there are often significant divisions. These are often based on gender and age differences. Children do not always accept their parents' decisions. Mothers and fathers do not always agree on what should be done. (On families and school choice, see Reay & Ball (1998).) See also chapters 2 and 3.

Social reproduction theory

This theory is especially useful in explaining the persistence of social structures and social hierarchies, including the reproduction of unequal social relations. It can help us to understand why many working-class and Aboriginal people, and others who are poor and disempowered, tend to remain so over a number of generations. Because the theory discusses the ways different people can be effective in different areas of society (*field*), and through family cultural characteristics and ways of doing things (*habitus*) go on to extract major benefit (*cultural capital*) from institutions with which they come into contact, the theory is useful for discussing school choice.

These elements are all important in affecting the ways parents might *read* (analyse and interpret) school prospectuses and advertisements. Can one read between the lines? What is not being mentioned? How confident do parents feel if they interview a school principal or members of staff? Can they ask the right questions, or feel comfortable in asking the uncomfortable questions that might evoke a better understanding of a school? What networks do parents have in order to harvest inside information on a school? Do they know some teachers at the school who might tell them the real story? And so on. Much of this power to effectively assess different schools in the school choice process is related to social class practices and knowledge. More highly educated middle-class parents are often in a better position to be astute players in the education market—but not necessarily in other markets, in other fields of practice (like buying a second-hand car). Chapter 6 discusses more comprehensively the ways that social class relations may affect schooling.

Liberal economic/political theory

Classic liberalism argued for the minimum of government intervention into the activities of its citizens. There should be considerable freedom of action, freedom of choice, and indeed freedom to fail or succeed. Economically, markets and free trade were trusted to produce economic growth. Understandably there were many opponents to classical liberalism, with its studied blindness towards the casualties of the free market. The New Liberalism, increasingly influential from the late nineteenth century was less concerned about active government interventions. The state should intervene, especially to modify the damage caused by the free markets. The state should provide, often as monopolies, certain services to produce a modicum of social fairness. (Laws providing old age pensions, compulsory schooling and the requirement that employers pay a basic wage can all be seen in this light.) In fact, the freedom of individuals to act and choose needed to be restricted in the interests of all. In Australia, this approach was somewhat common to both Labor and Liberal governments through to the 1980s.

At that point a new version of classical liberalism, hence *neoliberalism,* began its rise to major influence. It was characterised by the desire to cut back the welfare state as having produced welfare dependence and crippled individual initiative, to increase the sphere and power of markets to regulate social and economic activity, and in so doing, increase choice and competitive individualism, as a means of making a competitive economy and more self-reliant citizens (see Sawer, 2003).

So what we see in the rise of neoliberalism as it affects school choice is a belief that by extending the school market and encouraging choice, families and young people will take a new responsibility for their actions. They will find the schools that really suit them; both individual initiative and competitive behaviours will find their just rewards. In the process educational reform will occur, as those schools unresponsive to the market will either have to become market responsive, or fail.

There is no great concern here if social inequality is produced through persons or families choosing in a school market to a more or less skilled degree. People have to take responsibility for their own lives and their own decisions.

The reasons given by parents in surveys for choosing one school over another are fairly predictable—discipline, values, safety, opportunity, religion, the quality of the teachers and the students, and so on (Masters, 2004). The challenge is to go a little deeper and to see what some of these words and ideas might mean. The following text refers to the interview extracts (A-K) positioned over the next few pages. They come from a recent research project on school choice (Bagnall, Nicholls & Cuttance, 2004).

Interview A

Parent: He is a clever boy and he would have gone to a selective high school. He sat for the selective schools examination but he missed out … I thought he would struggle if he went to a selective high; it is not good being average in a selective high, it affects your self-esteem. Selective high school is my dream, but it is no use placing that on him. I work as a school teacher at [private school]. I would have liked him to come here as it is close, but he said 'No' … because none of his friends are going here … It is a user pays world. Schools where you pay have more responsibility … If he went to the local school he would be with those children who cannot get into other schools … If we lived in [X, a more middle class suburb] I would not mind, but not here.

In *Interview A* we can see the complexity associated with some school choice activity, especially when the parent has certain know-how (being a teacher) and ambitions for the child, but also a market-savvy approach to the relationship between what you get and what you pay. There is also a desire to avoid the local children by avoiding the local school and the necessity of taking into account the child's wishes—he refused to go to the school in which his parent worked. There is also a working knowledge of psychology—unrealistic expectations can affect self-esteem, with undesirable educational consequences.

Interview B

Parent: … the other negatives I heard were … the type of guys that were getting around the drug scene, that sort of thing … well what was most important was … welfare really.

In *Interview B*, child safety, travelling between home and school, and safety at school, were paramount in deciding against one school in this case. The other important thing about this extract is the source of the information. Rumours may or may not be true; often one incident can become wildly exaggerated as it gathers force.

Interview C

Parent: A friend who teaches at [selective school] had warned me of certain problems in the public system, at the moment, even though we're quite

> loyal to that system … And, ah, we discussed this a little bit and decided that because of the location—I live only five minutes away—it would mean that I could be more involved. [X] could travel easily on his own.

Interview C again shows the influence of intelligence gathering. It also points to the discomfort some parents have in considering other schools or systems than those to which they consider themselves 'loyal'. In this, opportunities for parental involvement, as well as ease of access to the chosen school, are important. Considerable research has shown that mothers, especially in middle-class families, believe that the choice of a good school is only the first step. There has to be close monitoring, participation, and intervention in the work of the school throughout the child's enrolment (Brantlinger, 2003; Devine, 2004; Reay, 1998).

Interview D

Parent: I was very impressed with the Headmaster at the school; he was a very young man, in his late thirties, enthusiastic, laughing and smiling, positive. I was very impressed. At his talk on Open Day he stressed there would be no weapons at the school—no graffiti. He was fantastic and he said there would be basic standards in the classroom and the playground. There was no rubbish and no chewing gum. It was very clean and neat.

What can be said for *Interview D*? Style over substance? Nevertheless it points to the importance of schools being marketable under the circumstances of neoliberalism. A Principal skilled in public relations, and the reassurances on safety and cleanliness—the idea of the school as a well-controlled environment—may be worth very many enrolments.

Interview E

Interviewer: They have hats there too!
Parent: Yeah! They still have, and they have to wear what they have to wear. And that's just like a discipline—and we believe that the education there … like with the discipline, conduct … how it is … their education. They can teach what they're supposed to be teaching … 'cos everything's sort of in control … They haven't got a whole class full of uncontrollable …

In *Interview E* there is the controlled environment again, but this time so that teachers can get on with teaching without disruption. The hats and the uniforms in this case symbolise the order and control that apparently occurs in the remainder of the school. In the market, *signs* and *symbolic practices* are important for communicating essential messages about what a school wishes a community to believe about it.

Interview F

Interviewer: Did academic standards concern you?
Parent: No.
Interviewer: What concerned you the most?
Parent: I think, that he goes somewhere where they will instil in him or exhort him to greater things, which without a watchful eye he may rather do other things. He needs that discipline, and I don't mean physical discipline. He needs that constant attention … He needs to keep his nose to the grindstone.

For *Interview F*, high academic achievement was not so much the point as the parent being able to trust the school, to draw the school into a purposeful child-rearing and educative strategy. The child is to be encouraged, but also watched. Some schools might be trusted to do this more than others.

Interview G

Parent: I thought they were getting far too personal with the information they wanted—'average income'! I thought: 'That's none of your business!' When it came to questions about the child's baptism the form asked for:'What colour the priest was wearing on the day he did it.' I mean for pity's sake, if they're going to be that sticky about religion on the questions on the application, what are they going to try to pump into her in school?

Interview G is interesting from at least three points of view. The first is the desire of the school (non-government of course) to choose its parents and students. Presumably where prospective enrolees are in good supply, parental choice is actually reduced because the school may not want them. The second is the reaction to the intrusive nature of the questions. Not only does the school set up the conditions for discriminating against enrolments on the ground of insufficient income or religious seriousness, but assumes the possibility that parents will lie in order to secure their children a place. If this is true, it points again to the competitive behaviours that are encouraged under market conditions. Finally of course is the issue of what it means to send a child to a church-owned school. In this case the assumption was that a church school might be trusted not to be too serious about religious training—but the parent had to revise that assumption quite rapidly.

Interview H

Parent: Right. Well, my choice would have been [X, non-local state high school]. But he was quite adamant he didn't want to go there. He wanted to go to [local state high school], so we've agreed that he can go there, and, providing he doesn't get into any trouble he can stay there. If his grades are well enough.

Interview H points to the power of the child in many families. Much of the research on school choice suggests that children are more powerful in working-class families than in middle-class families in determining the school they will attend.

Interview I

Parent: I'm not impressed with the types of kids who live around the area we live in. There's a lot of crime. I'm not sure about drugs but I know it's an area where children can be very disadvantaged and although it was an elitist decision, I decided that my child wouldn't have the strength maybe sometimes to choose friends who are going to help her …

The reason given for the choice of school in *Interview I* is the desire to engineer a child's peer group. This may well be an underrated factor in the school choice literature. Again research tends to suggest that family and peers are at least, if not more, influential in affecting school success than the nature of the school attended. Parents may or may not have a strong sense of this.

Interview J

Parent: Anyway she really wanted to go to the local high school. It is really close to us. She liked the fact that it seemed to be quite a liberal school. They don't wear a uniform. I think, probably, a single sex school would allow a girl to develop emotionally at her own speed … Whereas going to a co-ed school—having to develop with the guys being there; it is almost like forced feeding. They have to learn certain social skills, because they are forced into that situation, and that takes a lot of time away from their studies. She was very adamant … she wanted to go to [local high school] … she was probably not terribly open minded to any other school. So she openly said that 'I'll go there [state girls' school], but I am not going to like it.'

Interview J reveals an old strategy of middle-class parents, the attempt to delay the transition to adulthood, and its distractions, including boyfriends or girlfriends, in the attempt to channel the energy of their children into serious school work. This thinking seems a bit old-fashioned in the early twenty-first century. Single sex girls' schools are often chosen for other reasons—to produce social and educational advantages seen as increasingly accessible to women since second-wave feminism. In this case the child's wishes come second.

Interview K

Interviewer: Were the fees an issue?
Parent: Well, I figured that by the time they told us the fees—no. I mean, I haven't got them, but they're not an issue! They're not something that's going to stop me from sending her there.
Interviewer: And it will mean sacrificing something else?
Parent: Yeah, husband will do more overtime …

In the discourse of neoliberal educational policy, the response of the parent in *Interview K* is often highly respected. This parent may be a *battler* or from the *aspirational class* (see chapter 6, section 5). Families that take the tough decisions should be supported with government encouragement through a range of subsidies. In the United States, *voucher* schemes are sometimes used to support families to achieve the schools they desire. In Australia a sliding scale of government support to schools is based on the estimated wealth of the parents (based on post codes) who send their children to a non-government school, although Catholic schools often get block grants distributed by the relevant Catholic Education Office (Watson, 2003). The final point here relates to the husband's role in the school choice plan. Hopefully he had a chance to agree to his sacrifice! (Families are not always united in the development of family strategies.)

6 The social consequences of market-based school choice

There are several ways in which reasons for choosing schools might be analysed. In the mid 1990s, writing in the English context, Sharon Gewirtz and colleagues collected the choosers into four groups: the privileged, the frustrated, the disconnected, and the non-choosers (Gewirtz, Ball & Bowe, 1995).

For the privileged, the choice process was a time-consuming but vital process. Members of such families looked at the league tables of exam results, interviewed the principal, studied the brochures, and observed student behaviour. They acted as intelligent consumers—they utilised all their cultural and social capital in the process. The 'frustrated' group also had a consumerist approach, but they were limited by what they could afford and the need for school proximity. The 'disconnected' families were disconnected from the choice process. They did not understand it, and it was often the child who made the choice. They were often satisfied with the local school; there were family members already at the school, and it was close to home. The non-choosers felt alienated from the market for ideological and other reasons. They often felt uncomfortable with schools altogether and often had a low regard for school education.

These groups do not always line up with social classes, but there is some correlation. The first and last groups are more likely to be drawn from the middle and working class respectively. Stephen Ball's *Class Strategies and the Education Market* (2003) is a major contribution to this discussion. He develops the idea of *rational action* by groups within the markets of post-welfare societies (p. 16). He argues that class competition in education is historically contingent. At the present time there is intense competition for entrance to elite institutions. That has involved a shift away from *merit* as the main currency of access, to be replaced by *distinction*, even oligarchic 'goods' (p. 20). There is a new push for the importance of 'goods' that come from attending the most prestigious schools and universities. He argues that the insertion of choice and competition into strategic planning undermines an old middle-class desire for orderly and 'moral' progressivism (p. 22).

The root cause of this anxiety is the increasing difficulty and instability of all job markets, including those of the white-collar worker and professional. At least most in the middle class have the resources to develop strategies to deal with the new circumstances; other social groups are not necessarily as skilled or knowledgeable (Power et al., 2003, chapter 3).

In his discussion of the retreat of the middle class from the government comprehensive school, Ball argues that the social context of schooling is a crucial issue. For example, too many students from ethnically alien or poor areas become a threat to successful middle-class strategies. Parents expect to influence the school's practices in the interests of their children. While diversified state schools retain numbers of middle-class families in the government sector, the market pressures tend to undermine cooperation between schools. Parents are forced to intervene in and supervise the education of their children in ways unprecedented in living memory. Parents are partners and 'customers' (p. 166). Their approach, and the engagement of their middle-class skills is 'fearful, alert and strategic' (p. 168).

Although Ball's discussion is drawn on evidence from the United Kingdom, most of the argument resonates in Australia as we can discover from the work of Pusey (2003). He argues that the Australian middle class have, except for some wealthier cosmopolitan fragments, been forced into the behaviours of aggressive individualism and competitiveness as a result of the past 30 years of neoliberal economic reform. Pusey argues that as middle-class families have had to adjust themselves to the market, which only intrudes ever more insistently into family and social life, the market is looked to for the defence of important and surviving values and codes of behaviour. He argues that such families feel let down by institutions such as public schools that cannot be trusted to do the necessary work ensuring family security (p. 95). A common consequence is that the private school is identified as a means of protecting children against some of the many dangers and uncertainties of life in post-welfare Australia. Pusey refers to the 'guilt' felt by many of the middle-class parents in his surveys and interviews that they had found it necessary to depart from public institutions. Under these circumstances, sending one's children to a private or select government school becomes a positive though resented response to government cutbacks in the public sector.

Richard Teese (2000) develops a more radical critique of the consequences of producing school markets and their effects on many parts of the public school sector. In his analysis of how many private schools and some selective state schools operate in the market he develops a metaphor, that 'school failure' may be 'exported'. 'Private schools, operating on an assured platform of public grants, drain secondary education of the cultural resources represented by family education, life-style and know-how and pump these into the most profitable locations of the curriculum. The school system becomes polarized' (p. 204). (See also Watson, 2004, on wealth differentials between schools and systems.)

To conclude, the school choice activity that has developed over the last two to three decades in Australia is neither a simple nor natural phenomenon. It has been structured and promoted by government. Some families are more able to engage in it than others. Some families are more effectively able to benefit from the opportunities than others. Such families are often middle or aspiring middle class: they are able to mobilise their habitus and their social and cultural capital to make schools work for them more effectively than others. Education is a field in which they can expect to win.

Others experience alienation and powerlessness when confronted with school choice regimes. Their inability or unwillingness to play may lead to continuing disadvantage and possible school failure—indeed, in reproduction theory terms, the reproduction of social inequality. This raises serious problems for the future of Australian schooling and the fair availability of good schooling to all. We need to ask the question whether it will be sustainable to continue to commit large amounts of tax monies to non-government schools that cater to specific communities defined substantially by wealth, religion, and ethnicity without asking of them that they share the burden of children and families in poverty and in trouble.

Focus questions

1 Is it important that Australia should have a well-resourced government school system? Why?

2 What effect might the development of publicly funded schools based on specific religious and ethnic communities have on the development of Australian society?

3 Should all families, regardless of their wealth, have the right to tax-subsidised non-government schooling?

4 What are the advantages and disadvantages of the creation of school markets?

5 How well does Australia manage its schooling for children and youth? For example, is there a problem with the division of power over school funding and schooling between local, state, and federal governments?

6 Some people say that the effect of the creation of school markets is to make parents more competitive and less concerned about the welfare of all young people, and more devoted to extracting maximum benefits for their own children, sometimes at the expense of others. Is this true?

7 What impacts are likely to be felt by teachers if the schools in which they are employed need to compete quite intensively in an education market? Are they positive or negative impacts?

Notes

1. A resurgence of genuine 'for profit' private schools has been predicted. They may develop from the many private coaching colleges or child-care businesses. Certainly, if entrepreneurs are able to access government funding then the development could be quite swift. See Connors & Caro (2006).

2. Some non-government schools, for example the Presbyterian, were suspicious that state aid might mean the beginnings of government control; that is, the loss of autonomy. Those suspicions were rapidly overcome.

Further reading

Anderson, D. (1992).'The interaction of public and private school systems.' *Australian Journal of Education, 36*(3), 213–36.

Ball, S.J. (2003). *Class Strategies and the Education Market: The Middle Classes and Social Advantage.* London: RoutledgeFalmer.

Campbell, C. & Sherington, G. (2006). *The Comprehensive Public High School: Historical Perspectives.* New York: PalgraveMacmillan.

Marginson, S. (1993). *Education and Public Policy in Australia.* Cambridge: Cambridge University Press.

Pusey, M. (2003). *The Experience of Middle Australia: The Dark Side of Economic Reform.* Cambridge: Cambridge University Press.

Reay, D. & Ball, S. J. (1998).'Making their minds up: Family dynamics of school choice'. *British Educational Research Journal, 24*(4), 431–48.

Sherington, G. (2004).'Public commitment and private choice in Australian secondary education'. In R. Aldrich (ed.), *Public or Private Education? Lessons from History* (pp. 167–88). London: Woburn Press.

Teese, R. (2000). *Academic Success and Social Power: Examinations and Inequity.* Melbourne: Melbourne University Press.

Vickers, M. (2004).'Markets and mobilities: Dilemmas facing the comprehensive neighbourhood high school.' *Melbourne Studies in Education, 45*(2), 1–22.

Whitty, G. & Power, S. (2002).'The overt and hidden curricula of quasi-markets'. In G. Whitty (ed.), *Making Sense of Education Policy* (pp. 94–106). London: Paul Chapman Publishing.

Internet sources

Take into account that web sites often belong to organisations that have a particular interest in making an argument one way or another (e.g. the 'cis' site below is dedicated to supporting and expanding non-government schools while the 'aeufederal' site is dedicated to the support of public education). Look at the web sites of different schools, elite through to Catholic and public.

www.acer.edu.au/publications/newsletters/enews/04_enews21/Aug04_index.html
www.abs.gov.au/
www.aare.edu.au/confpap.htm
www.dest.gov.au/
www.cis.org.au/
www.aeufederal.org.au/Publications/index2.html#PAP

10
Curriculum

Margaret Vickers

1 'Why do we have to learn this, Miss?'

'Why do we have to learn this, Miss?' It's is a question that comes up all the time in the classroom. It is an entirely legitimate one, since young people do have learning intentions of their own. As Garth Boomer—one of Australia's most imaginative curriculum thinkers—argued, what we learn in school should recognise this and should arise out of negotiations in which students' learning intentions are taken seriously (Boomer et al., 1992). Students might respectfully suggest that their own ideas about what is worth learning might be taken into account, or they may simply be trying to get out of work. In either case, the questions they ask pose an implicit challenge to the entire web of stakeholders who have sought to influence what will be included in the curriculum. Was it the teacher who decided that this topic would be taught, or was she simply implementing a decision made by some state authority, such as the Board of Studies? Did this topic get to be on the curriculum because some special interest group lobbied to have it included? Or was the state Minister for Education influenced by a federal-level political initiative? Or the Minister may have amended the curriculum in order to gain a specific Commonwealth incentive grant. Between 1989 and 1993, the state and territory Ministers worked together to create a series of national agreements known as the curriculum statements and profiles, and, as discussed later in this chapter, these have had a considerable influence on what is learned in Australian schools.

Why do we have to learn this?

Faced with the challenge of explaining 'why we have to learn this' there are a number of answers a teacher might give, such as:
- 'My real goal is to develop your potential, and I think this project might be right for you, but we can discuss it, and try to locate something that better matches your interests.'

- 'If you don't develop these skills you will never get a good job', or alternatively, 'If you don't learn this material you will not be able to deal with the Year 11 and 12 curriculum.'
- 'This is stuff that every educated person knows. Systematic bodies of knowledge that are organised in terms of subject-matter disciplines are foundational to our culture.'
- 'I think the issues we are looking at here matter, but I am not asking you uncritically to accept the version in the textbook. It might be biased and reflect views of the dominant culture. Can you tell me how you see it?'

'Why do I have to learn this?' is daunting question because it opens up deeper philosophical issues about what kinds of knowledge matter, and why. Four alternative responses to this challenge are presented in the boxed text above. In a shorthand way, each of these answers points towards a fundamentally different philosophical stance about what school is for and what the curriculum should try to do. Reduced to their bare essentials, these stances relate to centuries-old arguments about the nature of reality, what schools are for, what it is possible to know, and what is worth knowing.

2 Four approaches to curriculum and pedagogy

Progressive pedagogies

The first example given above represents a progressivist stance, a philosophy that emphasises the active engagement of the learner, focusing on learning by doing rather than by listening. Progressivism can be traced back to the writings of the American pragmatist, John Dewey (1938, 1991). Teachers who are influenced by this approach consider that the purpose of education is to develop each individual's full potential; they argue that schools should provide rich opportunities for student-directed learning and group problem-solving (Oakes & Lipton, 1999). Australian progressivism combined a focus on the individual child as a unique human being with a concern for social justice, specifically but not exclusively in terms of giving all children a fair chance of succeeding at school. In an overview of curriculum change in Australian schools, Collins (1995) suggested that, taken together, these two factors 'resulted in a belief that real educational improvements occurred in the classroom, through committed, professionally educated teachers working with local communities to create a salient curriculum for each child'

(1995, p. 4). This form of progressivism was one of the main inspirations behind the school-based curriculum development (SBCD) movement that shaped what happened in many Australian schools from the late 1960s and on through the 1970s (Print, 1993). SBCD placed heavy demands on teachers, since they were required to be 'professional curriculum creators and resource choosers, not just dispensers of a handed-down syllabus' (Collins, 1995, p. 5). While this approach is no longer as dominant as it once was, there are many teachers whose early practice was shaped by progressivism and who still construct their work in this way.

An instrumental curriculum

When teachers justify what is on the curriculum by telling students that they must develop the skills that are being taught if they want a good job in the future, they are adopting an instrumentalist stance. Throughout our history Australians have mostly thought about education in instrumental ways; for most students and families, getting a job has always been the major aim of schooling (Collins, 2002). An instrumental curriculum is a tool-kit curriculum: the focus is on acquiring literacy and numeracy skills, while much less attention is paid to what is read or counted. My niece, then aged 6, summed it up succinctly when I asked her what she was doing at school. 'Mostly reading and writing' she said. When I asked 'What are you reading and writing?' she replied, 'Mostly sentences with full stops at the end.' It seemed that the real emphasis in her primary school was on acquiring skills, rather than developing a sense of excitement about knowing history, or connecting with the characters in a story or a play.

In some ways the skills-oriented curriculum represented a backlash against the broad and open-ended nature of progressive education. During the late 1970s economic restructuring in Australia led to an increase in youth unemployment rates and the situation worsened with the recession of 1981–83. Politicians played on parents' fears and the back-to-basics movement began. This gained strength over time so that, by 1989, New South Wales had introduced Basic Skills Tests for literacy and numeracy that were to be taken by all students in Years 3 and 5, in both government and non-government schools. At the same time, John Dawkins, who was then federal Minister for Education, Employment and Training, started a process that he hoped would lead to higher 'standards' and greater curriculum consistency among school curricula across the nation (Dawkins, 1988). The development of curriculum 'statements' that specify content and curriculum 'profiles' that specify outcomes were at the centre of this national effort. The influence of this mega-project on state-level curriculum development will be discussed later in this chapter.

By the end of the 1990s, the emphasis on teaching and testing basic skills had been taken further still. Starting in 1997, the Ministerial Council on Education, Training, Employment, and Youth Affairs (MCEETYA) established the National Literacy and Numeracy plan that led to the development of national benchmarks for reading, writing, and numeracy. These benchmarks are now being used to assess students in all states and territories at grade levels 3, 5, 7 and 9.

The skills-acquisition approach to justifying what is learned in school has now become so widespread that it is threatening to take over the entire curriculum. Reading, writing, and number skills have always been central to schooling, particularly at the primary level. However, these have now been joined by new skills such as information technology skills, interpersonal skills, problem-solving skills, project management and time management skills, and so on. As Collins notes, 'We have already reached the point where, if one mentions knowledge to teachers they often reply using the term "skills" and think they are talking about the same thing' (Collins, 2002, p. 45).

A curriculum based on subject-matter disciplines

The next broad stance on 'why we are learning this' demands that students acquire much more than generic literacy and numeracy skills. It represents perhaps the most abiding view of the real purpose of education, arguing that the real goal of education is to introduce students to systematic bodies of knowledge that are organised in terms of subject-matter disciplines. From a postmodern perspective, it can be argued that knowledge itself is not absolute but is constantly reconstructed as social and historical contexts change. One formulation that attempts to grapple with what a 'discipline' is comes from British philosopher Paul Hirst. He argued that subject disciplines involve much more than a collection of related topics. Rather, says Hirst, the disciplines represent fundamentally different ways of knowing (Hirst, 1973). He proposed that subject disciplines comprise a body of concepts and key ideas, a common vocabulary, and distinctive ways of relating these concepts and ideas. Each discipline has a characteristic way of establishing the truth of its claims: for example, scientists appeal to laboratory evidence, while historians cite documentary records. In addition, each discipline has distinct methods or forms of inquiry: physicists use linear accelerators to examine atomic and molecular structures, while chemists explore the similar materials but use X-ray spectroscopy.

Among educational researchers and policy advocates, there are at least two groups who argue that the subject disciplines matter. This is, however, a complex field, and the views of various groups regarding what should be taught and how it should be taught do not always coincide. The first group has been strongly influenced by an eminent line of cognitive psychologists, from Jerome Bruner (1960) to Robert Glaser (1984) to current researchers including Alan Schoenfeld, Lauren Resnick, Andrea diSessa, and Gaie Leinhardt. Their extensive research across a range of subject disciplines has at least two important implications. The first involves a reiteration of the constructivist position, emphasising the need to pay attention to children's initial conceptions about the phenomena being studied, and to explore any culturally specific views they may have about the topic in question. If this is not done, the danger is that children will hang on to what they already 'know' while at the same time memorising the collection of disconnected facts that they think they will be asked to regurgitate for their exams and assessments. The second implication of this cognitive research is that thinking is inextricably tied to specific domains and that disciplinary knowledge is central to intellectual life (this work is reviewed in Stevens et al., 2005).

Glaser, Resnick, and others who followed them urged teachers and researchers to identify the concepts that are central to their subject disciplines and study the different ideas children come up with as they grapple to construct an understanding of these concepts. Using this method, cognitive researchers have built up a considerable body of pedagogical knowledge that is specific to particular content areas. Taking his lead from this work, American teacher educator Lee Shulman (1986; Shulman & Quinlan, 1996) argued that the most important thing teachers need in order to promote students' intellectual development is pedagogical content knowledge. It is simply not the case, says Shulman, that a good teacher can teach anything. According to Shulman, 'a social studies teacher who believes that the history textbook is history cannot engage students in legitimate historical inquiry, no matter how qualified he or she might be in classroom management of generic questioning skills' (cited in Stevens et al., 2005, p. 133). It follows that teachers need a deep knowledge of the subjects they teach, for it is only then that they will be able to take their understanding of disciplinary content and use it flexibly to help children construct deep understandings of the core concepts.

This line of cognitive research suggests that an instrumental, skills-based approach falls short of what is required if we want to fully develop our students' intellectual capacities. All young people need to be able to think, analyse situations, and solve complex problems. This has always been on the curriculum for some students, but now it needs to be on the curriculum for all students. Even if deep thinking is mostly developed though connecting with challenging problems in specific subject matter domains, this does not necessarily mean that all aspects of the school curriculum at every level should be exclusively structured around the traditional disciplines. Lauren Resnick, one of the influential members of the group referred to above, is critical of many of the standard activities students are expected to carry out at school. In a widely cited paper titled 'Learning in school and out' (Resnick, 1988), she pointed out that thinking and problem-solving out of school tends to focus on problems that matter; these are often complex problems to which there are multiple possible solutions, all of which involve trade-offs and a need to make judgments. Often, these problems require sophisticated intellectual input from several different disciplinary perspectives. Problem-solving outside of school often involves groups of people coming together to discuss what to do. In contrast with this, the problems students are often given inside school tend to be simple ones; they lie within a single disciplinary area, and have single right or wrong answers. Furthermore, students are expected to answer these problems without reference to external data sources and they are expected to do their work in silence and alone.

Conservative politicians and educational activists also advocate the centrality of the traditional subject disciplines, but tend to do so within a very specific framework. John Howard neatly represented this position in his 2006 Prime Ministerial speech to the National Press Club on Australia Day (Howard, 2006). He said it was time for a renewal of the teaching of Australian history in our schools, both in terms of the numbers taking history and in terms of how it is taught. Within our schools the 'structured narrative of Australian history' has, he said, been replaced by a 'fragmented stew of themes and issues'. Along with other subjects in the humanities it has succumbed to a 'postmodern culture of relativism where any objective record of achievement is questioned or repudiated' (p. 5). He said that students should learn about 'the central currents of our nation's development … the great and enduring heritage of our Western civilization … the evolution of parliamentary democracy, and the ideas that galvanised the Enlightenment …'. Indigenous history should also be included, but only if it is treated as part of our 'whole national inheritance' (p. 5).

In an era of national uncertainties, dramatic migrations and demographic shifts, and struggles for racial and gender equality, it is understandable that there will be—among the older, established groups in our society—a nostalgia for the past. When these older Anglo-Australians went to school, they studied a 'modern' curriculum in which the idea of scientific progress was accepted as an unquestioned truth and the facts about Australian history that they were required to absorb were clearly known, and (incidentally) these 'facts' produced a narrative that protected a rather idealised view of Australian society. Postmodern conditions, including increased ethnic diversity; demands for recognition of the rights of Indigenous people; and an increase in women's independence and power have challenged the certainties of modernism. Inevitably, teachers and parents are asking, 'What knowledge and skills are most worth learning?' and 'Is there such a thing as a "single" Australian culture, and if not, whose culture or which aspects of our cultural life should we pass on to the young?' This brings us to the fourth stance on curriculum, which could be called postmodern, or constructivist, but since both postmodernism and constructivism come under the rubric of sociocultural theory, we will use this title for our fourth category.

Sociocultural approaches

Sociocultural theorists propose that knowledge only has meaning in specific cultural contexts. This gives the traditionalists fits for, according to them, the curriculum revolves around a canon:that is, a recognisable collection of ideas, values, and facts that have stood the test of time; are recorded in the classic works of history and literature; and are considered by some to be indisputable. In contrast with this, the concept of knowledge construction is central to sociocultural theory—so central in fact that it applies to both learning and knowledge. Knowledge (or the subject matter content of the school curriculum) is not fixed but changes over time. And as Resnick and other cognitive scientists explain, learning itself depends on giving children opportunities to actively construct their own understandings of phenomena. The shift towards a constructivist or sociocultural approach means that instead of (or as well as) asking, 'What is the answer?', a teacher may ask, 'Would you explain what you mean by that?' or 'Can you help me make sense of the way you see it?' For constructivists, children's own ideas about the nature of the world are never irrelevant, no matter how odd they might sound. The challenge for teachers is to get the child to explain the logic underlying their theory, to interrogate the underlying assumptions, and to help children to refine their theories. Over time, the child's own theory may begin to approximate more closely to some mainstream view. However, what is true of knowledge is also true of the ways we attain it, for knowledge can be constructed in many ways.

Sociocultural approaches have been trenchantly criticised by conservatives such as Kevin Donnelly, who wrote a populist treatise titled *Why our Schools are Failing*. Donnelly argued that the education system has been undermined by a series of ideologically driven changes (Donnelly, 2004, p. 16). He targeted the Key Learning Area (KLA)—known variously in New South Wales as HSIE, 'Human Society and its Environment' and as SOSE, or 'Studies of Society and Environment' (elsewhere)—for particular criticism. He wrote:

> Whereas education was once based on the assumption that there are some absolutes (truth telling, equal justice for all and the need for tolerance and compassion) in the brave new world … students are told that everything is tentative and shifting and that the purpose of education is to criticise (Donnelly 2004, p. 145).

> The European settlement of Australia is described as an invasion and Australia's Anglo/Celtic heritage is either marginalised or ignored … the syllabus fails to make

any mention of Anglo/Celtic figures, such as Captain Cook, Matthew Flinders, Edmond Barton or Sir Robert Menzies, who have made this nation what it is today (Donnelly, 2004, p. 134).

As Henderson (2005) points out, there are a number of ways to counter Donnelly's arguments. First, these arguments ignore the findings of constructivist cognitive science and assert (contrary to our current understandings of how children learn) that children can acquire knowledge by simply absorbing the facts and concepts presented to them. Second, he asserts that any curriculum based on critical pedagogy undermines the well-being of society, because instead of emphasising absolutes (like truth telling) the critical approach simply involves criticising everything and treating everything as arbitrary. Henderson (2005) counters this by arguing that critical pedagogy involves a thoughtful process of sifting, investigating, and questioning, leading to decisions about which components of a narrative should be accepted and preserved, and which ones should be revised or removed. Hence, she says, critical thinking can have radical effects, when people decide to make changes to some version of our historical narrative, but can also have conservative effects, when people decide to maintain parts of the narrative because they are relevant and valuable.

Donnelly's statements also assume that Australia's culture and history is made up of universal and fixed social truths, that it is a derivative strand of British colonial history, and that it should remain so. In asserting that the arrival of Europeans in Australia was a 'settlement' and not an 'invasion', Donnelly is aligning himself with the conservative side in the so-called History Wars. Historian Stuart McIntyre describes how the History Wars have drawn historians, politicians, and media commentators into a fierce controversy over how Australia's past should be interpreted (McIntyre & Clark, 2003). An early event in this sequence was the 'minting of the Black Armband epithet', which historian Geoffrey Blainey used, in a lecture delivered in 1993, to characterise what he thought was an 'excessive emphasis in recent historical writings on the wrongs of the past' (2003, p. 3). John Howard has often referred to this epithet, distancing himself from Australian historians who have documented the dispossession of Aboriginal people from their lands, the illegal massacres, the forced removal of Aboriginal children, and the denial of voting rights to Indigenous people until 1967. As material such as this found its way into the curriculum documents and textbooks used in schools, conservative parents also began to object. The account by McIntyre and Clark (2003) makes fascinating reading, since it shows that great passions are aroused when we seek to go beyond the traditional canon and ask, 'What knowledge is most worth learning? What is our national identity as Australians?' and 'Which aspects of our cultural life should we pass on to the young?'

3   The intended curriculum and the enacted curriculum

Up to this point, this chapter has outlined four of the main stances that influence curriculum policy and practice, and has provided some examples as to how different positions about what should be taught and how it should be taught have played out in the recent history of curriculum development in Australia's schools and school systems. The rest of the chapter will examine how the Australian system of curriculum development works, the authority of the states and territories in relation to the school curriculum, attempts over the past 25 years to produce some form of 'national consistency' in the curriculum, the role of the federal government in this process, and, finally, the nature of the senior secondary curriculum. Before moving on to these topics, it is important to note, however, that the development of curriculum policy and the pathway from policy to practice is never simple or linear, and it is rarely rational or straightforward.

The four main philosophical positions on the curriculum that are discussed above place varying emphases on progressive pedagogy, on an instrumental skills-based approach, on a deep knowledge of the subject-matter disciplines, or on socio-cultural theory and the idea of knowledge construction. These four positions are not mutually exclusive or water-tight, since their boundaries overlap. For example, there are plenty of socio-cultural theorists who love their subject disciplines, but they differ from the traditionalists by arguing that it is always important to question the canon and to produce a curriculum that shows respect for a range of alternative views about key topics. Everyone, from curriculum policy-makers to teachers and parents, agrees that children need to acquire the basic skills, but thoughtful educators on both the conservative and radical sides would say that, taken by themselves, the basic skills are not enough. The situation is also messy at the classroom level. Faced with the problem of motivating a disengaged student, teachers who are avowed subject-matter disciplinarians will lapse into a permissive stance, searching for topics that will spark the child's interest. And on the other side, there are many teachers who use progressivist methods but still seek to guide students along a pathway that leads to a coherent understanding of a disciplinary field. What happens in a classroom depends in part on the philosophical position a teacher holds on to, in part on how she reacts when what she had planned is not working, and in part on her students, whose moment-by-moment responses determine whether it will 'work' or not. What will happen is never exactly predictable, so in this sense the curriculum in practice is almost always different from what the curriculum writers had in mind.

In each state and territory in Australia, there is an official body that develops, mandates, and promulgates curriculum documents. These documents record what we might call the intended curriculum. However, there is always a gap between the intended curriculum and what actually happens in the classroom; that is, the curriculum as it is enacted by teachers. Given the diversity of contexts in which this enactment takes place, this is not at all surprising. A teacher in an expensive private school in leafy St Ives operates in an entirely different context from a high school teacher in industrial Campbelltown, or in rural Bathurst, yet they are all expected to work from the same curriculum documents. The challenge for curriculum writers is to give teachers adequate decision-making space to adapt the intended curriculum to local circumstances. If a new curriculum is imposed across a whole state without leaving spaces in which teachers can make adjustments to suit the contexts in which they work, then it is likely there will be a large gap between the enacted and the intended curriculum. Inevitably, this gap will tend to disadvantage students whose parents are poor and poorly educated, rather then children from families of well-educated professionals. We will return to this point later in the chapter.

A case study illustrating the process of curriculum enactment is provided by Harris (2005), who studied how teachers responded to the introduction of the 1998 NSW History syllabus for Stages 4 and 5. At the time, many history teachers, including the History Teachers Association of NSW, expressed the view that the vision of history promoted by the 1998 syllabus was traditionalist and limited. At the same time, a new external examination was introduced that would test students' mastery of this syllabus and the revised geography syllabus was to be added to the New South Wales Year 10 School Certificate. In passing, it is worth noting that NSW is now the only state in Australia that retains any form of external certificate at the Year 10 level and by adding more exams at this level, is moving in the opposite direction to the rest of the nation. Harris studied the reaction of the history department in a high school in Sydney's outer-western suburbs as they faced the task of implementing this curriculum. Their school, which Harris called *Illangara*, served students who were predominantly from families of low socio-economic status; a 'tough' school where high levels of student absenteeism, vandalism, and arson against school property, and a negative media image made life difficult for all the teaching staff.

The three teachers who formed the history department at Illangara felt that the new syllabus was unnecessary, as they were already teaching a program that conformed to the HSIE outcomes specified for stage 5. The new syllabus contained a huge amount of chronologically ordered content, and in the teachers' view, it did not respond to the needs of Illangara students. They were concerned that an additional external exam would also reinforce a failure mentality among students and the local community. Yet if they ignored these reforms they would be letting their students down. To the best of their ability, they had to prepare Illangara students for the Year 10 exam. Harris (2005) describes how these teachers worked together as a team to produce a modified version of the new syllabus that was not exactly what had been prescribed but that would work with the kids they were teaching. Harris concludes that in any curriculum reform, teachers need to have a decision-making space so they can exercise their professional autonomy and make modifications relevant to their own students and the circumstances in which they work. It is unrealistic to assume that the intended curriculum and the enacted curriculum can ever be more than loosely coupled.

4   Curriculum development and the role of state and federal governments

Anyone starting out on a study of Australia's official curriculum documents soon faces a confusing array of terms whose only rationale lies in history of the reforms and counter-reforms of the past 30 years. The main building blocks of the curricula are called KLAs (Key Learning Areas) rather than subjects, except that history and geography don't exist as such: these are 'options' in a KLA called SOSE (Studies of Society and Environment). The curriculum sequence runs over six stages, but since there are 2 years per stage in New South Wales, it is easy to translate the six stages into the 12 years of school education. There are eight KLAs except that in NSW there are only six at the primary school level. What you teach is specified in terms of 'statements' and what kids are supposed to learn is defined in the 'outcomes'. This kind of discourse has been pretty common around Australia for the past 10 years. However, some of the states and territories have recently taken a different turn and are framing their curriculum in terms of Essential Learnings (in Victoria, South Australia, and Tasmania and the Northern Territory) while in Queensland these are called the 'New Basics'. The older terms are still in currency as well, but curriculum is a constantly moving target, so more change can always be expected.

This section of the chapter provides a brief historical review of curriculum developments across Australia over the past 30 years or so. It reviews the failed attempts of the late 1980s and early 1990s to construct a national curriculum, then follows the current trends towards an instrumental curriculum where vocational training and basic skills testing are salient features. In this account we will see how different stakeholders at different levels in the state and federal systems have used the curriculum stances described in the first part of the chapter to legitimate the reforms they are promoting. Instrumentalism is a stance that media commentators and the lay public have no trouble understanding. In any case, a focus on 'the basics' allows politicians to side-step difficult questions about which knowledges count, such as, for example, whether gender studies should have any place at all and how much Aboriginal history there should be in the core curriculum.

Setting aside the early work of the Australian Schools Commission, it seems that whenever the Commonwealth has entered into the debate, it has generally used an instrumentalist stance to legitimate its claims. It is much harder to persuade the public that a sociocultural approach to the school curriculum is needed, but as we shall see, this is where the more radical state-level reforms are currently taking us. And the states have the running on this, since the constitution places responsibility for school education in their hands. Over the past two decades the states have successfully resisted being corralled into adopting a single, uniform model. Although there is a considerable amount of overlap in curriculum content, the states continue at both at the K-10 and Senior Secondary levels to sustain distinctly different approaches to pedagogy, school organisation, and assessment.

5   Waves of curriculum reform

The progressive wave of reform

There are at least three waves of reform that need to be considered in order to make sense of how school curricula in Australia are currently constituted. The first began in the 1960s, when rising expectations about the entitlement of every child to the kind of educational opportunities that had, in the past, been a privilege accorded to an advantaged minority, ushered in the popular progressive movement. A demographic boom and rapid postwar migration meant that school systems were expanding at breakneck speed, and as large numbers of baby boomers came of age they entered the teaching service in droves. As Collins (1995) described it, this was an era in which well-educated and energetic young teachers resisted the constraints of the prescribed curriculum and sought to craft projects that would be salient for each child. Early in its life the Whitlam government appointed an Interim Committee for the Australian Schools Commission, and its report, *Schools in Australia*, captures the spirit of the times:

> The fact that in industrial societies highly disciplined and abstract specialization requires high education and commands high income has obscured the wider value of activity of mind as a perspective in living which bears no necessary relationship to productivity or income … [the Committee] … sees no reason why schooling should not be regarded as a life enjoyable and satisfying in its own right rather than a credit note drawn down on the future (Schools in Australia, 1973, pp. 23–4).

Schools Commission funding under the Disadvantaged Schools Program led to greater levels of community participation in local curriculum decision-making. Open classrooms, alternative schools, and school 'annexes' sprung up in both public and non-government schools and many of these gained financial support from the Schools Commission's Innovations program. School-based curriculum development was allowed and then encouraged by education departments in Victoria and South Australia. In Victoria alternative courses were officially accredited as Year 12 qualifications (more detail on this is provided below). In NSW 'Other Approved Studies' had a relatively brief flowering during the 1980s but was eliminated in 1989 by a newly-elected Minister for Education who considered that these school-based options had 'mushroomed out of control' (Print, 1993, p. 20). Further manifestations of progressivism include the abolition of public examinations in Queensland and the founding of an entirely new experimental system in the ACT in which curriculum responsibility was left entirely in the hands of school communities.

In the late 1970s, an economic downturn and rising levels of unemployment among early school leavers led to a more cautious climate and a desire for more structure and security. At the primary and junior secondary levels, the open classrooms and annexes gave way to practices that involved a greater degree of curriculum control. Yet at the same time, the very rapid increase in high school completion rates that began in 1981 meant that systems could not ignore this change. Schools had taken on board the fact that many of the students now staying on had no interest in university studies. Rather, in the tougher labour market climate of the 1980s, they needed a Year 12 certificate as a qualification for a job in the growing service sector. The challenge that all education systems faced was to find a way of meeting the needs of these students while at the same time sustaining the traditional role of Year 12 as the 'gatekeeper' year for university admissions. This brings us to the second wave of reform.

Reforms to the senior secondary curriculum

Across the eight jurisdictions, there are three patterns of reform that amply illustrate the degree of diversity in senior secondary curriculum that emerged during the 1980s. The reforms introduced in Victoria were quite radical, and are described in some detail below. New South Wales adopted a conservative approach. Although some flexibility was afforded through the inclusion of 'Other Approved Studies' (OAS) in the Year 12 curriculum in some schools, these subjects remained marginal as almost all NSW students continued to follow a Year 12 program of study that led to the award of a tertiary entrance score. The main preoccupation in New South Wales was, it seems, to run a Year 12 that would prepare students for the university admission exam. At the same time a great deal of attention was paid to the technocratic goal of making sure that the processes of standarising and aggregating examination scores would provide a statistically valid basis for placing all students on the single scale of merit used for university admission.

Queensland followed a unique trajectory, eliminating external examinations altogether from 1973. In Queensland, the key question appears to be: 'How do we ensure access by all our young people to a postcompulsory schooling experience which will be of value to them?' In order to pursue that question, Queensland has made the assumption that a fair system of high school certification and university admission can be invented and adapted over time according to what is in the best interests of most young Queenslanders. The system has changed fairly radically three times since 1970, moving from a progressivist stance to one that is now more closely aligned with a socio-cultural stance. A similar trajectory can be described for Victoria.

Starting in the early 1970s, the Victorian education department permitted a wide range of alternative programs to develop within the public system. By the end of the 1980s, the state was a veritable mosaic of innovation. To take one example, the so-called 'STC' (its full title was the Schools Year 12 Tertiary Entrance Certificate) began as a school-based course that was designed to allow students to negotiate entry to College of Advanced Education courses. In 1981 it was accredited as a Year 12 certificate course and by 1987 there were 117 schools offering STC across Victoria (Freeman, 1987). STC had all the hallmarks of a progressivist curriculum: committed teachers flexibly negotiated with students to design a workplan that would promote each student's intellectual growth. Other examples included an alternative Year 12 offered through TAFE, and a raft of non-tertiary entrance subjects supported by the Victorian Institute of Secondary Education, which were also accepted as part of a legitimate Year 12 certificate. In 1991, the Victorian government made a heroic effort to bring the best of these innovations into the mainstream. At the same time, the Victorians attempted to reconstruct academic education in a postmodern frame, giving voice to the many cultural groups represented in the schools. This heroic effort has to some extent been dismantled, but nevertheless, a strong strand of school-based curriculum adaptation and school-based assessment persists in the now not-so-new Victorian Certificate of Education.

During the 1980s, Australia's national retention rate doubled, increasing from 36 per cent in 1982 to 74 per cent in 1992. At the same time, the proportion of students who completed Year 12 by taking a program of study that did not qualify them for a tertiary entrance score increased steadily in most states (Vickers, 1995). The differences between New South Wales, Victoria, and Queensland in terms of the proportions of students taking these alternative pathways are striking. By 1982 Victoria was already awarding a Year 12 certificate without a tertiary entrance score to 8 per cent of Year 12 candidates; by 1990 this figure had increased to almost 24 per cent. In Queensland, the equivalent figure had reached 18 per cent by 1990, but in New South Wales the proportion of students gaining a Year

12 certificate without a tertiary entrance score in 1990 was less than 2 per cent. One interpretation of these differences might be that NSW was sustaining high standards, and no-one there was doing a 'Mickey Mouse' Year 12. This might be so, but it also needs to be acknowledged that in 1992, the apparent retention rate from Year 7 to Year 12 was only 69 per cent in New South Wales, while in Victoria it was 81 per cent and in Queensland it was 84 per cent (ABS, 1993). Although this gap has closed somewhat in the past decade, it remains substantial, with New South Wales still having significantly lower completion rates than the other mainland states (Lamb et al., 2004; Vickers & Lamb, 2002).

The national curriculum project and its demise

Looking across Australia at the end of the 1980s, it was evident that the amount of variation in both the K–10 curriculum and the curriculum for Years 11 and 12 was quite substantial. In the past, this had not been seen as a problem by the state Ministers for Education. However, John Dawkins, who was then the Commonwealth Minister for Education, Employment and Training, saw things differently. Dawkins was an economic rationalist, a former Minister for Trade, who saw education as an important driver of Australia's economic performance. If we were to compete on the world stage, Dawkins argued, we needed a major overhaul of our education systems (Dawkins, 1988). In his view, an efficient system would demand less duplication of effort and greater curriculum consistency across the nation. At the 1988 meeting of the Australian Education Council (AEC) he persuaded the state and territory Ministers to undertake a comparison of school curricula across all jurisdictions. In response to this pressure, the Directors of Education commissioned a succession of curriculum mapping exercises. Initially, their intention was to demonstrate that considerable consistency already existed, and that further efforts to achieve national consistency were unnecessary. Support for this initiative, particularly from teachers, was obtained because neither national nor system monitoring was among its stated purposes.

At the April 1989 meeting of the AEC in Hobart, the State, territory, and federal Ministers of Education declared that they were 'willing to act jointly to assist Australian schools in meeting the challenges of our time' (cited in McGaw, 1994). They defined ten agreed national goals of schooling, setting out in what is sometimes referred to as the Hobart Declaration on Schooling (Department of Employment, Education and Training, 1990). Following the Hobart declaration, the AEC adopted a traditional conceptualisation of the curriculum in terms of a set of areas; by 1991 they had identified eight broad learning areas or KLAs. These were the arts, English, personal development, health and physical education, languages other than English, mathematics, science, studies of society and environment, and technology. Inevitably there has been considerable debate about this division. For traditional studies such as English, mathematics, and science, there was some logic to this division, since these can reasonably be dealt with as distinct learning areas, but others were less coherent. For example, the KLA called Studies of Society and Environment (SOSE) includes both history and geography, and therefore deals with questions that are fundamentally different epistemologically. The collection of activities and disciplines cobbled together in the KLA called Personal Development, Health, and Physical Education is even less coherent.

For each of the Key Learning Areas, the AEC commissioned the development of a set of statements and profiles. The statements divide the content of each learning area into strands, and the profiles set out the expected sequence of the progress of a typical student in each of the eight learning areas. Profiles refer to years or stages, but the way these have been defined varied, starting with four 'bands'; they were then re-defined in terms of six levels, and later in terms of eight levels. In June 1992, the AEC asked the states and territories to deliver a complete set of statements and profiles by mid 1993. Each jurisdiction had responsibility for one KLA, and all were under huge pressure as they attempted to conceptualise their curriculum area and then develop a profile of eight levels in every designated strand, through descriptions, exemplars, and pointers (Marsh, 1994).

Curriculum statements and profiles

Statements describe what should be taught in each Key Learning Area (KLA) by defining a set of strands that specify curriculum content and process. Statements provide a basis for a curriculum framework by suggesting a sequence for developing knowledge and skills within each strand across the school years.

Profiles set out what students are expected to know and be able to do. A profile is a description of the progression in learning outcomes typically achieved by students during the years of schooling, in each Key Learning Area.

Despite the huge effort that had been made to develop national statements and profiles for all eight Key Learning Areas, this effort at national curriculum construction fell apart at the July 1993 AEC meeting in Perth. Labor ministerial power had shaped education policy through much of the 1980s, and the discourse of the AEC meetings had been dominated by an image of national cooperation and partnership. Political changes in several states and territories meant that

Dawkins, the federal Minister, was in a minority position at the AEC for the first time in several years. At the July 1993 meeting the non-Labor state Ministers of Education ambushed the AEC policy processes and reasserted their constitutional rights. Dawkins's national curriculum initiative was seen by some as carrying risks for the autonomy of the state and territory systems. An alternative explanation attributes the states' withdrawal from full cooperation to proposals by federal authorities to use the profiles as a basis for national monitoring and reporting. A third explanation attributes the withdrawal to public criticisms of some of the statements and profiles. For example, a group of university mathematicians was publicly critical of the mathematics profile and generated some loss of confidence in that product (McGaw, 1994).

Nevertheless, when the state and territory Ministers left the July 1993 meeting, they took the statements and profiles home with them. Thus, the AEC's effort at national curriculum building has had a continuing impact, as the documents have been considered separately by each state and each state has made its own decisions about implementation. Most states and territories incorporated the statements and profiles into their own curriculum frameworks. Collaborative work on the development of curriculum resources is also facilitated by the Curriculum Corporation, which is a jointly owned company supported by all the states and territories. The residual effects of the reforms of the 1980s have probably brought the state and territory curricula closer together than they would have been had this effort at national curriculum construction not occurred (Brady & Kennedy, 2003).

Recent developments

Over the past 15 years, the systems have sustained an uneasy balance between state initiatives and federal imperatives in curriculum policy. In each state, the mandated curriculum documents have a distinctly local flavour, yet they remain based on elements that are commonly used across the nation. In Victoria, for example, the Curriculum and Standards Framework (CSF) is designed to 'provide sufficient detail for schools and the community to be clear about the major elements of the curriculum' across the eight key areas of learning (VCAA, 2005, p. 1). Within each KLA, the CSF specifies strands that are discipline-based or skills-based. For each strand the CSF sets six levels of learning over the 11 years of schooling, from the preparatory year to the end of Year 10.

The NSW Board of Studies promulgates documents that are distinct from those of Victoria's, but the common elements are easy to identify. In New South Wales, the mandated Curriculum Foundation Statements (CFS) 'have been written to help teachers manage the curriculum more effectively … by prioritising what needs to be taught in all primary schools (Board of Studies, 2005, p. 2). There are six (not eight) KLAs at the primary level, and six stages of learning over the 13 years from kindergarten to Year 12. As in Victoria, the KLAs are divided into strands.

Within all these documents, learning outcomes are specified for each strand, but recent investigations in Victoria suggest that teachers have found it difficult to establish priorities for student learning, since the number of outcomes to choose from is simply enormous. The newly introduced Victorian Essential Learning Standards (VELS) represent an attempt to provide further guidance to teachers as they consider what is most important for their students. Essential Learning Standards are also being introduced in the ACT, South Australia, the Northern Territory, and Tasmania. Queensland has introduced 'the New Basics' into a group of pilot schools, with the intention of exploring a multi-disciplinary approach that gives a special status to the use of new technologies. Essential Learnings do not appear to be on the agenda at this stage in New South Wales or Western Australia.

Federal intervention at the K–10 level has been most conspicuous in relation to the introduction of mandatory basic skills testing across the nation's schools. In 1993, the Australian Education Council (AEC) was folded into a larger body known as the Ministerial Council on Education, Training, Employment, and Youth Affairs (MCEETYA). As already noted, MCEETYA established the National Literacy and Numeracy plan in 1997, developing national benchmarks for reading, writing, and numeracy; and using these to assess students in all states and territories at grade levels 3, 5, 7, and 9. These benchmarks currently provide nationally comparable data indicating what percentage of students in each state and territory have achieved the national reading and numeracy benchmarks (MCEETYA, 2005). They also indicate what percentages of students achieved the benchmarks by gender, by language background other than English, and by Indigeniety. At the same time, Australia now participates in the Program for International Student Assessment (PISA), which means that the performance of Australian 15-year-olds on literacy, numeracy, and science tests can be compared with students from over twenty countries across the industrialised word (Lokan, Greenwood & Cresswell, 2000; Thomson, Cresswell & De Bortoli, 2003). Both the MCEETYA program and Australia's participation in PISA are underwritten by federal support. Widespread media attention to the results achieved by students on these testing regimes reinforces the popular belief in the instrumental purpose of the curriculum: that the acquisition of basic skills is the thing that really counts in school.

The other conspicuous change over the past 15 years has been the introduction of vocational education and training (VET) as a universal option within the senior secondary curriculum. VET has played an increasingly important role in senior secondary education in the past 15 years. The changes in the nature of the vocational subjects and programs offered in schools have been driven by the need to strengthen the links between senior schooling and employment, as well as by employer concerns that schools meet industry standards of VET (rather than offering non-accredited courses). In the context of improving retention and strengthening post-school options, student demand for vocational skills and training prior to leaving school, as well as demand for flexible options and choice in school programs, have also been important influences for change (Malley & Keating, 2000).

Since the mid 1990s the numbers of senior school students enrolled in VET in schools has more than trebled to the point where almost one in three students now undertake VET subjects (MCEETYA, 2002). But it is not only student numbers that have changed. The numbers of schools offering VET have increased markedly, from 70 per cent in 1997 to over 90 per cent in 2002 (MCEETYA, 2002). Changes have also occurred in the types of programs offered at a school level: how schools deliver VET has been transformed. The Australian Qualifications Framework (AQF) was introduced on 1 January 1995 and the system of national training packages established and endorsed through this framework was phased in over 5 years, with full implementation by the year 2000 (ANTA, 2002). Before the introduction of the AQF, vocational education in senior schooling was based on initiatives such as work experience programs, school–industry link programs, cooperative programs with TAFE, and formal career education. Mostly, technology and technical subjects did not provide workplace learning; some were recognised as subjects within Year 12 certificates, and some were not. The development of the AQF and changes to the senior secondary curriculum have allowed schools across the country to offer units of study that can contribute both to Year 12 certificates and to accredited VET; that is, to vocational qualifications at Certificate levels I–IV. Thus, under this new set of arrangements, what is known as 'VET in Schools' subjects or 'VETIS' are subjects that are undertaken by students as part of their Year 12 certificate but that also provide credits towards nationally recognised vocational qualifications within the AQF.

The development of national training packages through the AQF system has provided a broad framework for the delivery of VETIS. Training packages provide a clear specification of the student outcomes required for qualifications in each industry by specifying the units of competence applicable to each qualification (ANTA, 2002). For a school subject or a unit of study within a subject to gain accreditation in the VET system, the unit must deliver the competencies specified by a particular training package, and must conform to the prescribed assessment guidelines, which means that accredited assessors must evaluate student performance, usually under workplace conditions. This framework has made it possible for the Ministerial Council for Education, Employment, Training and Youth Affairs (MCEETYA) to establish agreed national principles and guidelines on the organisation, provision and delivery of VETIS programs (see MCEETYA, 2000). According to these principles, at a school level, VET programs should be based on the national competency standards incorporated in training packages, leading to certificates within the AQF system as well as Year 12 certificates endorsed by state and territory Boards of Studies (MCEETYA, 2002).

6 Concluding comments

By and large, it could be said that at the beginning of the twenty-first century, the dominant feature of Australian curriculum policy is its instrumentalism. Media commentary and political pronouncements place great emphasis on acquisition of 'the basic skills', on boys' literacy achievements compared with girls', and on Australia's competitive standing compared with other nations on standardised tests (Nelson, 2004; Rowan et al., 2002). At the same time, we are told that the nation is facing such a severe shortage of skilled workers that the federal government has decided to set up twenty-five new Australian Technical Colleges (DEST, 2006). All this rhetoric carries the message that literacy and numeracy counts, and that the main purpose of an education is to prepare youth for future employment. In many ways this emphasis seems democratic and down-to-earth. Ordinary families want to know that the local school can be relied on to deliver the basics. For a substantial proportion of young people, their pathway into a job is through vocational training, rather than through higher education.

Yet there is another dominant feature of the Australian secondary school, and that is the centrality of the academic curriculum and the role it plays in the processes of selection for university admission. As Teese (2000) explains, this curriculum is firmly attached to the knowledges that are valued by the universities. The academic curriculum is planned for upward integration into university studies, even if the students taking that curriculum are not intending to enter a university. As Teese (2000, p. 7) wrote:

> It is not the intellectual demands of the curriculum as such that are problematic, but their imposition without parallel improvements in how the weakest students learn and without controls over how power is exercised by the strongest students and their institutional patrons.

Earlier in this chapter we noted that as high school completion rates doubled during the 1980s, some school systems developed alternative curricula, introducing a double structure for the senior secondary years. While these options lasted, students who were not intending to enter a university studied a different English or a different mathematics from those who were university-bound, and were able to select a range of options that did not count towards a tertiary entrance score. During the 1990s, many of these options were weakened and in some cases they were removed altogether. The revised NSW Higher School Certificate that came out of the McGaw review of 1997 set common standards of achievement for all students. Yet not all students are equally prepared to meet these standards, since the advantages that come from a childhood spent with well-educated parents cannot easily be matched. Our public schools would need to be provided with far more resources than they currently receive if we were to make a serious attempt to compensate for the differences in cultural capital between the families of professionals and the families of process workers.

As Australia moves into the twenty-first century it is clear that economically advantaged families are increasingly segregating their children from the 'others' by placing them in well-endowed private schools. (See chapter 9 for further discussion of this issue.) These families also use their cultural capital to prepare their children well for the demands of the academic curriculum. In addition, the private schools they choose for their children contribute huge resources to reinforcing the ability of these children to respond correctly to the forms of questioning and other assessment requirements imposed at the Year 11–12 level by the examining authorities. It is totally unfair to sustain a high-stakes selective role for the academic curriculum in a context where the resources available to public and private schools are so grossly unequal. The use of government funds to provide exceptional educational resources to those who are already economically advantaged threatens to exacerbate the divisions in our society between the opportunities available to these families compared with the opportunities for those who must depend on what our public schools can provide.

Focus questions

1 This chapter began with descriptions of four distinct philosophical approaches that teachers might use to justify decisions made about what children should learn. Choose one topic from one KLA area, and illustrate how the approach taken to teaching this topic might vary, by comparing and contrasting how this topic might be treated using at least two of the philosophical approaches available. For example: (1) consider 'the Periodic Table' from an instrumental and from a subject discipline perspective; or (2) consider 'Australian immigration' from a progressive and from a socio-cultural perspective.

2 'The curriculum in practice is almost always different from what the curriculum writers had in mind.' Why is this? Why is it unrealistic to assume that the intended curriculum and the enacted curriculum can ever be more than loosely coupled?

3 If there is a high likelihood that the enacted curriculum will vary from what was laid down in the mandated documents, what can be done about this? What are the conditions for effective curriculum change?

4 As high school completion rates doubled during the 1980s, some school systems developed alternative curricula, introducing a double structure for the senior secondary years. This meant that students who wanted to complete year 12 but were not interested in university admission studied an easier English, and easier mathematics, and a less demanding social science than those who were aiming at university entrance. In recent years in NSW, there has been a return to a single structure, which leads to a UAI score. Discuss the advantages and disadvantages of the single versus the double structure approach to the Year 12 curriculum.

5 'It is totally unfair to sustain a high-stakes selective role for the academic curriculum in a context where the resources available to public and private schools are so grossly unequal.' Discuss.

Further reading

Collins, C. (ed.) (1995). *Curriculum Stocktake: Evaluating School Curriculum change*. Canberra: Australian College of Education.

McGaw, B. (1997). *Securing Their Future: The NSW Government's Reforms for the Higher School Certificate*. Sydney: NSW Minister for Education and Training.

Oakes, J. & Lipton, M. (1999). *Teaching to Change the World* (2nd edn). Boston: McGraw Hill.

Teese, R. (2000). *Academic Success and Social Power: Examinations and Inequity*. Melbourne: Melbourne University Press.

Internet sources

Each state in Australia will have its curriculum frameworks and policies available on the web, so will each of the councils supervising the senior school assessments and curriculum. For example, for Western Australia the url is www.curriculum.wa.edu.au/pages/framework/framework00.htm and for South Australia, the web address is www.sacsa.sa.edu.au/.

The following site provides links to many organisations involved in curriculum production and policy: www.curriculum.edu.au/fineprint/links.php.

Information on the senior secondary curricula in each state or territory is available from www.acaca.org.au/links.htm.

The Australian Curriculum Studies Association (ACSA) is the source of interesting papers and policies on socially engaged school curricula: www.acsainc.com.au/.

11
Teachers
Raewyn Connell

1   Images of teachers

In one sense, teaching is the best-known occupation of all. Almost every adult once had a daily view of people working as teachers. Our memories of childhood are likely to hold vivid images of the teachers we liked and the teachers we hated. When a school class holds a reunion, perhaps 20 years later, the person most want to meet is their former teacher.

Yet teaching is also a little-understood occupation. Many people in other jobs imagine that teaching is an easy task which they could do at the drop of a hat—but it's not, and they couldn't. Teachers' working conditions are often misunderstood. For instance, there is a widespread belief that teaching must be a soft job because classroom hours are shorter than the average working week in other occupations. Most people know little about teachers' work beyond the classroom, and don't understand how intensive the face-to-face teaching hours are.

The images of teachers that circulate in literature and mass media are puzzling. There are many portraits of teachers in novels and films, since stories about young people growing up are one of the great imaginative genres of our culture. There are also novels and films in which teachers are the central characters. The images of teachers that come through are curiously different.

Quite bitter pictures of teachers were painted in the nineteenth century by Charles Dickens, perhaps the first great novelist to write about schools. One is the sadistic Mr Creakle, principal of Salem House, in the autobiographical novel *David Copperfield*. Another is the picture of an industrialised classroom in *Hard Times*, where Mr M'Choakumchild the teacher, and his patron the factory owner Mr Gradgrind—who believed in 'fact, fact, fact' and no 'fancy'—killed the imagination and lectured the bored children to distraction.

But consider a more recent autobiographical novel, turned into a popular film—*To Sir, With Love* (Braithwaite, 1959). In this, the hero is a black West Indian engineer who, unable to get a job in his profession because of racism, becomes a teacher in a tough white working-class school in east London. By patience, humour, imagination, and humanity, he not only overcomes the pupils' prejudice against him, but establishes a deep connection and begins to open doors for them into the wider culture. Or consider the 1989 Hollywood hit directed by Peter Weir, *Dead Poets Society*. In this American story the teacher is a rebel, who helps the privileged boys in his classroom break out of the conventional mind-set of their elite private school.

Teachers in two famous novels

A best-selling English novel of the mid nineteenth century, *Tom Brown's Schooldays*, was the first famous 'school story'. An exciting narrative of a boy's adventures at a private boarding school, Rugby School, it also gave a vivid picture of the reforming headmaster Thomas Arnold (a real person). In this story 'The Doctor' appeared a moral hero, as in this description of his sermons:

> We listened, as all boys in their better moods will listen (aye, and men too for the matter of that), to a man who we felt to be, with all his heart and soul and strength, striving against whatever was mean and unmanly and unrighteous in our little world. It was not the cold clear voice of one giving advice and warning from serene heights to those who were struggling and sinning below, but the warm, living voice of one who was fighting for us and by our sides, and calling on us to help him and ourselves and one another. And so, wearily and little by little, but surely and steadily on the whole, was brought home to the young boy, for the first time, the meaning of his life (Hughes, n.d., p. 104).

Unusually for men in the nineteenth century, Arnold was pictured as a caring, sensitive man with a deep understanding of children's emotions.

Contrast the picture of a teacher in Erich Maria Remarque's great novel of World War I, *All Quiet on the Western Front* (which became a famous film). Herr Kantorek teaches a rigid academic curriculum with bullying and sarcastic methods. He is also a great patriot who, at the outbreak of war, pressures the young men in his senior class into volunteering for the army. Herr Kantorek seems to stand for everything narrow-minded and conventional that made the holocaust of the trenches possible. And even then, as his students find, his teaching was of no use:

> We remember mighty little of all that rubbish. Anyway, it has never been of the slightest use to us. At school nobody ever taught us how to light a cigarette in a storm of rain, nor how a fire could be made with wet wood—nor that it is best to stick a bayonet in the belly because there it doesn't get jammed, as it does in the ribs (Remarque, 1929, p. 97).

The images of teachers are not only different, they are also opposed. Teachers are sometimes represented as the upholders of convention and sometimes rebels against it; sometimes authoritarian and brutal, and sometimes free-thinking agents of others' freedom. Perhaps this reflects some contradictions in the occupation itself.

2   The teaching workforce

To an economist, education is an industry like any other, and teachers are the main part of its workforce. Indeed, from an economic point of view, education is one of the largest industries in any modern economy, and teachers are one of the largest occupational groups. Focusing on school teachers, there were 255,000 teachers in Australian schools in the year 2002, or 225,000 in full-time equivalent (FTE) terms. Some 114,000 (FTE) were in primary schools, 111,000 in secondary schools; 68 per cent of them were in public schools, 32 per cent in private schools—the proportion in private schools has been rising over recent decades.

Data from 1999 indicate that 81 per cent of school teachers were employed on a permanent full-time basis, 10 per cent on a permanent part-time basis, and 9 per cent on fixed term contracts. But this understates the casualisation of teachers, because there are also temporary teachers in schools, working as 'relief' teachers (called in from day to day when needed) or on some other casual arrangement (ABS, 2003).

As well as teachers in schools, the total teaching workforce also includes pre-school teachers, teachers in technical and further education (TAFE) colleges, teachers in private vocational schools and colleges, and teachers in higher education (mainly universities). There is also a more informally organised sector that includes teachers in private practice, such as many teachers of musical instruments, and a range of training officers and educational consultants in industry and government.

Teaching used to be a young person's game. But in the last generation, the average age of school teachers has risen significantly. At the 2001 Census, it emerged that the average (median) age of school teachers was 43 years—up from 34 years in 1986. Not all teachers are middle-aged, of course, but it seems that turnover, i.e. movement of people into and out of the teaching profession, has slowed a good deal. To put it another way, more people seem to be staying longer in teaching, so there are now more experienced teachers, and fewer youthful teachers, in Australian schools.

One of the most striking divisions in the teaching workforce is the pattern of gender. Women predominate in primary school and early childhood teaching. In the year 2002, for every male primary teacher there were 3.8 female primary teachers, and the predominance of women has been rising. There is a more equal balance of gender among secondary teachers. But secondary schools also show another gender division—by subject. Women predominate in teaching areas like language and literature, men in teaching areas like maths and technology. This kind of division is very marked in the TAFE sector, where, for instance, automotive mechanics courses are taught by men, hairdressing and beauty courses by women, and so on.

There is a striking predominance of men, and lack of women, among professors in universities, and among senior educational administrators. Further, women teachers are much more likely to be casualised, e.g. employed on a contract rather than a permanent basis, than men. These divisions among teachers—which mean that women in teaching get lower average incomes than men—reflect the gender-segregated character of the whole Australian workforce.

The informal sector of teaching is not rigidly separated from the formal sector. Sometimes people work in both sectors at the same time, or in succession. For instance a retired schoolteacher may take part-time work coaching. It is quite likely that the informal sector has been growing, especially in corporate business contexts. More teachers of computer skills, for instance, are needed as a result of the growth of information processing that is now an integral part of business.

Teachers of other kinds of skills—some very vaguely defined, such as the skills taught by 'life coaches' and management consultants—have also been in demand. It can be difficult to define where teaching ends and something else begins. Are professional sports coaches really teachers, for instance? Are the people who run yoga classes? And what about those people who offer to Increase your Brain Power, get you reading four times as fast, or Unleash the Giant Within? The registration of school teachers (see below) will draw a line of professionalism around one kind of teaching, but will not affect this grey area.

3 Teaching as an occupation

Teaching is often described as 'a profession'. This may be just a vague way of naming an honourable line of work, but sometimes it is meant more precisely.

Half a century ago, sociologists had a well-defined model of professions. Taking medicine and law as models, a 'profession' was supposed to be based on a body of technical knowledge, and to require long training. Practitioners were to be certified by a government body. Income came from fees, not wages, which was supposed to guarantee professional independence. Professional organisations maintained their own standards and disciplined members who stepped out of line.

Teaching matches this model in some respects. There is a body of knowledge. In fact there are two bodies of knowledge in teaching, because teachers have to know about pedagogy and also have to know about subject matter (for instance, teachers with a BA in English, which gives them content, and a Dip. Ed., which gives them method). This requires formal training, which has grown longer and is now mostly done in universities. There is, increasingly, formal certification of teachers. But most teachers do not work on a fee-for-service basis (the exceptions are mainly in the informal sector). Most teachers are employees; in fact, employees of the state. Teaching does not police itself. To the extent there are quality controls, they are imposed by employers. The main teacher organisations are unions, intended to negotiate with employers, not self-regulating associations of independent practitioners.

Faced with these facts, some sociologists created another category of occupations: the 'semi-professions'. This is not as odd as it sounds. There are a number of other occupations, including nursing, social work, and some technological occupations, which have many similarities to teaching. They have a body of knowledge, technical training, and employee status, as well as middle-level incomes, and high proportions of women. These occupations came to be seen as important in their own right, not just pale imitations of the 'real' professions. In fact, the old professions seem to be following the model of the semi-professions, as more and more doctors and lawyers have become salaried employees of big firms, and the numbers of women rise (Acker, 1983).

When advanced economies shifted their focus from the production of goods to the production of services, a 'new middle class' came to be seen as the dominant group in post-industrial society. Teaching, a large and expanding white-collar occupation with a high proportion of women, seemed to be the perfect example of the new middle class. Australia is often described as a middle-class society. Teachers are easily seen as models for this new world.

Yet a picture of teachers as middle-class conformists seems to miss something vital about teaching. The missing part is what the United States educational theorist Henry Giroux (1988) had in mind when he wrote a book called *Teachers as Intellectuals*. To use another sociological term that has come into use recently, teachers, like computer professionals, media workers, engineers, and scientists, are 'knowledge workers'. A knowledge worker must be constantly moving a little bit beyond what is immediately given, and must work in a way that is not quite conformist. The popular commentator Richard Florida (2002) sees teachers as members of a rising 'creative class'. Whether or not we agree with that, it is important to notice the creative and intellectual dimension of teaching.

But teachers are not the same as computer professionals. Their daily tasks, their conditions, and above all their human connection with their pupils, are very different from work in high-technology firms. That was the point made in *To Sir, With Love*, contrasting teaching with engineering. We therefore have to pay attention to what is distinctive in the world of teachers. Another group of researchers have addressed this by studying the 'occupational culture' of teaching. Teachers as a group, and teachers' organisations, hold distinctive traditions, customs, language, attitudes, styles of dress, manners, ways of seeing the world, and ways of dealing with problems.

This occupational culture is informal, and it cannot be taught in university courses, but it is very powerful in the actual work context. It gives teachers a sense of direction, a sense that problems can be solved. It is a basis of cooperation and solidarity among teachers in the face of outside pressures and problems within the school. Different groups of teachers (e.g. trade teachers, physical education teachers) have their own versions of the occupational culture (Lawn & Grace, 1987; Mealyea, 1993).

Beginning teachers need to learn the culture to become an effective part of the school staff. This usually takes time—it is part of their struggle in the 'first year out' (see section 8 below). I was once told of a school in Victoria where the older teachers took this in hand. They took young teachers who had just been appointed to their school off for a weekend on the coast, before the school year began. There they told them what it was really like on the job—as distinct from what they had learnt at university.

Teaching as an occupation is now being redefined by the formal 'registration' of teachers. Most state governments in Australia have now set up legal machinery for this, in the form of teacher registration boards. An example is the recently established Victorian Institute of Teaching (see boxed text on 'Teacher registration'). On the one hand, teacher registration seems a confirmation of professional status, because it resembles the registration of doctors and lawyers. On the other hand it represents new machinery of surveillance and control over teachers, in the name of child protection and quality control.

Teacher registration

This description of the Victorian Institute of Teaching was extracted in 2005 from the Institute's web site at www.vit.vic.edu.au.

What is the Victorian Institute of Teaching?

The Victorian Institute of Teaching is an independent professional body for the teaching profession. Established by an Act of Parliament in December 2001, the Institute is a statutory authority operating along similar lines to other professional bodies, such as the Medical Practitioners Board of Victoria, the Legal Practice Board, and the Nurses Board of Victoria. The Institute registers teachers working in Victorian government, independent, and Catholic schools. As with other professions occupying positions of trust and responsibility, teachers are required to be registered in order to practise their profession. All practising Victorian school teachers must be registered by the Institute.

What does the Institute do?

The Institute
- registers all teachers to ensure only qualified people are employed in Victorian schools
- celebrates the achievements of teachers
- works to raise the standing of the profession in the community
- works with teachers to develop high professional standards
- provides advice to teachers to assist their professional learning
- approves teacher education courses that qualify future teachers for entry to the profession
- investigates and makes findings on instances of serious misconduct to protect the integrity of the profession.

Please note: Industrial and employment matters are not within the Institute's jurisdiction. These are matters for teacher unions and teacher employers.

4   The daily work of teaching

Any occupation can be studied in terms of the labour process involved. Industrial sociologists launched such research in places like an electrical parts factory. They looked at the nature of work groups, the flow of work, and group influences on output. The same approach was then taken to other occupations, such as office workers, and eventually to teachers.

The daily work of teachers turns out—by comparison with an electrical factory—to be very diverse. The sheer range of tasks a teacher undertakes in the course of a day, or even an hour, is impressive. As an Australian study of high school teachers put it:

> Even talking at a blackboard implies time spent preparing the lesson, time spent getting the class settled and willing to listen, time spent supervising exercises and correcting them. Beyond this, running a class involves keeping order; dealing with conflicts between the kids; having a joke with them from time to time and building up some personal contact; discussing work with them individually; planning sequences of lessons; preparing handouts and physical materials; collecting, using and storing books and audiovisual aids; organising and marking tests and major exams; keeping records; liaison with other teachers in the same subject (Connell, 1985, p. 71).

And that is only one side of the job. There are many other tasks that teachers undertake around a school, ranging from supervising the playground and meeting parents to budgeting and organising excursions.

The labour process varies from one sector of the workforce to another. In primary schools, for instance, most teachers have the same group of children the whole day, so teacher/pupil relationships are relatively intensive. In high schools, it is more common for teachers and classes to circulate, so one teacher may see five or six groups of pupils during the working day. Here, teacher–pupil relations are likely to be less intensive, while teachers' commitment to a particular field of knowledge is greater.

In technical education there is an alternation between conventional classrooms (for 'theory') and the workshops where equipment and materials are kept (for 'practice'). Some teaching and supervision is also done 'on site', in workplaces away from the school or college. In universities there is a labour practice called the 'lecture', where one teacher may speak to several hundred students at once—but may never see any of them in other settings.

In some specialised areas, teaching is done on an intensive one-to-one basis. Examples are the teaching of musical instruments, remedial literacy teaching, and the supervision of PhD theses. In these cases the teaching sessions tend to be widely spaced—e.g. weekly or monthly—otherwise the teaching would be phenomenally expensive.

The labour process of teaching is subject to change, and some of the sharpest controversies about teaching concern this issue. Researchers studying the manufacturing industry detected a process of 'de-skilling', where occupational skills were gradually removed from the workers and placed in the hands of managers—for instance, by computer-controlled automation.

There is controversy about whether teachers have been subject to de-skilling. On the face of it, teachers are becoming *more* skilled. More and more teachers are university-qualified, and training programs have grown longer. Yet some researchers have seen a significant trend to de-skilling, in the rise of commercially produced textbooks and curriculum 'packages', and in 'computer-assisted instruction'. To the extent that the classroom itself is replaced by online instruction, the range of teachers' tasks and the nature of their contact with students is narrowed (Apple & Teitelbaum, 1986).

Teaching is increasingly under the pressure of commercialisation. Some sectors of education have been restructured to make them more 'efficient' in market (though not necessarily in educational) terms. In Australia these pressures have been most strongly felt in the TAFE and university sectors. Being more efficient in market terms translates into teaching more students, and therefore earning more fees, with the same, or fewer, teachers. This has resulted in larger classes, less personal contact, more online teaching, and a shift in curriculum towards commercial subjects. It has also resulted, as managers try to extract more value from their staff's work, in longer hours and intensification of teachers' labour.

Time demands are felt in school teaching too. In the 2001 Census, for instance, a majority of Australian school teachers reported working more than 40 hours a week. Contrary to the myth that teachers have very short hours, 19 per cent worked more than 50 hours a week. However, the school sector has been protected from pressure to teach more pupils with fewer staff. The overall ratio of pupils to teachers has improved in Australia over the last 20 years, especially in private schools—made possible by a large increase in government funding of private schools (ABS, 2003).

Why is teaching open to restructuring pressures and long hours? One reason, as shown above, is the difficulty of drawing a clear boundary around the teacher's tasks. Therefore the demands can easily increase. For committed teachers, burnout is a real risk. In a classic piece of research, Grace (1978) studied teachers in inner-urban British schools who were nominated as 'good teachers' by their principals. What characterised good teachers, Grace found, was 'immersion' in the job. This meant total involvement, expending time and energy to meet the endless expectations. A common outcome was that the 'good teachers' became exhausted.

These trends can be resisted, but not easily on an individual basis. Therefore teachers' control over change in their own work is very much bound up with trends in teachers' organisations (see section 7).

5 Wages and conditions

Teachers' incomes mostly sit in the upper half of the economic spectrum, but not among the wealthy. For instance, in the year 2005 an experienced classroom teacher in the New South Wales public school system, full-time on salary step 13, earned $66,348 per annum. This is comfortably above the average earnings in the whole economy. But teachers' pay is below the average for all professionals considered as a group, and it is certainly not in the same bracket as an experienced doctor, accountant, stockbroker, or corporate executive. You don't go into teaching in order to get rich.

Early career teachers earn less. In the salary scale just mentioned, a commencing 4-year-trained teacher in New South Wales would earn $46 234. There are also part-time and casual teachers, whose hourly rates are above those of their permanent full-time colleagues but whose annual incomes are likely to be a lot less. In the 'informal sector' (section 2 above), incomes may also be a lot less, depending on an unpredictable flow of fees or contracts. We can picture the economic condition of the teaching workforce as a core of reasonably well-paid permanent workers with a career structure, surrounded by groups of lower-paid and less secure workers.

Where does the money come from? Mainly from tax revenue. Teachers are basically employed by the public via government, and the income tax system is the main channel through which education is financed. Government expenditure on all levels of education in Australia totalled $41 billion in the financial year 2002–03. Public school teachers are directly paid by state governments, who get the money through a long-standing tax-sharing arrangement with the federal government. Private school teachers also get most of their income from taxation, mainly through subsidies from the federal government, most of which are channelled through the Catholic Education Offices in the respective states.

Fees from students and their families are the second main source of income for teachers. In certain settings fees are the main source of teachers' incomes: a small group of high-fee private schools; commercial vocational colleges; and individual coaching and skills teaching. In TAFE and universities, fees are a growing contributor to income. 'Sales of goods and services' (mainly fees) by tertiary institutions in 2002–03 totalled $6 billion.

The fact that school teachers' incomes mainly derive from the tax system makes them dependent on economic trends in the public sector as a whole. When the public sector was expanding, in the decades after World War II, teachers' incomes tended to rise even though the number of teachers was also rising fast. Since the 1980s, with governments trying to reverse the expansion of the public sector, the flow of funds into education has been limited and teachers' incomes have stagnated or, in some cases, experienced relative decline.

This is part of a broader trend. As social resources are shifted into the market sector by neoliberal regimes such as the Howard government in Australia, all groups working in the public sector are under pressure. Public investment in most kinds of infrastructure has relatively declined—for instance, public transport relative to private transport via cars. Teachers experience the decline of public sector investment as deterioration in the physical fabric of their schools, difficulty in getting new equipment, and decline in support services such as in-service training, as well as wage stagnation. In some areas such as TAFE, as recent research by Clark (2004) shows, shrinking resources and market-based restructuring have had a severe impact on teachers' morale.

Teachers' wages and conditions are determined in detail by industrial bargaining with employers—principally, state Departments of Education and Catholic Education Offices. Since school teachers are a highly unionised group (see section 7), their bargaining is mainly done by union officials. Union officials are almost always former school teachers themselves, and are therefore experienced participants in teachers' occupational culture.

Under Australia's traditional industrial arbitration system, this bargaining was conducted through industrial courts or tribunals, resulting in 'awards' that specified wages and conditions with legal force. In North America, by contrast, unions and employers have faced off directly in wage bargaining, with no mediation from industrial tribunals. This has often made the process more conflictual, with long and bitter industrial disputes. With the current wave of neoliberal 'industrial reform', Australia is now heading in the North American direction.

Since wages are by far the biggest cost in education systems, managers trying to improve their bottom line will try to shrink their wages bill. Hiring casual workers for shorter periods of peak demand, rather than full-time permanent workers, is a classic cost-cutting technique in business. Casualisation is already a massive trend in TAFE. A decade ago, casuals were less than 10 per cent of the TAFE workforce; now they are the majority (Forward, 2005).

In school teaching, so far, casualisation has not been a strong trend. This is partly because demographic trends and hence pupil numbers are very predictable from year to year. But to the extent that neoliberal governments succeed in forcing schools to compete against each other for funds and pupils (see chapter 9), each school's need for teachers will become less predictable, and pressure for casualisation will become stronger.

6   Supervision and management

Apart from the operators of personal and family businesses, all workers in a modern economy experience control, generally by a manager or supervisor. For most teachers, their work is managed by school principals or heads of departments. Above the immediate supervisors there may be a bureaucratic hierarchy of many levels, in large public school systems, or a more limited hierarchy, in TAFE colleges or private schools. Generally the managers are former teachers, though this is no longer universal. In church schools the religious authorities play a role in determining policy, though have only a limited role in day-to-day school management.

Management has always had difficulty exercising control over teachers. This is partly due to the labour process of teaching, which is so complex and difficult to define that the familiar techniques of 'Taylorist' industrial management (e.g. time-and-motion studies) cannot be applied. During the early industrial revolution, attempts were made to apply factory techniques to schools, in the Bell and Lancaster systems of instruction using monitors. These rigid and clumsy techniques were gradually abandoned as public school systems developed.

Therefore education systems have mostly relied on *indirect* controls over teachers. One of the first methods was checking teachers' work by checking the results obtained by their pupils. School inspectors used to do this, travelling around schools and testing spelling, arithmetic, etc. in each class. In the late nineteenth century system of 'payment by results', teachers' incomes were determined by this testing of their pupils. In time, travelling inspectors were replaced by public examinations and standardised ability tests, and the payment-by-results system was also abandoned.

As research by Lawn (1987) has shown, school systems increasingly relied for control on cultural pressures associated with teachers' semi-professional status. Teachers were required to show a conservative demeanour, with respectable speech and dress, and conventional opinions and behaviour. Teachers could be sacked for having an extra-marital affair, and could also be sacked for being too radical. Pressure for conformity still exists, though with the trend towards market forces it has taken a different tone. Teachers' demeanour is now part of a school's, or a system's, market image.

The pattern of supervision has changed in recent decades. From the 1960s to the 1980s Australian teachers gained an unprecedented freedom from management control. There was an emphasis on decentralisation and democracy in the education system, and a great deal of experimentation with teacher-based curricula and participatory management. From the 1980s, neoliberalism and 'new public management' began treating schools, colleges, and universities much more like firms in a market. The result was that principals, vice-chancellors etc. increasingly became defined as 'managers'. They gained in power, and increasingly behaved like corporate executives.

In TAFE and universities this trend has gone a very long way. Management is now widely seen as separate from, and often hostile to, the academic and teaching staff. The introduction of computer-based corporate accounting and personnel management systems has increased the staff's sense of distance from management.

In schools the separation has been much less—so far. This may change, with growing attempts by governments to introduce 'performance indicators' for teachers, based mainly on new tests of their pupils. There is even talk of bonuses for teachers who 'achieve' particularly well on such criteria—ironically, a return to the old logic of payment by results.

There is also some revival of cultural controls over teachers. Right-wing politicians and journalists regularly attack public school teachers for being hippies and leftists. Media and political panics about 'paedophiles' have led to renewed scrutiny of the sexual behaviour of teachers. Anyone working in schools now has to undergo a check of their criminal record. The Catholic church officially refuses to allow homosexual teachers who are 'out' to work in its schools, and has an exemption from anti-discrimination laws to do so. Other religious groups have followed suit. So far, these renewed pressures have had limited effects. One important reason is the continuing strength of teacher organisations.

7 Teacher organisations

Teacher organisations are of two main kinds: unions and professional associations. There is some tendency for the two to converge, as unions develop their concerns with issues about curriculum and other 'professional' issues. But for the most part, in Australia, they are distinct (Clarke, 2001).

Unions generally operate at two levels. At the grassroots level there are branches (in North America called 'locals') consisting of all the union members in a given workplace, e.g. a school. The members elect local officers including a branch president and secretary, and delegates to the union's conferences. The branch officers are unpaid. They are expected to represent members in any disputes they have with local management, and to raise issues such as occupational health and safety.

The other level is the union's 'head office', where there are full-time officials and support staff such as clerical workers, researchers, and lawyers. The officials are elected by the local branch delegates, usually at a statewide annual conference. They hold their jobs only so long as they maintain a reasonable level of support among the union's members. (The members are often called the 'rank and file', a traditional joke that compares the union movement to an old-style army.) Full-time officials come out to a school to meet members, and sometimes to bargain with management, if there is a dispute that cannot be resolved locally.

The key task of head office officials is to represent teachers in bargaining with employers. Therefore, in Australia, they are expected to be expert in the ways of industrial tribunals. Head office officials are also expected to play a wider public role, representing teachers in public debates about education, and in lobbying governments about education funding, curriculum, and other issues.

Because Australian school systems are mainly administered at state level, it is the state unions that do most of the bread-and-butter work. There is also a national level of teacher union organisation. The Australian Education Union has a national conference, elected from state organisations, and a few full-time national officials. So does the university sector's union, the National Tertiary Education Union. National union officials had some influence under Labor Party governments, but have been frozen out of educational policymaking under the Liberal/National Party government.

Effective unions have to maintain a delicate balance between grassroots democracy and central leadership. Too much power in the centre, and rank-and-file support for the union will wither. Loss of commitment or initiative in the centre, and the union will be unable to make long-term gains.

Unions, like other institutions, reflect patterns of privilege and marginality in the wider society. For instance, the union movement was long dominated by men, even in industries where the majority of the workforce were women. This, as we have seen, includes education. The women's liberation movement of the

1970s challenged this and led to a sustained struggle to increase women's presence in teacher union leadership, which has had considerable success (Francis, 2003). Women from teacher unions have provided the two latest presidents of the Australian Council of Trade Unions.

The most potent weapon for a union is withdrawing its members' labour, i.e. going on strike. This is always a risky move. If the strike fails, as well as losing on the immediate issue the union is weakened for future struggles. Australian teacher unions have generally been unwilling to call strikes, except very short ones where they hope for public support. Their more usual tactics have been to lobby governments, and bargain with employers either directly or through industrial tribunals.

In the last two decades, union membership has declined across the developed world, though unions have been growing in some developing countries. The reasons for decline are complex. They include economic restructuring under globalisation, anti-union legislation by right-wing governments, and perhaps also cultural change towards individualism. In this unfavourable environment, teacher unions have maintained their strength remarkably well. One reason is that teachers are mostly public sector workers, another is the continuing strength of the occupational culture in school teaching, which is interwoven with unionism.

The other main form of teacher organisation is concerned with specific aspects of teaching. The most familiar example is the subject association, concerned to promote a given area of learning and provide resources for its teachers. An example is the Victorian Association of Teachers of English, mainly consisting of secondary teachers. VATE sponsors in-service events such as an annual conference with workshops, lectures, and performances. Among university teachers, academic organisations such as the Australian Psychological Society play a similar role, though they are often more concerned with research than with teaching.

Another type of teacher organisation is the sporting association, whose primary task has been to organise inter-school sporting competitions. Teachers have also provided the personnel for special interest groups or events concerned with school pupils. Examples are inter-school chess competitions, debating and public speaking, the Rock Eisteddfod, and inter-school musical ensembles. These organisations reflect the diversity of teachers' labour process, and the complexity of life in and around schools.

8　Teachers' careers

Teachers enter and leave teaching for a wide variety of reasons. Some come in after half a working life in another occupation. Trade teachers are usually recruited from the trade itself. Most teachers start young and do their initial training when they are not long out of school. Some leave quickly, finding the work unsuitable; others leave after a few years. Some teachers experience burnout. Some leave to care full-time for their own children (this is still an unusual thing for men to do).

In the year 2002, among people in Australia with teaching qualifications (and under 65 years of age), 82 per cent were currently employed—but of those employed, more than one-third were employed in jobs outside teaching. Some who leave will return to teaching after a period away, but some are lost for good. There is significant turnover in the teaching workforce.

Life-history research with school teachers points to a common, though certainly not universal, career cycle (Goodson, 1992). This starts with a period of entry to the occupation, including the decision to become a teacher, and the time spent in preservice training. Then there is the beginning of work in the job, the famous 'first year out' (a stage that may last less than a year, or considerably more). The first year out is often experienced as an extremely stressful baptism of fire. Some leave teaching at this stage.

Those who go on will consolidate their basic teaching skills, find their feet in the classroom, learn how to manage the emotional stresses of teaching, and often find their first specialist role in the school. In subsequent years, teachers begin to specialise, and to position themselves for promotion. They may get further qualifications, and often become known informally as the school's expert in a given area (e.g. using computers, community relations, or dealing with difficult Year 9 boys).

Some then enter promotion pathways, becoming heads of department, deputy principals, system curriculum consultants, etc. Some, moving further along this track, will finish their careers as school principals or school system managers. Other teachers, however, wish to stay in the classroom, and spend the later stages of their careers teaching in their established specialties.

A teacher's early career

Margaret Blackall, one of the teachers interviewed for the project described in *Teachers' Work* (Connell, 1985), is a language teacher in a public high school with a mostly working-class catchment, Greenway High. This is her first school and she has been there for 6 years.

Margaret came from a working-class family that had only limited schooling but valued education. She did well, went to a selective state school, then went on to university and did an Arts degree. After a Diploma of Education she went straight into a full-time teaching position with her state's Department of Education.

In the 'first year out' Margaret had a difficult time controlling her classes, and like many teachers decided that the solution was to get tough, to get on top with heavy-handed discipline. But as she gained a little more experience, she modified her first response:

> After you have gone through the first year of teaching, you can organise yourself a bit better. You know what to expect, you care less what the kids think of you. In your first year out, you still treat them as monsters, or as you would treat any other adult. Now I treat kids more as I should treat them. I don't yell at them any more, or only rarely I suppose. And I like to cultivate a friendly but firm relationship with them, which I find works very well with most kids. A little bit like a big sister, but a strict big sister, who expects things.

Margaret thus achieved balances in her teaching life—between being too tough and being too slack, between caring for the kids and making herself too vulnerable. She now has a reputation at Rockwell High for being a little more formal than most teachers, a little 'prim and proper', demanding orderly behaviour from the students. But she still cares a great deal about them at a personal level.

She has also tried to think out her philosophy of education. She emphasises intellectual learning, rather than, say, training for jobs:

> For me, schools are to pass on knowledge, to make people grow intellectually, to civilise them, however you would like to see that done.

She thinks intellectual life has a vital part to play in society as a whole. This gives dignity to the teacher's role, and is integrated into the professional identity Margaret has formed. Margaret now sees teaching as her lifetime career. She is applying for her first promotion now, and looks forward to travelling and to broadening her experience in other schools.

This career cycle is modified by several influences. One is the specific sector or field. University teachers do not usually come in through a period of initial teacher training. Their point of entry is usually research, which is also the main promotion criterion for academics. Technical teachers are likely to enter the occupation significantly older than other teachers, having spent some time in industry working in their trade.

Another important influence on teachers' careers is the gender system. At earlier stages of history, women could not get promotion in the public schools at all, or were obliged to leave teaching if they got married (the 'marriage bar'). It took a long struggle to get women teachers equal promotion rights with men. Until quite recently kindergarten teachers, almost all of whom are women, could not become principals of the primary schools they worked in. Even now women are under-represented in senior positions across the education system.

Historically, school systems have not provided promotion for teachers who stayed full-time in the classroom. Promotion positions such as secondary head of department, and primary deputy principal, are based on administrative work, though they can be combined with classroom work. The craziness of forcing dedicated and skilful teachers to leave the classroom in order to get professional advancement is now recognised. Some systems give recognition to experienced classroom teachers by creating a category such as 'advanced skills teacher', and try to give such teachers a role as mentors.

Other changes in teachers' careers may be afoot. Indeed, some social comment-ators think the very idea of a 'career' is vanishing in a postmodern world. People's working lives may look less and less like 'careers' and more and more like a suc-cession of short-term contracts with different customers. The pressures of globali-sation and the neoliberal market agenda are certainly changing the environment of education systems, and this must have an impact on teachers' working lives (Robertson, 2000).

A massive disappearance of teaching careers is very unlikely. But given current trends, it is quite likely that the shape of teachers' working lives will change. There is likely to be more fixed-term contract work, greater differences in rates of pay, less long-term security, less predictable promotion pathways, and more blurring of public and private sectors. Whether such changes will lead to better education is open to argument.

Focus questions

1 How would you define 'teaching'? What distinguishes teaching from coach-ing, training, or counselling?

2 What are the advantages, and disadvantages, for teachers in claiming 'professional' status for teaching as an occupation? What effects might professionalism have on teachers' relations with pupils' families in (a) rich communities, and (b) poor communities?

3 What are the similarities and differences in the labour process of different groups of teachers—for instance, kindergarten teachers vs trade teachers?

4 Why, and when, do teachers go on strike? Examine a particular industrial dispute, involving some group of teachers, and work out the reasons for the teachers' actions.

5 What will be the shape of teachers' careers in the twenty-first century? (Sug-gestion: interview both an experienced teacher, and a new teacher, about their career stories and expectations.)

Further reading

Acker, S. (1983). 'Women and teaching: A semi-detached sociology of a semi-profession'. In S. Walker & L. Barton (eds), *Gender Class and Education* (pp. 123–39). Barcombe: Falmer.

Clarke, S. (2001). 'Reforming teachers' work and changing roles for unions'. *Education Research and Perspectives, 28*(2), 33–50.

Francis, R. (2003). 'Challenging masculine privilege: the women's movement and the Victorian Secondary Teachers Association, 1974–1995'. *Journal of Australian Studies, 78,* 59–70.

Goodson, I. (ed.). (1992). *Studying Teachers' Lives*. London: Routledge.

Mealyea, R. (1993). 'Reproducing vocationalism in secondary schools: marginalization in practical workshops'. In L. Angus (ed.), *Education, Inequality and Social Identity* (pp. 160–95). London: Falmer Press.

Internet sources

The web sites of the teachers' unions usually have all sorts of interesting material. The AEU (Australian Education Union) is the union of government school teachers. Look also at the sites of its branches in each state. Here is the federal site, which includes an excellent links page: www.aeufederal.org.au/.

The web site of the Independent Education Union can be found at www.ieu.org.au/.

It is worth keeping an eye on the government web sites, state and federal, for the latest reports on teachers and teaching. Australia's Teachers: Australia's Future concentrates mainly on issues to do with science and mathematics teaching, but also discusses the wider questions: www.dest.gov.au/sectors/school_education/policy_initiatives_reviews/reviews/teaching_teacher_education/.

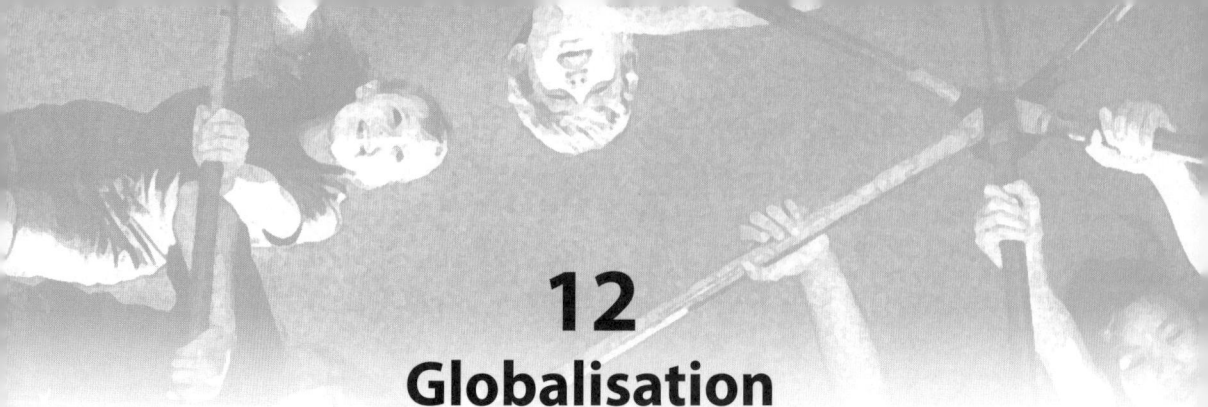

12
Globalisation
Nigel Bagnall

1   What is globalisation?

Globalisation, or as the French would say *la mondialisation*, affects us all. But what exactly is it? Is it something to do with the convergence of monetary systems and the shrinking of the world as technology and the travel industry make it possible to be physically anywhere in a short period of time, and to be *virtually* anywhere anytime? The significance of globalisation in the lives of Australians in the twenty-first century is evident in a number of implicit and explicit ways. When we sign up at the bank for a Visa card we are doing more than just looking for a way to pay our bills. We are becoming members of a global economy that enables us to travel throughout the world with just one card, if we believe the advertisers. The connection we make to the global economy is easily made, but what of our education? Why does globalisation affect the schooling that Australian students receive? How can it impact on the course we take at university and those that we took while at school?

This chapter will provide a brief history of the development of the concept of globalisation and offer a working definition of it. It will then show how the impact of this concept affects us as Australian educators and how we need to be cognisant of its potential as we enter the phase of globalisation that Robertson (1990) describes as *uncertainty*. The complexity of our lives today makes comparisons with previous generations difficult, if not impossible. One of the central themes underpinning this complexity or density is caused by globalisation:

> [Globalisation] reflects a widespread perception that the world is rapidly being moulded into a shared social space by economic and technological forces and that developments in one region of the world can have profound consequences for the life chances of individuals or communities on the other side of the globe (Held, 1999, p. 1).

There is often a perception that globalisation moves at its own pace and, like the dark riders in the *Lord of the Rings,* will catch up with you and destroy you if you are not very swift. Hopefully this chapter will give you a considered insight into the nature of globalisation and enable you to understand how to conceptualise the process. Before looking at a brief historical back ground to globalisation theory, let me introduce Shane (not his real name) to you. Interview 1, is taken from an interview in Hanoi, Vietnam, at an international school in November 2004.

International school (Interview 1)

Shane: OK, I was born in Western Australia, which makes me Australian. Born on a wheat and sheep farm, so from a country area. Moved to the city as a young child when I was 5 or 6, basically for family opportunities. The country, there wasn't much out there. Went through the government school system in Western Australia, in Perth. Then attended the University of Western Australia, did a Human Movement degree. Halfway through that I was a bit sick of studying. I was selected to attend the Royal Military College in Canberra for a one-year officer-training course. When the Labor government was in they had the military training where you could do one-year full time and then another year part time. So I graduated from there, spent a year in the military, went back to university, finished my degree. Spent a year teaching in rural Western Australia in a goldmining town and then moved to Melbourne in Victoria, Australia. I taught for 3 years in a very ethnic school, a lot of Middle-Eastern children and from there I got the opportunity to teach in Cambodia at the International School of Phnom Phen, where I worked for three years. Then I moved to Vietnam, since then this is my second year in Vietnam.

Interviewer (N. Bagnall): So you would definitely consider yourself an Australian?

Shane: Yeah, certainly.

Interviewer: Why did you make the transition, do you think, from teaching in a national school in Australia to an international school in Phnom Phen?

Shane: Mine was more about chance. I was looking for a bit of adventure and a bit of a challenge, something different to teaching in Australia. I thought, I don't want to be here and be 50, teaching Phys. Ed. in Australia. So I was looking to teach in America, just purely for the adventure of getting overseas and combining work and travel. While I was going through that process, the opportunity came up to teach in Cambodia through a company that was recruiting people in Australia and I went to the interview—didn't know anything about international education, it was all new to me. That's how I gained my job.

Interviewer: So I guess that begs the second question I was going to ask: had you had any formal training before you entered into the international school scene?

Shane: No, the only formal training I had was for Western Australian education. The focus in states in Australia is basically on that state. So no, nothing to do with international education.

Interviewer: Your experience is pretty much common. I mean, in reality there's not a huge amount of training out there. I can't think of any provider in Australia. There are some places in the [United] States but –

Shane: Yeah, most of it's all now Masters level, isn't it, in international education?

Interviewer: Yeah, that's true. So, talk to me about your experience here in Hanoi at the UNIS school of Hanoi.

Shane: In terms of what aspect?

Interviewer: How have you found it? What are the differences between here and maybe Cambodia? Is it … a walk in the park? Or is it really difficult?

Shane: I wouldn't say it's a walk in the park. The big difference that I say to people is in my original national system, in Australia, a lot of your teaching time is spent as a behaviour manager. There are a lot more behavioural management problems. In international education, I find that the job in terms of teaching—and for me, as a Phys. Ed. teacher organising sporting trips and lessons and competitions, that side of school is not really different. The big thing that I find is the students themselves and the way they interact with the teacher. That would be the biggest difference that I find.

It is likely that at some stage in your teaching career you will be offered an opportunity to teach outside the Australian school system. Whether you take up that possibility is up to you. I will talk more of that later in the chapter. Now

I would like to give a theoretical framework that will help your understanding of globalisation.

2   Historical background and theories of globalisation

The last 30 years have seen a plethora of literature relating to globalisation. In front of me as I write I have *Globalization and Fragmentation* (Clark, 1997), *Globalization* (Bauman, 1998), *Globalization, Tame it or Scrap it?* (Buckman, 2004), *Understanding Globalisation* (Schirato & Webb, 2003), *Globalization and its Outcomes* (O'Loughlin, Staeheli, & Greenberg, 2004), *The Globalization of World Politics* (Baylis & Smith, 1999) and *Empire* (Hardt & Negri, 2000) to name a few.

There is a strong argument that globalisation is not a new phenomenon but has increased in its intensity in the past 20 years. Held provides an analytic framework for understanding the historical forms of globalisation. In an attempt at measuring the dominant features of contemporary globalisation he identifies four spatio-temporal dimensions:

- the extensity of global networks
- the intensity of global interconnectedness
- the velocity of global flows
- the impact propensity of global interconnectedness (Held, 1999, p. 17).

The introduction of these categories enables Held and others to measure the forms taken by globalisation over time. He argues that sceptics of globalisation who do not see global interconnectedness as a novel phenomenon overlook the possibility that the form taken by globalisation may differ between historical eras. The creation of the four categories outlined above enables a framework for measuring these differences over differing historical eras.

What Held does particularly clearly is outline the three principal positions on the issues at stake in the globalisation debate. These may be summarised as:

- the hyperglobalist thesis
- the sceptical thesis
- the transformationalist thesis.

The hyperglobalists

The hyperglobalists believe that *transnational* networks of production, trade, and finance have replaced nation states:

> In this 'borderless' economy, national governments are relegated to little more than transmission belts for global capital, or ultimately, simple intermediate institutions

sandwiched between increasingly powerful local, regional and global mechanisms of governance (Held, 1999, p. 3).

Australia is certainly aware of the need to think about trade alliances in Asia as well as the more traditional links with Europe and America. The overwhelming belief among the hyperglobalists is that globalisation is primarily an economic phenomenon. The North/South[1] divide is no longer applicable as the labour market becomes more complex. Multinational corporations seek the cheapest labour with an ensuing division between rich and poor, winners and losers. One of the major casualties in such a deregulated market is the welfare state. The rules are no longer set by individual governments but rather by organisations such as the North American Free Trade Agreement, (NAFTA), the European Union (EU), or the International Monetary Fund (IMF):

> In this hyperglobalist account the rise of the global economy, the emergence of institutions of global governance, and the global hybridisation of cultures are interpreted as evidence of a radically new world order, an order which prefigures the demise of the nation-state (Held, 1999, p. 3).

The convergence of the economies of the world is a central feature of this argument that sees a homogenising of not only economic but also cultural and political aspirations of individual nations. The emergence of a 'global civilisation' is not far behind in this theoretical perspective. Schwartz (1996) warned of the emerging force of the 'Global Teenager'. He warned of the impact the 'Global Teenager' would have on technological, political, and economic forces in the twenty-first century due to the interconnectedness of the cohort. Some of his predictions about this group of almost 2 billion teenagers have come true. The iPod and Internet have brought new music, new images, and new fashions from unlikely corners of the globe. Playing virtual games with live audiences around the world makes the connection between the virtual world and the real one an even finer delineation. The wave of 'reality shows' such as *Big Brother, Who Wants To Be a Millionaire, Survivor,* and *You're Fired,* local versions of which play around the world, reflects a desire for audiences to be involved in the programs they are watching. The audience is encouraged to vote by sending a message on their phone to decide who goes and who stays for next week's show. Schwartz felt that the biggest uncertainty about technology as it was emerging in the 1990s was its impact on cultural differences between different nations. Would it be an homogenising agent or a cause for celebration of different cultures?

Undoubtedly the biggest casualty in the hyperglobalists' view of the world would be the 'sovereignty and autonomy' of the nation state. The small dent would become a huge hole as the emerging 'global civil society' took place.

The sceptics

The sceptics, by contrast to the hyperglobalists, believe that contemporary 'globalisation' is grossly exaggerated. They view the argument that national governments are being undermined by transnational organisations as a fallacy (see also chapter 1):

> The sceptics consider the hyperglobalist thesis as fundamentally flawed and also politically naïve since it under estimates the enduring power of national governments to regulate international economic activity. Rather than being out of control, the forces of internationalisation themselves depend on the regulatory power of national governments to ensure continuing economic liberalization (Held, 1999, p. 5).

Sceptics acknowledge the regionalisation of the world into economic zones of mutual benefit, but argue that this falls short of the economic situation prevailing in the late nineteenth century when the Gold Standard prevailed. The sceptics believe that the North/South divide has given way to a 'growing economic marginalisation of many "Third World" states as trade and investment flows within the rich North intensify to the exclusion of much of the rest of the globe' (Hirst & Thompson, 1996b, in Held, 1999, p. 6).

Sceptics downplay the significance of the multinational tendency to shift jobs to the South while de-industrialising the North. They do, however, acknowledge that there is an ingrained inequality and hierarchy that pervades the global economy and that this has been in place for the past century. This imbalance favours the wealthier nations; in particular what may be called the Western states. By downplaying the economic interdependence underlying the hyperglobalisers' argument, the sceptics challenge what they perceive as the myths surrounding globalisation.

The transformationalists

The third group, the transformationalists, believe that there is a blurring of boundaries between international and domestic, external and internal, as a result of contemporary processes of globalisation. There were many in Australia, for example, who felt that the decision by the ruling Liberal coalition party led by John Howard to enter the war with Iraq was merely an extension of the foreign policy of America. John Howard was cast as the Deputy Sheriff doing the work of the Sheriff, George Bush.[2]

In comparison with the sceptical and hyperglobalist accounts, the transformationalists make no claims about the future trajectory of globalisation; nor do they seek to evaluate the present in relation to some single, fixed ideal-type 'globalised world', whether a global market or a global civilisation (Held, 1999, p. 7).

The diminution in power of national governments is a direct result of the global economic processes resulting from globalisation. While states may still hold *de jure* power over the 'ultimate legal claim to effective supremacy over what occurs within their own territories', the *de facto* power imposed by the 'expanding jurisdiction of institutions of international governance and the constraints of international law is the more powerful force' (Held, 1999). Political decisions are no longer made by the governments of Canberra, Wellington, Paris, Montevideo, or Washington DC but in the offices of the World Trade Office (WTO), the World Bank, and the expanding array of international governance organisations and the requirements of international law. The sovereignty of nation states has never been total, but transformationalists believe that globalisation is making them redundant:

> Globalization is associated not only with a new 'sovereignty regime' but also with the emergence of powerful new non-territorial forms of economic and political organization in the global domain, such as multinational corporations, transnational social movements, international regulatory agencies, etc (Held, 1999, p. 9).

Inevitability, resistance and disruption

Taking into account the three theories outlined above, *hyperglobalist, sceptical,* and *transformationalist,* there seems to be an underlying inevitability about globalisation. The reduction in power of the nation state as outlined by the transformationalists, the emergence of the transnational networks of production, trade, and finance, as suggested by the hyperglobalists, and the more moderate position of the sceptics who acknowledge the regionalisation of the world into economic zones all suggest a steady move towards a global marketplace. One scholar who argues that the forces of economic globalisation are 'eminently reversible and hugely resistible' is Greg Buckman (2004). He would be heartened to hear of the recent (July 2005) 'No' vote in both France and Holland for an extension of power to the European Union. Buckman clearly sees the evolution of the 'global supermarket' as a potentially catastrophic event. A committed environmentalist, Buckman outlines the evolution and consequences of economic globalisation. He shows how the driving engines of globalisation are two groups of institutions. The first is the world's transnational corporations (TNCs) and the second is the World Trade Organization (WTO), the International Monetary Fund (IMF), and the World Bank (WB):

> So, today's global supermarket is the product of misguided free-market economic globalization ideology and a lot of opportunism, both of which have failed to take into account either the big world picture or our long-term future (Buckman, 2004, p. 16).

When I was training to become a teacher in New Zealand in the late 1970s, we were doing a module of work on board games and how they can be used in teaching complex ideas. One game we played involved using a series of coloured tokens. What we had to do was wander round the room and talk to each other and then swap tokens randomly. At the end of a certain amount of time we sat down and assigned values to each of the different colours. Now two groups were created, one whose token value was greater than the other. The group with the greater token value count made a series of simple rule changes that everyone had to adhere to. These people were then allowed to approach the members of the other group and take whatever tokens they wanted and give whatever they wanted back. Once again at the end of a period of time the token values were added up. Not surprisingly the group that had the greatest value after the first round had comprehensively accumulated all the tokens of value by the end of the second round. Buckman sees economic globalisation doing just this. Poorer nations are left with very little while the richer nations become ever richer:

> Nearly 70 per cent of world trade is currently controlled by the largest five hundred TNCs [trans-national corporations] in the world and about a third of world trade is conducted between different arms of the same company (Madeley, J. 2000). This means two dollars in every three dollars of world trade is controlled by TNCs, and one dollar in every three is represented by trade within the same company (Buckman, 2004, p. 16).

Buckman argues that the two groups of institutions that promote this unequal distribution of trade between rich and poor countries, TNCs and the WTO, IMF and WB, have a lot to answer for. These are the organisations that make the rules of the game. The poor countries are often unable to represent themselves at the meetings of these organisations: 'About thirty of the world's poorest countries, or roughly a quarter of all the poor countries that belong to the WTO, can't even afford to maintain delegations at the WTO's base in Geneva, and sub-Saharan African countries often only send one, or no, representative to key negotiations while rich countries send a small army' (Buckman, 2004, p. 47).

Buckman contends that the increase in intensity of flow of capital took place from the 1970s as a direct result of the floating of rich-country currencies. The 1950s and 1960s, he contends, were relatively stable with poor countries enjoying '... *steady increases in per capita wealth*' (Buckman, 2004, p. 52). The 1970s, however, saw a change in capital flow with poorer countries beginning to borrow heavily at a time when their development was faltering. The resulting interference in poorer economies with '*major policy-based strings attached*' eventuated in the 1982 Third World debt crisis. A further crisis in the guise of the East Asian meltdown not only further dented the reputations of the IMF and the World Bank but also showed how interconnected the economies of the global economy had become.

Without labouring the point, the rich countries have continued to increase their wealth while the poorest nations have suffered in the newly emerging global economic distribution system. Economic globalisation has not treated all players equally. Unlike the game I played with tokens when training to be a teacher, the tokens are real for the developing nations. The debts that were encumbered in the 1970s continue to haunt the borrowing nations. In recent meetings of the G8 (the Finance Ministers from the world's top eight economic powers), steps have been made to reduce or eliminate altogether the burden of debt of the poorest nations on earth. The series of concerts organised by Bob Geldof and his supporters in conjunction with the meeting of the G8 countries, on 25–26 June 2005, show how individuals can make a difference in fighting perceived negative impacts of globalisation. The concerts have been going since the mid 1980s and are a direct response from local supporters to oppose the global imbalance in the distribution of wealth.

3 How does Australia figure in the global marketplace?

The remainder of this chapter will focus specifically on the impact that globalisation has had in Australia, in particular on the provision of education within Australia. What are some of the consequences of the neoliberal economic policies of successive Australian governments on formal institutions such as schools and universities? How do schools and universities survive the budget cuts imposed by successive governments? Welch points to the backlash at the university level to the constant call for higher education institutions, in particular, to 'do more with less':

> Unending cost pressures on higher education have seen internationalization accomplished against a backdrop of declining staff-student ratios, with the massive growth in enrolments increasingly being sustained by resorting to marginal funding, the common substitution of tenure with contract and casual (teaching only) appointments, rising managerialism with a concomitant swell of resentment among academic staff, and a never-ending ethos of 'do more with less,' all leading to a declining morale among many staff members (Welch, 2002, p. 433).

Marginson (1997a) notes that it was the higher education sector that experienced the fuller implications of the 'efficiency imperative' (p. 213).

One of the most immediate impacts of globalisation on Australian society is felt by the creation of a global marketplace. The change in location of manufacturing to the country with the cheapest labour supply has meant that many traditional entry-level jobs have disappeared. This has had a major impact on those entering the work force for the first time, predominantly youth. This was dealt with in chapter 3. (See also Bagnall, 2005b.) One of the impacts on youth leaving school has been a higher retention rate as students realise that in order to get a job, they need to hold a high school leaving qualification at the very least, and a tertiary qualification for preference. As Te Riele and Wyn (2005) note:

> In response to increased youth unemployment during the 1970s the attention of Australian Commonwealth education policy was directed to young people and 'the government subsumed youth policy into its general macroeconomic program for education, employment and training' (Irving et al., 1995, p. 339). Policy encouraging retention to Year 12 for all students who wanted to was initially seen as 'inescapable' rather than necessary (p. 122).

The retention rates to Year 12 or equivalent across Australia show some of the implications of the reduction in entry-level jobs abailable to the youth cohort. As the jobs 'dry up' the option of staying on in school past compulsory leaving age (15 in all states except South Australia and Tasmania, where it is 16) is seen as a viable option. While the figures below do not show it, the percentage of females staying on till completion of Year 12 is generally 10 per cent higher than that for male students. This is possibly due to the increased range of entry-level jobs available to male students over female students.

Table 12.1   Apparent retention rates to Year 12, Australia, 1970–2004

Year	Retention to Year 12
1970	29.3
1975	34.1
1980	34.5
1985	46.4
1990	64.0
1997	74.5
1998	74.1
1999	74.4
2000	74.4
2001	75.4
2002	75.1

Source: ABS, 2004c

It is not only at the secondary level that participation in formal education is increasing in Australia.[3] Te Riele and Wynn (2005) suggest that higher education has become the '… "new" mass education sector' (p. 123). The so-called transition of higher education from an elite to a mass phenomenon has had a number of ramifications. The introduction of a higher education contribution scheme (HECS) levy has meant a growing number of students are now entering the workforce with a considerable debt. It has also led to an inflation of qualifications at the tertiary level as more students are participating in post-compulsory education.

Welch (2003) argues that globalisation 'has been influential in shaping the direction of contemporary educational reforms in Australia' (p. 272). He finds the increasingly diminished nature of the state highlighted in the dialogue process between government and electorate. The new agenda of reform at any cost may not be the sole responsibility of globalisation, but it is aggravating the chasm that is appearing in Australian society. In particular, Quiggin argues that there is a tendency for domestic and international economic frameworks to become intertwined. The resultant loss of autonomy in the international arena is significant for all economies, not just Australia's:

> Reductions in tariffs, together with the encouragement of new technology and its effects in the workplace, has been accompanied by substantial deregulation of the labour force, an increasing stance in favour of individual contracts over awards negotiated by trade unions … as well as by the progressive restriction of the 'government's role as a producer of many basic services, including education, health and welfare' (Quiggin, 1996, p. 2, in Mok & Welch, 2003, p. 266).

Mok and Welch contend that the increasing dependence of Australia's economy on the global market has had, and continues to have, considerable implications for fundamental principles underpinning governance within Australia. The major threat is evidenced in the replacement of the 'social good' by the imperative of the 'economic good': 'In education, as in other policy arenas, the relative weighting of social and economic concerns is sometimes seen as a contest between "quality", a major concern of structural adjustment proponents, and equality' (Mok & Welch, 2003, p. 263).

For Mok and Welch, the ensuing false polarisation applied to education (between quality and equality) has reduced notions of quality to economic indicators. While acknowledging that some of these indicators are of significance to some forms of quality education such as staff–student ratios, student progression rates, and year-by-year attrition rates, other important considerations are ignored:

> less often evident in such indices are the expressed aspirations of local people (Abu Duhou, 2000; Youngman, 2000), close considerations of the pedagogical relationship itself, and the extent to which such notions of 'quality', are tendentious

and fissiparous proposals about the introduction of user-pays principles, which impose the greatest penalties upon socially marginal families and individuals, least able to afford the fees entailed (Mok & Welch, 2003, p. 263).

The following section looks at some of these indicators and shows how they may be of value to you as you prepare to enter the teaching profession.

4 International educational standards

One consequence of globalisation is that government Ministers of Education are constantly trying to measure the success or failure of their policies against other countries. This is notoriously difficult to do, as education systems are not like car manufacturing plants. You cannot just tally up the number of units that are produced annually and measure that against another country. There are a number of ways that evaluation is undertaken on a global scale. The Organisation for Economic Co-operation and Development (OECD) publishes annually a set of indicators that make comparisons possible between countries. The table of contents usually contains several headings that evaluate a range of topics. They include:

- the demographic, social, and economic context of education
- financial and human resources invested in education
- access to education, participation, and progression
- the transition from school to work
- the learning environment and the organisation of schools
- student achievement and the social and labour-market outcomes of education.

The OECD 'continuously seeks to develop the indicators that can provide insight into the comparative functioning of education systems—focusing on the human and financial resources invested in education and on returns to those investments' (Centre for Educational Research and Innovation, 1998, p. 5). It is not always possible to put a dollar figure on educational outcomes but the OECD offer an impressive array of statistics that enable comparison of some aspects of different countries education systems to be compared.[4] (See also chapter 10.)

A less economic focus is taken in the Trends in International Mathematics and Science Study (TIMSS)[5] undertaken by the International Association for the Evaluation of Educational Achievement (IEA), an international organisation of national research institutions and governmental research agencies. These studies are an attempt to compare United States of America fourth-graders' and eighth-graders' maths and science results with those students from other countries. The data has been collected in 1995, 1999, and 2003 and will next be collected in 2007.

The results of the average mathematics achievement of eighth-grade students by nation in 1999 were: Singapore 604, USA 502 and South Africa 275, and the average of the 38 nations that took part was 487. The average of fourth-grade students in Table 12.2 shows some of the figures from the 2003 study.

Table 12.2 Average mathematics scale scores of fourth-grade students, by country: 2003

Country	Average Score
Singapore	594
Hong Kong#*	575
Japan	565
Chinese Taipei	564
Belgium-Flemish	551
Netherlands*	540
Latvia	536
Lithuania+	534
Russian Federation	532
England	531
Hungary	529
United States*	518
Cyprus	510
Moldova	504
Italy	503
Australia*	499
New Zealand	493
Scotland*	490
Slovenia	479
Armenia	456
Norway	451
Iran	389
Philippines	358
Morocco	347
Tunisia	339

Source: International Association for the Evaluation of Educational Achievement (IEA), Trends in International Mathematics and Science Study (TIMSS), 2003

Hong Kong is a Special Administrative Region (SAR) of the People's Republic of China.

* Met international guidelines for participation rates in 2003 only after replacement schools were included.

+ National desired population does not cover all of the international desired population.

Results of these surveys are useful for government planning agencies. When comparing results over a number of years it is possible to track general trends in a number of ways. The major problem in trying to evaluate how successfully particular programs are working—for example, mathematics teaching in fourth-grade schools—is that the surveys do not evaluate the same cohort in each evaluation period. The figures are not always as accurate and clear cut as the results may indicate. For example, in some of the schools surveyed, the percentage of students remaining at school to age 15 varies. The countries in this survey were required to sample students in the upper of two grades that contained the largest number of 9-year-olds. In the United States and most countries this corresponds to grade 4. It is reasonable to expect that in most developed countries all students of this age would be attending school as the compulsory attendance rate is on average from age 5–6 until age 15–16. In the developing world, however, actual attendance rates fall far short of these age ranges. What constitutes attendance at school varies widely also. In some developing nations a student who attends school for one day a month may be counted in a survey relating to school attendance. More rigorous criteria might be applied in the developed world.

The OECD looks at participation in education by estimating the number of years of full-time and part-time education that a 5-year-old child can expect to enrol in over her or his lifetime:

> This 'school expectancy' is estimated by taking the sum of enrolment rates across each single year of age over 4. Within the OECD, school expectancy varies from 12 years in Mexico to over 18 years in Australia, Belgium and Sweden; in most countries it falls in the range of 16–17 years' (Centre for Educational Research and Innovation, 1998, p. 149).

5   International curriculum

Another impact of globalisation on Australian schooling concerns international curricula. Australia does not have a unified education system, as each state is responsible for its educational provision. At the secondary level there is a formal leaving certificate that is particular to each state. Students in Victoria have the Victorian Certificate of Education (VCE) as their leaving certificate, New South Wales has its Higher Education Certificate (HSC) and students in the Australian Capital Territories (ACT) have their Year 12 leaving certificate. One certificate that can be sat in all states in Australia is the International Baccalaureate (Bagnall, 1997a, 1997b, 2005a). The first school to offer it in 1979 was a state school in Canberra, Narrabundah College. Since then a steady, if small, number of schools has experimented with it throughout Australia. There are currently over eighty-eight schools throughout Australia[6] offering programs that are entirely monitored and administered from outside Australia.

The reasons schools gave for offering the IB included its international focus, curriculum choice, and its ability to cater for an increase in overseas students. It was seen as a magnet for attracting other students. Principals sometimes felt concern about the lowering of standards in the local system and wanted their staff to be involved in an international curriculum. It was favoured for its apparent portability, its service to internationally mobile parents and for its academic excellence (Bagnall, 1994). The International Baccalaureate has also become an alternative curriculum in the primary and middle years of schooling in some Australian schools. It is acknowledged as a useful entrance qualification at the university level and since its inception as a high school leaving diploma in the early 1970s has helped many international students make the transition from an international school to a university. The addition of the primary years program (PYP) and middle years program (MYP) in the past 10 years have seen the evolution of a complete curriculum from primary school to high school. While the numbers are not huge,[7] it is significant that a reasonably substantial number of schools are choosing an international curriculum ahead of an Australian (Victorian/New South Wales/Western Australian etc.) curriculum.

It is possible to see an increasingly strong connection between the teachers within Australia and the rest of the world as curriculum and teacher training becomes more analogous globally. Shane (Interview 1—boxed text) found himself teaching in Hanoi after training to be a teacher in Western Australia. I include another excerpt from a colleague of his at the international school he is working in.

International school (Interview 2)

Interviewer (N. Bagnall): Now that I know your name's Susan and that you're Canadian, I'm going to ask you … a little bit about your teaching background, your teaching experience, how you got into international school education, and what other international schools, if any, you've taught at, and how long you've been here.

Susan: OK. Well, this is my third year here and I'm currently teaching music, grades 1 to 4, but next year I'll be moving into the classroom. Before I came here I was in the Middle East in a tiny country called Bahrain, and it wasn't an international school but it was a national school, mainly Bahrainis but some

Saudis, some Kuwaitis, and I taught music, grade 7 to 10 in my first year, and grade 7 to 9 in my second year, and before that I was in Toronto teaching in an inner-city school, and I taught grade 4, and I was (there to teach) music … Yes, it was a high ethnic population, a lot of recent immigrants to the country, mainly from Pakistan, Bangladesh … And how I got interested in international teaching was through my cousin. She had done it when I was still in university and she'd been in Kuwait for 5 years and then she went to Mexico for 2 years, and so I was listening to all her stories of all these great places she got to visit, and just the different lifestyle that she lived, and I thought that would be an interesting thing to try. When I left Toronto I had planned to just do 2 or 3 years and then go back, but I knew within my first 6 months I wasn't going back to teach in Ontario! I really enjoyed the lifestyle and enjoyed the schools. There was not as many hassles as we have with education in Ontario.

Interviewer: So, did you have any specific training in preparation for working in an international school?

Susan: Nothing. No. Although it was an area of interest, and I had always been interested in international education, and then I guess my training was teaching for 3 years in Toronto in a school where the population was so diverse and multicultural that everybody in there … I would look around my classroom and I would probably have only six students who were actually born in Canada, in Ontario, whereas the school across the street from where my mum lives, you'd be lucky to have one student in the school who was not born in Canada! And they're only 15 minutes apart, very close but very different. I'm currently doing my Masters in international education, and—

Interviewer: By distance?

Susan: Yes.

Interviewer: Through—

Susan: Endicott College in Beverley, Massachusetts. We did 4 weeks last July, intensively, in Madrid, and then two courses in the Fall and two courses in the Spring right now, and then another four courses again intensively in July in Madrid will be done, so it's 13 months when it's finished. But I'm finding it doesn't have enough of an actual international angle to it. It's a lot more local …

Interviewer: What they're doing is Massachusetts-based?

Susan: Not necessarily Massachusetts, but I guess I was looking more for intercultural, I think, than international, and I've just come across a program in Deakin, I guess they've got two programs: one's international development and the other is intercultural relations …? I can't remember.

Interviewer: … The curricula in this School is PYP [primary]?

Susan: Yes.

Interviewer: What role do you think the curricula have in promoting intercultural sensitivity?

Susan: In terms of the PYP it's just a framework, so the actual content is decided by the school, so it's just a matter of putting in as much cultural input into it … we looked at cultures from a musical perspective and we looked at them from an art perspective … It's not the PYP that sets that; it's the school who decides, and then our own school curricula. We've just written a music one, and I feel that there needed to be more cultural aspects to it, so we put that in, as well.

Susan (Interview 2) covers a range of significant issues for Australians entering the workforce in the twenty-first century. Her career path is typical of an increasingly large number of teachers who see their career from a global rather than a state (provincial) or national perspective. While her initial teacher training was undertaken in Canada, her continuing career path has taken her in a different direction, that of a teacher in an international school. Like Shane (Interview 1), she has benefited by the flexibility of a global education marketplace that accepts teachers from many different nationalities.

The International Baccalaureate Organisation (IBO) is an example of an international organisation that has the potential to change the way education is provided in a number of ways across a wide range of countries, including Australia. A visit to the web site shows how it sees its role as not only the provider of an educational qualification but also an educational philosophy. The early critics[8] of the IBO argued that it was not available to all countries and indeed favoured the developed countries over the developing world. The number of schools in the developing world that can afford to offer the IB some 30 years after its introduction is still small.

6 Conclusion

Globalisation is a complex phenomenon. It is also sometimes very simple. The 2005 London underground bombing brought the pictures of global terrorism into the homes of people all over the world. The media is truly globally connected and shows how events in one part of the world quickly become part of the global consciousness. The events of September 11 in New York were devastatingly global in their coverage and outcome. The ensuing war in Iraq and continuing war in Afghanistan brought the fight against terrorism onto a global stage. Why is it, however, that catastrophic events in some parts of the world, like London and New York, have more impact than those in other parts of the world, such as Rwanda and Bosnia?

As a teacher, you will be expected to have a position on events that take place outside the classroom. How would you react if a primary school student came to school the day after September 11 events with a poster saying that they were glad that the planes had been flown into the skyscrapers? Some teaching students at one Australian university were on practicum in a school where that occurred. Would you sit passively and say nothing?

The explanations given in this chapter have suggested that there is not one definition of globalisation that will please everyone. Globalisation is about power and how that power is distributed. It is about culture and the way that some cultural groups have more power than others. It is about money and how freely it flows between borders as if there were no such things as nation states. It is about the way that education is influenced by increasingly complex international standards of comparison such as the TIMSS survey and OECD education indicators that compare such things as access to education and transition to work.

It is likely that many of you reading this book will stay in teaching for a long time. Since the average age of teachers in Australia seems to be somewhere between 48 and 50 depending on your source, it seems likely that there will continue to be ample numbers of positions in this challenging profession. Many of you will probably spend some time teaching out of Australia. You will all, however, feel the influence of globalisation in your work as teachers.

Focus questions

1 Held (1999) suggests that there are three principal positions in the globalisation debate. Describe what they are and explain which camp you fit into?

2 How do you see the emerging drift between the minority of wealthy nations and the majority of poorer nations playing out in the next 10 years?

3 The diminishing role of the nation state is arguably one of the most significant outcomes of globalisation? How do you see Australia dealing with this aspect of *le mondialisation*?

4 Australia's economy is increasingly becoming a service economy. How do you see this affecting your future?

5 If you were to do a research project in this area, you may look at a number of problems. These could include: the impact of the internet, the role of information technology, and the role of qualifications such as the International Baccalaureate in Australian schools.

Notes

1. The North vs South divide was highlighted in the report of the Brandt Commission set up in 1977. The 'Independent Commission on International Development Issues' delivered its findings in 1980 in its report *North-South: A program for Survival*. The world was divided into two groups: the rich countries of the North (Europe, North America, Japan, Australia, New Zealand) and the developing countries of the South (Russia, China, most of Asia, Africa and South America). The recommendations of the Report were given under the headings: a new international economic order; a global food strategy; and population control. For a fuller account of the implications of the Brandt Report, see Alladin (1986).

2. Hardt & Negri (2000) argue that the collapse of the Soviet Union and the end of the Cold War reorganised the lines of hegemony within the imperialist world, accelerating the decline of the old powers (Britain, France) and raising up the US initiative of the constitution of an imperial order: 'This imperial project, a global project of network power, defines the fourth phase or regime of US constitutional history. In the waning years and wake of the cold war, responsibility "fell" squarely on the shoulders of the United States' (Hardt & Negri, 2000, pp. 179–80).

3. Between 1951 and 2001, the number of higher education students in Australia increased from 31,700 to 614,100 (ABS, 2002b; Te Riele & Wyn, 2005, p. 123).

4. See the OECD web site at www.oecd.org/home/0,2987,en_2649_201185_1_1_1_1_1,00.html.

5. For those interested in this study go to www.nces.ed.gov/nceskids/eyk/index.asp?flash=true.

6. As of February 2006 there were some 1722 schools in 122 countries offering three programs to approximately 200,000 students worldwide: www.ibo.org/ibo/index.cfm?page=/ibo/services/ib_worldsch [date accessed 6/7/05].

7. There are 73 schools listed in various programs of the IB as of 6 July, 2005. There are more waiting to come on line in the next 6 months. This total includes some schools that may have been included twice or three times if they offered the Diploma, MYP, and PYP programs: <www.ibo.org/ibo/index.cfm?page=/ibo/services/ib_worldsch> [date accessed 6/7/05].

8. See Uy's (1988) study and also Bagnall (1994) for a summary of the literature relating to the early years of the IBO.

Further reading

Abu-Ahou, I. (2000). 'The struggle to achieve quality.' In A. Welch (ed.), *Third World Education*. New York: Garland.

Alladin, I. (1986). 'North-South Cooperation: Educational Implications of the Brandt Report'. In R.R. Gillespie & C.B. Collins (eds), *Education as an International Commodity* (Vol. 1, pp. 170–83).

Australian Bureau of Statistics (ABS) (2002). *Education and Training Indicators. Australia. Catalogue number 4230.0*. Canberra: ABS.

Bagnall, N.F. (1997a). 'The International Baccalaureate in Australia.' *Melbourne Studies in Education, 38*(1), 129–44.

Bagnall, N.F. (1997b). 'The International Baccalaureate in Canada, 1980–93'. In K. Burridge, L. Foster & G. Turcote (eds), *Canada-Australia: Towards a Second Century of Partnership* (pp. 233–46). Carlton: Carlton University Press.

Bagnall, N.F. (2005a). 'The International Baccalaureate in Australia and New Zealand.' *Change, Transformations in Education, 8*(1), 39–57.

Bagnall, N.F. (ed.). (2005b). *Youth Transition in a Globalised Marketplace*. New York: Nova Science Publishers Inc.

Commonwealth Schools Commission (1980). *Schooling for 15 & 16 Year-olds*. Canberra: AGPS.

Hardt, M. & Negri, A. (2000). *Empire*. Cambridge: Harvard University Press.

Madeley, J. (2000). *Hungry for Trade: How the Poor Pay for Free Trade*. London: Zed Books.

Mok, K. & Welch, A. (eds) (2003). *Globalization and Educational Restructuring in the Asia Pacific region*. Basingstoke: PalgraveMacmillan.

Robertson, R. (2003). *The Three Waves of Globalization. A History of a Developing Global Consciousness*. London: Zed Books.

Schwartz, P. (1996). *The Art of the Long View: Planning for the Future in an Uncertain World*. New York: Doubleday.

Uy, V.T. (1988). *Determining the Relevance of the International Baccalaureate Program vis-à-vis the Third World Countries.* Columbia University.

Youngman, F. (2000). 'The state, adult literacy policy, and inequality in Botswana.' In A. Welch (ed.), *Third World Education. Quality and Equality*. New York: Garland.

Internet sources

Entering the key words 'globalisation' and 'education' into Google produces many sites of interest.

These significant organisations each have web sites that can be searched profitably:

OECD (Organisation for Economic and Cooperative Development) (Paris) at www.oecd.org

World Bank (Washington) at www.worldbank.org.

United Nations (New York) at www.un.org.

UNICEF—United Nations Children's Fund (New York) at www.unicef.org.

World Trade Organization (Geneva) at www.wto.org.

See also International Baccalaureate Organisation (IBO) at www.ibo.org/ibo/index.cfm?page=/ibo/services/ib_worldsch.

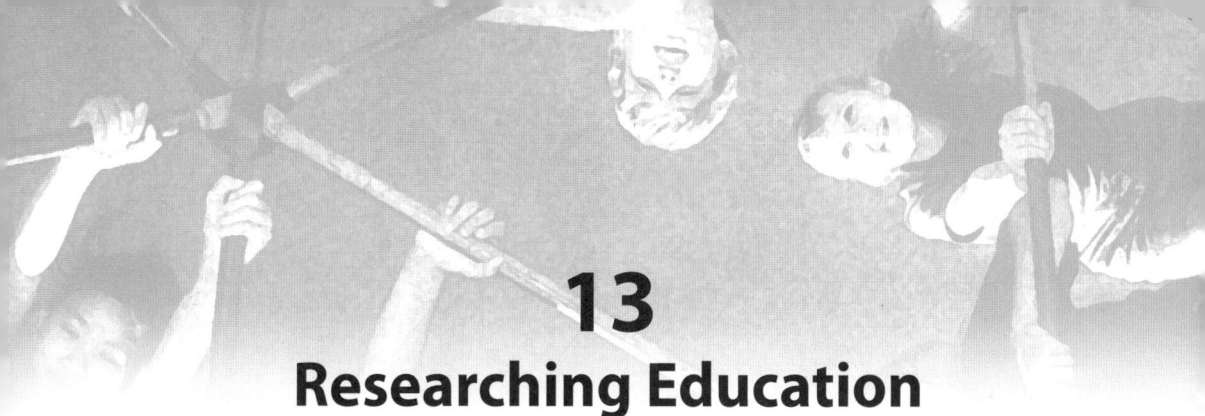

13
Researching Education

This chapter is divided into two parts. The first addresses some general questions about what educational research is, and what status the knowledge that it produces has. There is also the important discussion about why teachers might also be researchers, and to what end. The second part is aimed more specifically at students who might do a research project as part of course of study on the social, cultural, and policy contexts of Australian education.

Part I: Science, Research, and Teachers
Raewyn Connell

1   What is science?

In past generations there has been great enthusiasm for the idea that education can be transformed by science. Applying proper scientific method, it was thought, would determine how much intelligence different pupils have, what is the best way to teach and the best way to test, what is the best way to group pupils, and so forth. Do enough research, develop enough scientific knowledge, and we can deduce what to do in practice.

This optimism about science is still strong. At present it takes the form of a movement for 'evidence-based education', in which rigid scientific method—preferably randomised controlled trials, the 'gold standard' borrowed from medical research—will distinguish good methods from bad methods. Thus everyone can adopt international best practice. This is an idea that appeals strongly to some educational authorities (Hendery & Barratt, 2002).

These ideas rest on a particular understanding of science, which runs as follows. Scientific knowledge is sharply distinguished from all other forms of knowledge. It is uniquely reliable, because it is built up by accumulating facts.

After accumulating the facts, science states universal 'laws' (e.g. the laws of thermodynamics) that are true everywhere. It uses observational and logical methods that also apply everywhere.

In this model, *pure science*, consisting of research and theory, is sharply distinguished from *applied science*, which consists of practice governed by the laws established in pure science. The two cannot be mixed, since that would contaminate the methods of pure science. 'Bias' is the worst thing that can happen in research. Neutral observation of facts is the foundation of all scientific knowledge.

Though still popular, this is actually a very old-fashioned conception of science. Its essentials were stated in a famous book, *The Grammar of Science*, by the mathematician Karl Pearson, more than a hundred years ago. Since then, this picture of science has been called into question by philosophers and sociologists of science, and by the development of science itself.

The idea that we can have pure, neutral observation independent of the researchers' standpoint has been strongly rejected. This is now considered obsolete in fields as diverse as physics and anthropology. The sharp distinction between fact and theory has been overthrown. Theories of some kind are always involved in scientific observations. The sharp distinction between pure and applied research is untenable in some areas, such as psychiatry, and is probably pointless in many others. 'Laws' cannot, logically, be justified by piling up facts, however big the pile becomes. Statements about laws always involve an imaginative leap, a 'conjecture' as one philosopher put it (Chalmers, 1982).

Some writers go so far as to argue there is no fundamental difference between science and belief systems such as religion or astrology. There is, now, another popular view that the only thing that matters is what any individual believes. One person's beliefs have the same standing as any other's, and there is no way of proving any of them true or false. Instead of an authoritative science, we have a chaotic marketplace of beliefs, opinions, and values.

This anything-goes view may or may not apply to 'values', but it is certainly wrong in relation to *knowledge*. We should indeed get rid of nineteenth-century myths about science. But we should not throw out the concept of science itself. Rather we need a better, more realistic understanding of what science is and how knowledge develops.

It is important to maintain a distinction between research-based knowledge, which we call 'science', and knowledge that is not research-based. There are three key points.

1 Research-based knowledge is testable, and is actually tested. It is checked by observation and experiment, and also by logical critique. This does not mean it is certain; in fact, scientific knowledge never is certain. It simply means that science is systematically open to correction.

2 Scientific knowledge is open to growth. New ideas, new methods, and new observations, are constantly emerging—and constantly require discussion and correction. This is very much a social process. The participants in science form 'knowledge communities' in which both the innovation and the checking occur.

3 Therefore scientific knowledge is inherently public knowledge. It requires communication; it is brought out and tested in open forums. Hence the importance of what we correctly call 'publication' of research.

Because science is a social process, the questions it asks and the answers it gives are inevitably shaped by institutions, economics, interpersonal relations, and large-scale social structures. But science does not mechanically reflect social forces. The growth of knowledge requires the creation of many forums in which open-ended argument can occur. In such forums the final arbiter is not a President, a CEO, or a Pope but simply the force of the better argument. In the course of time, the better argument persuades informed participants that such-and-such a conclusion is the right one to draw. In this sense, science is inherently democratic.

2 Research and practice

This more contemporary view of science draws no sharp distinction between 'pure' and 'applied' research. In fact it points to the practical dimension in all research efforts. To this way of thinking, the method of science is substantially the same as the method by which reliable everyday knowledge is produced. This is not because we can substitute common sense for the organised research effort of science, but because both are essentially *learning processes*. One is more elaborate, formalised, and public than the other, but they still have a lot in common.

People and groups learn through their encounters with the world, through grappling with problems and obstacles while pursuing their purposes. Individual learning, like science, involves creating hypotheses, searching for facts, and testing solutions. The solutions arrived at are always subject to correction through further learning. Science, like individual learning, is provisional, tentative, and involves a certain amount of trial and error. But it is also progressive, building over time better solutions to intellectual problems.

This view of knowledge emphasises the links, rather than the divisions, between research and practice. It contests the view of science as a specialised activity conducted only in remote laboratories by white-coated specialists ignorant of the real world.

Certainly we should recognise the role of disinterested curiosity, or passion for understanding, in the development of knowledge. But we should also recognise that there is often a practical reason involved in a given expansion of knowledge, and much of our knowledge is appropriately tested by what can be done with it. There is, in fact, no reason why the researcher and the practitioner cannot be the same person, or the same group.

A number of movements emphasise the democratic possibilities in science and technology. Cooley's *Architect or Bee?* (1980) describes actions in a high-technology aerospace firm in Britain that revealed the creativity of production workers and their capacity to come up with alternative, more socially valuable, uses for technology. The 'green' movement is another important example, trying to link organised knowledge to social participation in decision-making about the environment. An example of democratising social science knowledge is the 'Dig Where You Stand' movement in Sweden, where working-class people researched the history of their own jobs. They dug out documents, photographs, official records, etc. that showed how their industries had developed, how particular firms had arisen, how machinery or techniques had changed, and how particular divisions between jobs had been created.

In social welfare and community action in Australia, community groups have often defined a need for knowledge and have organised themselves to produce it. The Australian sociologist Wadsworth wrote a bestselling book based on this experience, *Do It Yourself Social Research*. This is full of practical advice on how grassroots-based research can be done.

In education, there has also been strong interest in creating a new relationship between research and practice. This impulse has taken several forms:

- A self-study movement where teachers take their own practice as the object of research. Practitioners try to create systematic knowledge about practice as a basis for reflection, thus linking research and professional development. This can be done in all curriculum areas, including the 'hard' sciences (Tobin, 1999).
- An action research movement, which puts into effect an 'action research cycle'—the phases are plan, act, observe, and reflect—in which research and practice are linked in a continuing way (Kemmis & McTaggart, 1988). The action research cycle can be used by whole schools or community groups as well as by individual teachers. Indeed, it is now being done by virtual groups on the Web (Hughes, 2001).
- A strategy of creating researcher/practitioner teams, often linking universities with schools, in which the separation of roles is deliberately reduced. The goal is to investigate and improve practice by empowering teachers as researchers (Burns, Hood & de Silva Joyce, 1995–2001).

Research and practice in teaching

A striking illustration of how teacher research can link with teaching practice is given by Comber and Kamler (2004). One of the problems in promoting social justice in education is the prevalence of a 'deficit' view of working-class children. This is the idea that they, or their families, are lacking some cultural qualities needed for success in learning.

A very interesting project in Victoria and South Australia encouraged new teachers, in collaboration with their more experienced mentors, to look in greater depth at the families of particular children currently regarded as 'at risk' in their schools. The young teachers visited the families in their homes, talked to parents, and learned about the tensions and difficulties the families faced. This investigation began to turn around the new teachers' perceptions of the families and children involved. They also began to see that even poor and marginalised families have many resources and capabilities—for instance, knowledge of football and fishing, deep concern for the child's future—which the school system usually ignored. This insight made it possible to re-design their teaching methods to make more use of the resources these children could access rather than resources they could not.

3   Practitioner research and professional research

There is now a considerable body of writing about teacher research (e.g. Loughran, Mitchell & Mitchell, 2002). This is no longer an uncertain, pioneer field; there is much experience that teachers can draw from.

This experience shows problems as well as advantages in teachers doing their own research. Some of the practical issues are explained by Johnson (1999), the principal of a primary school in Adelaide that has been involved in a number of collaborative research projects. The busy pace of school life makes it difficult for teachers to find the time that university researchers are accustomed to. The practical focus of teachers' work means that 'outcomes' of research are defined in terms of local improvements in practice, rather than publication, i.e. the wider circulation of knowledge.

A practitioner such as a teacher in a school has limited time for research, and may find it difficult to get funding. Teacher education programs used to give no training in research skills at all. It is now more common to include such training, with a little practical research experience, in teacher education programs. But the time given to research training is severely limited by the many other demands on teacher education curricula. Many teachers in schools have little confidence in themselves as researchers.

Hence, when the idea of doing research comes up, the reaction may be to reach for a familiar, inexpensive procedure—'Let's do a survey on that!'—without much thought about how useable the information will be. Or, when some data have been collected, they get just a quick scan, with attention focused on some juicy high-lights. 'Cherry-picking' data is probably the commonest error in research. Cherry-picking usually reinforces the view of the problem that the researcher began with. Yet the whole point of research—whether practitioner research or professional research—is to challenge existing assumptions and gain new knowledge.

Practitioner research therefore needs to be concerned, quite as much as professional research is, with the *quality* of information, and with the way the information, once gathered, is processed, interpreted, and used.

The best way to do this is to use the standard quality control mechanism in science—publication. The forums may be different but the principle is the same. Practitioners can publish their findings and ideas to colleagues (for instance, fellow-teachers in the same school). They can debate appropriate methods, discuss the study with potential participants, circulate the findings, and put their interpretations into wider circulation (for instance via in-service conferences). This also maximises the chances of connecting practitioner research findings to other investigators' findings, and thus multiplying the information available on the problem itself.

Practitioner researchers can also access the findings of professional researchers, and use them to build on. It saves time and energy if someone else has already done some of the work. But it may take time to find the researcher or the report.

The main resource nowadays is the Internet. Most current published research does find its way onto the Internet. But so does a stunning amount of misleading, poor quality, distorted, or outright deceptive information. A general-purpose search engine such as Google cannot distinguish the quality of the information on the different web sites to which it leads. It will, in addition, be biased toward commercial sites.

For this reason, professional researchers usually go straight to databases where there is some control over quality (for instance, an emphasis on journals that 'referee' all papers, a common though not perfect quality-control mechanism). A good example is the 'Web of Science', a database of scientific publications that amalgamates many specific disciplines, including the social sciences. In educational research, the best-known database is ERIC (unfortunately now being de-funded by the United States government, which sponsored it for many years), and in Australia, the Australian Education Index.

These databases have their problems, too. The international ones are mostly based in the United States and are biased towards US material, which may not be relevant in Australia. They are not always up to date. And they can be difficult to search. Searching a database requires using key words, and limiting the search to prevent being flooded with irrelevant material. If you are having difficulty, ask a reference librarian for help.

How to find research reports on a given topic

- Search a database such as ERIC or the Web of Science, using key words that describe your topic.
- Ask an expert. Often a researcher in a related field can direct a practitioner to relevant studies or will know of relevant authors.
- Look at textbooks, encyclopedias and handbooks in the field, which usually have many references to research (though probably they will not be the most current).
- Look at the list of references in any highly relevant paper you have already found, and track back. This is constantly done by professional researchers, and there is even a tool, known as a Citation Index, to help track *forward* from a given publication.
- Skim the contents pages of journals that publish work in the field of interest. Contents of journals are usually on the Web. This is the best way to find very recent publications.
- Read practitioners' journals, and go to in-service events, which may provide guides to research relevant to a practical problem.

Practitioner research has the advantage of relevance and immediacy. It is directly connected with the problems that called for the research and with likely users of it. Professional research has the advantage of resources, research experience, and (often) technique. There is an obvious extra advantage, therefore, in *combining* them—doing practitioner research informed by the professional stuff, or doing professional research connected with investigations by practitioners.

Research is our basic tool for the growth of knowledge—at least, for the growth of public, testable knowledge. Research is necessarily risky. Projects often fail, or produce less than hoped for. Science, including social science, grows by a combination of imagination, debate, and hard grubbing for information, and the results are never guaranteed. It is important, then, to take a critical view of all sources (even those in refereed journals!) and test them against local experience, practice, and other research.

In that testing, the greatest asset is hands-on experience of doing your own research. Therefore we think it important for every student in education programs to have some experience of doing research projects. The experience will be of extra value if they become practitioner researchers later on.

Focus questions

1 Some people consider teaching an 'art' or a 'trade' in which practical know-how counts and there is little room for scientific research. What arguments can you find for and against this view?
2 What advantages are there in teachers being active researchers? What disadvantages are there?

Further reading

Johnson, K. (1999). 'Reflections on collaborative research from the realms of practice.' *Change: Transformations in Education, 2*(1), 12–25.
Loughran, J., Mitchell, I. & Mitchell, J. (eds). (2002). *Learning from Teacher Research*. Sydney: Allen & Unwin.
Wadsworth, Y. (1983). *Do It Yourself Social Research*. Melbourne: VCOSS and Allen & Unwin.

Part II: A Research Project
Craig Campbell

1   Why do a research project?

There are many different sorts of assignments one could write as a result of studying the material in this book. This section of this chapter supports a specific kind of research project that might be planned and conducted by students. Its purpose is to encourage a deeper personal and possibly local understanding of aspects of the topics discussed in this book.

The idea is to establish a way of thinking about the social contexts and impacts of educational activity. Included in the process are topic definition, proposal construction and presentation, literature search and writing a literature review, discussion of possible research methods and the kinds of knowledge or results different methods can produce, and finally, issues relating to the writing of a report and its presentation to a group.

The ideas discussed in this section are very modest; they simply support a first step in research. They introduce one of many ways of organising such an activity.

2   Choosing a topic and a partner; and what the project might eventually look like

This project has a very general organising statement:

> Report on your research project into an aspect of education and its social consequences and/or character.

The final report might look something like this:

a Title page including:
  i   Title of the project
  ii Names of investigation team.

b Report including the following sections:
  i   Brief introduction of topic and its importance or significance
  ii   Short literature review
  iii Description of research method
  iv   Ethical issues raised in the course of the project
  v   Results and discussion of results
  vi   Conclusion
  vii List of references.

This project has several sections, and therefore phases, associated with its development and writing. It is best to work through the process with a partner from a very early stage. Such partnerships support good learning as possible topics are planned, and finally the meaning and significance of the research results are discussed and written up.

In selecting a topic, the previous chapters of this book are a significant resource. It may be that you choose issues raised in a particular chapter to enquire into further. From a general topic area there needs to be a discussion whereby your research topic is converted into a *fairly specific question*. For example, from being interested in youth transition from school to work, a question might eventually emerge, such as: 'How do a group of young people still at school, but also employed on a casual basis at a Coles supermarket, understand the relationships between school and work?'.

Into such a question, one could build some possible answers (*hypotheses*) to be explored as a result of the research process; for example, in the supermarket scenario above, 'That students do not make many links, but are simply glad of the extra cash', or 'That students gain significant knowledge about work and casual work in particular, and that they are likely to adjust their approach to education and work as a result', and so on.

In the organising statement for this project there is a key word: that is 'social'. It is important to realise that this project should be based on the concerns of this book or similar. Sociology, and policy studies are the fields of educational study that sustain this book, and should help define your project topic. There is little in this book to support more technical pedagogical or psychological research projects; say researching the best techniques for teaching, or classroom management, or trying to understand the cognitive processes involved in individual learning. Such issues should wait for another day or another course.

The other thing that should probably be said is that some topics may cause some problems. There are at least four issues that have caused problems for students who have conducted this kind of project over the years:

1 Choosing a topic that is simply too large. Pick a topic of manageable size. Most students have very limited time to do these kinds of assignments. Choose a topic that can be explored with two or three interviews, or a very limited survey or a limited documentary or media study. This also relates to being circumspect in how much you can actually show or conclude in a very small study. (This is discussed below.) Choose an interesting topic, but choose one that you can explore with limited time and resources.

2 Choosing a topic that could lead to major ethical, relationship, and research problems. There is no doubt that the terrible phenomena of youth suicide or drug addiction among young people at school can be explored as social issues as well as from psychological points of view. It may be, however, that in the process of finding knowledgeable people to interview about such problems, you will come across a raft of problems. Many people will not wish to talk about the issues; some people will demand high levels of official ethics clearance and assurances, which universities are unlikely to grant undergraduate students. Sometimes in the process of exploring such a topic, student investigators can cause additional grief to people already damaged in some ways. It is usually sensible to choose other kinds of topics.

3 Choose a topic and approach that lessens your involvement with institutions such as schools, for example. It is sometimes tortuous and time-wasting to get involved in seeking permission from institutions to conduct a research project. Most schools, government departments and other organisations have strict guidelines or protocols about whom they will allow to conduct research. For a small student project, satisfying such protocols may waste precious time. There are plenty of possible project topics to be done that do not require involved negotiations with institutions. However, if you have close personal contacts with schools, for example, you may be able to cut through a little of the red tape.

4 Choose a topic area that clearly fits within the concerns and content of your course. This issue has been discussed in the paragraphs immediately preceding these four points.

The following list of questions and issues have often produced excellent research projects, but they should not be considered as limiting the more important process of independently arriving at a project topic.

The first group of possible topic areas can be thought of as *attitudinal studies*: why people think the things that they do is an important factor in trying to explain what happens, or why certain educational institutions or policies are developed. For example:

- attitudes to public schooling
- attitudes to non-government schooling
- attitudes to ethnically and religiously exclusive schooling
- attitudes to educational policies (multiculturalism, anti-racism etc.).

Such topics need to be made more specific. Then the particular kinds of people whose attitudes are to be surveyed are identified, and then, usually through interview or questionnaire methods, the study proceeds.

Another group of topics may centre on the needs and handling of different groups in education. Often the issue that links such topics to a social perspective is the often stated aim of educational policies and institutions that there be fair or equal access by different groups to educational services. Such groups could include sexual orientation minorities, specific ethnic or minority cultural groups, groups such as the disabled who often struggle for access, or even broader groups based on social class, gender, or region (urban or rural).

The same groups can form the basis for projects based on individual or group *life-histories* in education. These are often based on one or a number of interviews in which we try to understand the decisions, participation, and outcomes associated with persons' interactions with schools and education in general. A specialised form of this is the *generational study*. In such a study one might ask to interview three members of one family, perhaps of the same sex, of different generations. How did their expectations and experience of schooling differ in different time periods? What did it take in terms of education to get a good job in different generations?

Another group of topics can derive from the study of the way the mass media reports education. There are many different things that might be done here; for example:

- study the reporting and editorial stance of particular news media (newspapers are often the easiest to access) on particular issues; for example, voluntary student unionism, non-government school funding, Year 12 examination results, or the 'boy crisis' in education
- study the attitude of particular newspaper columnists to public and private education
- study local newspapers for their advertisements encouraging parents to enrol their children at a particular school
- compare the professional journals of public and non-government teacher unions on private schools and/or government funding.

Then there is the possibility of studying policies, policy-makers, and educational leaders. Web sites of government departments and school systems are good sources in the identification of these. In terms of policy-making, one could interview policy-makers in terms of the contexts and pressures in writing policy for governments or school systems. Which groups have their voices heard, or not heard? How are policies received by their targeted audiences? How well are they implemented? Do they have an effect? On whom, and how?

Another possibility is the regional study. What mix of schools and school markets occurs in this region? Why has it worked out this way? Which schools are better regarded than others, and why? Which groups use different schools, and how might their relationships to higher education and the labour market vary as a result?

Finally (only for the purposes of this discussion), there are possible topics associated with teachers and the curriculum. Again there should be a connection to the *social* rather than more technical approaches to pedagogy or curriculum design and implementation. One might ask questions about the social status of teachers in Australian communities and how this might affect their bargaining power in the labour market. One can imagine interview-based projects with teachers, asking them to what degree they see themselves as social justice workers. Do teachers in different government and non-government schools see their work differently in relation to the social purposes of education? How do teachers respond to refugee children in their classroom? In terms of the curriculum, there is always the possibility of studying in detail a particular curriculum and the way teachers implement it, from the point of view of the politics of curriculum. Who chooses what should be in a curriculum? What implicit and explicit assumptions and values underlay those choices?

The curricula associated with the social sciences are often easier to analyse in these terms. What are the politics associated with the Year 11 and Year 12 boards of studies and public examinations? Who is represented and has power on them? As the author is writing this chapter (early 2006), the 'history wars' have blown up again. What is at stake in the controversy over what should appear in the Australian history curriculum in Australian schools? See also chapter 10, pp. 244–5.

3   Searching the literature and writing a literature review

An important part of this project is the linking of your topic to what the academic literature (journal articles and books) has had to say about either your topic, or topics similar to it. Therefore the aim of your literature review is to situate your research questions and findings in relation to the existing research, but certainly not to be confined or intimidated by it.

There are several benefits to be gained by a *literature search*, and then writing up the results of the search as a *literature review*:

- developing a deeper understanding of the phenomena you are researching
- this enables the asking of better research questions
- it also enables the development of better ways of conducting the research; for example, if good questionnaires have been developed, you might be able to adapt them to your work (with acknowledgement of course; always avoid possible charges of plagiarism)
- developing better arguments and conclusions when you analyse your research results as you compare your results with those of others.

A literature review of this kind really concentrates on academic literature; writing that has been subject to some kind of 'quality assurance'. In the academic world this occurs more or less efficiently through the process of peer review. The danger with blithely typing your key words into an Internet search engine such as Google is that you may well turn up references that are of dubious authority. Rarely are newspaper or magazine articles acceptable in a literature review of this kind unless you are prepared to make a special case that they should. Beware also of web sites that look respectable enough but are in fact single-mindedly devoted to a particular policy outcome (for example, supporting private schools no matter what, or public schools no matter what, and so on). (See also pp. 306–7.)

To play it safe, these are the more reliable ways to get acceptable references for your literature review:

- using your university library catalogue, although not all books in university libraries are equally authoritative
- using the specific databases constructed to assist the academic study of education (see below)
- having found one or two good articles or books, using their reference-lists and end-notes to find other authoritative academic literature on your topic.

In terms of the databases, the most important Australian database is the Australian Education Index. Most university library catalogues will have a pathway through to the accessing of this. Similarly, the most important of the international databases is ERIC. This has an American bias, however, and if you are looking for more references from or about Asia, Africa, or Europe you might go to other databases that your library provides access to. Organisations like UNESCO, the OECD and the World Bank each have web sites and interesting reports on education that can be searched electronically.

When searching the different databases it is important to remember that most libraries have idiosyncratic holdings. If I was hoping to find five good references for my literature review, I would collect the details of at least fifteen on the assumption that my nearby libraries might not have the books or journals I have identified. Some may have been borrowed or gone missing, or my library may simply never have bought them, and not all journals are online to be found for direct downloading of articles.

Many databases containing journal articles provide you with *abstracts*, or summaries of their contents. They can be an excellent guide to the relevance of an article to your project. If you decide to use a particular article, however, you will need to read it rather than just the abstract, because you need to show how the article really contributes something to your understanding of your research project.

Other places that are useful for searching the academic literature relevant to your topic are the various international and national encyclopaedias and handbooks on education. There are new such works published every year and your university library should have a selection of them, often in a special reference section. Two excellent examples from the mid 1990s are Saha (1997) and Carnoy (1995).

If two partners in a research project get four to five good references each (eight to ten together), then the literature review can eventually be written up as a short essay. The point is not to provide a series of article or book summaries, but to craft an essay in which your constant organising question is: what do these articles or books contribute to my/our research topic? Some references will be dealt with in a sentence or two, while others may involve a paragraph and more. Try to relate the different material and arguments you find in one reference to the others. Try to establish what recent academic thinking has come up with in relation to your topic area. This then allows you to test the ideas and results in your own project against them, and allows you to develop a stronger argument about the significance of your results.

If you would like to look at some models for literature reviews, there are journals devoted to them. In education, one of the best comes from America, published by the American Educational Research Association: *Review of Research in Education*. The 1996 and 1997 issues, edited by Michael Apple, concentrate in particular on issues relevant to this book, such as creating markets in education, Indigenous education, race and education, gender and teachers' work, and the state and education.

Finally, something that the literature review may be able to help you with is the identification of the main theories that explain why the phenomena you are researching work the way they do. It may be that you and your partner may wish to test one or more of these theories out during the course of your project. It may be that you adopt a particular theoretical or explanatory framework and through the course of your research, you demonstrate its explanatory power (and possible weaknesses). In undertaking this approach you may come across small theories that explain very limited educational phenomena. Then there are the grander theories associated with feminism for example, or Marx or Weber, or Bernstein, Bourdieu or Foucault. Some of these are referred to in this book, but if you wish to develop the kinds of theoretical understandings and approaches associated with such thinkers, then more than this book will be required to prepare you.

4 Research methods and research results

There are a number of research methods and combinations of research methods that you could use in your project. It is not possible here to provide a full explanation of them. What we do is provide a brief description with a comment on the kinds of knowledge they might produce. As important, we provide further references if you wish to know more, and a statement about what you might say about your research results. This last point comes first.

In the first part of this chapter on research there was a discussion of the scientific basis of research in which the idea that some of the older kinds of scientific and experimental kinds of research were barely possible or credible in educational contexts, and especially where we are looking at the *social* character and impacts of educational activity. Therefore it is probably best to think of your research as being *suggestive* of how things might work, rather than *proving* hypotheses. Even where some professional education researchers continue to work in this scientific and experimental framework, the kinds of things they do to shore up claims to the scientific *reliability* and the *validity* of their conclusions are very rarely possible for beginning student researchers.

Consequently if we do a survey using questionnaires, we usually select our questionnaire respondents on the basis of *convenience* or *opportunity* (surveying our friends, family, and acquaintances rather than the random selection of a representative sample of, say, every person between the ages of 20 and 40 in the Northern Territory). Rarely would it be possible for students in this kind of project to develop a genuinely random and therefore representative sample of a broader survey population.

For the purposes of this project, it is acceptable to find people to talk to or survey on a convenience or opportunistic basis. But two things go with this:

- you must resist any tendency to say that you have definitively proven or shown something to be the case
- you should state upfront in your methodology section that if you have used interview or survey methods, that your respondents have been chosen on the basis of convenience or opportunity, and consequently your conclusions will be *suggestive* rather than *definitive*.

We discuss this issue a little further on in the part titled 'Writing up your project', but the other thing to remember is that in terms of understanding educational phenomena, especially the social, it is often through research methods such as interviewing people for their in-depth understandings of what education means to them that we as researchers get high-quality explanations of how education works socially. There is nothing to apologise for in research based on *qualitative* rather than *quantitative* methods.

Interviews

Interviewing as a research method gives us a unique opportunity to talk to participants in the educational process. Depending on the project, interviewees may be high-level policy-makers or managers, school principals, teachers, student counsellors, curriculum designers, and so on. They may also be ordinary people whose lives have been touched by schools and education, as students, as job applicants hoping to trade their educational credentials for a job, or as parents looking for a good school to advantage their children.

Interviews always have the capacity to surprise us, to upset our hypotheses, whether explicit or implicit. Interviewers listen carefully and respectfully to interviewees, but the process is rarely passive. Interviewers and interviewees respond to one another, elaborating or suppressing their explanations and questions as they assess the verbal and body language of the other. It is best to be open about the inevitability of this interactive process rather than construct an image of the interviewer as passive and objective, and the interviewee as a *subject*, responding only to the 'rational' stimuli of the interviewer.

Interviews are often conducted in line with one of three broad categories:

- structured
- semi-structured
- unstructured.

The *structured* interview requires a limited list of very carefully constructed questions. There is very limited opportunity to ask clarifying questions, or to interpret the questions. This kind of interview is very close to administering a questionnaire, but orally instead of in written form. Its advantages and disadvantages are obvious. If it is really important that a number of people are asked exactly the same questions, then structured interviewing is the way to go. If, however, one wishes to improve the depth, range, and quality of the answers being received, then this is not the way to go, since it is impossible to encourage interviewees to expand their answers with the use of follow-up questions, with the interviewer responding to the leads thrown out by the interviewee. If this kind of interviewing is envisaged it is obviously important to spend a lot of time on wording the questions carefully, and even giving them a test-run through a couple of *pilot interviews*, to make sure useful responses may be evoked.

Semi-structured interviewing can be very useful. The capacity to follow an agenda of questions that the interviewer wishes to proceed through is certainly there, but there is also a great capacity for interviewers to follow up on interesting leads thrown out by the interviewee. This form of interviewing recognises to a greater degree the individuality of the interviewee, and the valuing of his or her personal interpretations of their experience.

Unstructured interviewing transfers a great deal of the control over the interview to the interviewee. The interviewer starts the interview or discussion with a theme or topic, but then goes with what the interviewee makes of it. There is little attempt to control the topics covered or to direct the attention of the interviewees in the direction possibly desired by the interviewer. Such interviewing has the capacity to turn up all sorts of interesting material, but it is also time-consuming, and it may not give student interviewers on a tight assignment-production deadline enough 'useful' material or data for their purposes.

Finally, thought has to be given to recording an interview. If research partners are both present, one can talk, and the other can take notes. Otherwise digital or analogue recording machines with microphones may be used, with the interviewee's consent, to capture the voices. Either way, the interview will eventually need to be indexed, and some kind of transcript written. It is very time-consuming to write full transcripts. In this kind of student project it is more efficient to index the interview and only transcribe the sections that you wish to quote in the assignment.

In the age of widespread email access, it is also possible to conduct interviews by email. This has a great advantage of providing capturable written text for quotation and paraphrase without the additional task of transcribing. An email exchange has disadvantages as well as advantages in comparison to the person to person, voice-recorded interview.

For the kind of project envisaged here, the number of interviews undertaken should be strictly limited. Managing an interview project, even of five or so people, can be time-consuming, in terms of setting up appointments, travelling to interview sites acceptable to interviewees, and then dealing with recordings and transcripts.

Survey through questionnaire

Questionnaires can be given to a large number of people, so they have the advantage of producing numerous responses to the concerns of your project topic. Many of the questions are constructed in such a way that there are only a limited number of responses possible. For example, 'yes' or 'no'; or circle one of five possible statements; or do you 'strongly agree', 'agree', 'don't know', 'disagree', or 'strongly disagree' with a provided statement?

Such limited responses may be counted and subjected to various arithmetical and statistical procedures. 'The percentage of people responding in this way was 22 per cent', or 'The average response was 3.2 out of a maximum of 5.'

Such data does not provide the depth of response evoked by interviewing. Moreover, the levels of attention given by respondents to questionnaires vary enormously. Answers given in split seconds may differ from more considered answers. Clearly questionnaires need to be constructed very carefully, should be piloted, and the means of ensuring considered responses given great attention. Trying to maximise the numbers of questionnaires returned similarly requires good planning.

If you decide to conduct surveys through questionnaires you really are advised to follow up with the further reading texts at the end of this chapter. What is offered here is a very cursory discussion of some of the issues.

In constructing a questionnaire, what is often a useful thing to do is to try to find out some of the social background characteristics of the respondents. There is often a link between background characteristics relating to social class origin, age, gender, cultural or language group, kind of employment, place of residence, income, and so on, and the experiences people have of education.

Sometimes questionnaires are developed in three parts, though there may be no physical indication of the different parts on the actual questionnaire:

- questions that seek to reveal the social background or characteristics of the respondent
- limited response questions that explore the beliefs, attitudes, and experiences of the respondent
- open response questions that enable a respondent to write in their own words their responses to questions that are not easily summarised into limited response categories.

Examples of the first might be boxes to tick indicating the gender of the respondent: 'Male' or 'Female', or categories to circle indicating a person's income: 'Low', 'Medium', or 'High'. Examples of the second might include the use of an ordered scale of possible responses to a proposition, such as 'Well-funded public schools are important for the survival of a democratic society', with the 'Strongly agree' down to 'Strongly disagree' categories available for response. Sometimes questionnaires offer a list of factors relevant to a particular phenomenon and respondents are asked to indicate the ones they think are most important. The third, open response question is self-explanatory: 'In the space provided, explain how important your parents were in motivating you to do well at secondary school'.

When you come to report the results of a survey using questionnaires, it is likely that in part you will report using tables or charts. There is much software that assists in the production of these, not only in spreadsheet programs but also database and occasionally word-processing programs. Look at the recommended texts regarding the requirements for producing graphs and charts professionally. It may be that examples of these appear in articles and books used for your literature review.

How you construct your tables and charts will respond to the kinds of ideas or results you are reporting. In terms of tables, *cross-tabulations* are an obvious thing to do. So, in the table below you will see the results of an attitudinal survey presented in a cross-tabulation with the age of the respondent. Perhaps there was a hypothesis that older people would be more resistant to certain kinds of social education, such as anti-racist education or sex education in the school curriculum. In the fictional Table 13.1 below, there does indeed seem to be a relationship between the age of the respondent and their attitude. But even here where a relationship appears pretty clear it is important to remember that there may be other issues affecting the result. Moreover, we have only reported frequency of response here; we have not made any attempt to use more advanced statistics to measure *significance* in the statistical sense. Again, it is not appropriate for us to engage in a more advanced discussion of statistical procedures that might be used with the data you come up with. If you have this training there is every reason to use it, but otherwise the use of *descriptive statistics* (especially the basic frequencies, percentages, means, and perhaps range) are all that is required.

As mentioned before, the most important thing is to have a sense of the limitations of your analysis, not claiming too much from what you come up with. This is especially important to be aware of and to discuss, since your survey sample is likely unrepresentative of any envisaged population of respondents. It will likely have been put together through *convenience* or *opportunity*, rather than genuine random sampling.

Table 13.1 Attitude to anti-racism education in schools by age of respondent (N, %)

	15–24		25–34		35 plus	
Attitude	**N**	**%**	**N**	**%**	**N**	**%**
Should be compulsory	10	58.8	7	36.8	5	27.8
Should be optional	4	23.5	7	36.8	6	33.3
No place in the curriculum	3	17.6	4	21.1	5	27.8
Don't know	0	0	1	5.3	2	11.1
Totals*	17	100	19	100	18	100

* The effect of decimal rounding occasionally produces a disparity of up to 0.1 per cent between the percentage totals and the apparent sum of the percentages.

Source: survey conducted by Wendy Tran & Simon Habib, 2007 (Fictional example)

We have already mentioned the possibility that charts might also be used to display results. These could include bar, column, pie, line, and other kinds of charts.

Media study

The collection and analysis of newspaper or other media reportage and articles can also provide an excellent basis for understanding the ways that attitudes towards education and educational policy are developed. There are many different ways of going about this, but all involve the collection of relevant material over a certain period of time. Broad surveys can be time-consuming. It may be better to identify a particular incident or policy producing a great deal of media comment to confine the amount of time going into searching the media source. In the following discussion the writing will mainly refer to newspapers, but the text should be adaptable to other forms of media.

Some possible topics for media study have already been discussed on page 312, so we shall not repeat them here. There are some specific things to take into account in media studies, however, and as is true for other kinds of approaches to this project you would be wise to follow up with more specialised texts. A couple are recommended at the end of this section.

The first is to have a sense of the *political economy* of the mass media. It is important to understand that newspapers are produced in the main to produce profit for the companies that own them. Some owners have strong interests and views regarding different aspects of public policy. These can often be discerned by reading the *editorials* and the kinds of columnists they give most space to.

The other thing to be aware of is that newspapers are being sold to a public that has probably been analysed for its receptivity to certain kinds of messages and stories. A journalist is often a good story teller who can transform the facts of a fairly ordinary event into narrative that both entertains and suggests attachment to older patterns of story telling. For example, it is one of the oldest story-telling structures that once everyone was happy and things worked well. Then along came a disruptive stranger or strangers with strange ideas and activities; then there was chaos and decline, and maybe a return to order and happiness can be envisaged if only certain things are or could be done. Many stories about public education in the more conservative press follow this kind of narrative pattern. Once everyone could spell, teachers could teach, and naughty children would be punished and do the right thing thereafter. Then came along the 1960s and 1970s with new ideas such as feminism and progressive education and schools became chaotic. The future can be secured by the return to a concentration on the 'basics' of literacy and numeracy and the reform of teachers and schools by forcing them to compete for students in a new educational market.

There is no doubt that the reporting of 'crisis' helps sell newspapers. In terms of education reporting, isolated examples of school violence are quickly turned into crises associated with ethnic gangs, or the marginal drop of some percentage in various literacy scores becomes a 'literacy crisis', or the success of some girls at the Year 12 public examinations becomes proof of a 'boy crisis'.

So, a sense of the *discursive characteristics* of media stories, the interests of the owners, and their sense of the kinds of stories that are required to be written in order to make people buy the newspapers or watch their television news should inform projects based on studies of the media and education.

Otherwise, some of the comments made below in terms of document study as a project research method are also applicable to a media study.

Documentary study

This kind of study most approaches the kind of thing that is done in the more conventional academic essay. Nevertheless, there needs to be an identification of the list of documents that are to provide the *primary sources* for the research. These, in the context of this kind of study, are likely to be government or school system policies, government reports or perhaps extracts from parliamentary debates where certain controversial education bills are being discussed. It may be that the policies, press releases or speeches of a controversial Minister of Education are downloaded from their web sites for analysis of their thinking about educational reform. It may be that a series of school newsletters or discipline policies, say from a public, Catholic, and independent school, are collected and analysed. There are lots of possibilities here.

As is true for other kinds of research, it is important to organise the questions you wish to ask of your documents and establish frameworks of analysis. There is a strong academic literature in policy analysis, for example, that could be very useful if you concentrated on that area (see chapter 1.) Again you might find it useful to propose certain hypotheses about what you expect to find from documents of a certain provenance, and then test the contents against such expectations.

There are some very basic questions to ask in any documentary analysis that will provide a firm basis for your research activity:

- Who commissioned or authorised the writing of the document?
- Who wrote the document?
- What were the expectations of the document commissioners of what it should achieve?
- Who were the people expected to read or take note of the document?
- Were there any interest or pressure groups trying to influence the document?
- What were its hidden and explicit assumptions?
- What were its hidden and explicit intentions?
- What did the document actually say?
- What effect did it appear to have?
- What else was happening in the broader society at the time that may have affected the policy process?

And finally, how can the study of this or these documents assist our understanding of our research topic, and do we have any evidence of how the document was received, and whether it was influential?

5   Ethical practice in research

Besides the usual issues associated with plagiarism, there are some important requirements that must be met if you engage real people rather than documents in your research projects. These comments mostly apply to the interview and survey methods discussed above.

The basic points are associated with the recognition of certain rights that your interviewees or questionnaire respondents should have as you approach and work with them. They also derive from the fact that they are giving up time to help you, and that they deserve to be treated well, with honesty and respect.

Any research done with humans requires strong ethical procedures, including an absolute respect for the rights of the people helping you with your research. Minimally this would involve a full disclosure of the nature of the project, its aims, and the purposes to which the information gathered from respondents will be put. No pressure should be brought to bear on people to participate or, once having started, not to withdraw from the research, as they wish. Bell (2005), for example, goes into these issues in greater detail.

In some cases, where a project like this is being done as part of a university course, the coordinator may provide a letter for you if required, stating that you are a student of your university, describing the unit and the aims of the research assignment, and stating that you have had some basic advice in terms of ethical research practice and are seeking cooperation for your work.

Interviews

You need to prepare two documents. They should be brief and written in plain language.

The first is an *Information Sheet*. This should neatly set out:

- the topic of the research project
- the names of the researchers
- a contact address and perhaps an email address for the researchers
- the reason for the project (e.g. it is an assignment in my university course)
- the unit of study and the university the assignment proceeds from
- an assurance that the interview transcripts will not be published without the permission of the interviewees who will have been given a chance to check what they are reported as saying if there is an intention to publish
- that the names of interviewees and schools or other institutions will be changed to protect anonymity.

It is of course extremely important that having produced such an Information Sheet for interviewees to read that you follow through on all the commitments you have made.

The second is a *Consent Form*, which should also be neatly set out. This requires:

- the topic of the research project and 'Consent Form' as headings
- a statement along the lines of: 'I agree to be interviewed for this research project. I have read the *Information Sheet* and I understand that my name and

institution will be changed to protect my anonymity. I also understand that in the unlikely event that the researchers wish to publish extracts from this interview, they will give me an opportunity to check the transcript, and seek my permission to do so. I also understand that if I do not wish to proceed with the interview at any stage and for any reason, that I have the full right to do so.'

- an area on the form for the interviewee to sign and insert the date, with similar room for the interviewer to sign and date as a witness.

Warning: In some universities, there may be specific protocols governing student research, and these must necessarily be followed.

Survey questionnaires

A statement at the beginning of your questionnaire should be all that is required to satisfy most ethics requirements. In this you should provide the following information and make the following statements:

- the topic of the research project
- the names of the researchers
- a contact address and perhaps an email address for the researchers
- the reason for the project (e.g. it is an assignment in my university course)
- the unit of study and the university the assignment proceeds from
- an assurance that the questionnaires are conducted on the basis of complete anonymity for the person who fills it out
- no person approached to fill out a questionnaire is under any obligation to do so.

Warning: In some universities, there may be specific protocols governing student research, and these must necessarily be followed.

6   Writing up the project and presenting the results of your work

A pattern of writing your final report has already been suggested above on page 309. As is important in any written assignment, attention should be given to clear writing, competent referencing, and orderly formatting and presentation. The key to writing this assignment well occurs in:

- the linking of topic, literature review, and research activity and conclusions into a cohesive whole
- a demonstration that you know the limitations of your research methods and are able to qualify the claims you make in your conclusion as a result.

In some cases you will be presenting the results of your work to a workshop or wider group. It is important to present your work in ways that attract interest and that are both orderly and respectful of the time constraints given to you. It is often a good idea to highlight the differences between the expectations you had of what the research would produce and what you actually came up with. It is also occasionally a good idea to highlight some of the positive features, and difficulties you ran into using particular research methods.

Good luck.

Focus questions

1 What are the uses of a literature review in designing and conducting research in education?
2 Why is so much emphasis placed on ethical practice in research with humans, not only in education, but in the other social sciences as well?
3 Different research methods produce different kinds of data. In a general way discuss what kinds of knowledge we might gain from an interviewing, a questionnaire, or a documentary based study.

Further reading

Bell, J. (2005). *Doing Your Research Project : A Guide for First-time Researchers in Education and Social Science* (4th edn). Maidenhead: Open University Press.

Croteau, D. (2006). *The Business of Media: Corporate Media and the Public Interest*. Thousand Oaks: Pine Forge Press.

Henry, M., Lingard, B., Rizvi, F. & Taylor, S. (1997). *Educational Policy and the Politics of Change*. London: Routledge.

McMillan, J.H. (2004). *Educational Research: Fundamentals for the consumer* (4th edn). Boston: Pearson Education.

Street, J. (2001). *Mass Media, Politics, and Democracy*. New York: Palgrave.

Taylor, L. (1999). *Media Studies: Texts, Institutions, and Audiences*. Malden: Blackwell.

Wadsworth, Y. (1983). *Do It Yourself Social Research*. Melbourne: VCOSS and Allen & Unwin.

Whitty, G. (2002). *Making Sense of Education Policy: Studies in the Sociology and Politics of Education*. London: Paul Chapman Publishing.

References

ABC Online (2005). 'School's in for indigenous culture.' Monday 19 December. Retrieved 2 January 2005 from http://www.abc.net.au/news/newsitems/200512/s1533874.htm.

Aboriginal and Islander Independent Community School (2005). Retrieved 23 January 2006 from http://www.murrischool.qld.edu.au/school_history.html.

ABS, see Australian Bureau of Statistics.

Acker, J. (1990). 'Hierarchies, jobs, bodies: A theory of gendered organizations.' *Gender and Society,* 4(2), 139–58.

Acker, S. (1983). 'Women and teaching: a semi-detached sociology of a semi-profession.' In S. Walker & L. Barton (eds), *Gender Class and Education* (pp. 123–39). Barcombe: Falmer.

Ainley, J. & Marks, G. (1997). *Reading Comprehension and Numeracy among Junior Secondary School Students in Australia. LSAY Research Report No. 3.* Melbourne: ACER.

Alladin, I. (1986). 'North-South Cooperation: Educational Implications of the Brandt Report.' In *Education as an International Commodity, Vol I,* 170–83.

Alston, M. (2004). '"You don't want to be a check-out chick all your life". The out-migration of young people from Australia's small rural towns.' *Australian Journal of Social Issues, 39*(3), 299–313.

Alston, M. & Kent, J. (2001). *Young, Rural and Looking for Work.* Wagga Wagga: Centre for Rural Social Research, Charles Sturt University.

AMA, see Australian Medical Association.

Anderson, D. (1990a). 'Values, religion, social class and the choice of private school.' In J. Keeves & L. Saha (eds), *Schooling and society in Australia. Sociological Perspectives.* Canberra: Australian National University Press.

Anderson, D. (1990b). 'The public/private division in Australian schooling. Social and educational effects.' In J. Keeves & L. Saha (eds), *Schooling and Society in Australia. Sociological Perspectives.* Canberra: Australian National University Press.

Anderson, D. (1992). 'The interaction of public and private school systems.' *Australian Journal of Education, 36*(3), 213–36.

ANTA, see Australian National Training Authority.

Apple, M. (1982). *Education and Power.* London: Routledge.

Apple, M. (1990a). *Ideology and Curriculum* (2nd edn). London: Routledge.

Apple, M. (1990b). *Official Knowledge: Democratic Knowledge in a Conservative Age.* London: Routledge.

Apple, M. (1997). 'What postmodernists forget. Cultural capital and official knowledge.' In A. Halsey, H. Lauder, P. Brown & A. S. Wells (eds), *Education, Culture, Economy and Society* (pp. 595–604). Oxford: Oxford University Press.

Apple, M.W. & Teitelbaum, K. (1986). 'Are teachers losing control of their skills and curriculum?' *Journal of Curriculum Studies, 18*(2), 177–84.

Arnot, M., David, M. & Weiner, G. (1999). *Closing the Gender Gap: Postwar Education and Social Change*. Cambridge: Polity Press.

Aronowitz, S. & di Fazio, W. (1994). *The Jobless Future. Sci-tech and the Dogma of Work*. Minneapolis: University of Minnesota Press.

Asmar, C. (2001). 'Muslim students in Australian universities.' In A. Saeed & S. Abkarzadeh (eds), *Muslim Communities in Australia*. Sydney: University of New South Wales Press.

ATSIC (1998). *As a Matter of Fact*. Canberra: Australian Government Publishing Service.

Audas, R. & Willms, J. (2001). *Engagement and Dropping out of School: A Life Course Perspective*. Canada: Human Resources Development.

Austin, A.G. (1958). *George William Rusden and National Education in Australia 1849–1862*. Melbourne: Melbourne University Press.

Austin, A.G. (1961). *Australian Education 1788–1900: Church, State and Public Education in Colonial Australia*. Melbourne: Isaac Pitman.

Austin, A.G. (1963). *Select Documents in Australian Education: 1788–1900*. Melbourne: Isaac Pitman.

Austin, A.G., & Selleck, R.J.W. (1975). *The Australian Government School 1830–1914*. Melbourne: Pitman.

Australian Bureau of Statistics (ABS) (1993). *Schools Australia*. (Cat. No. 4221.0). Canberra: ABS.

Australian Bureau of Statistics (ABS) (1997, 2000). *Education and Training Experience Australia 1997, 2000*. (Cat. No. 6278.0). Canberra: ABS.

Australian Bureau of Statistics (ABS) (1999a). Population: Special Article—Aboriginal and Torres Strait Islander Australians: A statistical profile from the 1996 Census (Year Book Australia, 1999). *Year Book Australia, 1999*. No. 1301.0).

Australian Bureau of Statistics (ABS) (1999b). 'Population. Australian Social Trends 2002. Education—Participation in Education: Education of Aboriginal and Torres Strait Island peoples'. From http://www.abs.gov.au/Ausstats/abs@.nsf/2f762f95845417aeca25706c00834efa/e9edc3c77168a3d2ca2570ec000af328!OpenDocument

Australian Bureau of Statistics (ABS) (2002a). 'Australian social trends 2002: Education—participation in education: education of Aboriginal and Torres Strait Islander peoples.' (Cat. No. 4102.0).

Australian Bureau of Statistics (ABS) (2002b). *Education and Training Indicators, Australia*. Canberra: ABS.

Australian Bureau of Statistics (ABS) (2002c). *Education and Work, Australia*. (Cat. No. 6227.0). Canberra: ABS.

Australian Bureau of Statistics (ABS) (2003). *Australian Social Trends*. (Cat. No. 4102.0).

Australian Bureau of Statistics (ABS) (2004a). *Australia in Profile: A Regional Analysis* (Cat. No. 2032.0). Canberra: ABS.

Australian Bureau of Statistics (ABS) (2004b). *Family Characteristics Australia*. (Cat. No. 4442.0).

Australian Bureau of Statistics (ABS) (2004c). *Schools Australia*. (Cat. No. 4221.0).

Australian Bureau of Statistics (ABS) (2005). 'Value of Agricultural Commodities Produced, Australia'. From www.abs.gov.au/ausstats/abs@.nsf/b06660592430724fca2568b5007b8619/48788628e4fd7a3fca256d970021c495.

Australian Bureau of Statistics (ABS) (2006). *Worldfacts*. Canberra: ABS.

Australian Council for the Defence of Government Schools (2005). D.O.G.S. and the high court case. Retrieved 9 November, 2005 from http://www.adogs.info/dogs_high_court_case1.htm.

Australian Institute of Health and Welfare (2003). 'The health and welfare of Australia's Aboriginal and Torres Strait Islander peoples'. From http://www.aihw.gov.au/publications/index.cfm/title/9226.

Australian Medical Association (2005). Media release: 'Launch position statement on Aboriginal and Torres Strait Islander Health', 5 October. Retrieved 12 January 2006 from http://www.ama.com.au/web.nsf/doc/WEEN-6GV25A.

Australian National Training Authority (ANTA) (2002). *Australian Qualifications Framework Implementation Handbook*. Carlton: ANTA.

Bagnall, N., Nicholls, S. & Cuttance, P. (2004). *The 'Tough' Process of Parental Choice of Secondary Schools in Australia*. Unpublished manuscript.

Bagnall, N.F. (1994). *The International Baccalaureate in Australia and Canada: 1980–1993*. University of Melbourne.

Bagnall, N.F. (1997a). 'The International Baccalaureate in Australia.' *Melbourne Studies in Education, 38*(1), 129–44.

Bagnall, N.F. (1997b). 'The International Baccalaureate in Canada, 1980–93.' In K. Burridge, L. Foster & G. Turcote (eds), *Canada-Australia: Towards a Second Century of Partnership* (pp. 233–46). Carlton: Carlton University Press.

Bagnall, N.F. (2005a). 'The International Baccalaureate in Australia and New Zealand.' *Change, Transformations in Education, 8*(1), 39–57.

Bagnall, N.F. (ed.) (2005b). *Youth Transition in a Globalised Marketplace*. New York: Nova Science Publishers Inc.

Ball, S. (1990). *Politics and Policy Making in Education*. London: Routledge.

Ball, S. (1994). *Education Reform. A Critical and Post-structural Approach*. Buckingham: Open University Press.

Ball, S. (1998). 'Big policies, small world: An introduction to international perspectives in educational policy.' *Comparative Education, 34*(2), 119–30.

Ball, S.J. (2003). *Class Strategies and the Education Market: The Middle Classes and Social Advantage*. London: RoutledgeFalmer.

Bamberry, L. (2005). *Globalisation, Gender and Teachers' Employment.* University of Sydney.

Banks, O. (1955). *Parity and Prestige in English Secondary Education: A Study in Educational Sociology*. London: Routledge & Kegan Paul.

Barcan, A. (1980). *A History of Australian Education*. Melbourne: Oxford University Press.

Barlas, A. (2002). *'Believing Women' in Islam*. Austin: University of Texas Press.

Bartrop, P.R. (1994). *Australia and the Holocaust 1933–1945*. Melbourne: Australian Scholarly Publishing.

Batrouney, T. (2001). 'Muslim communities in Melbourne.' In J. Jupp (ed.), *The Australian People. An Encyclopedia of the Nation, Its Peoples and Their Origins* (pp. 567–69). Cambridge: Cambridge University Press.

Bauman, Z. (1998). *Globalization: The human consequences*. Cambridge: Polity Press.

Baxter, J. (2002). 'Patterns of change and stability in the gender division of household labour in Australia.' *Journal of Sociology, 38*(4), 399–424.

Baylis, J. & Smith, S.T. (1999). *The Globalization of World Politics. An Introduction to International Relations*. Oxford: Oxford University Press.

Beck, U. (1992). *Risk Society*. Sage Publications: London.

Bell, J. (2005). *Doing Your Research Project : A Guide for First-time Researchers in Education and Social Science* (4th edn). Maidenhead: Open University Press.

Bennett, C. (2004). *Muslims and Modernity. An Introduction to the Issues and Debates*. London: Continuum.

Bennett, S. (1999). *White Politics and Black Australians*. Crows Nest: Allen and Unwin.

Benyon, H. (1992). 'The end of the industrial worker?' In N. Abercrombie & A. Warde (eds), *Social Change in Contemporary Britain*. Cambridge: Polity Press.

Beresford, Q. (2003). 'The context of Aboriginal education.' In Q. Beresford & G. Partington (eds), *Reform and Resistance in Aboriginal Education: The Australian Experience* (pp. 10–40). Crawley: University of Western Australia Press.

Bernstein, B. (1997). 'Class and pedagogies: Visible and invisible.' In A.H. Halsey, H. Lauder, P. Brown & A.S. Wells (eds), *Education: Culture, Economy, and Society* (pp. 59–79). Oxford: Oxford University Press.

Bernstein, R. (1983). *Beyond Objectivism and Relativism: Science, Hermeneutics, and Praxis*. Philadelphia: University of Pennsylvania Press.

Bessant, B. (1984). 'The influence of the "public schools" on the early high schools of Victoria.' *History of Education Review, 13*(1), 45–57.

Best, S. (2005). *Understanding Social Divisions*. London: Sage.

Biddulph, S. (1998). *Raising Boys: Why boys are Different – And How to Help Them Become Happy and Well-balanced Men*. Sydney: Finch.

Blaug, M. (1972). *An Introduction to the Economics of Education*. London: Penguin.

Board of Studies (2005). NSW Primary Curriculum Foundation Statements. Sydney: NSW Board of Studies. [www.boardofstudies.nsw.edu.au]

Boomer, G., Lester, N., Onore, C. & Cook, J. (1992). *Negotiating the Curriculum: Educating for the 21st Century*. Sussex: The Falmer Press.

Bourdieu, P. (1983). *Distinction. A Social Critique of the Judgement of Taste*. London: Routledge and Kegan Paul.

Bourdieu, P. (1997). 'The forms of capital.' In A.H. Halsey, H. Lauder, P. Brown & A.S. Wells (eds.), *Education: Culture, Economy, and Society* (pp. 46–58). Oxford: Oxford University Press.

Bourdieu, P. & Passeron, J.-C. (1977). *Reproduction in Education, Society and Culture*. London: Sage.

Bourdieu, P. & Passeron, J.-C. (1990). *Reproduction in Education, Society and Culture* (R. Nice, Trans. 2 ed.). London: Sage.

Bourke, L. (2001). 'One big happy family? Social problems in rural communities.' In S. Lockie & L. Bourke (eds), *The Social and Environmental Transformation of Rural Australia*. Sydney: Pluto Press.

Bowe, R., Ball, S. & Gold, A. (1992). 'The policy analysis and the processes of policy.' In *Reforming Education and Changing Schools*. London: Routledge.

Bowen, J. (1985). 'Women's struggle to gain entry into universities in nineteenth century Australia.' *Discourse, 5*(1).

Bowles, S. & Gintis, H. (1976). *Schooling in Capitalist America: Educational Reform and the Contradictions of Economic Life*. London: Routledge and Kegan Paul.

Brady, L. & Kennedy, K. (2003). *Curriculum Construction*. New York: Pearson, Prentice Hall.

Brady, W. (1993). 'The education of Aboriginal women and girls in rural New South Wales.' In R. Petersen & G. Rodwell (eds), *Essays in the History of Rural Education in Australia and New Zealand* (pp. 129–49). Darwin: William Michael Press.

Braithwaite, E.R. (1959). *To Sir, With Love*. London: Bodley Head.

Brantlinger, E. (2003). *Dividing Classes: How the Middle Class Negotiates and Rationalizes School Advantage*. New York: RoutledgeFalmer.

Brenner, R. (1998). 'The economics of global turbulence: A special report on the world economy.' *New Left Review, 229*, 1–265.

Brett, J. (2003). *Australian Liberals and the Moral Middle Class: From Alfred Deakin to John Howard.* Cambridge: Cambridge University Press.

Bronfenbrenner, U. (1971). *Two Worlds of Childhood: U.S. and U.S.S.R.* London: Allen and Unwin.

Brownell, M. (2000). 'Who is an Indian? Searching for an answer to the question at the core of Federal Indian law.' *University of Michigan Journal of Law Reform, 34,* 273–320.

Bruner, J.S. (1960). *The Process of Education.* Cambridge: Harvard University Press.

Bryson, L. & Winter, I. (1999). *Social Change, Suburban Lives: An Australian Newtown 1960s to 1990s.* Sydney: Allen and Unwin and Australian Institute of Family Studies.

Buckingham, J. (1999). 'The puzzle of boys' educational decline: A review of the evidence.' Retrieved 9 December 2005 from www.cis.org.au.

Buckman, G. (2004). *Globalization, Tame It or Scrap It?* London: Zed Books Ltd.

Burns, A., Hood, S., & de Silva Joyce, H. (eds). (1995–2001). *Teachers' Voices.* Sydney: National Centre for English Language Research, Macquarie University.

Burnswoods, J. & Fletcher, J. (eds) (1980). *Sydney and the Bush: A Pictorial History of Education in New South Wales.* Sydney: NSW Dept. of Education.

Callahan, R. (1962). *Education and the Cult of Efficiency.* Chicago: University of Chicago Press.

Calwell, M. (2001). 'Post war migration.' In J. Jupp (ed.), *The Australian People. An Encyclopedia of the Nation, its Peoples and their Origins.* Cambridge: Cambridge University Press.

Campbell, C. (1993). 'Family strategy, secondary schooling and making adolescent: The Indian summer of the old middle class, 1945–1960.' *History of Education Review, 22*(2), 18–43.

Campbell, C. (1999a). 'Pioneering modern adolescence: The social significance of the early state high schools of Adelaide.' In C. Campbell, C. Hooper & M. Fearnley-Sander (eds), *Toward the State High School in Australia: Social Histories of State Secondary Schooling in Victoria, Tasmania and South Australia, 1850–1925* (pp. 55–77). Sydney: ANZHES.

Campbell, C. (1999b). 'The social origins of Australian state high schools: An historiographical review.' In C. Campbell, C. Hooper & M. Fearnley-Sander (eds), *Toward the State High School in Australia: Social Histories of State Secondary Schooling in Victoria, Tasmania and South Australia, 1850–1925* (pp. 9–27). Sydney: ANZHES.

Campbell, C. (2005). 'Changing school loyalties and the middle class: A reflection on the developing fate of state comprehensive high schooling.' *The Australian Educational Researcher, 32*(1), 3–24.

Campbell, C. & Sherington, G. (2006). *The Comprehensive Public High School: Historical Perspectives.* New York: PalgraveMacmillan.

Campbell, C., Hooper, C. & Fearnley-Sander, M. (eds). (1999). *Toward the State High School in Australia: Social Histories of State Secondary Schooling in Victoria, Tasmania and South Australia, 1850–1925.* Sydney: ANZHES.

Campbell, K.S.W. & Jell, J.S. (1998). 'Dorothy Hill 1907–1997, Australian Academy of Science biographical memoirs.' Retrieved 10 February 2006 from http://www.science.org.au/academy/memoirs/hill.htm.

Carnoy, M. (ed.). (1995). *International Encyclopaedia of Economics of Education.* New York: Pergamon.

Centre for Educational Research and Innovation. (1998). *Education at a Glance: OECD Indicators 1998.* Paris: OECD.

Cerny, P. (1990). *The Changing Architecture of the State: Structure, Agency and the State.* London: Sage.

Chalmers, A.F. (1982). *What is This Thing Called Science? An Assessment of the Nature and Status of Science and its Methods* (2nd edn). St. Lucia: University of Queensland Press.

Clark, I. (1997). *Globalization and Fragmentation International Relations in the Twentieth Century*. Oxford: Oxford University Press.

Clark, J. (2004). *'To hell in a handcart': Educational Realities, Teachers' Work and Neo-liberal Restructuring in NSW TAFE*. University of Sydney.

Clarke, J., Gewirtz, S. & McLaughlin, E. (eds). (2000). *New Managerialism, New Welfare*. London: Sage.

Clarke, S. (2001). 'Reforming teachers' work and changing roles for unions.' *Education Research and Perspectives, 28*(2), 33–50.

Cleverley, J. & Lawry, J. (eds). (1972). *Australian Education in the Twentieth Century: Studies in the Development of State Education*. Melbourne: Longman.

Clyne, M. (2005). *Australia's Language Potential*. Sydney: UNSW Press.

Codd, J. (1997). 'Education and the Role of the State: Devolution and Control Post Picot.' In A. Halsey, H. Lauder, P. Brown & A. Wells (eds), *Education, Culture, Economy and Society* (pp. 263–72). Oxford: Oxford University Press.

Cohen, R. (1998). *Global Diasporas. An Introduction*. London: Routledge.

Coleman, J.S. (1961). *The Adolescent Society: The Social Life of the Teenager and Its Impact on Education*. New York: Free Press.

Collins, C. (1988). 'Sex and Destiny.' *Australian Educator (Autumn)*, 22–5.

Collins, C. (ed.) (1995). *Curriculum Stocktake: Evaluating School Curriculum Change*. Canberra: Australian College of Education.

Collins, C. (2000). *Understanding the Relationship Between Schooling, Gender, and Labour Market Entry*. Paper presented at the DETYA Seminar on Educational Attainment and Labour Market Outcomes, Melbourne, 22–23 November 2000.

Collins, C. (2002). 'The content of the curriculum: What will young Australians be learning?' *Curriculum Perspectives, 22*(1), 44–9.

Collins, C., Kenway, J. & McLeod, J. (2000). *Factors Influencing the Educational Performance of Males and Females in School and their Initial Destinations After Leaving School*. Canberra: Commonwealth Department of Education, Training and Youth Affairs.

Collins, J., Noble, G., Poynting, S. & Tabar, P. (2000). *Kebabs, Kids, Cops and Crime*. Sydney: Pluto Press.

Comber, B. & Kamler, B. (2004). 'Getting out of deficit: pedagogies of reconnection.' *Teaching Education, 15*(3), 293–310.

Commonwealth of Australia (1973). *Schools in Australia: Interim Report of the Australian Schools Commission*. Canberra: Australian Government Publishing Service.

Commonwealth of Australia (2000). *What Works? Explorations in Improving Outcomes for Students*. Canberra: Australian Government Publishing Service.

Commonwealth Schools Commission (1975). *Girls, Schools, and Society*. Canberra: Commonwealth of Australia.

Connell, R.W. (1985). *Teachers' Work*. Sydney: Allen and Unwin.

Connell, R.W. (1993). *Schools and Social Justice*. Philadelphia: Temple University Press.

Connell, R.W. (1996). 'Teaching the boys: New research on masculinity, and gender strategies for schools.' *Teachers College Record, 98*(2), 206–35.

Connell, R.W. (2000). *The Men and the Boys*. Sydney: Allen and Unwin.

Connell, R.W. (2002a). *Gender*. Cambridge: Polity Press.

Connell, R.W. (2002b). 'Molloch mutates: Global capitalism and the evolution of the Australian ruling class, 1977–2002.' *Overland, 167*, 4–14.

Connell, R.W. (2003). 'Working-class families and the new secondary education.' *Australian Journal of Education, 47*(3), 237–52.

Connell, R.W. (2004). 'Working-class parents' views of secondary education.' *International Journal of Inclusive Education, 8*(3), 227–39.

Connell, R.W. (2005). *Masculinities* (2nd edn). Sydney: Allen and Unwin.

Connell, R.W. & Irving, T.H. (1992). *Class Structure in Australian History: Poverty and Progress* (2nd edn). Melbourne: Longman Cheshire.

Connell, R.W., Ashenden, D.J., Kessler, S. & Dowsett, G.W. (1982). *Making the Difference: Schools, Families and Social Division*. Sydney: George Allen and Unwin.

Connell, R.W., White, V.M. & Johnston, K.M. (eds). (1991). *Running Twice as Hard: The Disadvantaged Schools Program in Australia*. Geelong: Deakin University.

Connell, R.W., Wood, J. & Crawford, J. (2005). 'The global connections of intellectual workers. An Australian study.' *International Sociology, 20*(1), 5–26.

Connell, W.F. (1993). *Reshaping Australian Education 1960–1985*. Melbourne: ACER.

Connell, W.F., Stroobant, R.E., Sinclair, K.E., Connell, R.W. & Rogers, K.W. (1975). *12 to 20: Studies of City Youth*. Sydney: Hicks Smith.

Connors, L. & Caro, J. (2006). 'Learning to love the profit motive.' *Sydney Morning Herald,* 2 January, p. 11.

Conway, J.K. (1987). 'Politics, pedagogy, and gender (Reproduced from Daedelus)'. Retrieved 8 January 2006 from www.findarticles.com.

Cooley, M. (1980). *Architect or Bee? The Human/Technology Relationship*. Sydney: TransNational Co-operative.

Cox, P., Leder, G. & Forgasz, H. (2004). 'Victorian Certificate of Education: Mathematics, Science, and Gender.' *Australian Journal of Education, 48*(1), 27–46.

Cruickshank, K. (2003). *Literacy needs of students from non-English speaking backgrounds. Literature review submitted for ESL subgroup of the Director General's Advisory Group on Multicultural Education and Training*. Sydney: NSW Department of Education.

Da, W.W. (2003). 'Transnational grandparenting: child care arrangements among migrants from People's Republic of China to Australia.' *Journal of International Migration and Integration, 4*, 79–103.

Dale, R. (1997). 'The State and governance of education: An analysis of the re-structuring of the State-education relationship.' In A. Halsey, H. Lauder, P. Brown & A. Wells (eds), *Education, Culture, Economy and Society* (pp. 273–82). Oxford: Oxford University Press.

Dawkins, J. (1988). *Strengthening Australia's Schools: A Consideration of the Focus and Content of Schooling*. Canberra: Australian Government Publishing Service.

De Lepervanche, M. (1980). 'From race to ethnicity.' *Australian and New Zealand Journal of Sociology, 16*(1), 24–37.

Degan, M.J. (1986). *Jane Addams and the Men of the Chicago School, 1892–1918*. New Brunswick: Transaction Books.

Denborough, D. (1996). 'Step by step: Developing respectful ways of working with young men to reduce violence.' In C. McLean, M. Carey & C. White (eds), *Men's Ways of Being*. Boulder: Westview Press.

Department of Education and Training (DET) NSW (2001). *Vocational Education and Training for NSW Schools: Issues and Challenges for Distance and Rural Education*. Sydney: NSW DET.

Department of Education and Training (DET) NSW (2005). 'Teaching in rural and remote schools and the Rural School Teacher Plan'. From www.det.nsw.gov.au/employment/teachnsw/rural_remote.htm.

Department of Education, Science and Training (n.d.). 'Success for boys: Helping boys achieve'. Retrieved 17 November 2005 from www.dest.gov.au/schools/boyseducation/.

Department of Education, Science and Training (2003). 'Educating Boys: Issues and information'. Retrieved 25 July 2005 from www.dest.gov.au/schools/boyseducation/.

Department of Education, Science and Training (2005). 'Success for boys: Helping boys achieve'. Canberra: Commonwealth of Australia. Retrieved July 25 2005 from www.dest.gov.au/schools/boyseducation/.

Department of Education, Science and Training (2006). 'Australian technical colleges. Latest announcements of new Australian technical colleges.' Retrieved 14 February 2006 from www.australiantechnicalcolleges.gov.au.

Department of Education, Training and Youth Affairs (2001). *National Evaluation Report: Full Service Schools Program 1999 and 2000*. Canberra: Department of Education, Training and Youth Affairs.

Department of Employment, Education and Training (DEET) (1990). Australia's Common and Agreed Goals for Schoolng in the 21st Century. ('The Hobart Declaration.') From www. mceetya.edu.au/mceetya/default.asp?id=11578

DEST, see Department of Education, Science and Training.

DET, see Department of Education and Training.

Devine, F. (2004). *Class Practices: How Parents Help Their Children Get Good Jobs*. Cambridge: Cambridge University Press.

Dewey, J. (1938). *Democracy and Education in the World of Today. Essays*. New York: The Society for Ethical Culture.

Dewey, J. (1991). *School and Society*. Chicago: University of Chicago Press.

Dickens, C. (1962 [1849–50]). *The Personal History, Adventures, Experience & Observation of David Copperfield the Younger, of Blunderstone Rookery (Which He Never Meant to be Published on any Account)*. New York: Signet.

Dickens, C. (1969 [1854]). *Hard Times: For These Times*. Harmondsworth: Penguin.

Doherty, P., McGaw, B. & O'Loghlin, B. (2004). 'Level the learning field.' *The Australian*, 30 April, p. 13.

Dolby, N. & Dimitriadis, G. (eds). (2004). *Learning to Labour in New Times*. New York: RoutledgeFalmer.

Donnelly, K. (2004). *Why Our Schools are Failing*. Sydney: Duffy & Snellgrove.

Drewe, R. (2000). *The Shark Net: Memories and Murder*. Ringwood: Viking.

Eagleson, R., Kaldor, S. & Malcolm, I. (1982). *English and the Aboriginal child*. Dickson: The Curriculum Development Centre.

Edwards, C. & Read, P. (1989). *The Lost Children*. Sydney: Doubleday.

Encel, S. (1970). *Equality and Authority: A Study of Class, Status and Power in Australia*. Melbourne: Cheshire.

Ensminger, M. & Slusarcick, A. (1992). 'Paths to high school graduation or dropout: A longitudinal study of a first grade cohort.' *Sociology of Education, 65*(95–113).

Erikson, E.H. (1950). *Childhood and Society*. London: Imago.

Evans, R., Saunders, K. & Cronin, K. (1975). *Exclusion, Exploitation and Extermination. Race Relations in Colonial Queensland*. Sydney: Australia and New Zealand Book Company.

Fesl, E.M.D. (1993). *Conned*. Brisbane: University of Queensland Press.

Fine, M. (1991). *Framing Dropouts: Notes on the Politics of an Urban Public High School*. Albany: State University of New York Press.

Fisk, E.K. (1985). *The Aboriginal Economy in Town and Country*. North Sydney: Allen and Unwin.

Fitzgerald, R. (2003). *The Pope's Battalions: Santamaria, Catholicism and the Labor Split*. Brisbane: University of Queensland Press.

Fletcher, J. (1989a). *Clean, Clad and Courteous. A History of Aboriginal Education in New South Wales*. Marrickville: Southwood Press.

Fletcher, J. (1989b). *Documents in the History of Aboriginal Education in New South Wales*. Marrickville: Southwood Press.

Fletcher, J. & Burnswoods, J. (1980). *Sydney and the Bush*. Sydney: Department of Education, NSW.

Fletcher, J. & Burnswoods, J. (1988). *Government Schools of NSW since 1848*. Sydney: Department of Education, NSW.

Florida, R. (2002). *The Rise of the Creative Class: And How It's Transforming Work, Leisure, Community and Everyday Life*. New York: Basic Books.

Floud, J.E., Halsey, A.H. & Martin, F.M. (eds). (1957). *Social Class and Educational Opportunity*. London: Heinemann.

Foale, M.T. (1989). *The Josephite Story: The Sisters of St Joseph, Their Foundation and Early History 1866–1893*. Sydney: St Joseph's Generalate.

Fogarty, R. (1959). *Catholic Education in Australia, 1806–1950*. Melbourne: Melbourne University Press.

Foley, D. (2000). 'Too white to be black, too black to be white.' *Social Alternatives, 19*(4), 44–9.

Foley, D. (2006). *Indigenous Australian Entrepreneurs: Not Community and Not in the Outback. Discussion Paper: 279*. ANU, Canberra: Centre for Aboriginal Economic Policy Research.

Forward, P. (2005). 'Actively campaigning for job security.' *Australian TAFE Teacher, 39*(1), 12–13.

Francis, R. (2003). 'Challenging masculine privilege: the women's movement and the Victorian Secondary Teachers Association, 1974–1995.' *Journal of Australian Studies, 78*, 59–70.

Frankel, B. (2004). *Zombies, Lilliputians and Sadists. The Power of the Living Dead and the Future of Australia*. Fremantle: Curtin University Press.

Freeman, M. (1987). *One for All: Designing a Universal, Comprehensive and Challenging Senior Curriculum*. Canberra: Curriculum Development Centre.

Gadamer, H. (1975). 'Hermeneutics and Social Science.' *Cultural Hermeneutics, 2*, 307–16.

Gadamer, H. (1986). *Truth and Method*. New York: Crossroad Publishing.

Ganter, R. (1994). *The Pearl-shellers of Torres Strait*. Melbourne: Melbourne University Press.

Gee, J., Hull, G. & Lankshear, C. (1996). *The New Work Order. Behind the Language of the New Capitalism*. Sydney: Allen and Unwin.

Gerritsen, R. (2000). 'The management of government and its consequences for service delivery in rural Australia.' In B. Pritchard & P. McManus (eds), *Land of Discontent. The Dynamics of Change in Rural and Regional Australia*. Sydney: UNSW Press.

Gewirtz, S., Ball, S.J. & Bowe, R. (1995). *Markets, Choice, and Equity in Education*. Buckingham: Open University Press.

Giddens, A. (2000). *The Third Way and its Critics*. London: Polity Press.

Giddens, A. (2001). *Sociology* (4th edn). Cambridge: Polity Press.

Gilding, M. (1991). *The Making and Breaking of the Australian Family*. Sydney: Allen and Unwin.

Gilding, M. (1997). *Australian Families: A Comparative Perspective*. Melbourne: Longman.

Giroux, H.A. (1988). *Teachers as Intellectuals: Toward a Critical Pedagogy of Learning*. Granby: Bergin & Garvey.

Glaser, R. (1984). 'Education and thinking: The role of knowledge.' *American Psychologist, 39*(1), 93–104.

Goodson, I. (ed.). (1992). *Studying Teachers' Lives*. London: Routledge.

Grace, G. (1978). *Teachers, Ideology and Control: A Study in Urban Education.* London: Routledge & Kegan Paul.

Gray, I. & Lawrence, G. (2001). *A Future for Regional Australia. Escaping Global Misfortune.* Cambridge: Cambridge University Press.

Gronn, P. (1992). 'Schooling for ruling: The social composition of admissions to Geelong Grammar School 1930–1939.' *Australian Historical Studies, 25*(98), 72–89.

Gunn, S. & Bell, R. (2003). *Middle Classes: Their Rise and Sprawl.* London: Phoenix.

Habermas, J. (1971). 'Technology and science as ideology.' In *Toward a Rational Society* (pp. 81–122). London: Heinemann.

Habermas, J. (1976). *Legitimation Crisis.* Boston: Beacon Press.

Habermas, J. (1978). *Knowledge and Human Interests.* London: Heinemann.

Habermas, J. (1979). *Communication and the Evolution of Society.* Boston: Beacon Books.

Habermas, J. (1981). *The Theory of Communicative Action* (Vol. 1). Boston: Beacon Press.

Habermas, J. (1990). *Moral Consciousness and Communicative Action.* Cambridge: Polity Press.

Hall, S. (1983). 'The great moving right show.' In S. Hall & J. Martins (eds), *The Politics of Thatcherism* (pp. 19–39). London: Lawrence & Wishart.

Hardt, M. & Negri, A. (2000). *Empire.* Cambridge: Harvard University Press.

Harman, G. & Smart, D. (eds). (1982). *Federal Intervention in Australian Education: Past, Present and Future.* Melbourne: Georgian House.

Harris, C. (2005). 'Curriculum Theorising: Examining the Middle Ground of Curriculum.' *Curriculum and Teaching, 20*(2), 81–96.

Hattam, R. & Smyth, J. (2000). 'Listen to me, I'm leaving.' *Education Links, 61/62,* 25–7.

Hayes, D. (1996). *Sex in schools: How Gender Functions in the School Curriculum.* Paper presented at the Annual Conference of the Australian Association for Research in Education.

Held, D. (1999). *Global Transformations: Politics, Economics and Culture.* Cambridge: Polity Press.

Henderson, D. (2005). 'What is education for? Situating history, cultural understandings and studies of society and environment against new-conservative critiques of curriculum reform.' *Australian Journal of Education, 49*(3), 306–19.

Hendery, G. & Barratt, A. (2002). 'Evidence-based education: how can we decide on the best way to teach.' *Focus on Health Professional Education, 4*(1), 4–11.

Henry, M., Lingard, B., Rizvi, F. & Taylor, S. (2001). *The OECD, Globalisation and Educational Policy.* London: Pergamon.

Heitmeyer, D. (1998). 'The issue is not black and white: Aboriginality and education.' In J. Allen (ed.), *Sociology of Education: Possibilities and Practice* (pp. 195–214). Katoomba: Social Science Press.

Hesse, M. (1976). 'Theory and value in the social sciences.' In C. Hookway & P. Pettit (eds), *Action and Interpretation.* Cambridge: Cambridge University Press.

Hirsch, F. (1976). *Social Limits to Growth.* Cambridge: Harvard University Press.

Hirst, P. (1973). 'Liberal education and the nature of knowledge.' In R.S. Peters (ed.), *Philosophy of Education.* Oxford: Oxford University Press.

Holter, Ø.G. (2003). *Can Men Do It? Men and Gender Equality—The Nordic Experience.* Copenhagen: Nordic Council of Ministers.

Howard, J. (2006). 'Address to the National Press Club, Great Hall, Parliament House, January 25'. Retrieved 28 February 2006 from http://www.pm.gov.au/news/speeches.

HREOC, see Human Rights and Equal Opportunity Commission.

Hu, J. (2003). Speech to Federal Parliament, 24 October.

Hudspith, S. & Williams, A. (1994). 'Enhancing Aboriginal identity and self-esteem in the classroom.' In S.M. Harris (ed.), *Aboriginal Kids in Urban Classrooms*. Wentworth Falls: Social Science Press.

Hughes, I. (2001). 'Teaching action research on the web.' *Educational Technology & Society, 4*(3), 64–71.

Hughes, T. (n.d.). *Tom Brown's School Days*. London: Blackie and Son.

Hugo, G. (2005a). 'Australia's international migration transformed'. *Australian Mosaic, 9*(1).

Hugo, G. (2005b). *Chinese Intellectual Migration to Australia*. Paper presented at the HKUST Conference Chinese People on the Move.

Human Rights and Equal Opportunity Commission (HREOC) (2000). *'Emerging themes'. National inquiry into rural and remote education*. Sydney: HREOC.

Humphrey, M. (1998). *Islam, Multiculturalism and Transnationalism: From the Lebanese Diaspora*. London: Centre for Lebanese Studies and IB Tauris Publishers.

Humphrey, M. (2001). 'Muslim Lebanese.' In J. Jupp (ed.), *The Australian People. An Encyclopedia of the Nation, its Peoples and Their Origins* (pp. 564–7). Cambridge: Cambridge University Press.

Husen, T. (1974). *The Learning Society*. London: Methuen.

Hutchins, R.M. (1968). *The Learning Society*. New York: Praeger.

Hyams, B., Trethewey, L., Condon, B., Vick, M. & Grundy, D. (1988). *Learning and Other Things. Sources for a Social History of Education in South Australia*. Adelaide: South Australian Government Printer.

Hyndman, M. (1978). *Schools and Schooling in England and Wales. A Documentary History*. London: Harper and Row.

Inglis, C., Elley, J. & Manderson, L. (1992). *Making Something of Myself. Educational Attainment and Social Mobility of Turkish-Australian Young People*. Canberra: Office of Multicultural Affairs.

Inhelder, B. & Piaget, J. (1958). *The Growth of Logical Thinking from Childhood to Adolescence*. New York: Basic Books.

International Baccalaureate Organisation (IBO). Retrieved 6 July 2005 from http://www.ibo.org/ibo/index.cfm?page=/ibo/services/ib_worldsch.

Iredale, R. (1997). *Skills Transfer*. Wollongong: Wollongong University Press.

Jackson, B. & Marsden, D. (1986 [1966]). *Education and the Working Class*. London: Ark.

Jamal, N. & Chandab, T. (2005). *The Glory Garage. Growing up Lebanese Muslim in Australia*. Sydney: Allen and Unwin.

Jamrozik, A., Boland, C. & Urquhart, R. (1995). *Social Change and Cultural Transformation in Australia*. Cambridge: Cambridge University Press.

Johnson, K. (1999). 'Reflections on collaborative research from the realms of practice.' *Change: Transformations in Education, 2*(1), 12–25.

Jupp, J. (ed.). (2001). *The Australian People. An Encyclopedia of the Nation, Its Peoples and Their Origins*. Cambridge: Cambridge University Press.

Jupp, J. (2002). *From White Australia to Woomera. The Story of Australian Immigration*. Sydney: Allen and Unwin.

Jupp, J. (2005). Isolated and Angry. *The Australian*, 14 December.

Kabir, N. (2004). *Muslims in Australia. Immigration, Race Relations and Cultural History*. London: Kegan Paul.

Kalantzis, M. (1990). *Cultures of Schooling*. London: Falmer.

Karmel (Chair), P. (1973). *Schools in Australia: Report of the Interim Committee of the Australian Schools Commission*. Canberra: AGPS.

Kemmis, S. & McTaggart, R. (1988). *The Action Research Planner* (4th edn). Waurn Ponds (Vic.): Deakin University Press.

Kenway, J. & Kraack, A. (2004). 'Reordering Work and Destablizing Masculinity.' In N. Dolby & G. Dimitriadis (eds), *Learning to Labour in New Times*. New York: RoutledgeFalmer.

Kenway, J. & Willis, S. (1990). *Hearts and Minds: Self-esteem and the Schooling of Girls*. London: Falmer Press.

King, A. (1999). *The Cost to Australia of Early School-leaving. Prepared for the Dusseldorp Skills Forum*. Canberra: National Centre for Social and Economic Modelling, University of Canberra.

Klein, N. (2001). *No Space, No Choice, No Jobs, No Logo*. London: Flamingo.

Kyle, N. (1986). *Her Natural Destiny. The Education of Women in New South Wales*. Sydney: New South Wales University Press.

Lamb, S. & McKenzie, P. (2001). *Patterns of success and failure in the transition from school to work in Australia. Report No. 18*. Melbourne: Australian Council for Educational Research.

Lamb, S. & Vickers, M. H. (2003). *Part-time work during high school: What are its effects?* Paper presented at the AERA Annual Meeting, Chicago.

Lamb, S., Dwyer, P. & Wynn, J. (2000). *Non-completion of School in Australia. LSAY Research Report No. 16*. Melbourne: Australian Council for Educational Research.

Lamb, S., Hogan, D. & Johnson, T. (2001). 'The stratification of learning opportunities and achievement in Tasmanian secondary schools.' *Australian Journal of Education, 45*(2), 153–67.

Lamb, S., Walstab, A., Teese, R., Vickers, M. & Rumberger, R. (2004). *Staying on at School: Improving Student Retention in Australia*. Queensland Department of Education and the Arts on behalf of the MCEETYA National Fund for Educational Research.

La Nauze, J.A. (1940). 'Some aspects of educational opportunity in South Australia.' In J.D.G. Medley (ed.), *Australian Educational Studies* (pp. 29–61). Melbourne: Melbourne University Press.

Larum, J. & Beggs, J. (1989). 'What drives Australian labor force participation?' *Australian Journal of Statistics,, 31A*, 125–42.

Laughlin, A. (1997). *Mount Druitt High School: Review of 1996 Higher School Certificate performance*. Sydney: Department of School Education (NSW).

Lawn, M. (1987). *Servants of the State: The Contested Control of Teaching, 1900–1930*. London: Falmer Press.

Lawn, M. & Grace, G. (eds). (1987). *Teachers: The Culture and Politics of Work*. London: Falmer Press.

Lester, J. & Hanlen, W. (2004). *Report on the New South Wales Aboriginal Education Policy Review*: Umulliko Indigenous Higher Education and Research Centre, University of Newcastle.

Lewis, P. & Koshy, P. (1999). 'Youth employment, unemployment, and school participation.' *Australian Journal of Education, 43*(1), 42–57.

Lingard, B. (2000). 'Federalism in schooling since the Karmel Report (1973), "Schools in Australia": From modernist hope to postmodernist performativity.' *Australian Educational Researcher, 27*(2), 25–61.

Lloyd, C.B. (2005). *Growing Up Global: The Changing Transitions to Adulthood in Developing Countries*. Washington: National Academies Press.

Lo Bianco, J. (1987). *A National Policy on Languages*. Canberra: AGPS.

Lokan, J., Greenwood, L. & Cresswell, J. (2000). *15-up and counting, reading, writing, reasoning: how literate are Australian students?: PISA in Brief from Australia's Perspective.* Melbourne: ACER.

Long, M. (2005). *How Young People are Faring.* Paper presented at the Dusseldorp Skills Forum, Sydney.

Lopez, M. (2000). *The Origins of Multiculturalism in Australian Politics.* Melbourne: MUP.

Loughran, J., Mitchell, I. & Mitchell, J. (eds). (2002). *Learning from Teacher Research.* Sydney: Allen and Unwin.

Luke, A. (1993). 'The social construction of literacy in the primary school.' In L. Unsworth (ed.), *Literacy Learning and Teaching.* Macmillan: Sydney.

Lyotard, J-F. (1980). *The Postmodern Condition. A Report on Knowledge.* Minneapolis: University of Minnesota Press.

Maclure, J. (1973). *Educational Documents: England and Wales, 1816 to the Present Day.* London: Methuen.

Malley, J. & Keating, J. (2000). 'Policy influences on the implementation of vocational education in Australian secondary schools.' *Journal of Vocational Education and Training, 5*(4), 627–51.

Marginson, S. (1989) *Human Capital Theory and Education Policy.* Unpublished paper, Federated University Staff Association (FAUSA Melbourne, Australia).

Marginson, S. (1993). *Education and Public Policy in Australia.* Cambridge: Cambridge University Press.

Marginson, S. (1997a). *Educating Australia: Government, Economy and Citizen since 1960.* Cambridge: Cambridge University Press.

Marginson, S. (1997b). *Markets in Education.* Sydney: Allen and Unwin.

Marks, G. & Fleming, N. (1999). *Early School Leaving in Australia.* Melbourne: Australian Council for Educational Research.

Marks, G., Fleming, N., Long, M. & McMillan, J. (2000). *Patterns of participation in year 12 and higher education in Australia: Trends and issues. LSAY Research Report No. 17.* Melbourne: Australian Council for Educational Research.

Marr, D., & Wilkinson, M. (2004). *Dark Victory.* Sydney: Allen and Unwin.

Marsh, C. (1994). *Producing a National Curriculum: Plans and Paranoia.* Sydney: Allen and Unwin.

Martin, A. & Marsh, H. (2005). 'Motivating boys and motivating girls: Does teacher gender really make a difference?' *Journal of Education, 49*(3), 320–34.

Martin, B. (1998). 'The Australian middle class, 1986–1995: Stable, declining or restructuring?' *Journal of Sociology, 34*(2), 135–51.

Martino, W. (1998). '"When you only have girls as friends you got some serious problems": Interrogating masculinities in the literacy classroom.' In M. Knobel & A. Healey (eds), *Critical Literacies in Primary Classrooms.* Sydney: Primary English Teaching Association.

Martino, W. & Pallotta-Chiarolli, M. (2003). *So What's a Boy? Addressing Issues of Masculinity and Schooling.* Maidenhead: Open University Press.

Marx, K. & Engels, F. (1988 [1848]). 'The communist manifesto.' In F.L. Bender (ed.), *The Communist Manifesto: Annotated Text.* New York: W.W. Norton.

Masters, G.N. (2004). 'Public or private: Where's the evidence?' *ACER eNews.*

McCallum, D. (1990). *The Social Production of Merit: Education, Psychology and Politics in Australia 1900–1950.* London: Falmer Press.

McCalman, J. (1993). *Journeyings: The Biography of a Middle-class Generation 1920–1990.* Melbourne: Melbourne University Press.

McGaw, B. (1994). 'Standards from a civic and assessment perspective.' *Queensland Journal of Educational Research, 10*(3), 1–18.

McGaw, B. (1997). *Securing Their Future: the NSW Government's Reforms for the Higher School Certificate*. Sydney: NSW Minister for Education and Training.

McGregor, C. (2001). *Class in Australia* (2nd edn). Melbourne: Penguin Australia.

McIntyre, S. & Clark, A. (2003). *The History Wars*. Melbourne: Melbourne University Press.

McKnight, D. (2005). *Beyond Left and Right. New Politics and the Culture Wars*. Sydney: Allen and Unwin.

Mealyea, R. (1993). 'Reproducing vocationalism in secondary schools: marginalization in practical workshops.' In L. Angus (ed.), *Education, Inequality and Social Identity* (pp. 160–195). London: Falmer Press.

Menzies, G. (2002). *1421. The year China discovered the world*. London: Bantam.

Mickler, S. (1998). *The myth of privilege: Aboriginal Status, Media Visions, Public Ideas*. South Fremantle: Fremantle Arts Centre Press.

Miller, P. (1986). *Long Division: State Schooling in South Australian Society*. Adelaide: Wakefield Press.

Miller, P. (1998). *Transformations of Patriarchy in the West, 1500–1900*. Bloominton: Indiana University Press.

Miller, P., & Davey, I. (1988). 'The common denominator: Schooling the people.' In V. Burgmann & J. Lee (eds), *Constructing a Culture*. Melbourne: McPhee Gribble/Penguin.

Ministerial Council on Employment, Education, Training and Youth Affairs (2000). *New framework for vocational education in schools: Policy directions. A comprehensive guide about pathways for young Australians in transition*. Melbourne: Curriculum Corporation on behalf of MCEETYA.

Ministerial Council on Employment, Education, Training and Youth Affairs. (2002). *The growth of VET in Schools programs: A national overview. Report compiled by the MCEETYA Taskforce on Transition from School from data provided by States and Territories*. Melbourne: MCEETYA.

Ministerial Council on Employment, Education, Training, and Youth Affairs (2005). *National report on schooling in Australia. Preliminary paper. National benchmark results, reading and literacy, years 3, 5, and 7*. Melbourne: MCEETYA.

Mitchell, B. (1975). *Teachers' Education and Politics: A History of Organizations of Public School Teachers in New South Wales*. Brisbane: University of Queensland Press.

Mitchell, W., & Sherington, G. (1984). *Growing Up in the Illawara*. Wollongong: University of Wollongong.

Mok, K. & Welch, A. (eds). (2003). *Globalization and Educational Restructuring in the Asia Pacific region*. Basingstoke: PalgraveMacmillan.

Morgan, S. (1987). *My Place*. Fremantle: Fremantle Arts Centre Press.

Morrell, R. (2001). *From Boys to Gentlemen: Settler Masculinity in Colonial Natal, 1880–1920*. Pretoria: University of South Africa Press.

Mortimer, O. (1993). 'The Tasmanian area schools.' In R. Petersen & G. Rodwell (eds), *Essays in the History of Rural Education in Australia and New Zealand* (pp. 238–254). Darwin: William Michael Press.

Morton, T. (2001). 'Up the greasy pole.' *Sydney Morning Herald*, 16 June, p. 1.

Moses, A.D. (ed.). (2004). *Genocide and Settler Society: Frontier Violence and Stolen Indigenous Children in Australian History*. New York: Berghahn Books.

Moyle, D. (2005). *Report on a Survey of Schools on the Changes in Commonwealth Indigenous Education Funding*. Melbourne: Australian Education Union.

Murnane, R. & Levy, F. (1996). *Teaching the New Basic Skills: Principles for Educating Children to Survive in a Changing Economy*. New York: Free Press.

Musgrave, P. (1968). *The School as an Organisation*. London: Macmillan.

Musgrave, P.W. (1992). *From Humanity to Utility: Melbourne University and Public Examinations 1856–1964*. Melbourne: ACER.

My Future (2003) 'Aboriginal and Islander independent community school.' Retrieved 23 January 2006 from http://www.myfuture.edu.au/services/default.asp?FunctionID=5200&ProviderID=12360.

NALSAS statistics, program details. From www.dest.gov.au/nalsas.

National Centre for Vocational Education Research (NCVER) (2000). *Women in VET 2000*. From http://www.ncver.edu.au/statistics/aag/women00/women00.pdf.

National Centre for Vocational Education Research (NCVER) (2001). *Australian Apprenticeships: Facts, Fiction, and Future*. Adelaide: NCVER.

National Centre for Vocational Education Research (NCVER) (2003). *Australian Vocational Education and Training Statistics: VET in schools 2003*. Adelaide: NCVER.

National Economics (2000). *State of the Regions 2000*. Canberra: Australian Local Government Association.

NCVER, see National Centre for Vocational Education Research.

Neill, R. (2002). *White Out: How Politics is Killing Black Australia*. Crows Nest: Allen and Unwin.

Nelson, B. (2004). 'Lighthouse schools to lead the way in boys' education'. Media release, Department of Education, Science, and Training. Retrieved 25 July 2005 from http://www.dest.gov.au/sectors/school_education/policy_initiatives_reviews/key_issues/boys_education/ministers_media_releases.htm.

New Faces (2001). *New Faces, New Places. Review of the State-Specific Migration Scheme*. Canberra: Parliament of the Commonweath of Australia.

New South Wales Board of Studies (2005). NSW Primary Curriculum Foundation Statements. Retrieved 29 January 2006 from http://k6.boardofstudies.nsw.edu.au/foundation_statements.

Norst, M. (2001). 'Austrians.' In J. Jupp (ed.), *The Australian People. An Encyclopedia of the Nation, its Peoples and their Origins* (pp. 176–181). Cambridge: Cambridge University Press.

Oakes, J. & Lipton, M. (1999). *Teaching to Change the World* (2nd edn). Boston: McGraw Hill.

Oakley, A. (1976). *Housewife*. Harmondsworth: Penguin.

O'Connor, K., Stimson, R., Maude, A., Daly, M. & Dragovich, D. (2001). *Australia's Changing Economic Geography: A Society Dividing*. Melbourne: Oxford University Press.

O'Donoghue, T.A. (2001). *Upholding the Faith: The Process of Education in Catholic Schools in Australia, 1922–1965*. New York: Peter Lang.

Ogburn, W. (1923). *Social Change*. London: Allen and Unwin.

Ogburn, W. (1964). *On Culture and Social Change*. Chicago: Chicago University Press.

O'Loughlin, J., Staeheli, L. & Greenberg, E. (2004). *Globalization and its Outcomes*. New York: The Guilford Press.

Orellana, M. F., Thorne, B., Chee, A. & Lam, W.S.E. (2001). 'Transnational childhoods: the participation of children in processes of family migration.' *Social Problems, 48*(4), 572–91.

Organisation for Economic Cooperation and Development (OECD) (2003). *Trends in International Migration*. Paris: OECD.

Organisation for Economic Cooperation and Development (OECD) (2004). *Trade and Migration. Building Bridges for Global Labour Mobility*. Paris: OECD.

Ozolins, U. (1993). *The Politics of Language in Australia*. Cambridge: Cambridge University Press.

Painter, M. (1997). 'Public management: Fad or fallacy?' In M. Considine & M. Painter (eds), *Managerialism. The Great Debate* (pp. 39–43). Melbourne: Melbourne University Press.

Parliament of Australia (2004). 'Poverty rates by electorate. Research Note no. 49 2004–05.' From http://www.aph.gov.au/library/pubs/rn/2004-05/05rn49.pdf.

Parliamentary Library (2004). 'Investing in the economy's knowledge base. Research Note 24, 2004-5.' From http://www.aph.gov.au/library/pubs/rn/2004-05/05rn24.pdf.

Parliamentary Library (2005). 'Australia's migration programme. Research Note 48, 2004–5'. From http://www.aph.gov.au/library/pubs/rn/2004-05/05rn48.pdf.

Pearson, K. (1937 [1892]). *The Grammar of Science*. London: Dent.

Peel, M. (2003). *The Lowest Rung: Voices of Australian Poverty*. Cambridge: Cambridge University Press.

Peel, M. & McCalman, J. (1992). '*Who Went Where in "Who's Who 1988"': The Schooling of the Australian Elite*.' Melbourne: University of Melbourne.

Perkin, H. (1989). *The Rise of Professional Society: England Since 1880*. London: Routledge.

Perlez, J. (2004, April 17). 'Aborigines Say Australia Pushes Their Plight to Sideline.' *New York Times*, p.3.

Peters, M. (1992). 'Performance and accountability in "post industrial society": the crisis of British universities.' *Studies in Higher Education, 17*(2), 123–39.

Pitman, J. & Herschell, P. (2002). *The Senior Certificate: A New Deal*. Brisbane: Queensland Department of Education.

Pocock, B. (2003). *The Work/Life Collision: What Work is Doing to Australians and What to do About It*. Sydney: Federation Press.

Power, S., Edwards, T., Whitty, G. & Wigfall, V. (2003). *Education and the Middle Class*. Buckingham: Open University Press.

Poynting, S., Noble, G. & Tabar, P. (1998). 'If anybody called me a wog they wouldn't be speaking to me alone: Protest masculinity and Lebanese youth in Western Sydney.' *Journal of Interdisciplinary Gender Studies 3*(2), 76–94.

Poynting, S. et al. (2004). *Bin Laden in the Suburbs: Criminalising the Arab Other*. Sydney: Institute of Criminology.

Print, M. (1993). *Curriculum Development and Design*. London and Sydney: Allen and Unwin.

Productivity Commission (1999). 'Impact of competition policy reforms on rural and regional Australia. Report No. 8.' from www.pc.gov.au/inquiry/compol/finalreport/index.html.

Productivity Commission (2003). 'Social capital. Reviewing the concept and its policy implications.' From http://www.pc.gov.au/research/commres/socialcapital/socialcapital.pdf.

Purvis, J. (1991). *A History of Women's Education in England*. Philadelphia: Open University Press.

Pusey, M. (1991). *Economic Rationalism in Canberra. A Nation-building State Changes its Mind*. Cambridge: Cambridge University Press.

Pusey, M. (2003). *The Experience of Middle Australia: The Dark Side of Economic Reform*. Cambridge: Cambridge University Press.

Putnam, R. (1993). *Making Democracy Work*. Princeton: Princeton University Press.

Putnam, R. (2000). *Bowling Alone. The Collapse and Revival of American Community*. New York: Touchstone.

Read, P. (2002). 'The Stolen Generations, the historian and the court room.' *Aboriginal History, 26*, 51–61.

Reay, D. (1998). *Class Work: Mothers' Involvement in their Children's Primary Schooling*. London: UCL Press.

Reay, D. (2004). 'Finding or losing yourself? Working-class relationships to education.' In S. J. Ball (ed.), *The RoutledgeFalmer Reader in Sociology of Education* (pp. 30–44). London: RoutledgeFalmer.

Reay, D. & Ball, S.J. (1998). '"Making their minds up": Family dynamics of school choice.' *British Educational Research Journal, 24*(4), 431–48.

Remarque, E.M. (1929). *All Quiet on the Western Front*. London: Putnam.

Resnick, L. (1988). 'Learning in school and out.' *Educational Researcher, 16*(9), 13–20.

Retallick, J. (1991). 'Educational leadership in a critical theory of education.' *Discourse, 12*(1), 100–12.

RIRDC, see Rural Industries Research and Development Corporation.

Risman, B. (1986). 'Can men "mother"? Life as a single father.' *Family Relations, 35*, 95–102.

Robertson, R. (1990). 'Mapping the global condition: Globalization as the central concept.' In M. Featherstone (ed.), *Global Culture, Nationalism, Globalization and Modernity*. London: Sage.

Robertson, S.L. (2000). *A Class Act: Changing Teachers' Work, Globalisation and the State*. New York: Falmer.

Rodwell, G. (1992). *With Zealous Efficiency: Progressivism and State Primary Schools 1900–1920*. Darwin: William Michael Press.

Rothman, S. (2002). *Achievement in literacy and numeracy by Australian 14-year olds, 1975–1998. Longitudinal Surveys of Australian Youth Research Report No. 29*. ACER: Melbourne.

Rothman, S. & McMillan, J. (2003). *Influences on Achievement in Literacy and Numeracy. LSAY Research Report No. 36*. Melbourne: ACER.

Rothstein, V. (2002). 'Social capital in the social democratic state.' In R. Putnam (ed.), *Democracies in Flux: The Evolution of Social Capital in Contemporary Society*. New York: Oxford University Press.

Rowan, L., Knobel, M., Bigum, C. & Lankshear, C. (2002). *Boys, Literacies, and Schooling*. Philadelphia: Open University Press.

Rowse, T. (2002). *Indigenous Futures: Choice and Development for Aboriginal and Islander Australia*. Sydney: University of NSW Press.

Rural Industries Research and Development Corporation (RIRDC). (2002). *More Than an Education: Leadership for Eural School-Community Partnerships*: TIRDC and University of Tasmania.

Saeed, A. (2003). *Islam in Australia*. Sydney: Allen and Unwin.

Saha, L.J. (ed.). (1997) *International Encyclopedia of the Sociology of Education*, New York: Pergamon.

Sawer, M. (2003). *The Ethical State? Social Liberalism in Australia*. Melbourne: Melbourne University Press.

Schirato, T. & Webb, J. (2003). *Understanding Globalisation*. London: Sage.

Schools Commission. (1980). *Schooling for 15 and 16 Year-olds*. Canberra: Schools Commission.

Schools in Australia. (1973). *Report of the Interim Committee for the Australian Schools Commission*. Canberra: AGPS.

Schwab, R.G. (1999). *Why only one in three? The complex reasons for low Indigenous school retention. Centre for Aboriginal Economic Policy Research Research Monograph 16*. Canberra: ANU.

Schwartz, P. (1996). *The Art of the Long View: Planning for the Future in an Uncertain World*. New York: Doubleday.

Seidler, V.J. (2006). *Transforming Masculinities: Men, Cultures, Bodies, Power, Sex and Love*. London: Routledge.

Selleck, R.J.W. (2003). *The Shop: The University of Melbourne, 1850–1939*. Melbourne: Melbourne University Press.

Sharp, N. (1993). *Stars of Tagai: The Torres Strait Islanders*. Canberra: Aboriginal Studies Press.

Sherington, G. (1990). *Australia's Immigrants 1788–1988*. Sydney: Allen and Unwin.

Sherington, G. (2004). 'Public commitment and private choice in Australian secondary education.' In R. Aldrich (ed.), *Public or Private Education? Lessons from History* (pp. 167–88). London: Woburn Press.

Sherington, G., Petersen, R.C. & Brice, I. (1987). *Learning to Lead: A History of Girls' and Boys' Corporate Secondary Schools in Australia.* Sydney: Allen and Unwin.

Shulman, L.S. (1986). 'Paradigms and research programs in the study of teaching: A contemporary perspective.' In M.C. Wittrock (ed.), *Handbook of Research on Teaching* (3rd edn, pp. 3–36). New York: Macmillan.

Shulman, L.S. & Quinlan, K.M. (1996). 'The comparative psychology of school subjects.' In R.C. Calfee & D.C. Berliner (eds), *Handbook of Educational Psychology* (pp. 399–422). New York: Macmillan.

Simon, B. (1971). *Intelligence, Psychology and Education: A Marxist Critique.* London: Lawrence & Wishart.

Smart, D. (1982). 'The pattern of post-war Federal intervention in education.' In G. Harman & D. Smart (eds), *Federal Intervention in Australian Education* (pp. 15–34). Melbourne: Georgian House.

Smith, K.V. (1992). *King Bungaree.* Kenthurst: Kangaroo Press.

Snodgrass, A. (1992). 'Asian studies and the fusion of horizons.' *Asian Studies Review, 15*(3), 81–94.

Sommers, C.H. (2000). *The War Against Boys: How Misguided Feminism is Harming our Young Men.* New York: Simon & Schuster.

Spierings, J. (1999). *Why Australia Needs a National Youth Commitment: A Discussion Paper.* Paper presented at the Dusseldorp Skills Forum, Sydney.

Stevens, R., Wineburg, S., Herrenkohl, L.R. & Bell, P. (2005). 'Comparative understanding of school subjects: Past, present, and future.' *Review of Educational Research, 75*(2), 125–57.

Strintzos, M. (1984). 'To be Greek is to be good.' *Cultural Politics, Working Papers No. 5.*

Summers, A. (1994). *Damned Whores and God's Police.* Victoria: Penguin.

Swan, W. (2005). *Postcode. The Splintering of a Nation.* Melbourne: Pluto Press.

Tavan, G. (2005). *The Long Slow Death of White Australia.* Melbourne: Scribe Publications.

Taylor, S., Rizvi, F., Lingard, B. & Arnold, M. (1997). *Educational Policy and the Politics of Change.* London: Routledge.

Te Riele, K. & Wyn, J. (2005). 'Australia: Transformations in Youth Transition.' In N.F. Bagnall (ed.), *Youth Transition in a Globalised Marketplace.* New York: Nova Science Publishers Inc.

Teese, R. (2000). *Academic Success and Social Power: Examinations and Inequity.* Melbourne: Melbourne University Press.

Teese, R. (2002). *Early Leaving in Victoria: Geographical Patterns, Origins, and Strategic Issues.* Melbourne: Educational Outcomes Research Unit, University of Melbourne.

Teese, R. & Polesel, J. (2003). *Undemocratic Schooling: Equity and Quality in Mass Secondary Education in Australia.* Melbourne: Melbourne University Press.

Teese, R. et al. (1995). *Who Wins at school? Boys and Girls in Australian Secondary Education.* Melbourne: Department of Education Policy and Management, University of Melbourne.

Theobald, M. (1996). *Knowing Women: Origins of Women's Education in Nineteenth-century Australia.* Cambridge: Cambridge University Press.

Theobald, M. (2001). 'The Afghan Children of Oodnadatta: A reflection on gender, ethnicity and education in the interwar years.' *Paedagogica Historica, 37* (1), 211–230.

Theobald, M.R. & Selleck, R.J.W. (eds). (1990). *Family, School and State in Australian History.* Sydney: Allen and Unwin.

Thompson, J. & Held, D. (1982). *Haberma: Critical Debates.* London: Macmillan.

Thomson, P. (2002). *Schooling the Rustbelt Kids: Making the Difference in Changing Times*. Sydney: Allen and Unwin.

Thomson, S., Cresswell, J. & De Bortoli, L. (2003). *PISA in Brief from Australia's Perspective*. Melbourne: ACER.

Tiffen, R. & Gittins, R. (2004). *How Australia Compares*. Cambridge: Cambridge University Press.

Tilmouth, T. (2005, September 28). 'How Aboriginal Funding Gets Lost.' *Sydney Morning Herald*. Retrieved 29 September 2005 from http://www.smh.com.au/news/opinion/how-aboriginal-funding-gets-lost/2005/09/21/1.

Tobin, K. (1999). 'The value to science education of teachers researching their own praxis.' *Research in Science Education, 29*(2), 159–69.

Toner, P. (2005). *Getting it Right: Responding to What Employers and Apprentices Have to Say*. Paper presented at the Dusseldorp Skills Forum, Sydney.

Troy, J. (1993). *King Plates. A History of Aboriginal Gorgets*. Canberra: Aboriginal Studies Press.

Turney, C. (Ed.) (1969). *Pioneers of Australian Education*. Sydney: Sydney University Press.

United Nations Education Scientific and Cultural Organization (UNESCO) (1996). *Learning. The Treasure Within*. Paris: UNESCO.

Uy, V.T. (1988). *Determining The relevance of the International Baccalaureate Program vis-à-vis the Third World Countries*. Columbia University.

VCCA, see Victorian Curriculum and Assessment Authority.

Vickers, M. (1995). *Why State Policies Matter: The Uneven Rise of Australia's High School Completion Rates*. Harvard University, Cambridge.

Vickers, M. (2004). 'Markets and mobilities: Dilemmas facing the comprehensive neighbourhood high school.' *Melbourne Studies in Education, 45*(2), 1–22.

Vickers, M. (2005). 'School, work and social change: Revisiting the gender equity debate.' *Pacific Asian Education, 17* (2), 46–58.

Vickers, M. & Lamb, S. (2002). 'Why state policies matter: the influence of curriculum policy on participation in post-compulsory education and training.' *Australian Journal of Education, 46*(2), 172–88.

Vickers, M. & Lamb, S. (2003). *Part-time work during high school: What effects does it have on drop-out rates, post-school employment, access to vocational training, and participation in higher education?* Paper presented at the American Education Research Association (AERA) Annual Conference, Chicago, 15–20 April.

Vickers, M., Lamb, S. & Hinkley, J. (2003). *Student workers in high school and beyond: The effects of part-time employment on participation in education, training, and work. LSAY Research Report No. 30*. Melbourne: ACER.

Victorian Curriculum and Assessment Authority (2005). 'About the CSF II, years prep to 10.' Retrieved 29 January, 2006, from http://www.vcaa.vic.edu.au/prep10/csf/aboutcsf2.html.

Vinson, A. (1999). *Unequal in Life: The Distribution of Disadvantage in Victoria and New South Wales*. Melbourne: Ignatius Centre.

Vinson, A. (2004). *Community Adversity and Resilience. The Distribution of Social Disadvantage in Victoria and New South Wales and the Mediating Role of Social Cohesion*. Melbourne: The Ignatius Centre for Social Policy and Research.

Vinson, A. & Esson, K. (2005a). *Audit*: New South Wales Teachers Federation, and Federation of P&C Associations of New South Wales. .

Vinson, A. & Esson, K. (2005b). *Audit Overview*: New South Wales Teachers Federation, and Federation of P&C Associations of New South Wales.

Vinson, A. & Esson, K. (2005c). *Audit. Inquiry into the Provision of Public Education in New South Wales*. Sydney: NSW Teachers' Federation, and Federation of Parents and Citizens Associations of NSW.

Vinson, A., Esson, K. & Johnston, K. (2002). *Inquiry into the Provision of Public Education in NSW. Report of the 'Vinson Inquiry'*. New South Wales Teachers' Federation and the Parents and Citizens Council.

Wadsworth, Y. (1983). *Do It Yourself Social Research*. Melbourne: VCOSS and Allen and Unwin.

Walker, J.C. (1988). *Louts and Legends: Male Youth Culture in an Inner City School*. Sydney: Allen and Unwin.

Watson, L. (2003). *A Critique of the Federal Government's Recent Changes to Private Schools Funding. Discussion Paper No. 3*. Canberra: University of Canberra.

Watson, L. (2004). *The Total Operating Resources of Australian Private Schools in 2004 (No. Discussion Paper No. 4)*. Canberra: University of Canberra.

Weaver-Hightower, M. (2003). 'The "boy turn" in research on gender and education.' *Review of Educational Research, 73*(4), 471–98.

Weiss, L. (1998). *The Myth of the Powerless State: Governing the Economy in a Global Era*. Ithaca: Cornell University Press.

Welch, A. (1981). 'Curriculum as institution and ideology. A comparative essay in the legitimation of educational knowledge.' *New Education, 2 and 3*(1), 71–83.

Welch, A. (1993). 'Class, culture and the State in comparative education.' *Comparative Education, 29*(2), 7–28.

Welch, A. (1996a). 'Aboriginal education as internal colonialism.' In A. Welch (ed.), *Australian Education. Reform or Crisis?* (pp. 24–53). Sydney: Allen and Unwin.

Welch, A. (1996b). *Australian Education: Reform or Crisis?* Sydney: Allen and Unwin.

Welch, A. (1996c). 'The politics of cultural interaction: multicultural education in Australia.' In A. Welch (ed.), *Australian Education. Reform or Crisis?* (pp. 105–31). Sydney: Allen and Unwin.

Welch, A. (1998). 'Education and the cult of efficiency. Comparative reflections on the reality and the rhetoric.' *Comparative Education, 34*(3), 157–76.

Welch, A. (2002). 'Going global? Internationalising Australia's universities at a time of global crisis.' *Comparative Education Review, 46*(4), 433–71.

Welch, A. (2003). 'Globalization, structural adjustment and contemporary educational reforms in Australia.' In K.-H. Mok & A. Welch (eds), *Globalisation and the Re-Structuring of Education in the Asia Pacific* (pp. 262–301). London: Palgrave Macmillan.

Welch, A. (2004). *Educational Services in South East Asia, Building Institutional Capacity in South East Asia (BICA) project*. Research Institute for Asia and the Pacific (RIAP) and Ministry of Finance Japan.

Welch, A. (2005). 'Korean higher education in international perspective: Internationalised or globalised?' In K.-H. Mok & R. James (eds), *Globalization and Higher Education in East Asia* (pp. 99–136). London: Marshall Cavendish.

Welch, A. & Mok, K.-H. (2003). 'Deep development or deep divisions.' In K.-H. Mok & A. Welch (eds), *Globalisation and the Restructuring of Education in the Asia Pacific* (pp. 333–356). Basingstoke: PalgraveMacmillan.

Welch, A. & Zhang, Z. (2005). 'Zhongguo de zhishi liusan – haiwai zhongguo zhishi fenzijian de jiaoliu wangluo (Communication networks among the Chinese knowledge diaspora, in the global era).' *Comparative Education Review*.

White, R. (ed.) (1999). *Australian Youth Subcultures: On the Margins and in the Mainstream*. Hobart: Australian Clearinghouse for Youth Studies.

Whitehead, K. (1993). '"A small share of pioneering work." The relationship between provisional teachers and rural communities in South Australia, 1875–1915.' In R. Petersen & G. Rodwell (eds), *Essays in the History of Rural Education in Australia and New Zealand* (pp. 150–167). Darwin: William Michael Press.

Whitehead, K. (2003). *The New Women Come Along: Transforming Teaching in the Nineteenth Century*. Sydney: Australian and New Zealand History of Education Society.

Whitehead, K. (2005a). 'Advertising advantage: The International Baccalaureate, social justice and the marketisation of schooling.' Retrieved 7 February 2006 from http://www.aare.edu.au/05pap/whi05426.pdf.

Whitehead, K. (2005b). *Why Teach? Representing Prospective Teachers' Dispositions Towards their Future Occupation*. Unpublished manuscript, Flinders University.

Whitty, G. (1997). 'Creating quasi-markets in education.' *Review of Research in Education, 22*, 3–47.

Whitty, G. & Power, S. (2002). 'The overt and hidden curricula of quasi-markets.' In G. Whitty (ed.), *Making Sense of Education Policy* (pp. 94–106). London: Paul Chapman Publishing.

Williams, R. (1961). *The Long Revolution*. London: Penguin.

Williams, R. (1977). *Marxism and Literature*. Oxford: Oxford University Press.

Williams, R. (1983). *Keywords. A Vocabulary of Culture and Society*. London: Fontana.

Willis, P. (1977). *Learning to Labour: How Working Class Kids Get Working Class Jobs*. New York: Columbia University Press.

Willis, P. (2003). 'Foot soldiers of modernity.' *Harvard Education Review, 73*(3), 390–415.

Wooden, M. (1996). 'The youth labour market: Characteristics and trends.' *Australian Bulletin of Labour, 22*(2), 137–60.

Woodhall, M. (1972). *Economic Aspects of Education*. Windsor: National Foundation for Educational Research.

Woods, K. (Director) (2000). *Looking for Alibrandi*. (Motion picture). Australia: Roadshow.

World Bank (1994). *Priorities and Strategies in Education*. Washington: World Bank.

Wyn, J. & Rennie, P. (2002). 'Who are the learners?' In R. McDonald & J. Figgis (eds), *Knowledge Builders: Fresh Thinking About Learners and Their Teachers*. Brisbane: ANTA.

Wyn, J. & White, R. (2000). 'Negotiating social change: the paradox of youth.' *Youth and Society, 32*(2), 165–83.

Wynhausen, E. (2005). *Dirt Cheap. Life at the Wrong End of the Job Market*. Sydney: Pan Macmillan.

Yarwood, A. (1964). *Asian Migration to Australia. The Background to Exclusion*. Melbourne: Melbourne University Press.

Yeatman, A. (1987). 'The concept of public management and the Australian State in the 1980s.' *Australian Journal of Public Administration, 46*(4), 339–53.

Yeatman, A. (1990). *Bureaucrats, Technocrats and Femocrats: Essays on the Contemporary Australian State*. Sydney: Allen and Unwin.

Yeatman, A. (1993). 'Corporate managers and the shift from the welfare to the Competition State.' *Discourse, 13*(2), 3–9.

Yeatman, A. (1994). 'The reform of public management: An overview.' *Australian Journal of Public Administration, 53*(3), 287–95.

Yeatman, A. (1997). 'The concept of public management and the Australian State in the 1980s.' In M. Considine & M. Painter (eds), *Managerialism. The Great Debate*. Melbourne: Melbourne University Press.

Young, M. (1958). *The Rise of the Meritocracy 1870–2033*. London: Thames & Hudson.

Zuboff, S. (1988). *In the Age of the Smart Machine: The Future of Work and Power*. New York: Basic Books.

Zweig, D. & Fung, C. (2004). 'Redefining the brain drain: China's diaspora option.' Centre on China's Transnational Relations Working Paper No 1. From http://www.cctr.ust.hk/articles/pdf/WorkingPaper1.pdf.

Index